DATE DUE			

EARLY
AMERICAN
HISTORY

An eighteen volume series reproducing
over three hundred of the most
important articles on all aspects of the
colonial experience

EDITED WITH INTRODUCTIONS BY
PETER CHARLES HOFFER
UNIVERSITY OF GEORGIA

A Garland Series

THE PACE OF CHANGE

Selected Articles
on Politics and Society
in Pre-Revolutionary America

EDITED WITH AN INTRODUCTION BY
PETER CHARLES HOFFER

DISCARD

Garland Publishing, Inc.
New York & London
1988

Library of Congress Cataloging-in-Publication Data

The Pace of change : selected articles on politics and society in pre-
revolutionary American / edited with an introduction by
Peter Charles Hoffer.
p. cm.—(Early American history)
Reprint of previously published articles.
ISBN 0-8240-6244-2 (alk. paper)
1. United States—Politics and government—Colonial period, ca.
1600–1775. 2. United States—Social conditions—To 1865. I. Hoffer,
Peter C. II. Series.
E188.5.P33 1988
973.2—dc19   87-17211
                                                                               CIP

The volumes in this series are printed on
acid-free, 250-year-life paper.

Printed in the United States of America

CONTENTS

PREFACE

This volume carries the themes of Volume Twelve to the eve of the American Revolution. In the colonies, the pace of change had increased—slavery had spread, cities had grown, free population expanded west and south—but awareness of that pace, and its consequences, was still fixed in an older world of ideas and norms. This, perhaps, created one of those "biformities" that Michael G. Kammen explored so brilliantly in his *People of Paradox* (1973).[1] A biformity is an inherent contradiction, a polar opposition of two ideas, which are nevertheless simultaneously held. Such biformities include the colonists' commitment to personal liberty and their willingness to exploit slaves, their love of nature and their compulsion to transform wilderness into farmland, their submission to English royal authority and their apprehension that a conspiracy brewed within the court to destroy American rights.

The last decades of colonial life were certainly filled with such apparent contradictions. Some of these may reduce, upon closer examination, to disputes among modern historians over what really was happening. One of these disputes runs through the articles in this volume. Gary Nash has uncovered a growing maldistribution of wealth in the colonial cities, a declining buying power for the working classes that he believes led them into the streets. Economic grievances led the poor to join in political unrest in their own interest. This argument corresponds to suggestions by Philip Greven and Kenneth Lockridge, confirmed in part by Robert Gross, that declining wealth and increasing pressure on available land in the old New England towns also drove young people to the streets. James Henretta has recently disputed these findings, arguing that the maldistribution of wealth occurred in the early eighteenth century. If there was also an emerging urban proletariat, it was not a significant factor in colonial politics or economic development. He also finds no evidence that local stagnation led to revolutionary agitation in New England.[2]

No one now disputes the existence of a large landless class. Day laborers, servants, young people on the road, and vagrants passed through parish and town in endless array. Whether they were symptomatic of the breakdown of earlier colonial communities' values, or the inevitable byproduct of a modern society, no one has yet determined.

Peter Charles Hoffer
University of Georgia

Notes

1. Michael Kammen, *People of Paradox: An Inquiry Concerning the Origins of American Civilization* (New York, 1972). This was no "calculated ambiguity" (218); it went to the unresolved heart of Americans who made a new world while yearning for an old one.

2. James Henretta, "Wealth and Social Structure," in Jack P. Greene and J.R. Pole, eds., *Colonial British America* (Baltimore, 1984), 262–89.

College Founding in the American Colonies, 1745-1775

By Beverly McAnear

In the year 1745 there were but three colleges in all of British North America. Yet by the beginning of the Revolution the virus that Ezra Stiles labeled "College Enthusiasm" [1] had so widely infected the American colonists that seven new colleges had been firmly established; plans had been laid for three more which were to open during the Revolution; and at least six abortive projects had been undertaken by responsible people. Thus by 1776 every province and nearly every popular religious sect was planning and had arranged for financial backing for a school of its own. In addition to the older three — Harvard, Yale, and William and Mary — those actually giving instruction were: Dartmouth College in New Hampshire; the College of Rhode Island, now Brown University; King's College, from which Columbia University has descended; Queen's College, soon to bear the name of Rutgers; the College of New Jersey, destined to become Princeton University; the Academy and College of Philadelphia, still living as the University of Pennsylvania; and Newark Academy, ultimately to reappear as the University of Delaware.

This interest in the founding of colleges coincided with a growth of the spirit of rationalism that sought intellectual stimulation in sources other than theological — a spirit eagerly capitalized on by college promoters who urged the establishment of non-sectarian institutions. Sectarian discussion, such as the Old Light-New Light controversy, further spurred on the founding of colleges consecrated to the religious approach of the partisans. Finally, college founding was helped along by the years of prosperity after 1748, which made fund raising easier, and by the growth of civic and humanitarian

[1] Franklin B. Dexter (ed.), *The Literary Diary of Ezra Stiles* (3 vols., New York, 1901), I, 45-46.

spirit, which provided the stimulus. Between 1745 and 1765 most of the campaigns were organized by Yale graduates; after 1765 College of New Jersey men began to take the lead. Men educated in Great Britain and some who were not college men were also among the founders of the new colleges. Except for the role of Harvard graduates in the founding of Dartmouth and the part played by the College of Philadelphia in the establishment of Newark Academy, the graduates of the other American colleges did not figure prominently in the movement.[2]

2   Regardless of their educational background, college promoters became interested in advancing higher education through affiliation either with a library company or with a church. Most organizers — and they were the most successful — were ministers interested in the advancement of their own sect. Clerical leaders campaigned for Dartmouth, Queen's, New Jersey, Newark, and, in their final stages of organization, for Rhode Island and King's. The reasons emphasized by clerics for establishing colleges were to educate ministers, to raise the level of general culture and morals through the influence of the clerical alumni, and to convert the Indians.[3] They maintained that a college was a religious society whose basic and chief duty was to train its students to be religious and moral men. The study of nature was to be subservient to the inculcation of religion; the one was only a threshold to the other, and religious instruction therefore was to be emphasized. They freely promised toleration to all Protestant Trinitarian sects, but they demanded clerical administration and the dominance of one sect.[4]

[2] Yale University, *Catalogue of the Officers and Graduates of Yale University* (New Haven, 1924), 115-21; Thomas J. Wertenbaker, *Princeton, 1746-1896* (Princeton, 1946), 16, 27; Leon B. Richardson, *History of Dartmouth College* (2 vols., Hanover, 1932), I, 90; Beverly McAnear (ed.), "The Charter of the Academy of Newark," *Delaware History* (Wilmington), IV (September, 1950), 153.

[3] See, for example, John Ewing and Hugh Williamson, *To the Charitable and Humane Friends of Learning . . .; The Memorial . . . of the Academy of Newark* (London, 1774), 1-2; [Samuel Blair], *An Account of the College of New-Jersey* (Woodbridge, N. J., 1764), 6; *Charter of a College to Be Erected in New-Jersey, by the Name of Queen's College* (New York, 1770), 5-6; Frederick Chase, *History of Dartmouth College* (2 vols., Cambridge, 1891), I, 296-98.

[4] Richardson, *History of Dartmouth College*, I, 89; Herbert and Carol Schneider (eds.), *Samuel Johnson, President of King's College: His Career and Writings* (4 vols., New York, 1929), I, 154, IV, 56, 115-16, 223-24; Horace W. Smith, *Life and Correspondence of the Rev. William Smith* (2 vols., Philadelphia, 1879), I, 59; [Blair], *Account of the College of New-Jersey*, 24, 28-29, 46-47; [William P. Smith], *A General Account of the Rise and State of the College, Lately Established in the Province of New-Jersey* (New York, 1752), 5-6.

Those promoters identified with one of the library companies were usually laymen, often without much formal education. Colleges and libraries were at that time a natural conjunction of interests, for some of the library companies were originally designed as organizations which would not only circulate books but which would also provide popular lecture courses, particularly on scientific subjects. Men affiliated with libraries were concerned with the foundation of Rhode Island, King's, and Philadelphia, and with abortive proposals for colleges at Newport and Charleston.[5] They argued that a college should properly be considered a civil society committed to the duty of training youths for service to the commonwealth, and the value of any type of training was to be measured according to its ultimate usefulness to the graduates in civil life. The best attribute of an educated man was an independent mind; free inquiry was therefore to be encouraged and religious instruction prohibited. To assure freedom, religious toleration and non-sectarianism were to be maintained, and even direct state control was proposed.[6]

To their basic appeal for support each group of promoters added virtually the same arguments. College alumni would provide superior public servants and the very presence of the college and its faculty would raise the cultural level of the province. The students' love of their native province would be protected against the alienation that might result from new attachments formed during their school years in distant parts, and thus the best minds of the colony would be saved for the service of their birthplace. Money would not flow out of the province to enrich the residents of college towns in other provinces. And, finally, a local school would provide a less expensive education for ambitious sons of residents.[7]

[5] The Charter, Laws, Catalogues of Bookes ... of the Juliana Library-Company in Lancaster (Philadelphia, 1766), ii-iii, viii-xi, 55-56; J. Harold Easterby, History of the College of Charleston (Charleston, 1935), 4-6, 10-13; The Charter, Laws, and Catalogue of Books of the Library Company of Philadelphia (Philadelphia, 1770), 4-5; Reuben A. Guild, Early History of Brown University (Providence, 1897), 129-34; Beverly McAnear, "American Imprints Concerning King's College," Papers of the Bibliographical Society of America (New York), XLIV (1950), 326-27; Thomas H. Montgomery, History of the University of Pennsylvania (Philadelphia, 1900), 20.

[6] New York Independent Reflector, March 22, 29, April 5, 12, 19, 1753; [Archibald Kennedy], A Speech Said to Have Been Delivered ... by a Member Dissenting from the Church (New York, 1755), 13, 16-17, 28; Richard Peters, A Sermon on Education (Philadelphia, 1751), 33-41; Carl Van Doren, Benjamin Franklin (New York, 1938), 190-91; Montgomery, History of the University of Pennsylvania, 46-47, 503; Easterby, History of the College of Charleston, 15.

[7] [Blair], Account of the College of New-Jersey, 6; [William Smith], A Poem on

Almost inevitably a movement to launch a college aroused religious and political rivalries. Many of the quarrels concerned the sectarian affiliation of the proposed college; and in these contests the Anglicans and Presbyterians were the most combative. In addition to their involvement in the Old Light-New Light controversy raging in the Calvinistic churches,[8] some of the schools became involved in provincial or imperial political questions which had nothing to do with higher education,[9] and some college promoters were confronted with the monopolistic claims of institutions already established.[10] Once aroused by these contentions, factions which had been aligned in the opening days of a college lived on to blight its growth. These feuds account in great measure for the failure of all the newer colleges to gain annual provincial appropriations, and they caused the failure of many of the proposals for new colleges even though neither money nor public interest was lacking.

Factional division usually began with a dispute over the terms of a charter of incorporation and the nomination of the first trustees. Incorporation was necessary to protect the institution's property and to permit the granting of degrees; and the religious loyalties of the trustees usually determined the ecclesiastical affiliation of the college. The founders of New Jersey and Dartmouth objected so stubbornly to the inclusion of royal officers of Anglican faith among the trustees that they were almost denied their charters. A furious battle over the method of organization of the college cost King's

Visiting the Academy of Philadelphia (Philadelphia, 1753), 14-15; New York *Gazette, or Weekly Post-Boy*, February 4, 1751; Annapolis *Maryland Gazette*, March 21, 1754, November 7, 1771; Allen D. Candler *et al.* (eds.), *The Colonial Records of the State of Georgia* (26 vols., Atlanta, 1904-1916), IX, 259-61; William Allen to Thomas Penn, October 8, 1767, Penn Papers (Historical Society of Pennsylvania, Philadelphia), Official, X, 116-18.

    [8] George Whitefield, *A Letter to His Excellency Governour Wright* (Reprint, Charleston, 1768); Franklin B. Dexter (ed.), *Extracts from the Itineraries . . . of Ezra Stiles* (New Haven, 1916), 429-30, 557-60; Walter C. Bronson, *The History of Brown University, 1764-1914* (Providence, 1914), 14-27; William H. S. Demarest, *A History of Rutgers College, 1766-1924* (New Brunswick, 1924), 69-72, 77-80; Chase, *History of Dartmouth College*, I, 247-48, 272-74.

    [9] McAnear, "American Imprints Concerning King's College," *Papers of the Bibliographical Society of America*, XLIV (1950), 301-39; Easterby, *History of the College of Charleston*, 8, 12, 337 n.; Charles A. Barker, *The Background of the Revolution in Maryland* (New Haven, 1940), 330-31, 355-56, 366.

    [10] Henry Lefavour, "The Proposed College in Hampshire County in 1762," *Massachusetts Historical Society, Proceedings* (Boston), LXVI (1942), 53-74; Thomas Coombe to William Smith, March 12, 1770, Dr. William Smith Papers (Archives of the Protestant Episcopal Church, New-York Historical Society), I, 70; Guild, *Early History of Brown University*, 134; Richardson, *History of Dartmouth College*, I, 35.

thousands of pounds of endowment and all hope of future provincial support.[11]

In drafting their charters, King's, Dartmouth, and Queen's used the College of New Jersey charter of 1748 as a model; Rhode Island drew upon the Harvard and Yale charters, in addition to New Jersey's; and Newark turned to the charter of Pennsylvania. Ironically, no one seems to have known at the time whether the colonial governors had the power to grant charters of incorporation and therefore whether the college charters were valid.[12]

The building lot for the college was invariably provided by a public or semi-public organization in order to attract the college to its town. The difficulties that New Jersey College experienced in its attempts to secure a sizable sum in four different New Jersey villages indicate that the custom was not well established in the 1740's. But it caught on quickly, and Queen's was embarrassed by bids from New Brunswick, Tappan, and Hackensack, while Rhode Island felt obliged to hold an auction to terminate five months of competitive controversy.[13]

As soon as money was available, a college hall, containing classrooms and a dormitory, was erected. To supervise construction, some colleges relied on artisans or amateur architects, but Rhode Island, New Jersey, and Philadelphia retained the services of the

[11] Jonathan Belcher to Gilbert Tennent, June 18, 1748, Jonathan Belcher Letter Books (Massachusetts Historical Society, Boston), 1747-1748, pp. 371-72; McAnear, "American Imprints Concerning King's College," *Papers of the Bibliographical Society of America*, XLIV (1950), 334-35; William L. Saunders (ed.), *The Colonial Records of North Carolina* (10 vols., Goldsboro, 1886-1890), VIII, 486-90, IX, 250, 254, 284; Chase, *History of Dartmouth College*, I, 115-21.

[12] A copy of the New Jersey charter is among the King's College Papers in the Columbia University Library, as is a copy of the first draft of the King's College charter. Many passages of the latter are identical with or paraphrase clauses in the New Jersey charter; and many similarities remained after the revision of the King's charter at the order of Lieutenant Governor James DeLancey. See also Bronson, *History of Brown University*, 14, 28-29; McAnear (ed.), "Charter of the Academy of Newark," *Delaware History*, IV (September, 1950), 152; John Maclean, *History of the College of New Jersey* (2 vols., Philadelphia, 1877), I, 90-97; and for the question of power, Joseph S. Davis, *Essays in the Earlier History of American Corporations* (2 vols., Cambridge, 1917), I, 10-15; Elmer B. Russell, *The Review of American Colonial Legislation by the King in Council* (New York, 1915), 78; and Chase, *History of Dartmouth College*, I, 639-49.

[13] Belcher to Committee of West New Jersey Society, September 18, 1747, and Belcher to William Allen, October 12, 1748, Jonathan Belcher Letter Books, 1747-1748, pp. 52-53, 491-92; Minutes of the Trustees of the College of New Jersey (Princeton University Library), September 26, 1750, September 25, 1751, September 27, 1752; Demarest, *History of Rutgers College*, 31-32, 69-70, 77-81; Bronson, *History of Brown University*, 43-50.

Philadelphia architect and builder, Robert Smith. The plans drawn by Smith and William Shippen, a physician and amateur architect of Philadelphia, were repeated elsewhere and virtually created in America the collegiate Georgian style. Essentially their design was an adaptation of that for King's College, Cambridge University. During the twenty-five years before the Revolution, five of these schools spent approximately £15,000 sterling for the erection or remodeling of buildings.[14] "This they chose to do," President John Witherspoon of the College of New Jersey wrote, "though it wasted their Capital, as their great Intention was to make effectual Provision, not only for the careful Instruction, but for the regular Government of the Youth."[15] A pretentious building was also desirable because it afforded publicity, and its inclusion of dormitory space and commons reduced student expenses.[16]

The cost of the original hall invariably reduced the college to a state of near insolvency. Indeed, Philadelphia and Rhode Island invested in their buildings literally the last penny in the till.[17] As a result, trustees tended to limit the materials for classroom demonstrations in physics, surveying, and astronomy. Thanks to the

[14] For the expenditures of the Academy and College of Philadelphia, see Account of Robert Smith, Academy of Philadelphia, Treasurer's Ledger, 1749-1779 (University of Pennsylvania Archives), folios 4, 20-21, 27, and Minutes of the Trustees of the College of Philadelphia (University of Pennsylvania Archives), I, 3 (February 1, 1749 [1750]); for King's College: Schneider and Schneider (eds.), *Samuel Johnson*, IV, 55; for the College of New Jersey: Accounts and Receipts of Robert Smith, Jonathan Sergeant, and Richard Stockton, Princeton University Papers, and Minutes of the Trustees of the College of New Jersey, November 23, 1758, May 9 and September 27, 1759, and September 30, 1762; for the College of Rhode Island: Account of College of Rhode Island with Nicholas Brown, March 11, 1771, Brown Family Papers (John Carter Brown Library, Brown University), and Bronson, *History of Brown University*, 57; for Dartmouth College: Richardson, *History of Dartmouth College*, I, 104, and Chase, *History of Dartmouth College*, I, 269. Queen's College and Newark Academy did not own buildings prior to the Revolution.

[15] John Witherspoon, *Address to the Inhabitants of Jamaica* (Philadelphia, 1772), 15.

[16] See, for example, [Thomas B. Chandler], *Candid Remarks on Dr. Witherspoon's Address* (Philadelphia, 1772), 23; [Blair], *Account of the College of New-Jersey*, 11-13; Aaron Burr to George Whitefield, February 16, 1757, Princeton University Papers; and Minutes of the Trustees of the College of Philadelphia, I, 137, 147 (March 10 and November 28, 1761). For a discussion of the use of the term "college yard" in connection with this arrangement, see Albert Matthews, "The Use at American Colleges of the Word 'Campus'," Colonial Society of Massachusetts, *Publications* (Boston), III (1895-1897), 431-37.

[17] Guild, *Early History of Brown University*, 152; Richard Peters to Smith, June 10, 1762, Dr. William Smith Papers, II, 88-89. See also Schneider and Schneider (eds.), *Samuel Johnson*, IV, 55, and Burr to William Hogg, December 3, 1755, Princeton University Papers.

persistence of their presidents, however, by 1775 the scientific instruments of King's, New Jersey, and Philadelphia were equal to or better than those possessed by Harvard, Yale, and William and Mary. The other new colleges owned little or no scientific apparatus.[18]

A greater handicap was the inadequacy of libraries. By the time of the Revolution, the Harvard library, with more than 4,000 volumes, was probably the largest college library in the colonies. Yale was not far behind, but William and Mary must have had less than 3,000. While Philadelphia, King's, and New Jersey, with perhaps 2,000 books each, made at least a respectable showing, library facilities at the other newly established institutions were either virtually or completely non-existent.[19]

Nearly all the books in the libraries of the newer colleges had been presented: none customarily bought more than occasional titles. The only important purchases were three consignments for New Jersey, one of which was so costly that the trustees deemed it an extravagance and charged the bill to the president.[20] To make matters more difficult, these libraries were largely the gifts of benevolent clergymen, and the weight of theology hung heavy upon them. "But few modern Authors, who have unquestionably some Advantages above the immortal ancient, adorn the Shelves," wrote a college official in 1760. "This Defect is most sensibly felt in the Study of Mathematics, and the Newtonian Philosophy."[21] Phila-

7

[18] Account of Books and Instruments, Academy of Philadelphia, Treasurer's Ledger, 1749-1779, folio 8; Inventory of the Philosophical Apparatus Belonging to the University of Pennsylvania, December 3, 1779, University Papers (University of Pennsylvania Archives), I, 7; Schneider and Schneider (eds.), Samuel Johnson, IV, 55; Wertenbaker, Princeton, 107-109. Harvard's equipment had been destroyed in the fire of 1764 and was only partially replaced before the Revolution. Samuel E. Morison, Three Centuries of Harvard, 1636-1936 (Cambridge, 1936), 95-96. For Yale, see Dexter (ed.), Literary Diary of Ezra Stiles, II, 348-49, 446; and for William and Mary, "Papers Relating to the College," William and Mary Quarterly (Williamsburg), Ser. I, Vol. XVI (January, 1908), 164-68.

[19] The histories of the individual colleges contain general information on the beginnings of their libraries. For more details in some cases, see [Samuel Davies], A Catalogue of Books in the Library of the College of New-Jersey (Woodbridge, N. J., 1760); "Library of the College of William and Mary," William and Mary Quarterly, Ser. I, Vol. XIX (July, 1910), 48-51; Carl Bridenbaugh, "The Press and the Book in Eighteenth Century Philadelphia," Pennsylvania Magazine of History and Biography (Philadelphia), LXV (January, 1941), 22; Austin B. Keep, History of the New York Society Library (New York, 1908), 90-94.

[20] Minutes of the Trustees of the College of New Jersey, April 9, 1793.

[21] [Davies], Catalogue of Books in Library of College of New-Jersey, iv.

delphia and New Jersey sought to remedy matters by assessing the students a library fee, but the income must have been small.[22]

By the time the trustees of a college had built the hall and provided furniture, scientific equipment, and a library, they had invested approximately £5,000 — perhaps the equivalent of $350,-000 today. By 1776 the physical properties of all the infant colleges probably represented the expenditure of something approaching £25,000 — an investment which produced virtually no income, since student rents could hardly have paid for maintenance.

In assembling a faculty, the trustees were apt to seek a president who had been trained in a British university, but since the necessary income was often lacking they were forced to be content with the product of an American college. The president bore the heaviest share of the burden of the school. He did a good part of the teaching and conducted the college's religious exercises. He was also the chief and sometimes the only administrative officer, and he was obliged to gather money and recruit students. To supplement his income, he often served as the pastor of a neighboring church. Such arrangements were discouraged by the trustees, however, and as the college grew more prosperous, pressure was placed on the president to confine himself to college affairs.[23]

The other members of the faculty (seldom more than three) were usually younger men destined within a few years to be clergymen. Most were American trained, though Anglican schools secured some British-educated tutors. Lack of money prevented the hiring of a more stable, better trained faculty, since almost any profession promised greater returns and better social status. The hardest position to fill was that of the science instructor. Few men with the necessary training were to be found in the colonies, and hence the post was often vacant. Each instructor normally was assigned a given class of students to whom he imparted knowledge on all subjects except the natural sciences. This arrangement demanded, however, that a faculty member undertake a considerable degree of specialization of subject matter, because the cur-

[22] Minutes of the Trustees of the College of New Jersey, September 27, 1765; William Smith, Notes for Commencement, November 17, 1767, Dr. William Smith Papers, VI, 28.

[23] Smith to Peters, June 4, 1763, Dr. William Smith Papers, II, 135; Schneider and Schneider (eds.), Samuel Johnson, IV, 99-100; Maclean, History of the College of New Jersey, I, 164. See also George P. Schmidt, The Old Time College President (New York, 1930), 54-64.

ricula emphasized given branches of learning in different years.[24]

One of the president's most perplexing tasks was the enrollment of students. To an even greater extent than the present-day college, colonial institutions relied upon income from tuition to provide vitally needed revenue. But to recruit students, it was necessary to popularize the value of higher education. Prior to 1745 not many parents in the British North American colonies sent their sons to college. This was especially true for the Middle Colonies. To attract public attention, some use was made of printed publicity. Ministers were pressed to act as recruiting agents for the college identified with their sect. Alumni, especially where they were schoolmasters or pastors, were able to help the recruiting for New Jersey, but most of the other colleges were too young to have many graduates.

9

The overwhelming majority of entrants were attracted by the college nearest their homes. The difficulty and expense of travel, the emotional complications inherent in distant separation from home, and local pride perhaps influenced students and furnished talking points for recruiting agents. But provincialism could be defeated if a distant college offered a cheaper education. Those colleges which grew most rapidly and attracted most students from other provinces were those which charged least. New Jersey and Rhode Island had the lowest charges, and Eleazer Wheel k permitted some Dartmouth students to work for their expenses. Hence these three colleges showed the most rapid increase in enrollment. Apparently New Jersey was also aided by its custom of admitting applicants as juniors, thus waiving costly residence at college for the first two or three years of a boy's work. Philadelphia and King's were the most expensive and therefore always had small student bodies, largely drawn from their immediate vicinity.[25]

Despite ardent campaigning, the enrollment in all these infant colleges was small. The opening class in any of them could hardly have been more than five to eight boys. Succeeding classes naturally increased enrollment, and the prosperous years of the early

[24] Schneider and Schneider (eds.), *Samuel Johnson*, I, 38, IV, 55-57; Peters to Smith, May 28, 1763, and Smith to Peters, February 25, 1764, Dr. William Smith Papers, II, 130-32; Minutes of the Trustees of the College of Philadelphia, I, 125 (January 13, 1761).

[25] Beverly McAnear, "The Selection of an Alma Mater by Pre-Revolutionary Students," *Pennsylvania Magazine of History and Biography*, LXXIII (October, 1949), 429-40; Richardson, *History of Dartmouth College*, I, 106-107, 118-19.

1770's greatly aided recruitment. Even so, most of the newer schools prior to the Revolution had at best an attendance of only forty or fifty students. By all odds, the most successful was New Jersey, which grew to an enrollment of about one hundred. Yet, despite this rapid growth, New Jersey was still smaller than her older rivals, for after 1755 the student bodies of Harvard and Yale had often exceeded one hundred and fifty. Approximately four sevenths of all college students of 1775 were enrolled in the three oldest institutions.[26]

Upon appearance at college, the prospective student was required to pass an entrance examination, usually administered by the president. The requirements of the new colleges seem to have been copied from those of Yale; for Rhode Island, King's, and New Jersey the requirements were almost identical. Essentially, the test demanded ability to translate elementary Latin and Greek and a knowledge of arithmetic — this last being a contemporary innovation. It is doubtful that an applicant was ever sent home, though sometimes extra work was prescribed.[27]

Many of the students admitted were mere boys. From 1750 to 1775 the median age of the entrants at Yale was only sixteen or seventeen; at Philadelphia it was sixteen; and at King's only fifteen. Eleven- and twelve-year-old freshmen were not unknown, and John Trumbull satisfied the Yale entrance examination at the age of seven years and five months. Because of the competition for students the colleges were in danger of becoming grammar schools. As a step toward remedying this difficulty, the governors of King's in 1774 ruled that after the admission of the class of 1778 entrance would be refused any applicant younger than fourteen "except upon account of extraordinary qualifications." [28]

[26] Enrollments for 1775 have been estimated as follows: Dartmouth, 60; Harvard, 180; Rhode Island, 41; Yale, 170; King's, 50; Queen's, 20; New Jersey, 100; Philadelphia, 30; Newark, 25; William and Mary, 80. Grammar school students, often counted by contemporary administrators, are not included in these estimates. *Dunlap's Pennsylvania Packet* (Philadelphia), November 1, 1773, October 24, 1774, October 9, 1775; *Catalogue of the College of William and Mary* (Williamsburg, 1859), 29-46; John R. Williams (ed.), *Journal and Letters of Philip Vickers Fithian, 1767-1774* (Princeton, 1900), 10.

[27] Columbia University, *Early Minutes of the Trustees* (1 vol. published, New York, 1932), I, June 3, 1755, March 2, 1763; Montgomery, *History of the University of Pennsylvania*, 236; Thomas Clap, *The Annals or History of Yale College* (New Haven, 1766), 81; [Blair], *Account of the College of New-Jersey*, 33; Bronson, *History of Brown University*, 101-102.

[28] Draft Minutes of the Governors of the College of the Province of New-York,

As a general rule, only freshmen were admitted. Though there were exceptions in every college, only Dartmouth, New Jersey, and possibly Philadelphia made a practice of admitting students to advanced standing. These boys had usually studied with a minister because such a training was less expensive than college residence. For admission to advanced standing, the college required payment of fees for the earlier years and passage of an entrance examination. The examination seems to have been largely a formality. Writing to a friend, one such candidate at New Jersey reported: "After examinations on the usual *authors*, when I and they, who were examined with me, received admission into the junior-class, we were told, that we should have been examined on the *Roman antiquities*, if it had not been forgotten." Witherspoon disliked the system and unsuccessfully sought to abolish it.[29]

Rhode Island, King's, and New Jersey also patterned their curricula after the Yale model, a program that reflected the course of study developed in the English dissenting academies. Actually colleges, these institutions had broken away from complete concentration upon the classics and Aristotelianism and had instituted Newtonianism, social sciences, and modern languages.[30] All four colleges required the same course of studies in the first two years: principally Latin, Greek, and Hebrew. That they assigned much more time to these subjects than did the English academies indicates an effort to repair the deficiencies of their matriculants who, compared to their English counterparts, were retarded about a year and a half. In the final two years, the American colleges emphasized natural sciences, mathematics, and metaphysics. President Samuel Johnson at King's apportioned three fourths of the time of juniors and seniors to mathematics and the natural sciences, while Yale

11

March 29, 1774, and File of Alumni (Columbia University Library). See also Franklin B. Dexter, *Biographical Sketches of the Graduates of Yale College* (6 vols., New York, 1885-1912), III, 253.

[29] John Leake to Enoch Green, February 11, 1775, Princeton University Papers; Witherspoon to Samuel Hopkins, February 27, 1775, Emmet Collection (New York Public Library); Yale College Records (Yale University Library), I, 164 (November 22, 1764); Schneider and Schneider (eds.), *Samuel Johnson*, IV, 243-61.

[30] The Yale curriculum had been revised by Samuel Johnson and President Thomas Clap. William L. Kingsley (ed.), *Yale College* (2 vols., New York, 1879), II, 496-500. For similar changes at Harvard, see Morison, *Three Centuries of Harvard*, 80-92, *passim*; and at the College of New Jersey, Wertenbaker, *Princeton*, 80-83. A general statement concerning the changes is in Theodore Hornberger, *Scientific Thought in the American Colleges, 1638-1800* (Austin, 1945), 40-43.

provided but one year, and Rhode Island and New Jersey considerably less than a year. To complete the studies for the senior year, Yale provided metaphysics and divinity, and New Jersey and Rhode Island oratory, composition, and almost certainly divinity. This difference in emphasis is partly explained by the desire of the dissenting colleges to train preachers and in part by the lack of scientific equipment and instructors. All devoted some time to logic, ethics, geography, and public speaking.

At Philadelphia a more independent approach to the curriculum was undertaken by President William Smith, who was influenced by Dr. Samuel Johnson, the great English writer, and by Robert Dodsley's *Preceptor*.[21] Nonetheless, the subjects prescribed by Smith were much the same as those offered elsewhere, except that he placed much greater stress upon oratory and the social sciences and did not regularly offer courses on religion.

Between 1765 and 1775 the American institutions showed great capacity to adapt their curricula to trends appearing in the English academies. Stress was placed on English grammar and composition by requiring polished written translations and original products of the students' pens, and greater weight was placed on oratory. English literature, however, was never taught formally. Some schools began to offer modern foreign languages as electives, and with their growing popularity classes in Hebrew were deserted. Greater attention was also paid to history by Witherspoon at New Jersey and by President James Manning at Rhode Island, though, as was the case in England, apparently only ancient history was taught. In brief, during these thirty years the college moved to some degree from ancient to modern languages, from divinity to the social sciences, and from metaphysics to natural sciences. Only Dartmouth and King's seemed to find the older ideas the better.[22]

Most colleges organized their courses into a four-year curriculum.

[21] Theodore Hornberger, "A Note on the Probable Source of Provost Smith's Famous Curriculum for the College of Philadelphia," *Pennsylvania Magazine of History and Biography*, LVIII (October, 1934), 370-75.

[22] Witherspoon, *Address to Inhabitants of Jamaica*, 15-16; Witherspoon to Marquis de Barbé-Marbois, July 18, 1783, Emmet Collection; Joseph Shippen, Jr., to Edward Shippen, February 3, [1752], Shippen Papers (Historical Society of Pennsylvania), I, 31; Bronson, *History of Brown University*, 102-107; Montgomery, *History of the University of Pennsylvania*, 236-43, 473-74; Richardson, *History of Dartmouth College*, I, 119-20; Schneider and Schneider (eds.), *Samuel Johnson*, I, 314, 409; IV, 56-57.

Smith, however, instituted at Philadelphia the then current English innovation of a three-year college. In actual fact, Philadelphia's program of study was abbreviated by pushing back into the academy some of the courses taught elsewhere to college freshmen. Newark also seems to have required only three years' residence, but similar experiments in truncation by Witherspoon at New Jersey and Manning at Rhode Island were soon abandoned.[33]

Classes began early and lasted through the day, punctuated by morning and evening prayers. Instruction was based upon recitations from and elaborations of textbooks, though the lecture method was used by some presidents in teaching the seniors. The college library was rarely used by undergraduates, and New Jersey claimed distinction for its policy of encouraging seniors to browse in the library.[34] To stimulate scholarship, King's, New Jersey, and Philadelphia set up prizes to be awarded for excellence in specified subjects, and Manning wanted to adopt the plan at Rhode Island. But the system proved ineffective, and it was allowed to die.[35]

Regular attendance, payment of fees, and proper deportment — or due regret for improper deportment — seemed almost invariably to yield a diploma on the scheduled day. "To the frequent scandal, as well of religion, as learning," wrote a contemporary critic, "a fellow may pass with credit through life, receive the honors of a liberal education, and be admitted to the right hand of fellowship among the ministers of the gospel. . . . Except in one neighbouring province, ignorance wanders unmolested at our colleges, examinations are dwindled to mere form and ceremony, and after four years dozing there, no one is ever refused the honors of a degree, on account of dulness and insufficiency."[36] In 1756 there were 172 students enrolled at Yale, and all but seven eventually received degrees. Elsewhere, virtually automatic progress by the student like-

13

---

[33] Montgomery, *History of the University of Pennsylvania*, 236-40; McAnear (ed.), "Charter of the Academy of Newark," *Delaware History*, IV (September, 1950), 156.

[34] [Blair], *Account of the College of New-Jersey*, 28-29.

[35] Smith to Peters, October 2, 1762, and Thomas Penn to Smith, March 7, 1767, Dr. William Smith Papers, II, 51, 99; Witherspoon, *Address to Inhabitants of Jamaica*, 17; Guild, *Early History of Brown University*, 173; McAnear, "American Imprints Concerning King's College," *Papers of the Bibliographical Society of America*, XLIV (1950), 336.

[36] [John Trumbull], *The Progress of Dulness, Part First* (2nd ed., New Haven, 1773), v.

wise seems to have been the rule; only at King's and Philadelphia was the mortality rate high.[37]

All the younger colleges claimed to be non-sectarian and insisted that full religious toleration was granted to all Protestants. Therefore all were advertised as "free and Catholic" or as "Catholic, Comprehensive, and liberal." Nevertheless, all students were required to take courses in divinity or the Bible, and all attended college prayers twice a day. College laws also required attendance at church on Sunday. Tolerance demanded that the student be permitted to attend the church of his own choice, though in some instances there was only one church in town. Thus while sectarians could and did freely accuse each other of proselytizing, none could charge these college administrators of ignoring the injunction laid down by one of their trustees that "*Liberty* be not made a Cloak of *Licentiousness.*" [38]

Most students lived in the college hall, two or three to a room or suite of rooms. Meals were served in the college refectory, usually situated in the basement of the college hall. The only important meal came at mid-day; it consisted essentially of meat and potatoes. The evening meal was based upon left-overs from noon, and breakfast brought only bread and butter. While this community life was recommended by the college authorities, many students preferred the more expensive but freer method of boarding out in adjacent homes. Such freedom, however, sometimes created special problems of discipline.[39]

Relations between the faculty and the students seem to have been reasonably good, although there were, of course, exceptions. Provost William Smith, of Philadelphia, gained a reputation for harshness; Eleazer Wheelock, of Dartmouth, ruled with the care but without the indulgence of a father; and Robert Harpur, the science instructor at King's, was hated and tormented on general

[37] See, for example, Ezra Stiles to Nathaniel Lardner, December 6, 1766, Stiles Papers (Yale University Library), Quarto Bound Letters, IV, 212-18; Schneider and Schneider (eds.), *Samuel Johnson*, IV, 244-61; "Notes and Queries," *Pennsylvania Magazine of History and Biography*, XXXII (October, 1908), 511.

[38] [Smith], *General Account of the College of New-Jersey* (London ed., 1754), 5-6.

[39] See, for example, Minutes of the Trustees of the College of Philadelphia, I, 146-50 (November 28, 1761), 280 (September 11, 1764); II, 61 (March 8, 1773), 63 (May 25, 1773); William Smith to Peters, December 2, 1771, Richard Peters Papers (Historical Society of Pennsylvania), VII, 93; Columbia University, *Early Minutes of the Trustees*, I, March 2, 1763; Minutes of the Trustees of the College of New Jersey, June 26 and September 25, 1766, October 1, 1772, April 22, 1773.

principles. But the newer colleges were free of the student riots which occurred at Harvard and Yale.[40]

The students found their college days profitable and enjoyable, and letters written after graduation to former schoolmates bore the impress of nostalgia. Extra-curricular activities revolved around clubs devoted to literary and bibulous exercises. Oratory was perhaps the most popular interest, and students sharpened their oratorical prowess in nightly practice for the seniors' grand performance on commencement day. Singing and the writing of verse were also fashionable; and the score for the New Jersey commencement of 1762 is one of the earliest examples of college music now extant. In their songs and some of their poetry the students frequently gave expression to sentiments which suggest that college pride had already been born.[41]

15

However valuable students found college life to be, their fathers regarded the expense of maintenance with no little concern. During the years between 1746 and 1772 the charges of the College of New Jersey for room, board, and tuition — £9 per year — were the lowest of any college. But college fees gradually increased, and after 1772 an economical parent found that the lowest bill, £12, was presented by the College of Rhode Island. The highest annual charges made by any of the newer colleges were those of King's — £18. And room, board, and tuition, of course, represented only a fraction of a student's total expenses. Firewood, candles, and washing cost £3 more; books and stationery, clothing and travel, and pocket money, too, increased the cost. Thus in 1775 the lowest cost of educating a boy ranged from £25 to £35 a year; it might easily amount to £55 or even more for spendthrifts. But the highest expense in America was mild compared to charges in England, where advanced education cost over £100 annually.[42]

[40] Columbia University, *Early Minutes of the Trustees*, I, May 13, 1766; Yale College Records, I, 147 (July 21, 1761), 170-71 (July 31 and September 11, 1765), 174 (July 5, 1766); Morison, *Three Centuries of Harvard*, 117-18; Chase, *History of Dartmouth College*, I, 294-98; Wertenbaker, *Princeton*, 103-104.

[41] The allusions to Nassau Hall in Hugh Henry Brackenridge, *A Poem on Divine Revelation* (Philadelphia, 1774), 21-22, serve to illustrate the growth of college pride. See also Claude M. Newlin, *The Life and Writings of Hugh Henry Brackenridge* (Princeton, 1932), 8-33; Lewis Leary, *That Rascal Freneau* (New Brunswick, 1941), 18-21, 24-25, 30-31; and Nathaniel Evans, *Poems on Several Occasions* (Philadelphia, 1772). Jacob N. Beam, *The American Whig Society of Princeton University* (Princeton, 1933), 7-23, throws light on the activities of student clubs.

[42] See, for example, Henry Livingston to Robert Livingston, Jr., February 10, 1764,

For colonial days these were large sums in terms of personal cash income. An able carpenter with good employment earned about £50 a year; a captain in the royal army, £136; a college instructor, £100; and a good lawyer, £500. Some relief was afforded by the extension of credit, and only too often greater relief was gained by parents who defaulted payment of the indebtedness. A little money for needy students was raised through church collections and subscriptions by the Baptists at Rhode Island and the Presbyterians at New Jersey. But none of the infant colleges had annually appointed scholars, and it appears that only at Dartmouth did any number of students work to pay their expenses. Therefore, sooner or later, the father had to pay, and clearly only the well-to-do could easily afford to do so. Indeed, some contemporary commentators believed that only the sons of the wealthy should go to college.[42]

The greatest problem faced by the college administrators was that of getting the money necessary to keep the college open, for students' fees paid only a small part of the cost of a boy's education. In their search for the requisite funds, promoters of the new colleges found that tapping the provincial treasury yielded only a trickle of cash. Harvard, Yale, and William and Mary all had been given both grants and annual subventions by their respective provincial governments or by the King. Among the newer colleges, only Dartmouth, King's, and Philadelphia were voted money from public treasuries, and King's alone was treated generously. None ever received an annual public subsidy, despite repeated applications.

Appeals to the general public by means of subscription lists and lotteries brought some funds, and occasional bequests added more; but the receipts from these sources were usually needed to meet

Livingston-Redmond Papers (Franklin D. Roosevelt Library, Hyde Park, N. Y.); Jacob Rush to Benjamin Rush, January 24, 1771, Benjamin Rush Papers (Library Company of Philadelphia), XXXIV, 44; and McAnear, "Selection of an Alma Mater by Pre-Revolutionary Students," *Pennsylvania Magazine of History and Biography*, LXXIII (October, 1949), 432-34.

[43] Aaron Burr Account Book (Princeton University Papers), 130-31, 247, 264; Minutes of the Trustees of the College of New Jersey, September 25, 1760, September 30, 1761, June 20, 1764, September 28, 1769; William M. Engles (ed.), *Records of the Presbyterian Church* (Philadelphia, 1841), 342-43; John Rutherfurd, "Notes on the State of New Jersey, 1776," *Proceedings of the New Jersey Historical Society* (Newark), Ser. II, Vol. I (1867-1869), 89; and Richardson, *History of Dartmouth College*, I, 106, 107, 118-19.

recurring deficits. To gain capital for investment, efforts were made to raise funds in Europe and the West Indies. Between 1745 and 1775 the seven new colleges received well over £72,000 in gifts from thousands of people solicited by hundreds of well-wishers. Over the same period approximately two sevenths of these funds were invested in income-producing endowment; about three sevenths were used in meeting current operating expenses; and the remaining two sevenths were absorbed in the erection of buildings. With the exception of King's, which was able to meet its running expenses with the income from its investments, all were operating on deficit budgets after 1770; and at the same time the raising of funds for colleges became increasingly difficult.[44]

17

The most obvious effect of the work of the pioneer educators who were responsible for the establishment and operation of these newer colleges was the great increase in the number of college-trained men in the colonies. From 1715 through 1745 the three older colleges graduated about fourteen hundred men, but in the following thirty-one years over thirty-one hundred gained bachelors' degrees in British North America. Almost nine hundred of these degrees (28 per cent of the total number) were granted by the seven new colleges. These schools therefore were responsible for about half the increase of college-trained men during these decades.

Behind the growing interest in college attendance was increasing economic prosperity. Each advance in college enrollment followed by three or four years the initial point on a rise of the index of commodity prices. Mounting colonial wealth aided the establishment of colleges in provinces from which the older colleges had drawn few students. Probably over 90 per cent of the graduates of Harvard, Yale, and William and Mary came from eastern New Hampshire, Massachusetts, Connecticut, and Virginia.[45] Rhode Island and the middle provinces were relatively fallow fields, and to the boys in those areas the younger colleges represented opportunity. Therefore, the advance in enrollment beginning in 1769 redounded to the advantage of the newer rather than the older

[44] For a fuller discussion of this problem see Beverly McAnear, "The Raising of Funds by the Colonial Colleges," *Mississippi Valley Historical Review* (Cedar Rapids), XXXVIII (March, 1952), 591-612.

[45] Dexter, *Biographical Sketches of the Graduates of Yale College*, I, 773, II, 783, III, 715; Morison, *Three Centuries of Harvard*, 102; Montgomery, *History of the University of Pennsylvania*, 267.

colleges, and from 1769 through 1776 they graduated approximately 40 per cent of the bachelors of arts.

This sudden popular interest in a college degree brought repeated demands that college bills should not be so high as to exclude the sons of the less well-to-do. This insistence sprang in part from a belief that the duty of the college was to open the gates of opportunity to youths of merit regardless of their fathers' social and economic position. One of the college propagandists argued: "The great Inducement to Study and Application . . . is the Hope of a Reward adequate to the Expence, Labour and Pains, taken. In Countries where Liberty prevails, and where the Road is left open for the Son of the meanest Plebeian, to arrive at the highest Pitch of Honours and Preferments, there never will be wanting such Emulation, and of Course great Men. . . . Such at this Day, is Great Britain." Some extended the argument, maintaining that all classes of society needed some type of education beyond that of the common school.[44]

These democratic concepts of education were being applied at the time to a class society which it was assumed educated men would buttress. Such efforts as were made to reduce the barrier of high cost came from the dissenting colleges. Groups of dissenters in England had long aided poor students financially, and the Baptists and Presbyterians in America followed the custom. Furthermore, ministers were badly needed in the colonies and usually they could be recruited only among the sons of farmers. A costly education, therefore, would handicap the Presbyterian and Baptist churches. Inevitably the administrators of dissenting colleges were forced to yield to pressure to keep their fees down, and hence their graduates included a goodly number of sons of artisans and farmers of modest means. Thus the requirements of religious sects gave effect to the demand for democratization of higher education.[47]

One concern of this increased interest in higher education was the improvement of professional training. New Jersey was the first of the younger colleges to build a curriculum designed to train

---

[44] [Kennedy], *Speech . . . by a Member Dissenting from the Church,* 13-14; New York *Journal, or General Advertiser,* January 8, 1767; Minutes of the Trustees of the College of Philadelphia, I, 86 (June 14, 1757).

[47] Philadelphia *Pennsylvania Chronicle,* June 27, 1768; New York *Post-Boy,* October 17, 1768; Ewing and Williamson, *To the Charitable and Humane Friends of Learning,* 2; Engles (ed.), *Records of the Presbyterian Church,* 342-43.

preachers, and it is not surprising, therefore, that about half of the pre-Revolutionary graduates of New Jersey entered the ministry. Rhode Island and Newark followed New Jersey's precedent, and President Smith at Philadelphia read lectures in divinity as a special course for candidates for the ministry. Through the influence of President Witherspoon, New Jersey was also the first of the new colleges to introduce formal graduate training in divinity, a program already long established at William and Mary.[48]

Philadelphia in 1765 and King's in 1767 undertook to supply professional training in medicine, though on an undergraduate level. But physicians had a poor economic and social status, and so the medical schools were never overflowing with students. By 1776, Philadelphia had graduated but ten students and King's twelve. Perhaps it was as well, for one of the abler graduates of King's recommended in his thesis the prescription of a specific he had not the courage to administer.[49]

This advance in educational standards also influenced the legal profession, and in 1756 the New York bar began to demand college work as a requisite for admission. By 1776 one third of those entitled to plead before the provincial courts held the degree of bachelor of arts. Formal training in civil law, the common law, or municipal law was never undertaken in any colonial college, although King's, Philadelphia, and the advocates of the proposed college at Charleston all dreamed and planned for the establishment of such courses.[50]

The colleges likewise raised the standards of secondary education. Throughout the period, criticism of the preparation of college matriculants was constant, and, in an effort to gain more satisfactory material, all the new colleges maintained their own grammar

19

48 Maclean, *History of the College of New Jersey*, I, 155, 274, 299, 357; Bronson, *History of Brown University*, 104, 129; Lyon G. Tyler, "Early Courses and Professors at William and Mary College," *William and Mary Quarterly*, Ser. I, Vol. XIV (October, 1905), 72-73.

49 Samuel Kissam, *An Inaugural Essay on the Anthelmintic Quality of the Cow Itch* (New York, 1771). See also Columbia University, *Early Minutes of the Trustees*, I, August 14, 1767; Schneider and Schneider (eds.), *Samuel Johnson*, IV, 255-60; and Edward P. Cheyney, *History of the University of Pennsylvania, 1740-1940* (Philadelphia, 1940), 96-104.

50 Paul M. Hamlin, *Legal Education in Colonial New York* (New York, 1939), 37-38, 116-17, 133; Maximilien LaBorde, *History of the South Carolina College* (Charleston, 1874), 4-5; John B. Pine, "A Forgotten Benefactor," *Columbia University Quarterly* (New York), X (March, 1908), 148-53.

schools. These secondary schools were also essential to the colleges as "feeders" of matriculants. As the years passed, the number of independent grammar schools in the middle and southern provinces increased sharply, and the graduates of the newer colleges, particularly New Jersey, were in great demand as masters.[51]

These college founders also made significant contributions to colonial interdependence. Hundreds of students crossed provincial boundaries to enroll in their alma maters. Half of Newark's enrollment came from provinces other than Delaware; 40 per cent of Philadelphia's from homes outside of Pennsylvania. New Jersey attracted men from North Carolina and Massachusetts. So heavy a migration was a significant change, for the three older colleges had drawn nearly all their students from relatively restricted areas. In the years immediately preceding the Revolution, students migrating northward were passed by northern-born graduates, particularly of Yale and New Jersey, moving to southern provinces. In Virginia and North Carolina, New Jersey men began a new cycle of college founding. Thus the younger colleges stimulated interprovincial migration of able men, trained in much the same intellectual pattern.[52]

The history of higher education during these three decades, then, is dominated by the establishment of successful colleges and the development of promotional techniques. Each successive college was founded more easily and with better planning than its predecessors; problems were foreseen and precedents were available and accepted. Once opened, they carried on until subjected to military interference during the Revolution. These colleges significantly

[51] New York *Journal,* September 8, 1768; Philadelphia *Pennsylvania Chronicle,* October 31, 1772; New York *Mercury,* October 24, 1774; [Blair], *Account of the College of New-Jersey,* 35; McAnear (ed.), "Charter of the Academy of Newark," *Delaware History,* IV (September, 1950), 149-56; Columbia University, *Early Minutes of the Trustees,* I, March 1 and August 24, 1763; Witherspoon to Benjamin Rush, January 25, 1773, Rush Papers, XLIII, 11. For the interests of individual colleges, see also Cheyney, *History of the University of Pennsylvania,* 27-45; Wertenbaker, *Princeton,* 90-91; Richardson, *History of Dartmouth College,* I, 119; Demarest, *History of Rutgers College,* 69-72, 84; Bronson, *History of Brown University,* 36, 58.

[52] Wertenbaker, *Princeton,* 112-15; McAnear, "Selection of an Alma Mater by Pre-Revolutionary Students," *Pennsylvania Magazine of History and Biography,* LXXIII (October, 1949), 430; Address of President and Trustees of Liberty Hall Academy in Mecklenburg County, North Carolina, April 18, 1779, copy enclosed with Alexander Macwhorter to Elisha Boudinot, November 18, 1780, Emmet Collection; "List of Southern Graduates of the University of Pennsylvania from 1757-1783," *William and Mary Quarterly,* Ser. I, Vol. VI (April, 1898), 217-18; Dexter, *Biographical Sketches of the Graduates of Yale College,* I, 773, II, 783, III, 715.

increased the cultural level of the population and raised the educational standards of the professions. The founders advanced the practice and idea of democratic higher education. They transplanted the essentials of the educational system of the English dissenting academies and saw the system take root; and virtually the entire task had been the accomplishment of men born and bred in America.[33] They believed that they were strengthening the bonds of an empire in which America should be subsidiary, not subordinate to England. From the beginning many had hoped the colleges would further the creation of cultural autonomy in America. In 1770, for example, Ezra Stiles tabulated the various degrees granted by the several American colleges and concluded: "Thus all the learned degrees are now conferred in the American Colleges as amply as in the European Colleges."[34] As the colonial epoch closed, many Americans proudly felt that they had achieved educational self-reliance.

[33] William Smith and Francis Alison at Philadelphia, John Witherspoon at New Jersey, and Myles Cooper at King's were the only prominent educators trained in Europe, though some of the faculty members, particularly at King's, were also immigrants.

[34] Dexter (ed.), *Literary Diary of Ezra Stiles*, I, 71-72. See also Ewing and Williamson, *To the Charitable and Humane Friends of Learning*; [Smith], *General Account of the College of New-Jersey* (London ed., 1754), 6-7; and John Morgan, *To the Inhabitants of Jamaica and British West Indies* ([Kingston, Jamaica], 1772).

21

THE RISE OF A COLONIAL GENTRY:
A CASE STUDY OF ANTIGUA, 1730–1775

By R. B. SHERIDAN

22

THE story is told of George III, who, whilst driving with the elder Pitt at Weymouth, met a splendidly accoutred carriage that far outshone the one carrying the royal person and his chief minister. Upon learning that the occupant was a West Indian, the King turned to his companion and said: 'Sugar, sugar, eh? All that sugar. How are the duties, eh, Pitt, how are the duties?' [1] Other examples might be cited of West Indians who cut a fine figure at centres of fashion and used their wealth to purchase seats in parliament, to build town houses and country mansions, and, in a few cases, to form marriage alliances with members of the landed aristocracy.

Whilst the literature is replete with accounts of repatriated West Indians, it is far from adequate in explaining how these absentees acquired their estates. Little has been written, for example, of the relative importance of sources of wealth and income, such as agriculture, trade, shipping, finance, government, and the professions.[2] Furthermore, it is not clear whether the advantage lay with the descendants of pioneer families, with enterprising late comers, or possibly a combination of both in the form of marriage alliances. One contemporary maintained that the estates of absentees had been raised not by their own efforts, but 'by the hardship, sweat, and toil of their forefathers, among few capable competitors, in the infancy of colonies'.[3] Of a contrary opinion was the West Indian who wrote that 'When Merchants who settle here, or Men of the Learned Professions, of the Law especially, have got a little before hand let them but once get Footing on a Piece of Land or on a Plantation ever so poorly settled, whether by Marriage, Purchase, or otherwise, and they seldom fail (as their other Business or Practice is daily bringing them in Money) of soon becoming considerable Planters....' These individuals were said to be 'able to return to *Europe* and to live there in affluence and Splendour' on their plantation profits, 'whilst the *mere* Planters, who make the Bulk, are so far (some excepted) from being rich, that too many of them owe more than their Estates are worth'.[4]

To ascertain the historical accuracy of these accounts one would need to investigate the political economy of the West Indies, on an island by island basis, over a span of years long enough to resolve such questions as the nature

---

[1] Noel Deerr, *The History of Sugar* (London, 1950), II, 429, n. 15.
[2] The works of the late Professor Richard Pares are a notable exception to this generalization. See his *A West India Fortune* (London, 1950), and *Merchants and Planters*, The Economic History Review Supplements (Cambridge, 1960).
[3] *Some Observations; Which May Contribute to Afford a Just Idea of Our New West-India Colonies* (London, 1764), p. 22.
[4] Rev. Robert Robertson, *A Detection of the State and Situation of the Present Sugar Planters of Barbados and the Leeward Islands* (London, 1732), pp. 51–2.

342

of the plantation economy, the organization of trade and finance, and the rôle of government and the professions in economic life.

Although such a study is beyond the scope of this paper, it does seem possible to focus attention upon a single West India island and gain some insight into the forces that enabled a small, but not inconsiderable, group of inhabitants to accumulate modest fortunes and retire to England.

Owing to the relative abundance of source materials, the island of Antigua is suited to such a study. Dr Vere Langford Oliver, a descendant of a leading Antigua family, compiled a monumental genealogical *History of Antigua*, and edited *Caribbeana*, a magazine of West India genealogy.[1] Supplementing this source are the extant letter books of planters and merchants, the Board of Trade papers in the Public Record Office, and the works of the late Professor Pares.[2]

23

I

There is little question that the economy of Antigua underwent a remarkable transformation during the first three quarters of the eighteenth century. This was the period when the large sugar plantation became the dominant unit of production; when the race to acquire land, slaves, and sugar works sometimes made for conditions approaching a Hobbesian state of nature. In the brief compass of this paper a few statistics will highlight this transformation. The white population increased from approximately 2,300 in 1678 to 5,200 in 1724. From this peak it then declined to 2,590 in 1774, as the process of consolidating small farms and plantations into large sugar estates gained momentum. The slave population, on the other hand, experienced an almost continuous growth; it was reported in scattered census returns at 570 in 1672, 2,172 in 1678, 12,943 in 1708, and 37,808 in 1774.[3] Sugar production increased markedly under a system of near-monoculture, although not in proportion to the slave population. Approximately 4,900 tons were produced annually in the decade 1711–20, as compared with 9,200 in 1761–70.[4]

Though sugar might be produced on plantations of a hundred acres or less, economies of scale threw the balance in favour of the planter who possessed several hundred acres of arable land, an improved sugar works, and a labour force of from 200 to 400 or more Negro slaves. Few plantations fell in the latter category in 1734, when John Yeamans reported that very few persons were 'possest of Above, or even so Much as 300 Acres of Land fit for Sugar; and not without such a quantity or Something near it, no Planter can be enabled to bear the great Expence of the Buildings & Utensils necessary for making sugar ...'.[5] Some thirty years later Antigua was said to contain more than 300 sugar estates of an average value of approximately £10,000 sterling; the average plantation contained approximately 200 acres and 100 slaves.[6]

[1] Vere L. Oliver, *The History of the Island of Antigua* (London, 1894–9); ———, *Caribbeana, Being Miscellaneous Papers Relating to ... the British West Indies*, I (1909–10), VI (1919).

[2] *Samuel Martin Letter Books*, 1750–76, B. M. Add. MSS. 41,346–41,351. (I am indebted to the heirs of Sir Francis J. Davies for permission to quote extracts from the Martin letters). *Walter Tullideph Letter Books*, 1734–67. (I am indebted to Sir Herbert Ogilvy for permission to use the Tullideph letters.)

[3] Frank W. Pitman, *The Development of the British West Indies 1700–1763* (New Haven, 1917), p. 379. Deerr, *op. cit.* I, 174. Mrs Flannigan, *Antigua and the Antiguans* (London, 1844), II, 284. Oliver, *History of Antigua*, I, lvii, lxi, lxxviii.

[4] Deerr, *op. cit.* I, 195.

[5] John Yeamans to the Board of Trade, 27 May 1734, London, P.R.O., C.O. 152/20, V29.

[6] *Some Observations ... of Our New West-India Colonies*, p. 50.

Now these calculations leave many questions unanswered. They say nothing of the range and distribution of plantations in terms of acreage, labour force, and investment in sugar works. Yeamans states a minimum criteria in terms of acreage; however, the average plantation in 1764 was well below this minimum. If we accept Yeamans's minimum figure of 300 acres, then we are left to seek additional data in an effort to compile a frequency distribution of sugar estates.

Several problems arise in compiling a frequency table. The first and most obvious is the paucity of statistical data. Scattered statistics of estate valuations and individual ownership of land and slaves appear in the Board of Trade papers and the letter books of planters and merchants. The most fruitful sources, in the judgment of the writer, are the indentures and wills in Oliver's *History*. These figures, although rather tedious to extract, are more meaningful than raw data because they are related to property transfers.[1]

Another problem is to determine the unit of plantation ownership and control. The individual proprietor might be regarded as the logical unit. But when it is considered how often plantations changed hands through inheritance or sale and how many mergers were effected, the difficulty of this approach becomes apparent. Furthermore, it was not uncommon for plantations to be in control or possession of life tenants, trustees, administrators, attorneys, mortgagees, and share or cash tenants, with the actual proprietor assuming a passive rôle.

Prior to the age of steam power, limited companies, and free labour, the unit of production in the West Indies was the family-owned plantation, buttressed by the ancient institutions of primogeniture and entail. Moreover, the relationship between master and slave was not unlike that of the patriarchal family system. Antigua was a family-centred society where the great families were units of considerable permanence and power. Indeed, it was the rare outsider who made a fortune without also adding his name to the pedigree of a local family of prominence.

If the family is taken as the basic unit, several limitations and qualifications must be made explicit. In the first place, care must be taken to include individuals whose wealth and influence cannot be explained in the context of family. Secondly, not all family ties were salutary. Instead of helping one climb the economic ladder, one's family may have been a millstone around one's neck. Elder sons sometimes inherited plantations that were overburdened with fixed payments to annuitants. Thirdly, it should be remembered that the identity of small plantations was often lost in the process of consolidation. Owing to these limitations, it will not be possible to say how many plantations were owned by the leading families. All that can be done is to compile scattered statistics of landownership on a family basis, arrive at a maximum figure for the period from 1730 to 1775, and use this as one of several criteria for membership in the Antigua gentry.

Table I summarizes the landownership data for the 65 leading families.

---

[1] Besides the numerous indentures and wills, see the lists of plantations with names of proprietors and taxable acres and slaves in Oliver's *History of Antigua*, III, 355–392, 393–6.

TABLE I *Frequency Distribution of Landed Estates in Antigua, 1730-1775, Showing Maximum Acreage Held by the 65 Leading Families*

Number of Families	Acres of Land Owned
3	2,000–2,699
7	1,500–1,999
10	1,000–1,499
7	800– 999
5	700– 799
7	600– 699
11	500– 599
9	400– 499
6	300– 399
Total 65	

Source: See Appendix I.

25

The above table shows concentrations in the 500–599 and 1,000–1,499 frequencies, a decline in the intervening frequencies, and a tapering off at the extremities. The median family estate falls between 600 and 699 acres.

What other criteria are relevant to this study? Certainly, the statistics of slave ownership and plantation valuations are most useful, however infrequent their appearance in the literature. It is known, for example, that the Christians had 1,489 acres and 750 slaves in 1779; [1] the Fryes, in 1763, owned 1,350 acres and 562 slaves; [2] the Brookes, in 1767, had 821 acres and 260 slaves; [3] the Tullideph plantation, in 1755, contained 536 acres and 271 slaves; [4] and the Martin plantation, which was valued at £32,000 sterling in 1768, contained 605 acres and 304 slaves.[5] Estate valuations for the 65 families probably ranged between £20,000 and £80,000 sterling, and slave holdings between 200 and 800.

Other criteria are presented in Appendix I. By way of summary it can be said that approximately 33 families came to Antigua in the period from 1632 to 1679, 12 from 1680 to 1706, 18 from 1707 to 1775, and two at an unascertained period. Proprietary or crown land grants, a factor of some importance in the rise to wealth and influence, were made to 29 families, mainly in the period before 1670.

National origin can not be ascertained in all cases, but it is fairly certain that at least 36 families came from England or Wales, 13 from Scotland, and five from Ireland. Moreover, two were of Anglo-Irish origin, and one each of Dutch or French extraction. Except for the Irish-Catholic group, national origin was apparently no barrier to intermarriage, for all but eight families were intermarried with at least one other gentry family.

These families did many things besides oversee their plantations. In the period from 1730 to 1775 they dominated the local assembly and council where 50 and 39 families were represented respectively. Then there were at least 40 individuals, representing 27 families, who held a variety of public offices. Other families combined mercantile and professional vocations with planting. Included in these categories were at least 29 local merchants, 14

[1] Oliver, *History of Antigua*, I, 134–6.
[2] *Ibid.* I, 280–3; III, 396.
[3] *Ibid.* III, 396.
[4] *Walter Tullideph General Ledger*, ff. 17, 107, 190, 255.
[5] *Samuel Martin Letter Book*, B.M. Add. MS. 41,353, ff. 84–7.

lawyers, and 18 doctors. Though higher education was by no means essential for posts in government and the professions, 13 lawyers received some training at the Inns of Court, six individuals received university degrees, and 13 met Oxford matriculation standards.

Whilst the group's influence was parochial in the main, a number of families linked the island with the metropolis by ties of trade, politics, marriage, or mere social intercourse. At least 52 families had members away from the island for protracted periods in the years from 1730 to 1775. Included among them were 20 London-West India merchants, 12 members of parliament, one lord mayor of London, and nine titled persons.[1]

II

However useful the above survey may be in underlining the diverse origins and activities of the gentry, the larger task remains of showing what forces and qualities brought these families to the front. For purposes of analysis the 65 families can be divided into three groups according to period of settlement in Antigua.

The first group included approximately 33 families who came to Antigua before 1680.[2] Since this was a most troublesome period in the colony's history, family origins need to be seen against the background of historical developments. Antigua was settled by a group of colonists from St. Kitts under the leadership of Philip Warner, son of Sir Thomas Warner who was the first governor and colonizer of the Leeward Islands. Arriving about 1632, the colonists encountered the usual problems of pioneer settlement aggravated by troubles with Carib Indians.[3]

From the standpoint of the gentry, it is noteworthy that the infant colony, although ostensibly under the proprietorship of the Earl of Carlisle, was directed by a group of London merchants who dominated the Caribbean and North American trades. Included in this group were Martin Noell, Thomas Povey, and Maurice Thomson, who were key actors in shaping the colonial policy of the Protectorate and early Restoration periods. In Antigua one of the early land grants was made to Captain Rowland Thomson, probably a son or brother of Maurice Thomson.[4]

During the Civil War the inhabitants of Antigua sided with the Royalists until they were subdued by Commonwealth forces in 1652. Meanwhile, Dutch merchants entered the British Caribbean where they transmitted knowledge of sugar production, supplied planters with slaves and equipment, and carried off their tropical produce. Among the Dutch factors or agents who settled in Antigua was Sebastian Baijer, who later took out naturalization papers and founded one of the leading families of the island.[5] By the treaty of Breda in 1667 England acquired the colony of New York in exchange for that of Surinam.

---

[1] See Appendix I. Families with two members of parliament were CODRINGTON-Bethell, MARTIN, and WEBB.

[2] Families who ranked high in wealth and influence before 1680 but who failed to qualify for gentry status by the period 1730-75 are not included in this study.

[3] Oliver, *op. cit.* I, viii, xix; Aucher Warner, *Sir Thomas Warner, Pioneer of the West Indies, A Chronicle of his Family* (London, 1933).

[4] Charles M. Andrews, *British Committees, Commissions, and Councils of Trade and Plantations, 1622-1675* (Baltimore, 1908), pp. 33, 39. Oliver, *loc. cit.* I, xviii, xix.

[5] Oliver, *loc. cit.* I, 18-22, 37, 47, 137; II, 124, 242; III, 146, 248, 301, 329.

Among the families who came from Surinam to Antigua as a result of this settlement were the Willoughbys, of whom two members were West India governors-general. Francis, Lord Willoughby of Parham, lessee of Lord Carlisle's patent to the Caribbean Islands, settled in Antigua where he and his family acquired large landholdings. In 1679 the Willoughby plantations were purchased by the Tudways and Turneys, both London mercantile families; the Tudways who later purchased all of these estates have retained lands in Antigua to this day.[1]

The Martins and the Byams also came to Antigua from Surinam. William Byam wrote to a friend in 1668: 'I have deserted our unfortunate colony of Surinam, war and pestilence having almost consumed it. As it is to revert to the Dutch, I have with great loss removed to Antigua, where I am hewing a new fortune out of the wild woods.'[2]

Whilst these were families of some means, connexion, and plantation experience, others would appear to have started in more humble circumstances. In the latter group were small planters, retired soldiers and sailors, former shipmasters, government officials, lawyers, and merchants. Gentry families were recruited from all these occupational groups and possibly others. If it be asked which group was in the vanguard, it appears that locally based merchants, traders, and factors were most strategically placed to transform mercantile wealth into plantation wealth.

The nature of this transformation can best be explained in terms of the trading and agricultural organization of the period. In the infancy of the colony travelling merchants brought cargoes to exchange directly for island produce. However, as trade expanded, resident merchants and factors began to receive goods on consignment, thus constituting a group of permanent middlemen. In terms of comparative wealth and economic power, the merchants were generally superior to the planters, who, with few exceptions, cultivated small tracts of from ten to twenty or thirty acres of land. Even the locally based factor who was without personal means served as a channel through which wealth passed from merchant to planter. It would be realistic to assume, and there is some evidence to show, that factors found ways to divert, for a time at least, some of this wealth to their personal use. This might be done by complaining to the principal in England that planters were slow to pay their debts or that ships were not available to carry home the remittance. In the meantime the factor might have the remittance invested in lands, slaves, and sugar works. Governor Stapleton wrote to the Lords of Trade in 1682 that 'Many considerable adventurers from London and elsewhere have sent their factors there [Antigua], and converted their employers' goods into acquisitions of plantations and slaves, by which means ships went home empty.'[3]

Even before his plantation was fully settled, the merchant would be anxious to assume the title of gentleman planter. Only freeholders who could meet a rather stiff real property qualification were eligible to vote or become members of the local assembly, and it was this body, together with the council and governor, which enacted legislation. Planter governments, apart from the overriding concern of military defense, were interested in a variety of questions. These concerned such things as the titles to their estates, the disposal of govern-

_27_

---

[1] *Ibid.* III, 146–153, 166, 240–8. N. Darnell Davis, *The Cavaliers and Roundheads of Barbados, 1650–1652* (Georgetown, British Guiana, 1887), pp. 163, 172–5, 193–9.
[2] Pym Letters, *Hist. MSS. Comm.* 10th Report, Part VI, p. 96.
[3] *Cal. S. P. Col.* 1681–5, p. 276.

ment lands and escheated estates, laws to regulate the collection of debts, the
rate and incidence of taxation, and local enforcement (or unenforcement)
of the Acts of Trade. In a broad sense, planters were concerned to shift the
cost of local government, to the greatest extent possible, upon the broad back
of the mother country.

Besides numerous internal conflicts, differences arose between the islanders
and the mother country. Whilst the governors-general and patentees—customs
collectors, provost marshals, etc.—were charged with upholding the prerogative of the crown, authority might be undermined if assemblies voted money
to supplement the governors' income from the crown. From time to time
these local grants were cut off when governors incurred the displeasure of the
planter oligarchy. Most governors seem to have steered an uneven course
between the two extremes, with a tendency to lend a ready ear to leading
planters.[1]

Governors not only furthered the careers of favourites, but they also en-
dorsed certain planter measures that were inimical to outsiders. The land
disposal policy was one point at issue. After the French invasion of Antigua
in 1666, three acts were passed under the government of Lord Willoughby.
The first declared all old titles to land void and lost; the second confirmed the
land titles of present possessors; and the third put a limit of six hundred acres
on future grants or sales of land and provided that the lands of absentees
should be forfeited unless settled within a specified period.[2] Several London
merchants with large holdings in Antigua petitioned against these acts,
complaining that their land was unjustly held by inhabitants.[3]

The 33 families who settled in Antigua before 1680 not only survived a
century or more of fluctuating fortunes, but a majority of them also continued
to rank among the first families of the island. Using landownership as a criteria,
we find 11 of the 20 leading families, each owning more than 1,000 acres, in
this group. In government these families contributed four governors-general,
two lieutenant-governors, and one deputy-governor in the period before 1776,
not to mention other officials, councillors, and assemblymen. Since Antigua
was the seat of government for the Leeward Islands by the 1680's, this was a
factor of no mean influence in the rise of certain families.[4] Besides local politics,
these families were represented in parliament by Samuel Martin, Jr. Sir Henry
Martin, Clement Tudway, and the younger Richard Oliver.[5] These were
the men who upheld the cause of the sugar colonies in the mother parliament.

The mercantile and financial connexions of these families were a major
element of strength. These connexions were not confined to Antigua, for it
was customary for younger sons to take up residence in London to market the
family's sugar, purchase plantation supplies, and perform numerous services
connected with trade, shipping, and finance. In other words, direct access was
gained to the commodity and money markets of the metropolis, by which

[1] Vincent T. Harlow, *Christopher Codrington*, 1668–1710 (Oxford, 1928), pp. 188–201. Pares,
A West India Fortune, pp. 29, 343, n. 32. Oliver, *op. cit.* I, lxxvi–lxxxv.
[2] *Acts of Assembly, Passed in the Charibbee Leeward Islands* (London, 1734), pp. 25–30.
[3] Oliver, *loc. cit.* I, 37–40, 278–83; III, 30–2, 146–53, 268–77.
[4] In the period 1685–1783, nine of the fifteen governors-general of the Leeward Islands
belonged to families who already owned estates in this group of islands, and at least one more
acquired a plantation during his administration. Pares, *op. cit.* pp. 29, 343, n. 32.
[5] Oliver, *loc. cit.* II, 240–1, 318–19; III, 153.

means the dependence upon middlemen was reduced to the lesser branches of trade with the English outports, Africa, and North America.[1]

III

In a minor category, by comparison, were twelve families who made their way into the gentry after taking up residence in Antigua in the period from 1680 to 1706. In origin and occupation this group was most diverse. The Irish constituted one minor group. Four families (BROWNE, KIRWAN, LYNCH, SKERRETT) came from Galway, the west coast port that carried on an extensive trade with the West Indies in the seventeenth century.[2] From Drumcree came Walter Nugent, of an old Anglo-Irish family. After fighting in the Battle of the Boyne in 1690, he made three successful trading voyages to Antigua and eventually settled in the island as a landed proprietor.[3] Peter Gaynor, also from Ireland, was a merchant and planter in Antigua before his death in 1738. His large fortune of approximately £200,000 was inherited by his son-in-law, Sir George Colebrooke, who was chairman of the East India Company, member of parliament, and a London banker.[4]

Among the English families who came in the middle period, one (CHESTER) was founded by an agent of the Royal African Company; one (WEATHERILL) was founded by the commander of a privateer sloop that captured a large and valuable Spanish ship; and another (PEARNE) intermarried with the powerful Warner family.[5] From Barbados came the Codringtons, who contributed two governors-general of the Leeward Islands in the period 1689–1703. In the eighteenth century Sir William Codrington was a member of parliament. His brother-in-law, Slingsby Bethell, was a prominent London-West India merchant, lord mayor of London and member of parliament.[6]

Two events, closely associated in time, brought new elements into the Antigua gentry. The first was the Act of Union in 1707, which enabled young Scots lads to make their way to the British colonies. The second was the Treaty of Utrecht in 1713, which ushered in a peacetime period of expansion in the sugar industry. It was in this setting that the tempo of economic life quickened. Great prizes brought newcomers into the race. Whilst a number of old families continued to hold a commanding lead, some eighteen newcomers entered the Antigua gentry.

IV

From the standpoint of national origin the Scots were prominent after 1706. By 1775 some thirteen Scotsmen had established family dynasties of some importance. Numbered among these families were at least ten doctors and

---

[1] For an account of absentees from Antigua see Philip C. Yorke (ed.), *The Diary of John Baker 1751-1778* (London, 1931). Baker, a lawyer who had lived for some years in the Leeward Islands, was intimate with the London mercantile families of Bannister, Kirwan, Oliver, Skerrett, and Manning.

[2] Oliver, *loc. cit.* I, 74–8, 84–6; II, 9–11, 128–130, 206–209, 212–220, 240–7, 309–15; III, 87–9, 118–121. Oliver, *Caribbeana*, II, 336. Rev. Aubrey Gwynn, 'Documents Relating to the Irish in the West Indies,' *Irish MSS. Comm.* (Dublin, 1932), No. 4, pp. 139–277.

[3] Oliver, *History of Antigua*, II, 310–314.

[4] *Ibid.* II, 9–11. Lucy S. Sutherland, 'Sir George Colebrooke's World Corner in Alum, 1771–73', *Economic History*, III (1936), 237–258.

[5] Oliver, *loc. cit.* I, 126–133; II, 119–122; III, 16–19, 209–13.

[6] *Ibid.* I, 41–4, 144–153. Harlow, *op. cit.*

nine merchants. Broadly speaking, these young men combined skills and professional attainment with the desire to make their way in the world. In the changing economic environment of the West Indies they moved with ease from one vocation to another, often combining several vocations in one crowded career.

A brief sketch of Walter Tullideph's career will shed light on the forces which enabled one Scots family to gain admittance into the Antigua gentry. The son of a minister of the gospel at Dumbarny, Tullideph went to the high school at Edinburgh and in 1718 was apprenticed to a chirurgeon of that city. About 1726 he went to Antigua where several friends and relatives were already established as doctors, merchants, and government officials.[1]

With these connexions and his professional skill, Tullideph was able to combine several vocations during his early years in the island. As his brother's factor, he sold goods to the planters. Moreover, he received consignments from other merchants in England and Scotland. As a doctor, he treated both white and Negro inhabitants, but mainly the latter on a contract basis. When he travelled from plantation to plantation to minister to slaves he carried merchandise to sell to planters. A happy combination of these occupations was his wholesale and retail business in drugs and medicines. Much of his time was taken up in collecting debts, for planters were notoriously slow to pay.[2]

After a time Tullideph began to trade on his own account. He became a correspondent of William Dunbar, an uncle who was a sugar factor in London. This not only made it possible to by-pass local middlemen in buying English goods and selling island produce, but it also enabled Tullideph to borrow money on the promise of future consignments. The young doctor then began to make loans to needy planters, sometimes borrowing at five per cent in London and lending the funds locally at eight or ten per cent. By 1733 he held one planter's mortgage for £620, and numerous smaller debts on the security of personal bonds and judgments.[3]

Whilst some merchants and professional men purchased plantations in this period, others found an easier way to become planters. Our young doctor-merchant fell in the latter group, for in 1736 he wrote to his brother that he had 'married an agreable young Widow by whom I have gott Possession of a very fine Estate to which I am making additions & improvements and am likely to have a heir of my Own'.[4]

After taking up residence on the estate Tullideph retained his medical practice in the neighbourhood and began to devote most of his time to plantation affairs. Since his newly acquired plantation contained only 127 acres and 63 slaves, his overriding concern was to make 'additions and improvements'. An expansion program was launched with the earnings of trade and medicine, reinvested profits, and advances from his London merchant. By 1757 he had 536 acres and 271 Negro slaves. A conservative estimate places the value of his plantation at £30,000 sterling in 1763.[5]

Intricate financial transactions were involved in these acquisitions. In the long run resort was had to reinvested profits; however, loans and advances of

---

[1] Charles B. Boog Watson (ed.), *Register of Edinburgh Apprentices*, 1701–1755, *Scot. Rec. Soc.* (Edinburgh, 1929), p. 88. Tullideph to Andrew Aiton, 16 May 1757, Antigua, *Tullideph Letter Book*, II. Oliver, *op. cit.* I, 223–5; III, 128–133, 155–162.

[2] *Tullideph Medical Ledger*, ff. 1–156.

[3] *Tullideph General Ledger*, ff. 1–12.

[4] Tullideph to Thomas Tullideph, 28 April 1736, Antigua, *Tullideph L. B.* I.

[5] *Tullideph Medical Ledger*, f. 156. *General Ledger*, f. 255. Tullideph to Dr Sydserfe, 30 August 1755, Antigua, *Tullideph L. B.* II.

credit made it possible to speed up the process. On occasion Tullideph reduced the balance of his sterling running account to less than £500, but in most years he owed his London merchant between £500 and £2,000. Besides this source, he borrowed from his Scots friends and relatives in Antigua.[1] The impression is often given that sugar planters were chronic debtors, almost totally dependent upon their London merchants. This is only one side of the coin, if the Tullideph letters are a true indicator, for planter-merchants had offsetting credits in the colonies where borrowed money yielded higher returns than the five per cent normally paid to the London merchant.

The ownership of a large sugar plantation opened up new opportunities for our subject. After gaining the confidence of his neighbours, Tullideph was asked to write home for Scots doctors, merchants, and indentured servants; to superintend the estates of absentees; to purchase shares of ships and join with other planters in purchasing imported supplies in cargo lots; to engage in privateering ventures; to serve as an executor, administrator, guardian or trustee. On the estates of absentees, for whom he acted as attorney, he placed his Scots friends and relatives as doctors, plantation managers, attorneys and lessees. When an estate came up for sale he might help a friend to finance the purchase.[2]

No less important were Tullideph's trading activities. The management of numerous plantations enabled him to buy slaves and supplies at wholesale rates and to consign sugar and rum to the London merchant who would supply his growing financial needs. Besides the West India and London markets, he had correspondents in North America, Ireland, Scotland, and the English outports. With these contacts he developed a commercial intelligence system, however crude by modern standards, which enabled him to take advantage of the most favourable markets in making remittances and ordering supplies.[3]

Political preferment was to be expected for the planter-merchant on the make. Like a number of his colleagues, Tullideph climbed the island political ladder as his wealth and influence grew. He became, in order of succession, parish vestryman, justice of the peace, assemblyman, and councillor. These honours made him the social equal of the island's first families.[4]

Lest it be thought that these honours were the touchstone of a successful career, the reader of the letter books will learn that the young doctor was making enquiries about estates in Fyffeshire as early as 1734. After several short visits to England and Scotland, Tullideph became a semi-permanent absentee in 1757, thereafter making only short business trips to Antigua. Besides his Antigua plantation, he purchased a Scottish estate that cost approximately £10,000; and his two daughters, one of whom married a baronet, each had dowries of £5,000. This son of a rural minister lived his later years as a Scottish laird, taking great pride in his grandchildren. From planter on the make, *via* the route of doctor and merchant, we leave him now in Scotland as a successful planter, drawing income from his plantation in Antigua.[5]

---

[1] Tullideph to Dr Sydserfe, 19 June and 11 July 1749, 25 March, 14 June, and 15 July, 1752. Same to Slingsby Bethell, 11 November 1749. Same to Richard Oliver, 25 March, 14 June and 7 July, 1752, Antigua, *Tullideph L. B.* I. Same to Dr Sydserfe, 11 February 1754, London, *ibid.* II.

[2] R. B. Sheridan, 'Letters from a Sugar Plantation in Antigua, 1734–1758,' *Agric. Hist.* 31 (July, 1957), 3–23.

[3] *Idem. Tullideph L. B.* I–III.

[4] Oliver, *op. cit.* III, 155–62.

[5] *Idem. Tullideph L. B.* II–III.

V

Though similar in several respects the career of Samuel Martin affords points of striking contrast with that of Walter Tullideph. Both men owned plantations of approximately the same size and capitalized value, both had a marked influence upon the economic and political life of Antigua, both spent a substantial part of their adult lives away from the island, and both were able to pass on a larger estate to their survivors than they inherited. But here the parallel ends. Samuel Martin moved on a wider stage. He and his three sons had political and social connexions of some importance in England and North America. Since Martin inherited a large sugar plantation, he was not compelled to purchase land, build sugar works, and procure a fresh supply of labour. Whilst it is true that he added to the capitalized value of his estate, he already had a substantial base upon which to build. Martin's interests were directed chiefly towards plantership and he conformed more closely to the image of a gentleman planter than his friend Walter Tullideph.

32

The Martins came to Antigua by way of France, England, Ireland, and Surinam. Members of the family participated in the Norman Conquest, the Elizabethan conquest of Ireland, and, as Royalists, in the Civil Wars. Colonel Samuel Martin of Greencastle estate in Antigua was the eldest son and heir of Major Samuel Martin, a prominent planter who came to Antigua before 1680. He was born in Antigua in 1693, and after a long and eventful life which included many years' residence in England, he died in his native island in 1776. After his father's untimely death at the hands of his slaves, Samuel was sent to live with relatives in northern Ireland. At the age of fifteen he entered Cambridge University.[1] In the last year of his life Martin wrote to a friend: 'I have lost two wives & sixteen children out of one and twenty.'[2] Of the five who survived, four were sons and one a daughter.

Three of Samuel Martin's sons gained positions of some distinction. Samuel and Henry were members of parliament and Josiah was governor of North Carolina.[3] Other relatives were prominent in Antigua. Josiah Martin, a brother, was president of the council and the proprietor of a sugar plantation. William Thomas Martin, another brother, was a doctor. A half-brother and close business associate, William Byam, married Anne, daughter of John Gunthorpe. Both Byam and Gunthorpe were councillors, whilst Samuel Martin was speaker of the assembly from 1753 to 1763.[4]

Unlike Walter Tullideph who retired to Scotland after devoting his best years to his Antigua estate, Samuel Martin returned to Antigua in his fifty-seventh year to spend most of his remaining years on his plantation. Upon arrival in 1750, he met with a dismal prospect; his gang of Negroes reduced in numbers, his sugar works in a state of disrepair, and the fertility of his soil greatly diminished. In several letters Martin complained of the evils of absenteeism of which he was a sufferer.[5]

[1] Evangeline W. Andrews and Charles M. Andrews (eds.), *Journal of a Lady of Quality* (New Haven, 1923), pp. 103–06, 259–62. Oliver, *loc. cit.* I, lxxiv, xcii–xciv, xcvii–xcviii, cxix–cxx; II, 240–8; III, 297–302. Martin L. B., B.M. Add. MS. 41, 474, f. 56.
[2] Martin to Christopher Baldwin, 22 February 1776, Antigua, *Samuel Martin L. B.* B.M. Add. MS. 41, 351, f. 65.
[3] Andrews, *loc. cit.* pp. 262–70.
[4] *Ibid.* pp. 271–3. Oliver, *loc. cit.* I, 31–2, 96–104; II, 37–40.
[5] Martin to Samuel Martin, Jr., 14 and 16 June 1758, Antigua, *Samuel Martin L. B.*, B.M. Add. MS. 41, 346, ff. 208, 210.

An ambitious program of reconstruction was soon under way. In 1752, Martin wrote: 'I am in debt here, and must still lay out 3 or 4 thousand pounds before my Plantation can be brought into order'.[1] In a five-year period he purchased fifty slaves, most of them young Negroes from twelve to fifteen years of age. Moreover, he rebuilt his sugar works and increased his stock of cattle and mules. These additions and improvements were financed chiefly out of plantation profits.[2]

A major undertaking was to make his worn out lands more productive. This was not only a matter of applying more animal manure, but also of discovering other types of fertilizer and improved crop techniques. In the bed of a stream he found abundance of topsoil to spread over his cane lands. Marl pits and sand pits were opened in other parts of his plantation. By a process of trial and error Martin developed a rudimentary system of agronomy. He learned what ingredients to add to different types of soil; how to improve his lowlands by better drainage systems; how to space the rows of canes to take advantage of variations in moisture and soil types. The English system of husbandry was introduced, and Samuel Martin was probably the first planter in Antigua to use the plough in place of hand-hoe husbandry.[3]

So successful were most of these experiments that Martin's reputation as a planter spread to other parts of the island. In 1758 he said that his common rules of plantership had become generally established by his example and advice.[4] Planters in neighbouring islands learned of his achievements, especially after he published *An Essay Upon Plantership* about 1754.[5]

Prefacing the *Essay* is a dedication to all planters of the British sugar colonies in which Martin explains that his little tract was written for the instruction of a young planter. Over the years a number of young planters came under Martin's tutelage. He wrote for Scots servants or English farm boys who were trained in the English system of husbandry. Graduation from the Martin school of plantership opened up a wide field of opportunity. John Luffman observed in 1787 that 'poor Scots lads ... by their assiduity and industry, frequently become masters of the plantations, to which they came out as indentured servants'.[6] In fact, under the able guidance of planters like Martin and Tullideph a group of young men were trained to manage and superintend the estates of absentees, as they accumulated funds to achieve full ownership.

Actually, there were too few planters who were willing to devote time and energy to this pedagogy. The reason appears to be twofold. First, there were a growing number of absentee proprietors in the mid-century years of sugar prosperity. Secondly, planters remaining on the island were so taxed to superintend their friends' estates that little time remained to instruct young planters. Samuel Martin was in the diminishing group of resident proprietors who superintended the estates of absentees, minors, and superannuated planters.

By 1775 the sugar economy of Antigua and the social system it had spawned was already on its course of decline. After 1763 the Ceded Islands attracted a growing number of young planters who carried off seasoned slaves to carve

---

[1] Martin to Samuel Martin, Jr., 12 November 1752, Antigua, *ibid.* f. 40.

[2] Same to same, 24 June 1753, 14 and 16 June 1758, Antigua, *ibid.* ff. 70–71, 207, 210.

[3] Same to same, 18 October 1750, 14 June 1758, Antigua, *ibid.* ff. 11, 206–08.

[4] Same to same, 16 June 1758, Antigua, *ibid.* f. 211.

[5] Seven editions and several reprints of Martin's *Essay* were published in the period from 1754 to 1802. See Joseph Sabin, *A Dictionary of Books Relating to America* (New York, 1879), XI, 239.

[6] John Luffman, *A Brief Account of the Island of Antigua* (London, 1789), reprinted in Oliver, *op. cit.* I, 99.

new plantations out of wild woods. A disaster that struck more swiftly was the American War of Independence which brought real privation to this foreign fed colony. Working more slowly, but no less menacingly, were the eroding effects of absentee landlordism.

VI

We may now reconcile the conflicting accounts of absenteeism that appeared early in this paper. The evidence suggests that both accounts were true as far as they went, but that they were only half truths. Instead of absentees coming from a single source, we found both successful planters and planters on the make as absentees. Our analysis of the gentry from 1730 to 1775 revealed one group of families who traced their origin back to the early decades of the colony. The Martin family was in this group. Samuel Martin's career underlines the fact that it was no easy matter to preserve a plantation in its full productive power without the painstaking attention of a resident proprietor. When to this management problem we add the growing burden of fixed charges that was levied on plantations to support absentees, annuitants, and other rentiers, we can see that the margin between solvency and bankruptcy might be very slim indeed.

On the other hand, when we go back to the origin of the first group of families, a pattern not unlike that of later periods is revealed. Forming a nucleus were the families who brought capital and plantation experience from other colonies. To these were added families of diverse origin, with the mercantile group probably acting as the catalytic agent in the process of economic development.

Much the same process occurred in subsequent decades; however, the pace quickened after the early years of the eighteenth century. New families began to come forward, of which the group from Scotland was the most active. Walter Tullideph probably typified the members of this group, who, by means of scarce professional skills and mercantile connexions, accomplished in a few decades what for other families may have required a century.

As a final comment, a close investigation of Antigua marriage alliances reveals a process of intermixture. Families of long standing in the colony frequently intermarried with those who arrived late. From a business standpoint these alliances often proved rewarding. When, for example, the daughter of a saturated planter married a young merchant, a planter-merchant bond of mutual benefit might be established. This was especially the case when the merchant moved to that wider field of activity in London, for it was the metropolis that came to direct most aspects of the sugar economy. If such a move was made, the planter branch of the family might use its influence in the colony to secure correspondents for the merchant, whilst the merchant used his influence in the City to secure loans and advances for the planters. Loans and advances were merely a stopgap, however, for when the sugar economy moved into a period of secular decline the day of reckoning could not be indefinitely postponed. Eventually, it was the London-West India merchants who, through mortgage foreclosures, came into possession of a substantial number of West India estates.

Thus we have closed the circle; from merchant-planter to planter-merchant to gentleman-planter and finally, in the closing period of this study, to the merchant-planter again. Since the last mentioned phase is beyond the scope of this paper, it remains for another study to reveal the features of the Antigua gentry in the period subsequent to 1775.

University of Kansas

APPENDIX I

Classification of Gentry Families of Antigua, 1730–1775

Families / In Antigua before 1680	Acreage [1]	Slaves [1]	National Origin [2]	Land Grants [3]	Assembly [4]	Council [4]	Government Officials [4]	Antigua Merchants [4]	London-W.I. Merchants [4]	Lawyers [4]	Doctors [4]	Absentees [4]	M.P.s [4]	Titles [4]
1. WARNER-Johnson [5]	2697		Eng.	X	X	X	X	X	X	X	X	X		
2. BLIZARD	2618		?		X	X	X	X	X	X				
3. BAIJER-Otto	2102		Dutch	X	X	X						X		
4. LANGFORD-Redwood	1579		Eng.	X	X			X				X		
5. THOMAS	1523		Eng.	X	X	X	X		X			X		X
6. BYAM	1515		Eng.	X	X	X	X	X	X	X	X	X		
7. FRYE	1350	562	Eng.	X	X	X			X			X		
8. MORRIS	1326	284	Eng.	X		X						X		
9. WILLIAMS	1275	250	Eng.	X	X				X		X	X		
10. Willoughby-TUDWAY	1096		Eng.	X								X	X	
11. GUNTHORPE	1039		Eng.	X	X	X	X					X		
12. FREEMAN-Willis	900		Eng.		X	X				X		X		
13. GRAY	830		Eng.		X	X	X					X		
14. OLIVER	780		Eng.	X	X	X	X			X		X	X	
15. HORNE	750		Eng.	X	X		X				X			
16. NIBBS	740		?		X									
17. LYNCH	693	253	Irish		X		X					X		
18. TANKERD-Tyrrell	625	265	?	X		X						X	X	X
19. YEAMANS-Laroche	606	305	Eng.	X	X	X	X		X	X	X	X	X	X
20. MARTIN	605	304	An.-Ir.	X	X	X	X			X		X		
21. TOMLINSON	600		Eng.	X	X	X	X					X		
22. KING-Lavicount	554		Eng.	X	X	X	X	X				X		
23. COCHRAN	545		?	X		X		X				X		
24. BROWNE	500		Irish	X				X				X		
25. CARLISLE-Payne	500		Eng.	X	X	X	X	X		X		X	X	X
26. LUCAS	500		Eng.	X		X	X	X				X		
27. VAUGHAN-Voguell	500		Eng.	X								X		
28. BURKE	450		Irish	X	X					X		X		
29. WINTHROP-Lyons	426	219	Eng.	X	X							X		
30. DUER	410		Scots	X	X	X						X		
31. VERNON	400	242	Eng.	X	X			X				X		
32. WATKINS-Alexander	390		Eng.	X	X	X		X	X			X		
33. KERBY	358		Eng.	X	X	X		X	X			X		
Totals				28	25	22	15	13	9	9	5	29	5	4

35

Note: See p. 357 for source notes.

Families, 1680–1706

	Acreage[1]	Slaves[1]	National Origin[2]	Land Grants[3]	Assembly[4]	Council[4]	Government Officials[4]	Antigua Merchants[4]	London-W.I. Merchants[4]	Lawyers[4]	Doctors[4]	Absentees[4]	M.P.s[4]	Titles[4]
1. PEARNE	1830		Eng.									X		
2. CODRINGTON-Bethell	1734	799	Eng.	X					X			X	X	X
3. CHRISTIAN	1489	750	Eng.		X	X	X	X	X			X		
4. MACKINEN	1210	219	Scots		X	X								
5. THIBOU-Jarvis	1064		French		X	X	X	X			X			
6. WEATHERILL	925		Eng.		X	X						X		
7. KIRWAN	700		Irish						X			X		
8. GILBERT	513		Eng.		X	X	X			X	X			
9. Nugent-SKERRETT	500		An.-Ir.		X	X			X			X		
10. CRUMP	480		?		X	X	X	X		X	X	X		
11. CHESTER	423		Eng.		X			X	X			X		
12. FARLEY-Laforey	423		?		X	X		X				X		X
Totals				1	9	8	4	5	5	2	3	9	1	2

Families, 1707–1775

	Acreage[1]	Slaves[1]	National Origin[2]	Land Grants[3]	Assembly[4]	Council[4]	Government Officials[4]	Antigua Merchants[4]	London-W.I. Merchants[4]	Lawyers[4]	Doctors[4]	Absentees[4]	M.P.s[4]	Titles[4]
1. GORDON-Brebner	1891	460	Scots		X	X	X			X	X	X		
2. DELAP-Halliday	1655		?		X		X	X						
3. GRANT	1288	242	Scots					X			X	X		
4. HARVEY	1196	500	Scots					X			X			
5. Lessly-LIVINGSTON	885	256	Scots		X	X	X	X			X	X		
6. DUNBAR	846		Scots		X	X	X	X	X		X	X		
7. WILLOCK	824		Eng.		X			X						
8. BROOKE	821	260	Eng.		X	X								
9. REDHEAD	740	264	Eng.		X									
10. YOUNG	655	325	Scots		X	X					X	X		X
11. GAYNOR-Colebrooke	643		Irish						X		X	X	X	X
12. SYDSERFE	570		Scots		X						X	X		
13. TULLIDEPH-Ogilvy	536	271	Scots		X	X		X		X		X		X
14. DOUGLAS	510		Scots		X	X	X					X	X	
15. MAXWELL	461	300	Scots		X			X	X		X	X		
16. DOIG	320		Scots		X			X				X		
17. WEBB	320		Eng.		X		X			X	X	X	X	
18. MATHEWS	315	227	Eng.		X	X	X	X				X		
Totals					15	8	7	10	3	3	10	13	3	3

Note: See p. 357 for source notes.

	Acreage[1]	Slaves[1]	National Origin[2]	Land Grants[3]	Assembly[4]	Council[4]	Government Officials[4]	Antigua Merchants[4]	London-W.I. Merchants[4]	Lawyers[4]	Doctors[4]	Absentees[4]	M.P.s[4]	Titles[4]
Period of Arrival Unascertained														
1. BANNISTER	346		Eng.		X		X	X	X			X		
2. LIGHTFOOT	460		Eng.			X								
Totals					1	1	1	1	1			1		
Grand Totals				29	50	39	27	29	18	14	18	52	9	9

37

[1] Vere L. Oliver, *The History of the Island of Antigua* (London, 1894–99), I–III (see especially vol. III, 355–92, 393–6); ————, *Caribbeana, Being Miscellaneous Papers Relating to . . . the British West Indies*, I (1909–10), VI (1919); *Samuel Martin Letter Book*, B.M. Add. MS. 41, 353, ff. 84–87; *Walter Tullideph General Ledger*, ff. 17, 107, 190, 255; Robson Lowe, *The Codrington Correspondence*, 1743–1851 (London, 1951), pp. 19, 26; Richard Pares, *Merchants and Planters* (Cambridge, Published for the *Economic History Review*, 1960), p. 69, n. 66. The above figures represent the maximum ascertainable acreage and slave population for the period 1730–75.

[2] Oliver, *History of Antigua*, I–III. See pedigrees of families.

[3] *Ibid.* III, 285–305.

[4] *Ibid.* I–III. 'X' indicates one or more members of a family in the above classifications in the period 1730–75.

[5] Hyphenated surnames are used to designate: (1) families whose plantations were inherited through the female line, e.g. SMITH-Jones – the male line (SMITH) preceding the female line (Jones); and (2) the proprietors of plantations that were transferred by deed of sale or mortgage foreclosure, e.g. (White-BROWN) – the grantor or mortgagor (White) preceding the grantee or mortgagee (BROWN).

The Progress of Inequality in Revolutionary Boston

Allan Kulikoff*

ON February 2, 1785, the *Massachusetts Centinel* in Boston complained that "We daily see men speculating, with impunity, on the most essential articles of life, and grinding the faces of the poor and laborious as if there was no God," yet five months later to the day, Sam Adams wrote to his cousin John, "You would be surprizd to see the Equipage, the Furniture and expensive Living of too many, the Pride and Vanity of Dress which pervades thro every Class, confounding every Distinction between the Poor and the Rich."[1] As these quotations suggest, opinion divided sharply in post-Revolutionary Boston on the direction of major social change, and impressionistic evidence can be found to sustain a broad range of interpretation. Relying on this material, historians have perpetuated the contemporary diversity of opinion. Scholars of the Progressive era, like J. Franklin Jameson, tended to agree with Adams that the Revolution had a leveling effect, while more recent studies have found some change as whigs replaced tories and a new propertied class emerged, but less democratization than had been supposed.[2]

This essay attempts to discover the magnitude of change in Boston from 1771 to 1790 by testing controllable, quantitative materials to answer the following questions: How did the town's occupational structure change? Did the distribution of wealth become more or less equal? How closely related were wealth and status? Did political power become more democratically shared? By how much did population increase?

* Mr. Kulikoff is a graduate student at Brandeis University. He would like to thank Stuart Blumin, M. I. T.; John Demos, Marvin Meyers, and members of the graduate seminar, Brandeis University; Kenneth Lockridge, University of Michigan; and Paul Kleppner and Alfred Young, Northern Illinois University, for their advice and criticism. David Fischer, Brandeis University, who directed the paper, made numerous helpful criticisms.

[1] *Massachusetts Centinel* (Boston), Feb. 2, 1785; Samuel Adams to John Adams, July 2, 1785, *The Writings of Samuel Adams,* ed. Harry Alonzo Cushing, IV (New York, 1908), 315-316.

[2] J. Franklin Jameson, *The American Revolution Considered As a Social Movement* (Princeton, 1926); Richard D. Brown, "The Confiscation and Disposition of Loyalists' Estates in Suffolk County, Massachusetts," *William and Mary Quarterly,* 3d Ser., XXI (1964), 534-550, surveys the relevant historiography.

What social and economic patterns of residence could be found? What changes occurred in the rate of geographic and economic mobility?

Before the Revolution, Boston had been an intensely unequal society. Wealthy men of high status dominated government and social life. The top 10 per cent of the taxpayers in 1771 owned nearly two-thirds of the wealth and held most of the important town offices. While demanding respect from the poor, many of the wealthy lived in the center of town, segregated from the impoverished. Poorer men possessed no significant political power, but held numerous minor town offices. And largely because many poor men and women were migrating from nearby towns, the poor in Boston were becoming more numerous.[3] These trends continued and accelerated during the war and the Confederation period. Not a less stratified, but an even more unequal society developed in Boston after the Revolution.

Late eighteenth-century Boston was a typical "consumer city" in Max Weber's phrase. It was a town of under 20,000 inhabitants in which "the purchasing power of its larger consumers rests on the retail for profit of foreign products on the local market . . . the foreign sale for profit of local products or goods obtained by native producers . . . or the purchase of foreign products and their sale . . . outside."[4]

The economy of Boston still rested squarely on foreign trade. Close to a quarter of her workers—merchants, mariners, captains, chandlers, and wharfingers—earned their livelihood from commerce. Another 15 per cent were indirectly concerned with trade. Retailers sold and distributed foreign goods; coopers made barrels bound for the sea; laborers supplied the manpower necessary to unload ships; and distillers used foreign sugar in their product.

Unlike Weber's "producer city," Boston was not an exporter of the goods she produced.[5] Most of those not engaged in commerce produced goods and services for the local market. No industrial group included large numbers of workers. About 7 per cent worked with cloth, 4 per

[3] James A. Henretta, "Economic Development and Social Structure in Colonial Boston," *Wm. and Mary Qtly.*, 3d Ser., XXII (1965), 75-92.

[4] Max Weber, *The City*, trans. and ed. Don Martindale and Gertrud Neuwirth (New York, 1958), 69.

[5] *Ibid.* Philadelphia closely resembled a "producer city." See James T. Lemon, "Urbanization and the Development of Eighteenth-Century Southeastern Pennsylvania and Adjacent Delaware," *Wm. and Mary Qtly.*, 3d Ser., XXIV (1967), 504-510.

TABLE I

BOSTON'S OCCUPATIONAL STRUCTURE, 1790[a]

Occupational Group	Number in Group	Number of Trades in Group	Percentage of Work Force
Government Officials	67	4	2.6
Professionals[b]	105	8	4.1
Merchants-Traders	224	3	8.7
Retailers	184	7	7.1
Sea Captains	114	1	4.4
Other Business[c]	66	6	2.6
Clerks and Scribes	66	2	2.6
Building Crafts	245	7	9.3
Cloth Trades	182	8	7.1
Leather Crafts	113	5	5.1
Food Trades	175	11	6.8
Marine Crafts	219	13	8.5
Metal Crafts	132	11	5.1
Woodworkers	106	7	4.1
Other Artisans	105	35	4.1
Transportation	80	6	3.2
Service	103	4	4.0
Mariners	117	4	4.5
Unskilled	183	4	7.4
Total Artisans	1,271	96	49.1
Total Other	1,314	49	50.9
Total Employed	2,585	145	100.0
Servants (white)	63		
Unemployed and Retired[d]	106		
Total	2,754		

Notes: [a] Boston Tax Taking and Rate Books, 1790, City Hall, Boston, Mass. Hereafter cited as Tax and Rate Books, 1790. These records were checked with the Boston city directories for 1789 and 1796, *Report of the Record Commissioners of the City of Boston* (Boston, 1876–1909), X, 171–296. Hereafter cited as *Record Commissioners' Report*. A total accounting of each trade is found in the Appendix.
[b] Includes 20 untaxed clergymen counted in Thomas Pemberton, "A Topographical and Historical Description of Boston, 1794," Massachusetts Historical Society, *Collections*, 1st Ser., III (1794), 256–264.
[c] Includes groups such as wharfingers, chandlers, brokers, and auctioneers.
[d] Includes 23 gentlemen, 27 poor, 28 sick and poor, and 28 little or no business.

cent with leather, and 5 per cent with metals. Construction workers were under a tenth of all those employed. The small proportion of innkeepers (3 per cent) and men in the food trades (7 per cent) showed that Boston was not a major food market; nor had a large bureaucracy developed, since only 3 per cent of the labor force was employed in government— and many of these worked only part-time.

Large enterprises were uncommon: the median number of workers in ninety-six artisan crafts was only three, and the mean number thirteen. The typical middling artisan employed his sons and several other workers. These young apprentices and journeymen lived with the families of master craftsmen, not alone in rented rooms.[6]

There was an excess population in the working ages, composed mostly of women and including many widows, who were outside the occupational structure. Between 1765 and 1800, the proportion of people in the productive ages above fifteen years increased by 17 per cent, thereby providing workers for any factories that might open. There were 19 per cent more women than men of working age in 1765, and 14 per cent more in 1800. About a tenth of these women were widows, and three-quarters of them supported dependents.[7]

[6] Tax and Rate Books, 1790, compared with *Heads of Families At the First Census, 1790. Massachusetts* (Washington, 1906), 188-195; and "Names of the Inhabitants of the Town of Boston in 1790," *Record Commissioners' Report*, XXII, 443-511. Numerous dependent males over 16 years of age are found in the census, but not in the tax lists. Almost all of them were in homes of artisans of middling wealth. This suggests that many of them were transient journeymen and apprentices and not older sons hidden from the assessor. Tax and census records are the source for any uncited comments.

[7] Lemuel Shattuck, *Report to the Committee of the City Council Appointed to Obtain the Census of Boston for the Year 1845*, . . . (Boston, 1846), 4, 45. A sample of every sixth column of the Washington edition of the census was checked for widows; three-quarters had dependents. Joseph J. Spengler, "Demographic Factors and Early Modern Economic Development," *Daedalus*, XCVII (1968), 440-443, defines productive ages as from 15 to 65 years. Data in Shattuck does not allow such fine distinctions, but the percentage of people over 65 is probably too small to materially change the following statistics:

Age Ratios	Percentage over 15 yrs. old			Sex Ratios	Number of Men/100 Women		
	1765	1790	1800		1765	1790	1800
Total	44.30	...	61.93	All ages	95.48	82.07	90.27
Male	41.71	56.13	60.42	Over 15	81.42	...	86.14
Female	47.26	...	63.31				

41

Two small factories were operating in 1790, but they were not part of a general industrialization, and only one of them utilized this surplus laboring population. At a "duck cloth manufactory" employing four hundred workers in 1792, there were only seventeen male employees two years before. A few of the others were young girls; the rest were women. The factory had been established to promote American manufactures and at the same time to aid the poor. According to the *Massachusetts Centinel* in 1788, it and a small glass works "promise soon to be completed and to give employment to a great number of persons, especially females who now eat the bread of idleness, whereby they may gain an honest livelihood." By 1800, the duckcloth factory was out of business.[8]

42

About three-quarters of the one thousand workers in the other large enterprise, a cotton and wool card factory, were children. About a fifth of all the children in Boston from eight to sixteen years of age were probably employed there. The owners chose to hire them rather than women, since children could easily run the machinery and were paid less.[9]

At least until 1820, Boston's occupational structure remained close to the "consumer city" model. Less than one-tenth of 1 per cent of men listed in the 1820 directory were manufacturers, and the proportion of merchants, retailers, and building tradesmen remained almost the same. Domestic commerce was becoming more important as foreign trade declined. A reduction in the percentage of mariners, captains, and marine tradesmen from 17.4 per cent in 1790 to 10.6 per cent in 1820 illustrates the trend. Meanwhile, the town had become more important as a food market, with the proportion of men in the food trades climbing from 6.8 per cent to 10.7 per cent.[10]

Most of Boston's taxable wealth—real estate, stock in trade, and income from trade[11]—rested in fewer and fewer hands as time passed.

[8] *Mass. Centinel* (Boston), Sept. 6, 1788, quoted in William R. Bagnall, *The Textile Industries of the United States, . . .* (Cambridge, Mass., 1893), 112-116; Pemberton, "Description of Boston," Mass. Hist. Soc., *Collections*, 1st Ser., III (1794), 252-253, 279; Samuel Breck to Henry Knox, Sept. 12, 1790, Knox Papers, Mass. Hist. Soc., Boston.

[9] Nathaniel Cutting, "Extracts from a Journal of a Gentleman visiting Boston in 1792," Sept. 6, 1792, Mass. Hist. Soc., *Proceedings*, 1st Ser., XII (1871-1873), 61-62.

[10] See Table I; David Reed, Membership in the Massachusetts Peace Society, 1816-1820 (unpubl. seminar paper, Brandeis University, 1968), 60-63.

[11] *The Acts and Resolves, Public and Private, of the Province of Massachusetts Bay*, V (Boston, 1886), 1163, 1165.

Boston followed a pattern similar to both American towns and rural areas. Although in the seventeenth century wealth in American towns was typically less concentrated than in sixteenth-century English towns, where the poorer half of the population owned less than a tenth of the wealth and the richest tenth owned between half and seven-tenths, the English pattern soon reappeared in America and intensified.[12]

TABLE II

A. DISTRIBUTION OF TAXABLE WEALTH IN BOSTON, 1790[a]

Assessment in Pounds	Number in Category	Percentage of Taxpayers in Category	Wealth in Category in Pounds	Percentage of Wealth in Category
0	892	29.8	0	0.0
25	388	12.9	9,700	1.0
26–50	240	8.0	11,162	1.2
51–75	148	4.9	11,012	1.2
76–100	167	5.6	16,662	1.8
101–150	186	6.2	24,938	2.7
151–200	147	4.9	27,887	3.0
201–300	186	6.2	49,113	5.3
301–400	128	4.3	46,713	5.0
401–500	116	3.9	54,300	5.9
501–700	124	4.1	75,775	8.3
701–999	71	2.4	58,775	6.1
1000–1,999	122	4.1	159,875	17.2
2000–4,999	58	1.9	165,250	17.8
5000+	22	0.8	217,775	23.5
Totals	2,995	100.0	928,937	100.0

[12] W. G. Hoskins, *Provincial England* (London, 1963), 90-91; J. F. Pound, "The Social and Trade Structure of Norwich 1525-1575," *Past and Present*, No. 34 (July 1966), 50-53; Donald Warner Koch, "Income Distribution and Political Structure in Seventeenth-Century Salem, Massachusetts," *Essex Institute Historical Collections,* CV (1969), 54, 59; James T. Lemon and Gary B. Nash, "The Distribution of Wealth in Eighteenth Century America: A Century of Changes in Chester County, Pennsylvania, 1693-1802," *Journal of Social History,* II (1968-1969), 9-12; Stuart Blumin,

B. DISTRIBUTION OF WEALTH IN BOSTON, 1687 TO 1830[b]

Percentage of Taxpayers	Percentage of Wealth Held			
	1687	1771	1790	1830
Bottom 30	2.48	0.10	0.03	0.00
Low-Mid 30	11.29	9.43	4.80	7.92
Upper-Mid 30	39.63	27.01	30.47	26.94
Top 10	46.60	63.46	64.70	65.14
Total	100.00	100.00	100.00	100.00
Top 1%	9.51	25.98	27.14	26.15
Schutz Coefficient	.4896	.5541	.6276	.6370

44

Notes: [a] Tax and Rate Books, 1790. Group at 0 paid only poll tax; £25 was the first assessment. Untaxed widows found on the census are not included.
[b] See Table II A for 1790 figures; 1687 and 1771 figures are from Henretta, "Economic Development and Social Structure," *Wm. and Mary Qtly.*, 3d Ser., XXII (1965), 80, 82, with those paying only poll tax added; 1830 figures were estimated from imprecise, grouped data in Shattuck, *Report*, 95. The Schutz coefficient of inequality measures income concentration—0 equals total equality, 1 total inequality. Robert R. Schutz, "On the Measurement of Income Inequality," *American Economic Review*, XLI (1951), 107–122; Blumin, "Mobility and Change," in Thernstrom and Sennett, eds., *Nineteenth-Century Cities*, 204.

From 1687 to 1790, Boston's wealth became very concentrated. A glance at the Lorenz curves shows that the amount of change between 1687 and 1771 was similar to that between 1771 and 1790. Statistically, changes in the distribution of wealth measured by increases in the Schutz coefficient (see Table II B) were greater between 1771 and 1790 (.0735) than during the preceding 87 years (.0647). However, the proportion of wealth held by the richest tenth of the taxpayers had almost reached its peak by 1771 and 29 per cent were without taxable property both before and after the Revolution. The wealth of the lower middle group, where assessments

"Mobility and Change in Antebellum Philadelphia," in Stephan Thernstrom and Richard Sennett, eds., *Nineteenth-Century Cities: Essays in the New Urban History* (New Haven, 1969), 204-206; Robert E. Gallman, "Trends in the Size Distribution of Wealth in the Nineteenth Century," in Lee Soltow, ed., *Six Papers on the Size Distribution of Wealth and Income* (New York, 1969), 22-23; Merle Curti, *The Making of an American Community: A Case Study of Democracy in a Frontier County* (Stanford, Calif., 1959), 78.

Chart I
Distribution of Wealth in Boston, 1687-1790*

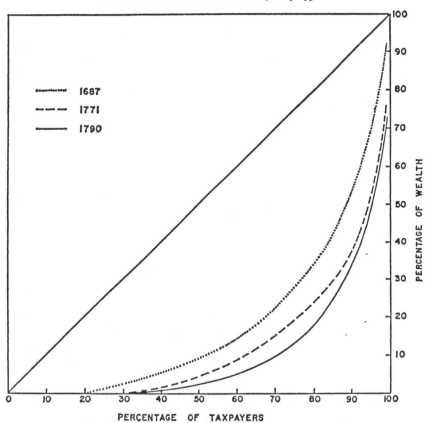

45

Note: *Drawn from Table II. The diagonal indicates an equal distribution; the area
between the dotted and dashed lines shows change between 1687 and 1771;
and the space between the dashed and solid lines shows change between 1771
and 1790.

ranged from £25 to £100, was cut in half. Three-quarters of this decline
was gained by the upper middle group, assessed between £100 and
£500.

The sale of forty-six loyalist estates in Suffolk County to ninety-six
men, two-thirds of whom already owned land in the county, had little effect on the overall distribution. The sale may have permitted a few poorer

men to enter the upper middle group, but the small gain in wealth between 1771 and 1790 made by the top tenth suggests that a wealthy group of patriots replaced an equally wealthy group of tories.[18]

Were the relatively poor becoming poorer? Brissot de Warville discovered full employment in Boston in 1788 and "saw none of those livid, ragged wretches that one sees in Europe, who, soliciting our compassion at the foot of the altar, seem to bear witness ... against our inhumanity."[14] Brissot's European standard of comparison allowed him to underestimate the extent of poverty in Boston. At this time, a fifth to a third of those living in English and French towns were beggars, paupers, and others who could not make a living for themselves. Another third were the near poor of the English towns and the *sans-culottes* and *menu peuple* in French towns—persons who could become destitute in times of crisis.[15]

The poor and near poor were growing more numerous in Boston. The percentage of poor can be roughly estimated at 7 per cent of the population in 1771 and 10 per cent in 1790. The change is illustrated by the slow increase in the numbers of destitute, old, and sick men and women, and dependent children in the poorhouse at a time of relatively little population increase (see Table V): 146 in 1742, never over 180 before the Revolution, and 250 in August 1790, with 300 to 400 expected the following winter.[16] Because personal property was not taxed, it is difficult to determine the percentage of near poor, but an estimate can be made.[17] Composed of widows, blacks, seamen, laborers, and poorer arti-

[18] Brown, "Confiscation of Loyalists' Estates," *Wm. and Mary Qtly.*, 3d Ser., XXI (1964), 546-349.

[14] Jacques Pierre Brissot de Warville, *New Travels in the United States of America, 1788*, trans. Mara Soceanu Vamos and Durand Echeverria, ed. Durand Echeverria (Cambridge, Mass., 1964), 87, 98-100.

[15] In this paper, "poor" refers to the destitute, "near poor" to those living at or near the minimum level of subsistence. For Europe see Hoskins, *Provincial England*, 90-93; Hoskins, *Industry, Trade and People in Exeter, 1688-1800,* . . . (Manchester, Eng., 1935), 119; Pound, "Structure of Norwich," *Past and Present*, No. 34 (July 1966), 50-51; George Rudé, "La population ouvrière de Paris de 1789 à 1791," *Annales Historiques de la Révolution Française*, XXXIX (1967), 21-27; Jeffry Kaplow, "Sur la population flottante de Paris, à la fin de l'Ancien Régime," *ibid.*, 7-8; Pierre Deyon, *Amiens, Capitale Provinciale. Etude sur la Société Urbaine au 17ᵉ Siècle* (Paris, 1967), 349-357. I am indebted to Gerald Soliday, Brandeis University, for the French materials.

[16] See Table VI; *Record Commissioners' Report*, XXXI, 239.

[17] Since the total amount of property remains unknown, any "poverty line" chosen from Table II would be arbitrary. Instead, estimates of poor have been calculated by adding poorhouse and unemployed figures from Table I and of near poor

sans who might dip below the minimum level of subsistence when unemployment increased, this group probably ranged from 30 to 40 per cent
in 1771 and from 37 to 47 per cent in 1790.

Unemployed, old, or sick, most of the poor and their families lived
outside the poorhouse. Alexander Lord, a poor laborer, had "gone broke,
wife as broke"; they had a son under sixteen to share their misery. Jacob
Bull, an old shoemaker, and his wife were both ill, but two other women
lived in their household. And Samuel Goddard, "shoemaker, no business,
poor and supported by charity," could provide his family of five with
few comforts.[18] Only the very old, the totally destitute, and the terminally
ill entered the poorhouse, for the social conditions there steadily declined.
In 1790, the poorhouse was filthy, dark, crowded, and odoriferous. "Persons of every description and disease are lodged under the same roof and
in some instances in the same or Contiguous Apartments, by which
means the sick are disturbed, by the Noise of the healthy, and the infirm
rendered liable to the Vices and diseases of the diseased, and profligate."[19]

The lives of the near poor were only somewhat better than those of
the poor. While the number of people per dwelling declined from 9.53 in
1742 to 7.58 in 1790 (see Table V), many of the near poor lived in grossly
inferior housing. The tax assessors found 90 families living in single
rooms. Sixty-five of the same families were also counted by the census
taker; three-quarters of this group had families of fewer than five members. Joseph Blayner, carpenter, lived with his wife and two children in
a kitchen chamber while John Cartwright, cooper, his eight children,
wife, and a boarder, crowded into the back of a house. Elijah Tolams,
a "very poor carpenter," lived in one room with his three children, and
Ebenezer Pilsbury, shoemaker, slept and worked with his six children
in only two rooms.

There was a close relationship between wealth and status. Although
status was not legally defined as in England, and the reputations of vari-

47

by adding the number of widows from the census to the number of persons without
taxable property and of those in the lowest category of taxpayers. A fifth of the
propertyless and 15% of the lowest category have been subtracted from the near
poor figure to account for upward mobility. The figures, especially for 1771, are very
rough, but the direction of change they indicate is accurate, and the estimates are
minimal figures of the extent of poverty.
[18] "Gone broke, wife as broke," and all similar short comments are marginalia
from the Tax and Rate Books, 1790.
[19] *Record Commissioners' Report*, XXXI, 239.

ous trades were unstable,[20] the order of precedence in a parade honoring President Washington in 1789 gives some indication of the prestige of various groups. The military, town and state officers, professional men, merchants and traders, and sea captains led the parade. They were followed by forty-six different artisan crafts, "alphabetically disposed, in order to give general satisfaction." No mechanical art was deemed better than the next. Sailors brought up the rear, and laborers were not included in the line of march.[21]

As Table III shows, the eleven wealthiest occupations included professional men of high status, merchants, retailers, along with several arti-

48

TABLE III

MEAN ASSESSED WEALTH OF SELECTED OCCUPATIONS IN BOSTON, 1790*

Rank	Occupation	Mean Assessment in Pounds	Number of Persons in Category
1	Merchant	1,707	206
2	Lawyer	846	21
3	Doctor	795	26
4	Apothecary	657	17
5	Distiller	642	47
6	Broker	622	16
7	Retailer	601	133
8	Taverner	522	26
9	Grocer	472	33
10	Chandler	347	17
11	Wharfinger	335	24
12	Tobacconist	260	17
13	Boarder-keeper	258	24
14	Printer	247	17
15	Sea Captain	240	114
16	Hatter	233	29
17	Clerk	232	28
18	Chaisemaker	188	16
19	Baker	170	64
20	Goldsmith	166	23
21	Painter	154	34

[20] Jackson Turner Main, *The Social Structure of Revolutionary America* (Princeton, 1965), *passim*, esp. 200-211.
[21] Committee to Arrange a Procession, *Procession* (Boston, 1789).

Rank	Occupation	Mean Assessment in Pounds	Number of Persons in Category
22	Cabinetmaker	131	15
23	Cooper	130	70
24	Founder	120	15
25	Sailmaker	112	30
26	Mason	95	44
27	Carpenter	92	140
28	Schoolmaster	89	16
29	Truckman	84	50
30	Blacksmith	83	59
31	Shipwright	78	65
32	Scribe	77	38
33	Barber	65	42
34	Blockmaker	63	16
35	Tailor	61	100
36	Caulker	53	14
37	Sea Cooper	46	16
38	Shoemaker	45	78
39	Mate	41	20
40	Ropemaker[b]	35	37
41	Duckcloth maker	25	16
42	Fisherman	15	37
43	Sailor	9	58
44	Laborer	6	157

Notes: [a] Computed from Tax and Rate Books, 1790.
[b] Excludes 5 ropewalk owners with a mean wealth of £760.

san trades. Most of those in the economic elite—men assessed over £1,000 —were in these groups. Sea captains, with a mean wealth of £240, were lower on the list than their status might indicate. Most others whose wealth fell between £100 and £260 were artisans. Immediately below a mean of £100 were the building trades, schoolmasters, and shipwrights. Other sea artisans, and such traditionally poorer trades as tailor, shoemaker, and barber, fell between £40 and £75. Bringing up the rear were the industrial trades of ropemaker and duckcloth maker, and mariners and laborers.

An analysis of variance showed a highly significant relationship between occupation and wealth, but the magnitude of this relationship was small. Only about 19.4 per cent of the variations in the wealth of all the individuals included in Table III was accounted for by differences between occupations. The rest of the variation was within each occupation.[22] In most trades, a few men had wealth far above the group mean; a number of hatters, printers, and bakers, for example, owned large establishments. As a result, in all but three trades below chaisemaker on the table, the median wealth was fifty pounds or less. Most fishermen, sailors, and laborers had no taxable wealth at all.

50   Those who possessed the highest status, reputation, and wealth expected visible differences of "Equipage, Furniture, . . . and Dress" between themselves and the rest of society. They socialized mostly with each other and separated themselves from the masses by forming exclusive organizations. One of these, a dinner club that encouraged members to relax and enjoy good conversation, was open to only sixteen men, each admitted by a unanimous vote. Another, the Massachusetts Historical Society, was incorporated in 1794 by ministers, doctors, lawyers, and a scientist to diffuse historical learning. This group limited its membership to thirty.[23]

Wealthy artisans were granted substantial respect. In the parade honoring President Washington, each trade was led by a member whose wealth averaged 225 per cent more than the mean wealth of his group: the leader of the tailors, Samuel Ballard, was assessed £500; goldsmith

[22] An F test was significant at less than the .01 level. This means there is less than a 1% chance that the differences shown in Table III are random. The test is a comparison of two quantities: 1. the sum of the squared variations of each case in each occupation subtracted from the group mean; and 2. the sum of the squared variations of each group subtracted from the grand mean. Eta^2, calculated from the same data, tests the strength or degree of relationship. In this case, Eta^2 was .194, which means that about 19.4% of the difference between the means in Table III is accounted for by the differences between occupational groups. See Herbert M. Blalock, Jr., *Social Statistics* (New York, 1960), 242-252, 255-257. Stuart Blumin's calculations of Eta^2 on Philadelphia data from 1860 were almost identical (.17). "The Historical Study of Vertical Mobility," *Historical Methods Newsletter*, I, No. 4 (Sept. 1968), 8-10.

[23] Brissot de Warville, *New Travels*, 90; *Handbook of the Massachusetts Historical Society* (Boston, 1949), 1-3. On the continuation of deference see Josiah P. Quincy, "Social Life in Boston: From the Adoption of the Federal Constitution to the Granting of the City Charter," in Justin Winsor, ed., *The Memorial History of Boston, Including Suffolk County, Massachusetts, 1630-1880*, IV (1886), 2, 4; David Hackett Fischer, *The Revolution of American Conservatism: The Federalist Party in the Era of Jeffersonian Democracy* (New York, 1965), xiv-xv, 4-10.

Benjamin Bert, £400; shoemaker Samuel Bangs, £500; and carpenter
William Crafts, £400. Nathaniel Balch, who was assessed £925, not
only led his fellow hatters in the parade, but his shop was described as
"the principle lounge even of the finest people in the town. Governor
Hancock himself would happen into this popular resort, ready for a joke
or a political discussion with Balch."[24]
While poorer groups were expected to defer to the elite, they in turn
were accorded little respect. Not only did poorer artisans have less
status than those who were richer, the elite tolerated insults and attacks
on black men and old black women by lower-class whites. Prince Hall,
leader of the black masonic lodge, nevertheless urged Boston's Negroes to
ignore their white attackers and trust "men born and bred in Boston,"
because we "had rather suffer wrong than to do wrong, to the distur-
bance of the community and the disgrace of our reputation."[25]
Did the elite demonstrate any sense of social responsibility toward the
poor? Noblesse oblige was practically nonexistent. The Massachusetts
Humane Society, founded mainly to save people from drowning, chose
to build three small huts on islands where shipwrecks were common,
rather than aid the poor sailors who populated Boston's North End.[26]
Men often complained to the assessors that they were poor, sick, lame,
or had "little or no business." The only relief granted them was tax abate-
ment; seventy men found on both the 1790 census and 1790 tax lists
paid no taxes.
However, benevolence to widows was considered a community responsibility. A husband's death, commented one minister, "deprives a
weak and helpless woman . . . of the sole instrument of her support,
the guide of her children's youth, and their only earthly dependance."[27]
Any charity granted by town or church went to them. The overseers of

51

[24] *Independent Chronicle* (Boston), Oct. 28, 1789 (I am indebted to Alfred
Young for the source); Samuel Breck, *Recollections of Samuel Breck with Passages
from His Note-Books (1771-1862)* (London, 1877), 108.
[25] Prince Hall, *A Charge Delivered to the African Lodge* . . . (Boston, 1797),
10-11; and Hall, *A Charge Delivered to the Brethren of the African Lodge* . . .
(Boston, 1792). About half the blacks were servants and therefore had little choice
but to be respectful.
[26] M. A. DeWolfe Howe, *The Humane Society of the Commonwealth of Massachusetts: An Historical Review, 1785-1916* (Boston, 1918), Chaps. 1-2; *The Institution of the Humane Society of the Commonwealth of Massachusetts* . . . (Boston,
1788).
[27] Peter Thacher, *A Sermon, Preached in Boston, . . .* (Boston, 1795), 13.

the poor distributed minimal aid from bequests. In 1787, for example, they gave money to sixty-six different widows, most receiving nine or twelve shillings, and only fifteen women were helped more than once. The First Church, perhaps typical, collected donations for the poor quarterly and on the Sunday before Thanksgiving. Several dozen women received a pittance of two or three shillings each month from this money.[28]

Who held political office in Boston after the Revolution? In pre-Revolutionary Boston, wealthy men of high social status monopolized important positions. Minor offices went to those of less wealth and status and gave their holders a sense of belonging in the community. After the Revolution, recent research indicates, the Massachusetts legislature included more moderately wealthy men than before the war.[29] Did Boston officeholding become more widely distributed?

TABLE IV

ASSESSED WEALTH OF BOSTON OFFICEHOLDERS, 1790[a]

Office	Mean Wealth	Median Wealth	Number in Group
State Legislators	4,044	1,750	9
Overseers of Poor	3,398	1,610	12
Fire Wards	2,850	1,350	15
School Committee	1,633	1,000	9
Clerks of Market	954	875	12
Selectmen	642	500	9
Cullers of Hoops and Staves	208	175	21
Assessors, Collectors	207	200	9
Fire Companies	125	50	138
Constables	115	75	12
Surveyors of Boards	78	50	15

Note: [a] Tax and Rate Books, 1790; Record Commissioners' Report, XXXI, 217-224; X, 207-211. Information for a few officers could not be determined. These included 14 members of the fire companies, 4 cullers of hoops, 3 surveyors of boards, and 3 untaxed ministers who were members of the school committee. Four legislators are missing from the table: 3 were Suffolk County senators, probably residents of other parts of the county, and the other was a representative whose name was too common to identify. All other officers are included.

[28] Record Commissioners' Report, XXVII, 11-12, 15, 20, 25-26, 31, 33, 37, 40; First Church Poor and Sacramental Fund, First Church, Boston.
[29] Henretta, "Economic Development and Social Structure," Wm. and Mary Qtly., 3d Ser., XXII (1965), 84, 89; Jackson Turner Main, "Government by the

As Table IV shows, the economic elite still dominated the most important town offices. All the state legislators from Boston were assessed over a thousand pounds and were among the wealthiest 6.8 per cent of the population. Four were merchants, two were wealthy gentlemen, one was a doctor, one a lawyer, and one a hardware store owner. Only a quarter of the firewards, who protected valuable property in case of fire, dipped below a thousand pounds; most of them were merchants, wharfingers, and wealthy shipwrights. The school committee, a newly created agency of the government, included three clergymen, three lawyers, three doctors, and two businessmen.

53

Probably the two most important town offices were the selectmen and the overseers of the poor. In 1790, only one of the overseers was assessed below a thousand pounds. From 1785 to 1795, eight merchants, three hardware store owners, one auctioneer, two distillers, one apothecary, one ropewalk owner, and a wealthy baker served as overseers. During the same period, selectmen included five merchants, two lawyers, the county treasurer, a captain, a retailer, an apothecary, a wharfinger, and a wealthy hatter. Five others were probably retired businessmen, whose low assessments reduced the selectmen's mean wealth.[30]

Remarkably little turnover occurred in these two time-consuming, nonpaying positions. From 1760 to 1770, the average selectman served between three and four years; there was a small rise in tenure between 1785 and 1795. Overseers served even longer terms. In the decade 1760 to 1770, the average overseer served four or five years; after the war tenures increased to from six to eight years. At annual elections, both before and after the Revolution, typically only one or two selectmen or overseers were replaced. Bostonians served longer and replaced their officials less frequently than did the citizens of many other Massachusetts towns before the Revolution.[31]

People: The American Revolution and the Democratization of the Legislatures," *Wm. and Mary Qtly.*, 3d Ser., XXIII (1966), 404; and Main, *The Upper House in Revolutionary America, 1763-1788* (Madison, Wis., 1967), 162-174.

[30] The profile of officers was drawn from sources cited in Table IV; Boston city directories, 1789 and 1796, *Record Commissioners' Report*, X, 171-296; XXXI, 53, 59-60, 65, 97, 102, 133-134, 147, 160-161, 185, 200, 217, 224, 232, 243-245, 253, 276-277, 283, 319, 349-350, 384, 391; "Assessors' 'Taking Books' of the Town of Boston, 1780," *Bostonian Society Publications*, 1st Ser., IX (1912), 9-59. Hereafter cited as Assessors' Books, 1780.

[31] See n. 30; Robert Francis Seybold, *The Town Officials of Colonial Boston, 1634-1775* (Cambridge, Mass., 1939), 289-305. For other Massachusetts towns before

The middling artisans, assessed between £100 and £500, were a group far larger than the economic elite, yet after the war they still held only a small percentage of major offices. Assessors and tax collectors, full-time paid officials who determined and collected taxes, were the only powerful officers of middle-class wealth. Other positions gave artisans some recognition of their special talents, but no political power. Carpenters, joiners, and cabinetmakers dominated the position of surveyor of boards; shoemakers were sealers of leather, and coopers were cullers of hoops and staves. Marine artisans formed a majority in the fire companies, the only agencies dominated by the poor and near poor. These jobs, dirty and unpaid, gave the economic elite an opportunity to share civic participation while keeping political power in its own hands.

The elite was suspicious of any attempt to organize the laboring force politically, however deferential the organizers initially were. Artisans of middle wealth, whose share of the town's taxable property had increased since 1771, founded the Mechanics Association in 1795. Only two members of the group had belonged to the economic elite in 1790, at which time the assessments of 63 per cent of those who became members fell between £100 and £500. In 1796 the group petitioned the General Court for incorporation because "the disconnected state of the mechanics of the town of Boston . . . retarded the mechanic arts of the state" whose "situation as a manufacturing country promised the greatest extension." Twenty leading merchants were personally urged to support the petition, "to patronize an institution formed for the reciprocal benefits of the merchant and mechanic." But despite the Association's broadly conceived purpose, the legislature feared the group's potential political power and three times

---

the Revolution, see Michael Zuckerman, *Peaceable Kingdoms: New England Towns in the Eighteenth Century* (New York, 1970), 274-276. Boston turnover and service rates were as follows:

Years	Number of Offices	Number of Officeholders	Years of Service		Rate of Turnover/Year	
			mean	median	mean	median
			Selectmen			
1760–70	7	19	4.0	3.0	1.7	1.5
1785–95	9	23	4.3	4.0	2.2	1.0
			Overseers of the Poor			
1760–70	12	28	4.7	4.0	1.6	1.0
1785–95	12	23	6.3	8.0	1.2	0.5

refused to grant incorporation. The Association finally succeeded in obtaining a charter in 1806.[32]

The poorer sort commanded no political resource other than ineffective deferential appeals to the wealthy. The accumulated grievances of poor mechanics were partially relieved by harassing the black population; only the middling artisans were able to organize successfully. Pressure from below on the elite was nonexistent after the Revolution, and criminal activity was rare. Between 1787 and 1790, nine men were hanged, all for robbery, while twenty-six were punished for other crimes.[33]

55

Boston's population steadily increased from 1630 to 1740 as the townsmen settled the entire Shawmut Peninsula, but after 1740 people migrated from eastern New England in large numbers, so that from 1742 to 1790 Boston's population grew only 8.4 per cent, a gain of 1.68 per cent per decade. (See Table V) During the same period, the American population overall expanded at the Malthusian rate of 34.7 per cent per decade. Migration patterns bypassed eastern New England; people generally traveled up the Connecticut Valley into western Massachusetts, New Hampshire, and Maine. The results may be seen in the differential population growth of areas of Massachusetts between 1765 and 1790: Massachusetts's total population increased 54.1 per cent; Boston's (based on the smaller population of 1765) 16.2 per cent; the surrounding towns of Brookline, Cambridge, Charlestown, Chelsea, and Roxbury, 18.3 per cent; and the eastern Massachusetts counties of Suffolk, Essex, Plymouth, and Middlesex, 28.5 per cent.[34] Boston's population fell after 1742 but recovered by 1771 until the British occupied the city in 1776, when people left en masse for the countryside and only slowly returned. The exodus postponed major population growth until after recovery from the effects of the war. Between

[32] Joseph H. Buckingham, *Annals of the Massachusetts Charitable Mechanics Society* (Boston, 1853), 6-10, 12-14, 57-58, 80, 94-97.

[33] Edward H. Savage, *Police Records and Recollections; or, Boston by Daylight and Gaslight* . . . (Boston, 1873), 40-42. Savage lists only punishments, not unsolved crimes.

[34] J. Potter, "The Growth of Population in America, 1700-1860," in D. V. Glass and D. E. C. Eversley, eds., *Population in History: Essays in Historical Demography* (London, 1965), 636-641; Evarts B. Greene and Virginia D. Harrington, *American Population Before the Federal Census of 1790* (New York, 1932), 21-24, 46; Herman R. Friis, *A Series of Population Maps of the Colonies and the United States, 1625-1790*, American Geographical Society Mimeographed Publication, No. 3 (New York, 1940), 16 and maps 10a, 10b, 12a, 12b.

1790 and 1820 the town's population increased at the rate of 31.3 per cent per decade.[85]

Although the population remained nearly stationary until 1790, Bostonians began to live in less settled areas. Most, however, still crowded onto about two-thirds of the peninsula. Streets in the North End and the center of town were filled with houses; yet many areas remained uninhabited, and the empty common was almost as large as the entire North End. In 1794, Boston was still "capable of great increase as many large spots of land remain vacant." Without the pressure of large population growth, there was no need to build on inaccessible areas like Beacon Hill. The relatively high population density that resulted allowed people to conduct their business with ease by walking.[86]

56

TABLE V

POPULATION AND DENSITY IN BOSTON, 1742 TO 1810[a]

Year	Population	Number of Houses	Number of People Per House
1742	16,528	1,719	9.53
1752	15,731	...	...
1760	15,631	...	...
1765	15,520	1,676	9.26
1771	16,540	1,803	9.12
1776	2,719	...	...
1780	10,000	...	...
1784	14,000	2,178	6.43
1790	18,038	2,376	7.58
1800	24,937	3,000	8.31
1810	33,788	3,970	8.51

Note: [a] Shattuck, *Report*, 5, 54; Greene and Harrington, *American Population*, 31; Worthington C. Ford, ed., *Writings of John Quincy Adams*, I (New York, 1913), 62; Valuation of Towns, 1768–1771: Boston, 1771, Massachusetts Archives, Statehouse, Boston, CXXXII. The 1771 figure was derived by multiplying the number of polls by 5.75, a figure suggested by the larger number of houses that year, and the large immigration between 1765 and 1771.

[85] Leo F. Schnore and Peter R. Knights, "Residence and Social Structure: Boston in the Ante-Bellum Period," in Thernstrom and Sennett, eds., *Nineteenth-Century Cities*, 250.

[86] Pemberton, "Description of Boston," Mass. Hist. Soc., *Collections*, 1st Ser., III (1794), 249-250. The North End (wards 1-5) and the West End (ward 7) were contemporary geographical areas (*ibid.*, 267). To allow analysis the South End of

Boston expanded slowly, gradually consuming her open spaces. The mean number of people per dwelling decreased from 9.53 in 1742 to 7.58 in 1790. From 1740 to 1760 few houses were built, and many were destroyed in the 1760 fire, but from 1765 to 1790 a net total of 700 new houses were constructed. A small housing boom took place between 1771 and 1790 when an average of 28.7 houses per year were built.

The new housing was probably built mostly in the open West and South Ends. As Table VI shows, these areas were gaining population. In 1742 61 per cent of the people lived in the small, crowded North End and the center of town; the remaining 39 per cent resided in the West and South Ends, about two-thirds of the town's area. Population slowly moved west and south. Ward twelve, closest to the Roxbury Neck, gained 73 per cent from 1742 to 1790; the West End gained 21 per cent; and the center of town lost population. As a result, only 43 per cent of the population lived in the North End and the center by 1790. In 1802, William Bentley, a minister from Salem, while on a walking tour, "saw the increasing wealth of the south end, so called, but the growth of West Boston by the new Bridge from Cambridge is very great. Where the popu- 57

TABLE VI

POPULATION OF BOSTON'S NEIGHBORHOODS, 1742 TO 1790[a]

	1742	1771	1790	Percentage of Change, 1742–1790
North End	6,229	6,165	6,331	+2
West End	1,204	1,386	1,456	+21
Center	3,843	3,796	3,304	−14
South End	5,106	5,193	6,625	+30
Other[b]	146	...	322	+120
Total	16,528	16,540	18,038	+8

Notes: [a] Shattuck, *Report*, 3–5; Valuation of Towns, Mass. Archives, CXXXII; Tax and Rate Books, 1790; *1790 Census*. For 1771, total polls in ward were multiplied by 5.75; the 1790 figure is based on name-by-name comparison of tax and census records, with interpolations where necessary.
[b] Poorhouse in 1742; poorhouse and jail in 1790.

the 1790s was divided into the center of town (wards 6, 8, and 9) and the South End (wards 10-12). Houses are drawn on Price's 1769 map reprinted as frontispiece to *Bostonian Society Publications,* 1st Ser., IX (1912).

58

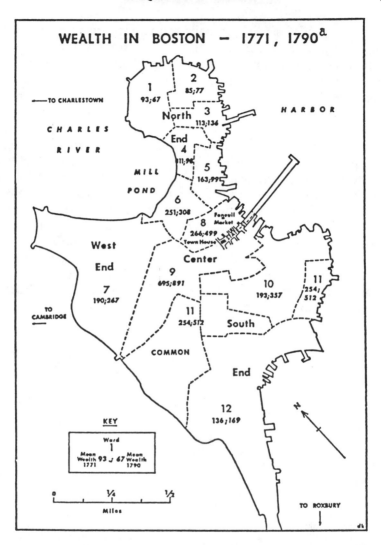

WEALTH IN BOSTON — 1771, 1790[a]

TO CHARLESTOWN

CHARLES
RIVER

HARBOR

1
93;67

2
85;77

North
3
113;136

End
4
111;98

MILL
POND

5
163;99

6
251;308

Faneuil
Market

8
266;499
Town House

West
End

Center

9
695;891

7
190;267

10
193;357

11
254;
512

TO
CAMBRIDGE

11
254;512

South

COMMON

End

12
136;169

N

KEY

Ward
1
Mean
Wealth 93 ⌡ 67 Mean
1771   Wealth
1790

0   ¼   ½

Miles

TO ROXBURY

dk

[a] Mass. Archives, CXXXII; Tax and Rate Books, 1790; *1790 Census.* The 1771 means were calculated by dividing the wealth of the ward by the number of polls; the 1790 means by dividing the ward's wealth by the number of people taxed with the addition of widows from the census. Untaxed widows were not included in the 1771 list, but the two sources are comparable because all polls (including each poll in multiple poll households and "polls not rateable") were included in the 1771 figure, but not in the 1790 figure. This seems to have underestimated the 1771 wealth.

lation was thin . . . and there were fields and marshes, are now splendid houses and crowded Streets."[37]

Boston's social geography was similar to other preindustrial towns. In those towns, wealthy merchants, lawyers, retailers, and noblemen lived on or near the main business streets. Residents of middling wealth generally lived next to them. On the outskirts, farthest away from the economic center of town, resided poor artisans and laborers.[38] In Boston, both before and after the Revolution, the farther one walked from State Street, the lower the ward's mean and median wealth became.

The center of town, with a median wealth of £125 in 1790, was the richest section. The Massachusetts Bank, the Statehouse, the market, and various retail shops were located there, mostly along State and Cornhill Streets. Families of retailers lived over their shops. Unlike

59

TABLE VII

RESIDENTIAL PATTERNS OF ECONOMIC AND OCCUPATIONAL GROUPS, BOSTON, 1790[a]

A. ECONOMIC GROUPS

1790 Assessment in Pounds	Percentage by Area				Number in Group
	North End	West End	Center	South End	
0	46	6	14	34	1,364
1–75	41	10	13	36	776
76–275	33	8	21	38	627
276–999	20	7	35	38	498
1000+	6	9	40	45	202
Total of All Groups	37	8	18	37	3,467

[37] William Bentley, *The Diary of William Bentley, D.D.*, II (Gloucester, Mass., 1962 [orig. publ. 1907]), 426.

[38] Gideon Sjoberg, *The Preindustrial City, Past and Present* (Glencoe, Ill., 1960), 95-102; Deyon, *Amiens*, 247-252, 543, 566; Hoskins, *Exeter*, 113, 116-117; Hoskins, *Provincial England*, 92-93; D. V. Glass, "Notes on the Demography of London at the End of the Seventeenth Century," *Daedalus*, XCVII (1968), 583; Richard L. Bushman, *From Puritan to Yankee: Character and Social Order in Connecticut, 1690-1765* (Cambridge, Mass., 1967), 57-58; Charles A. Beard, *Economic Origins of Jeffersonian Democracy* (New York, 1915), 384-386; Blumin, "Mobility and Change," in Thernstrom and Sennett, eds., *Nineteenth-Century Cities*, 186-190.

B. OCCUPATIONAL GROUPS

Occupation	North End	West End	Center	South End	Number in Group
	Percentage by Area				
Bakers	38	18	5	39	66
Blacksmiths	46	3	8	43	59
Building Trades	31	10	11	48	245
Coopers	70	0	3	27	70
Laborers	47	7	8	38	157
Leather Workers	33	5	10	52	108
Mariners	68	5	8	19	117
Marine Crafts[b]	72	2	6	20	193
Merchants[c]	9	12	28	51	206
Professionals	15	13	38	34	68
Retailers[d]	28	4	46	22	144
Sea Captains	46	10	16	28	114
Tailors	41	11	16	32	100
Transportation	32	4	14	50	80
Total of All Groups	40	7	16	37	1,727

Notes: [a] Tax and Rate Books, 1790. Variations in residential patterns can be seen by comparing the percentage of the total of all groups in each area with the percentage of each subgroup in the area. In Table VII A, widows from the census are included; Table VII B includes about two-thirds of all employed. A Chi Square test run on the raw data of Table VII A yielded a result that was significant at less than the .01 level. This means the probability that the distribution occurred by chance is less than 1%.
[b] Excludes ropemakers, concentrated in the West End.
[c] Includes only merchants, not other groups included under "Merchants-Traders" in Table I.
[d] Retailers and hardware store owners only.

those in the rest of the town, the buildings were predominantly brick.[39] Ward nine, on the south side of State Street, was the wealthiest in town, with a fifth of its residents assessed over a thousand pounds each, but it was closely followed by surrounding wards. The richest merchants and professional men and almost half the retailers lived in these wards, but in proportion to their numbers in the total population, fewer artisans made their homes there.

[39] Pemberton, "Description of Boston," Mass. Hist. Soc., *Collections,* 1st Ser., III (1794), 248-250.

Part of the South End was far from the center of town and quite poor, but a number of retailers and merchants, mostly of middling wealth, lived in wards ten and eleven. The area's median wealth in 1790 was only fifty pounds; but over half the people in ward twelve were assessed twenty-five pounds or less. This ward, almost as populous as the two others together, contained large numbers of laborers, truckmen, and leather workers. In 1790, the ward must still have seen intense building activity, because a third of the town's masons, carpenters, and painters resided there.

The undersettled West End, with a median wealth of twenty-five pounds, was poorer than the South End. Most of the town's ropemakers lived there, close to the ropewalks. This was the only part of town not to lose black population between 1742 and 1790; in 1790 blacks were most concentrated there. As the area became more densely settled, merchants and professional men also moved into the area; by 1790 both groups were settled there in greater proportion than throughout the town generally.

The North End was the poorest section of town in 1771, and by 1790 the wealth of its inhabitants seems to have declined. The median wealth of the area in the latter year was twenty-five pounds, but over half the people in the remote wards one and two were without taxable wealth. Most of the town's transient sailors, shipwrights, sailmakers, and other marine artisans lived there. An area dominated by marine interests, it also housed proportionately higher percentages of coopers, sea captains, laborers, tailors, and poor widows than there were in the population as a whole.

How strong was this pattern? Even though the town was small, and a few members of every economic and occupational group lived in every section, substantial economic segregation could have existed. As Table VIII shows, no group was as segregated as blacks are today.[40] There was no necessary relationship between occupation and degree of segregation. Professional men were more integrated than merchants; blacks, laborers, and tailors clustered far less than their lower-class status might indicate. Marine artisans, with their special ship-related functions, were the most segregated trade. Wealth rather than occupation determined

[40] For figures in Philadelphia see Sam Bass Warner, Jr., "If All the World Were Philadelphia: A Scaffolding for Urban History, 1774-1930," *American Historical Review*, LXXIV (1968-1969), 36-37. Figures for the index of dissimilarity for blacks in ghettos 1940-1960 run between 75 and 90. Karl E. and Alma F. Taeuber, *Negroes in Cities: Residential Segregation and Neighborhood Change* (Chicago, 1965), 37-41.

TABLE VIII

INDEX OF DISSIMILARITY OF ECONOMIC AND OCCUPATIONAL GROUPS, BOSTON, 1790[a]

Unpropertied	56.8	Marine Crafts[b]	35.5	Transportation	11.6
Assessed £1–75	26.4	Merchants	25.9	Professionals[c]	9.8
Assessed £76–275	16.7	Building Crafts	18.6	Sea Captains	8.8
Assessed £276–999	41.7	Mariners	17.3	Tailors	8.8
Assessed £1000+	28.5	Retailers	16.7	Leather Crafts	8.3
Blacks	10.4	Laborers	15.2	Bakers	6.7
Widows	19.1	Coopers	11.8	Blacksmiths	6.4

Notes: [a] Tax and Rate Books, 1790. For details on the construction of the index, which measures the average deviation within wards of the percentage of each group from its mean percentage in the total population and runs from 0 (perfect integration) to 100 (total segregation), see Taeuber and Taeuber, *Negroes in Cities*, 235-237.
[b] Excludes ropemakers, concentrated in the West End.
[c] Lawyers, doctors, an accountant, an apothecary, and an architect.

residence. Boston's propertyless residents—nearly 40 per cent of the population—were the most segregated group and mostly lived in economic ghettos at either end of town. Wealthier, and thus smaller, economic groups were less concentrated and spread more evenly across the city.

In late eighteenth-century Boston, individuals were becoming increasingly more mobile, moving from place to place and from one economic position to another, while society itself was becoming more stratified. Almost all newcomers to Boston were "warned out," officially informed that the town would not care for them if they ever needed charity.[41] Since there is no indication that warnings out were limited to the poor, they are rough measures of migration into Boston. While the scrutiny of the overseers may have increased over the period, the pattern found in Table IX is too strong to be discounted. The number of migrants remained small until 1755, then in terms both of numbers and rates, rapidly increased. After 1765, at least a tenth of Boston's residents had been in town five years or less.[42]

[41] Josiah Henry Benton, *Warning Out in New England* (Boston, 1911), 55-62; *Record Commissioners' Report*, XXV, 28, 34, 166, 212, 242.
[42] Rates for 1765-1790 were almost as great as in early modern London, but less than those in antebellum Boston. E. A. Wrigley, "A Simple Model of London's Importance in Changing English Society and Economy 1650-1750," *Past and Present*, No. 37 (July 1967), 45-49; Peter R. Knights, "Population Turnover, Persistence and

TABLE IX
WARNINGS OUT IN BOSTON, 1745 TO 1792[a]

Year	Number Warned	Number Warned/1000 Population
1745–1749	363	23.1
1750–1754	528	33.6
1755–1759	1,160	74.2
1760–1764	765	49.3
1765–1769	2,499	151.1
1770–1773	1,587	95.9
1791–1792	2,405	133.9

63

Note: [a] Warnings Out in Boston, 1745–1792, Records of the Overseers of the Poor of Boston, Mass., Mass. Hist. Soc. From 1745 to 1773, children and wives were listed with husbands; the 1791–1792 lists often include many entries under a single family name, but the relationships are not indicated. The 1791–1792 number/1000 population is comparable with the others; at that time a resident could be warned until he resided in the town four years. Robert W. Kelso, *The History of Public Poor Relief in Massachusetts, 1620–1920* (Boston, 1922), 59. This table represents minimum migration into Boston.

What would explain this dramatic change in the intensity of migration? Migrants in most modern societies tend to travel short distances, going from remote villages to nearby towns and from towns to more distant cities. They stop and settle at the first place where a job is offered, and travel farther only if the opportunity disappears.[43] These generalizations apply to post-Revolutionary Boston. Almost three-quarters of the migrants entering Boston in 1791 came from Massachusetts, and a third traveled ten miles or less. In point of origin, the other quarter principally divided between foreign lands and more distant American cities like New York and Philadelphia.

The migrants formed three distinct streams. Twenty-eight per cent arrived from foreign ports. The other two groups, totaling 71.2 per cent of all migrants, traveled from Massachusetts towns. Most of them,

Residential Mobility in Boston, 1830-1860," in Thernstrom and Sennett, eds., *Nineteenth-Century Cities*, 258-274.

[43] E. G. Ravenstein, "The Laws of Migration," *Journal of the Royal Statistical Society*, XLVIII (1885), 167-227, esp. 198-199; Ravenstein, "The Laws of Migration: Second Paper," *ibid.*, LII (1889), 241-305; Samuel A. Stoffer, "Intervening Opportunities: A Theory Relating Mobility and Distance," *American Sociological Review*, V (1940), 845-867; George Blackburn and Sherman L. Ricards, Jr., "A Demographic History of the West: Manistee County, Michigan, 1860," *Journal of American History*, LVII (1970), 616-617.

TABLE X
BIRTH PLACES OF THOSE WARNED OUT OF BOSTON, 1791[a]

Foreign	237	*Other States*	62	*Massachusetts*	740
England	84	Philadelphia	28	Within 10 miles of Boston	341
Ireland	52	New York City	19	Southeast of Boston	181
Scotland	31	Carolina	4	North of Boston	143
Africa	29	Maryland	3	West of Boston	75
Germany	16	New Hampshire	3		
France	14	Albany	3		
Nova Scotia	3	Hartford	2		
West Indies	8				

Total: 1,039

Note: [a] Warnings Out in Boston, Overseers of the Poor Records, Mass. Hist. Soc.

39.8 per cent of the total, migrated from nearby coastal areas such as Charlestown, Plymouth, Cape Cod, Ipswich, Salem, and Newburyport. This seaport-to-seaport stream probably brought numerous marine artisans and mariners into Boston. If the mobility of this group was as great in the 1760s, it may help to explain the number and volatility of the crowds in pre-Revolutionary Boston.[44] The final group, constituting 31.4 per cent of all migrants, came from neighboring agricultural areas that were experiencing population pressure on land. In these areas during the late eighteenth century, poverty and geographical mobility increased as the average size of landholdings fell.[45] Forced off the land and unaccustomed to urban life, these men at least temporarily joined and augmented the number of poor and near poor.

Though Boston drew many people from smaller ports, declining agricultural areas, and foreign lands, her own opportunities were limited. By 1790, 45 per cent of the taxpayers in town in 1780 had dis-

[44] Pauline Maier, "Popular Uprisings and Civil Authority in Eighteenth-Century America," *Wm. and Mary Qtly.*, 3d Ser., XXVII (1970), 3-35.
[45] Kenneth Lockridge, "Land, Population and the Evolution of New England Society 1630-1790," *Past and Present*, No. 39 (Apr. 1968), 62-80; Philip J. Greven, *Four Generations: Population, Land, and Family in Colonial Andover, Massachusetts* (Ithaca, N. Y., 1970), 212-214; Charles S. Grant, *Democracy in the Connecticut Frontier Town of Kent* (New York, 1961), 94-103; Bruce E. Steiner, "New England Anglicanism: A Genteel Faith?" *Wm. and Mary Qtly.*, 3d Ser., XXVII (1970), 122-135.

appeared from tax lists. Some had died; the rest left town. The figure is higher than that found in stable, rural communities where land is plentiful, but is low· compared to nineteenth-century American cities or frontier areas.[46] Those who moved out of Boston were the poorest and least successful members of the community. As Table XI shows, only 42 per cent of those without real estate (rents) in 1780 remained in town in 1790. In Newburyport between 1850 and 1880, 41 per cent of the laborers persisted during each decade, a rate almost identical to that of the unpropertied in Boston seventy years earlier.[47] As the amount of rent reported increased, the rate of persistence rose; only one-quarter of the upper 10 per cent of those listed in 1780 had moved or died by 1790. Even if the death rates of the poor were higher, and their slippage from one list to another greater, this table suggests that a larger proportion of the poor than the rich were mobile.

65

TABLE XI

GEOGRAPHIC MOBILITY IN BOSTON, 1780 TO 1790[a]

Rent in Pounds in 1780	Number Reported in 1780	Number Missing in 1790	Persistence Rate
0	546	318	42
1–20	448	215	52
21–40	360	169	53
41–60	217	83	62
61–80	219	83	62
100–199	226	78	66
200+	209	54	74
Total	2,225	1,000	56

Note: [a] Assessors' Books, 1780, compared with Tax and Rate Books, 1790. The persistence rate is the percentage of the number reported in 1780 found on the 1790 list.

[46] Other rates, all expressed in terms of per cent per decade: 51% in 17th-century English towns; 22% in Dedham, Mass., 1670-1700; 56% in Boston, 1830-1860; 73% in Trempealeau Co., Wis., 1860-1880. Peter Laslett and John Harrison, "Clayworth and Cogenhoe," in H. E. Bell and R. L. Ollard, eds., *Historical Essays 1600-1750, Presented to David Ogg* (London, 1963), 173-177; Kenneth Lockridge, "The Population of Dedham, Massachusetts, 1636-1736," *Economic History Review*, 2d Ser., XIX (1966), 322-324; Knights, "Population Turnover," in Thernstrom and Sennett, eds., *Nineteenth-Century Cities*, 262; Curti, *American Community*, 68.

[47] Stephan Thernstrom, *Poverty and Progress: Social Mobility in a Nineteenth Century City* (Cambridge, Mass., 1964), 85.

Inward and outward mobility suggests a small, but significant, floating population of men and women at the bottom of society who moved from seaport to seaport and town to town in search of work. Many of the 278 men who were assessed for only the poll tax in 1790, but who disappeared before the census was taken, were probably among them.[48] The nature of this floating population was very similar to that in nineteenth-century Newburyport.[49] Impoverished, unemployable men dominated the wanderers in both places. The fifteen men whipped for various offenses in Boston in September 1790 were transients who had not been listed by the assessors a few months earlier.[50] Other migrants from Boston landed in the poorhouses of neighboring towns, triggering angry correspondence between their overseers and those of Boston.[51]

Uprooted, unwanted, unhealthy migrants could call no town their home. The potent identity given an individual by his community was not theirs. Thomas Seymore, an old man living off poor relief in Abington in 1805, was born and attended school in Boston, and later moved to Barnstable, Sandwich, Weymouth, and Abington, but never "gained a settlement" by paying taxes for five successive years. In his whole life, he never found a home. Similarly, Braintree demanded in 1804 that Boston "remove Stephen Randal belonging to your town." Since his arrival there in 1802, he had received relief from the town. "He has been wandering about from place to place. . . . Some part of the time chargeable. About four weeks ago he froze himself very bad in the feet and is att the Expense of two Dollars and 50 cents per week, Besides a Dollar attendance, there is no prospect of his being better very soon."[52]

After the Revolution, the old laws used to deal with migrants fell apart. Even though the state accepted responsibility for transients without legal residence anywhere in the commonwealth, the time limit for towns to present migrants with warnings out was extended from two years to three, four, and ultimately five years between 1790 and 1793.

[48] The census was taken between Aug. 2 and 22 (*Record Commissioners' Report* edition of census); when assessments were made is unknown, but assessors were elected in March and some widows of men who were taxed appear in the census.

[49] Thernstrom, *Poverty and Progress*, 84-89.

[50] *Boston Gazette* (Mass.), Sept. 20, 1790.

[51] Overseers of the Poor of Boston, Mass., Miscellaneous Papers, 1735-1855, Mass. Hist. Soc. Most letters are from the period 1800-1805; for similar examples in the 1760s see *Record Commissioners' Report*, XX, 201-202, 281-289.

[52] Overseers of the Poor, Misc. Papers, 1735-1855, Mass. Hist. Soc.

In 1794, when the state became responsible for all migrants, warnings out were finally eliminated. Instead, legal residency required payment of taxes on an assessed estate of sixty pounds for five successive years. A former apprentice who practiced his trade for five years or anyone over twenty-one years of age who lived in town for ten years and paid taxes for five became a resident. The law discouraged transients, but encouraged artisans with capital to remain.[53]

But did "expensive Living . . . [pervade] thro every Class, confounding every Distinction between the Poor and the Rich," as Samuel Adams insisted? Enough examples could be found to keep him worried. Thomas Lewis was a shoemaker assessed for £40 rent in 1780 and a wharfinger taxed on £700 in 1790; Josiah Elliot was an agent for a merchant in 1780 and owned no real estate, but in 1790 he operated a hardware store and was assessed for property worth £450; Robert Davis was a leather dresser with £30 rent in 1780, and a merchant assessed £600 in 1790.

Adams failed to see more modest gains. "Mechanics of sober character, and skilled in their trades, of almost every kind, may find employment, and wages equal to their support," wrote the Boston Immigrant Society.[54] The society was partially right. When the Mechanics Association, open only to master craftsmen, was founded in 1795, a fifth of its original members were not on the 1790 tax list; they had either been apprentices in 1790 or had entered town since that time.

A comparison of 1780 and 1790 tax lists shows that occupational mobility was very moderate and that opportunity may well have been declining. Since only those who remained in town for ten years are considered, the results are biased toward success. Only 28 per cent changed jobs, while merely 14 per cent made even minor changes in status. Changes from one artisan job to another and changes among merchants, grocers, retailers, and captains were typical—and rather trivial. Other changes resulted in new status; and about the same number rose as declined. Seventeen artisans became small shopkeepers, wharfingers, and merchants, and four advanced to professional status, while thirteen declined to laborer status. Twenty-eight tradesmen and professionals declined to artisan status, and one became a laborer.

Some new men from outlying areas probably migrated to Boston, bought tory estates, and joined the elite classes immediately after the

[53] Kelso, *Public Poor Relief*, 55-61.
[54] Immigrant Society in Boston, *Information for Immigrants to the New-England States* (Boston, 1795).

TABLE XII
OCCUPATIONAL MOBILITY IN BOSTON, 1780 TO 1790[a]

Occupation in 1790	Occupation in 1780				Total in 1790
	Pro-fessional	Tradesman	Artisan	Marine-Laborer	
Professional	42	15	4	0	61
Tradesman[b]	0	162	17	0	179
Artisan	5	23	311	9	348
Marine-Laborer	0	1	13	24	38
Total in 1780	47	201	345	33	626

68

Notes: [a] Assessors' Books, 1780; Tax and Rate Books, 1790. Table XII represents only about half the people who remained in Boston during the decade. Wards 5, 6, and 10 do not have occupations listed for 1780, and Negroes and widows were rarely listed. The columns are 1780, the rows 1790 (e.g., 61 professionals in 1790, 47 in 1780, 311 artisans remained artisans over the decade, 23 tradesmen became artisans). Lateral changes within the groups, which included no change in status, involved 4 professionals, 37 tradesmen, 42 artisans, 4 marine-laborers. Total changes of status: 87. Total lateral changes: 87. Total changes: 174.
[b] Retailers, merchants, businessmen.

Revolution,[55] but opportunity soon diminished and the situation became critical. As population grew, more men competed for fewer jobs; many, according to Samuel Breck, became unemployed, "so much so that several gentlemen who associated for the purpose of building three ships had solely in view the occupation of the carpenters and tradespeople."[56] Breck may not have greatly exaggerated. The percentage of laborers and other unskilled men more than doubled: between 2 and 3 per cent were in the group in 1780; the number had grown to 7.4 per cent in 1790.[57] Within the groups staying in town for the ten years, opportunities seem to have been slightly closing at the top and opening at the bottom. While ten merchants and traders became government functionaries (all

[55] Brown, "Confiscation of Loyalists' Estates," *Wm. and Mary Qtly.*, 3d Ser., XXI (1964), 546-549; Oscar and Mary F. Handlin, "Radicals and Conservatives in Massachusetts after Independence," *New England Quarterly*, XVII (1944), 352-355.
[56] Breck, *Recollections*, 178.
[57] Laborers constitute 6.1% of the people whose occupations in 1780 are known. However, the three wards from which there is no occupational data housed only 11% of the laborers in 1790. The figure of 6.1% is therefore far too high. A number of

but one in a full-time position), the total number of tradesmen declined by 11 per cent. On the other hand, the number of men in the marine-laborer category declined 12 per cent.[58]

Upward mobility among sons of artisans was somewhat greater. Jackson Main discovered that the fathers of about a quarter of the merchants sampled from the 1789 directory had been artisans such as brewers, coopers, hatters, carpenters, and tailors. Since each of these trades included a few wealthy members whose sons should have risen in the normal course of events, and Main discovered none from his sample among the wealthiest merchants, his findings, like mine, point to very modest upward mobility.[59]

While a small minority changed their status, almost two-thirds of the group changed their relative economic position in the community. Table XIII shows that 30 per cent lost and 31 per cent gained wealth. However, these figures are deceptive; probably most of those who moved during the decade feared economic decline. When geographic mobility is considered, more men lost than gained wealth. In each of the three middle categories of Table XIII, the number who fell slightly approximated the number who gained slightly. Unpropertied men who left town were probably those who could not gain a foothold in Boston, for 71 per cent of those who remained became property owners. Most made minor gains; the twenty-eight men who entered the top categories were mostly merchants who had not yet bought property in Boston in 1780. The very top category—as Sam Adams asserted—was in a state of flux; less than half the men in that group in 1780 managed to remain there in 1790, but men from the next lower category rushed to fill their places.

What all these changes meant to most workers was buying—or losing—a small piece of real estate, finding a new, somewhat different job, or receiving a small profit from one's trade. Joseph Snelling, an unpropertied joiner in 1780, gained £25 of real estate by 1790; John Scutter,

69

---

others in other wards have no occupations listed, and some of them may have been laborers. For a conservative estimate of the proportion of laborers, I added 30% to the number listed (38), and divided that number (50) by 2,225, the total number of males on the 1780 list. The result was 2.3%.

[58] These percentages, based on a small number of cases, must be taken as indicative only of the direction of change, not of the extent of change. It is probable that some of the difference is random. However, the figures may be minimums; Table XII probably underestimates the extent of downward mobility. See note to Table XIV.

[59] Main, *Social Structure*, 191-192.

a propertyless fisherman in 1780, was a journeyman goldsmith with £25 of real estate in 1790. Tailor Samuel Beales owned £12 10s. of real estate in 1780; by 1790, he owned property assessed at £125 and had six children and four apprentices or journeymen in his house. Small losses were equally common. John Douglass, a cooper with real estate worth £12 10s. in 1780, was a combmaker without taxable property in 1790. Samuel Clark, tailor, lost real estate worth £20 over the decade, and Richard Salter, a merchant with a rent of £180 in 1780, was a small shopkeeper with property worth only £25 in 1790.

70 What pattern explains these small changes? Men in some trades—merchants, professional men, builders, coopers—tended to gain wealth, while others—bakers, shoemakers, tailors—tended to lose it. Whole classes, however, neither rose nor fell; some individuals in most groups became prosperous and some poor.[60] As Table XIV illustrates, over 70 per cent of Boston's workers assumed different occupations or economic conditions over the decade. While there is a significant (and expected) ten-

TABLE XIII

PROPERTY MOBILITY IN BOSTON, 1780 TO 1790[a]

1790 Income Groups	1780 Income Groups					Total in 1790
	High 1	2	3	4	Low 5	
High 1	55	39	15	3	7	119
2	43	85	63	7	21	219
3	12	46	107	59	39	263
4	4	17	51	87	55	214
Low 5	7	14	32	71	51	175
Total in 1780	121	201	268	227	173	990

Note: [a] Assessors' Books, 1780; Tax and Rate Books, 1790. Some persons could not be ranked. Columns are 1780, rows 1790. The income groups were determined by comparing 1780 rents (hypothetically 1/6 of the real estate assessment) with total assessments in 1790. In the table, 1 is the highest and 5 the lowest group. The real figures for each group in 1780 and 1790 respectively are: 1, £200+ and £1000+; 2, £75–£199 and £276–£999; 3, £30–£74 and £76–£275; 4, £1–£29 and £1–£75; 5, £0 for both years.

[60] The problem is discussed in Blumin, "Historical Study of Mobility," Hist. Meth. Newsletter, I, No. 4 (Sept. 1968), 1-13.

TABLE XIV

OCCUPATIONAL AND PROPERTY MOBILITY IN BOSTON, 1780 TO 1790[a]

	Occupation Up	Occupation Same	Occupation Down	Total
Wealth Up	32	164	14	210
Wealth Same	26	186	33	245
Wealth Down	12	84	52	148
Total	70	434	99	603

71

Note: [a] Assessors' Books, 1780; Tax and Rate Books, 1790. Occupations in Table XIV are ranked as in Table III, and ranks for other occupations have been interpolated to determine direction of mobility. The occupational mobility figures are not identical to those of Table XII because of the differences in the categories of Table III; the method used here allowed inclusion of cases of lateral mobility mentioned in n. *a* to Table XII. Some cases have been lost, and several cases of men employed in 1780 and unemployed in 1790 added. Ratios of downward/downward and upward mobility in Tables XII-XIV show that Table XIV may be biased toward upward property mobility (51.7% downward/downward and upward mobility in Table XIII and only 41.3% downward in Table XIV). Since Table XIII has the larger number of cases, it should be more accurate. But with its more exact methodology, Table XIV points to a bias toward upward occupational mobility in Table XII (48.2% downward mobility in Table XII, 58% in Table XIV). Chi Square was significant at less than .01.

dency for some to rise or fall both in wealth and occupation, 74 per cent of those changing in one variable did not change the other.

Though occupational mobility had little relationship to economic mobility, age in most occupational groups was probably related to wealth.[61] A young man might begin working with little money, gain wealth, and perhaps change occupations as he grew older, lose wealth when he became an old man, and leave his widow with few worldly goods. Some impressionistic evidence supports this thesis. John Hooton followed his father's trade of oarmaker in 1780 and lived at home, but by 1790 he was a wharfinger taxed for £275. In 1780 Benjamin Jervis was a propertyless journeyman working for merchant Pascol Smith; by 1790 Jervis had set up as a merchant himself and was assessed £450. Aged Joseph Morton, propertyless in 1790, had been a taverner with a rent of £200 in 1780; John Maud, an old tailor, had a £30 rent in 1780 but was propertyless in 1790.

[61] Age and mobility were related in 19th-century Canada. Michael Katz, "The Social Structure of Hamilton, Ontario," in Thernstrom and Sennett, eds., *Nineteenth-Century Cities*, 209-244.

The social condition of the town's widows also supports this thesis. In 1790, only 76 of Boston's 575 widows owned any taxable property. Widows of very successful men managed to hold on to some property: of the widows taxed, 17 were assessed under £125, 23 from £125 to £200, 21 from £201 to £500, 10 from £500 to £1,000, and 5 over £1,000. Probably some husbands lost wealth before they died; widows quickly lost the rest. Their decline in wealth and status was steeper than almost any experienced by their husbands; the resulting loneliness and unhappiness appear in the assessor's marginal comments. Widow Gray was a "dogmatic lady," and Widow Turrell was a "talking woman." A number of widows followed callings that allowed contact with the public. Twenty-eight of them combated poverty and isolation by operating boarding houses; five others owned taverns; three managed millinery shops; and eight owned other types of retail establishments.

72

Inequality rapidly advanced in Boston during the Revolutionary period. Wealth was less evenly distributed than before the war, and the proportion of wealth held by the poor and middling classes declined. The growth of poverty was a major problem. As continued migration increased the numbers of poor, a surplus female population of working age was only temporarily helped by the duckcloth factory. Many citizens were able to gain economic security, but unsuccessful families lived in crowded housing or wandered from place to place in search of employment.

Rich and poor were divided by wealth, ascribed status, and segregated living patterns. Individuals could rarely breach a status barrier in fewer than two generations. While social mobility may have been relatively easy for a few immediately after the Revolution, these extraordinary opportunities tended to disappear as population returned to its pre-Revolutionary size. Since political power was monopolized by the wealthy, the poor could only deferentially appeal for aid. The economic elite socialized only among themselves, never showed visitors the semi-ghetto of the North End, and rode through the South End without seeing the poor. But increased segregation could eventually undermine deference by eliminating opportunities for the lowly to defer to their superiors.

A class system based primarily on economic divisions slowly developed. Occupation and wealth determined a man's position in the community; the few titles that survived became functional descriptions of groups, not indicators of a special status. Tax records show that "gentleman"

ceased to be a social distinction, but was instead a term reserved for
retired tradesmen; "esquire" was a title generally limited to lawyers and
public officials. Increased wealth alone could bring higher status to tradesmen and artisans—a fact probably behind Samuel Adams's complaints.

At the same time Boston was becoming more stratified, a new political
philosophy emerged. Whig theory divided society and government into
three orders, democracy, aristocracy, and monarchy, and demanded that
each be perpetually a check and balance on the others. After the Revolution this theory slowly gave way to a model that put the people above
the entire government. They held "constituent power," enabling them
to call conventions to write constitutions restraining the powers of
government. Sovereignty was transferred from the king (or a branch
of the legislature) to the people, and political equality was enshrined in
the country's legal documents.[62]

Yet the city of Boston, increasingly democratic in theory, and increasingly stratified and divided economically and socially, managed
to avoid major civil disturbances after the Revolution. Not only did social
and political trends seem to run in opposite directions, but the groups of
near poor who manned preindustrial crowds in Europe—apprentices,
journeymen, and artisans—lived in greater profusion in Boston than in
contemporary European towns.[63] What social forces kept these groups
quiet after the Revolution?

Definitive answers to this question await further research, but at least
some speculation is in order. Before the Revolution, crowd action was
considered a legitimate means for producing social change and protecting
the community. When the monarchial order seemed to deny the people
their liberties, the people took to the streets. The resulting disturbances
were not class conflicts, for pre-Revolutionary crowds in America were
supported by the upper classes and peopled by the near poor.[64]

After the Revolution, the ideological props for violence slowly dis-
integrated. If the people were sovereign, if they held "constituent
power," crowd action was a revolt against the people, not a conflict to

[62] Robert R. Palmer, *The Age of the Democratic Revolution: A Political History
of Europe and America, 1760-1800* (Princeton, 1959), I, Chap. 8; Gordon S. Wood,
The Creation of the American Republic, 1776-1787 (Chapel Hill, 1969), Chaps. 8-9.
[63] George Rudé, *The Crowd in History: A Study of Popular Disturbances in
France and England, 1730-1848* (New York, 1964), passim, but esp. Chap. 13; Ralf
Dahrendorf, *Class and Class Conflict in Industrial Society* (Stanford, Calif., 1959),
216-218.
[64] Maier, "Popular Uprisings," *Wm. and Mary Qtly.*, 3d Ser. XXVII (1970), 3-30.

restrain one branch of government. This change did not eliminate violence, but it altered its nature.[65] Crowds would no longer be the weapons of one order, composed of elements from many economic classes, to be directed against another, but would be revolutionary instruments of class conflict.

Post-Revolutionary Boston, however, provided several structural restraints against this development. The possibility of moderate economic success and the safety valve of short-distance migrations probably limited the chance for confrontation. Unless economic disaster strikes a large number of men (and there is no evidence of this in Boston at this time), group conflict can be generated only when two organized interests compete for the same goods or power.[66] But Boston's only organized society of workers—whose members were of firm middle-class standing—willingly deferred to their social superiors.

[65] *Ibid.*, 30-33.
[66] Dahrendorf, *Class and Class Conflict*, Chaps. 5-6.

APPENDIX
OCCUPATIONS OF BOSTON MALES, 1790[a]

Occupation	Number	Occupation	Number
I. Government[b]	67	Peddler	6
Federal Officers	11	Retailer	133
Law Enforcement	10	Stationeer	5
State Officers	13	Tobacconist	17
Town Officers	33	Trader	13
		Underwriter	1
II. Professional	219	Wharfinger	24
Accountant	3		
Apothecary	17	IV. Clerical	66
Architect	1	Clerk	28
Dentist	1	Scribe	38
Doctor	26		
Lawyer	21	V. Artisans A to G	1,271
Minister	20		
Schoolmaster	16	A. Building Crafts	245
Sea Captain	114	Carpenter	140
		Glazier	12
III. Tradesmen	474		
Auctioneer	7	Mason	44
Banker	1	Painter	34
Broker	16	Joiner	5
Bookseller	2	Sawyer	7
Chandler	17	Stonecutter	3
Hardware Shop	11		
Lemondealer	10	B. Cloth Trades	289
Lumber Merchant	5	Cardmaker	24
Merchant	206	Combmaker	2

Occupation	Number	Occupation	Number
Duckcloth Maker	17	Carver	4
Furrier	3	Chairmaker	11
Hatter	29	Cooper	70
Leather Dresser	13	Turner	1
Shoemaker	78	Upholsterer	4
Shoedealer	6	Woodsealer	1
Silkdyer	3	G. Misc. Crafts	5
Tailor	100	Bookbinder	103
Tanner	10	Chaisemaker	16
Weaver	3	Huckster	4
C. Food Trades	175	Instrument Maker	3
Bacon Smoker	1	Musician	3
Baker	64	Paper-stainer	3
Bonecutter	1	Printer	17
Butcher	10	Saddler	6
Confectioneer	1	Soapboiler	6
Distiller	47	Watchmaker	8
Gingerbread Baker	2	Wheelwright	8
Grocer	33	Misc. Trades	28
Miller	4	VI. Service	183
Slop Shop	4	Barber	42
Sugar Boiler	8	Boarder-keeper	24
D. Marine Crafts	219	Carter	9
Blockmaker	16	Chaise-letter	3
Caulker	14	Coachdriver	6
Head Builder	5	Hackdriver	7
Mastmaker	7	Sexton	11
Rigger	11	Stablekeeper	3
Sailmaker	30	Taverner	26
Sea Cooper	16	Truckman	50
Oarmaker	1	VII. Mariners	117
Pumpmaker	4	Fisherman	37
Shipjoiner	7	Mate	20
Shipwright	65	Pilot	2
Staysmaker	1	Sailor	58
Ropemaker	42	VIII. Unskilled	188
E. Metal Crafts	132	Chimney Sweeper	6
Blacksmith	59	Gardener	15
Coppersmith	4	Laborer	157
Founder	15	Lightman	7
Goldsmith	23	Total Employed:	2,585
Gunsmith	1	Unemployed and Retired	106
Ironmonger	1		
Jeweler	3	Gentlemen	23
Silversmith	5	Poor (no trade)	27
Tinner	14	Poor, sick, lame	28
Whitesmith	1	Unemployed	28
Pewterer	6	Servants (white)	63
F. Woodworkers	106		
Cabinetmaker	15	Grand Total	2,754

75

Notes: * Tax and Rate Books, 1790; *Record Commissioners' Report*, X. The groups are in approximate order of status. There is some unavoidable overlapping in the appendix; a few trades in parts III and VI might well be placed under the artisan category.
 ᵇ Includes only those with no other listed occupation.

THE JOURNAL OF ECONOMIC HISTORY

VOLUME XXXI   SEPTEMBER 1971   NUMBER 3

Food Surpluses and Deficits in the American Colonies, 1768-1772

SCHOLARS are gradually piecing together the puzzle of the economic development of the American colonies through quantitative studies designed to clarify and measure economic variables having theoretical relevance for the wider process of economic growth and development. Recently, researchers such as Jones,[1] Land,[2] Shepherd,[3] Walton,[4] and Thomas[5] have been helping others to build a base that one day may permit the writing of a comprehensive study of the process of early American economic development which may even include reliable estimates of economic growth and living standards. The data problems for the colonial period of American economic history are severe, and much of the research has tended to concentrate on the important role of international trade, where the extant data sources are capable of yielding rich lodes of quantitative information. Customs 16/1, en-

---

[1] Alice Hanson Jones, "Wealth Estimates for the American Middle Colonies, 1774," *Economic Development and Cultural Change*, XVIII, No. 4, Part II (July 1970).

[2] Aubrey C. Land, "Economic Base and Social Structure: The Northern Chesapeake in the Eighteenth Century," THE JOURNAL OF ECONOMIC HISTORY, XXV (Dec. 1965), pp. 639-54. Land, "Economic Behavior in a Planting Society: The Eighteenth Century Chesapeake," *Journal of Southern History*, XXXIII (Nov. 1967), pp. 469-85.

[3] James F. Shepherd and Gary M. Walton, "Estimates of 'Invisible' Earnings in the Balance of Payments of the British North American Colonies, 1768-1772," THE JOURNAL OF ECONOMIC HISTORY, XXIX (June 1969), pp. 230-63. James F. Shepherd, "Commodity Exports From the British North American Colonies to Overseas Areas, 1768-1772: Magnitudes and Patterns of Trade," *Explorations in Economic History*, VIII (Fall, 1970), 5-76.

[4] Gary M. Walton, "New Evidence on Colonial Commerce," THE JOURNAL OF ECONOMIC HISTORY, XXVIII (Sept. 1968), pp. 363-89. Shepherd and Walton, "Estimates of 'Invisible' Earnings in the Balance of Payments," pp. 230-63.

[5] Robert Paul Thomas, "A Quantitative Approach to the Study of the Effects of British Imperial Policy Upon Colonial Welfare," THE JOURNAL OF ECONOMIC HISTORY, XXV (Dec. 1965), pp. 615-38.

titled the *Ledger of Imports and Exports for America, 1768-1772*, has been the most valuable source of trade data, since it is the only comprehensive document which shows the trade of the American colonies with all parts of the world and not just with the British Isles.[6] Still yet to be mined are the rich sources of data buried in the naval office lists for the various colonies.[7] These sources also give the trade of each colony with all parts of the world although they are more tedious to work with than the better collated Customs 16/1.

One of their principal assets is that the naval office lists show global trade for periods of time prior to 1768-1772, yet many years are missing or rendered worthless through incomplete entries by the naval officers who were charged with the task of record keeping in the various ports. The present study also relies on Customs 16/1 and on the Massachusetts naval office lists to focus attention on an important aspect of the colonial domestic economy: the magnitude, geographic distribution, and the size relative to consumption requirements of basic food surpluses and deficits in the American colonies. The study concludes with a range of per capita income estimates.

A comprehensive study by James F. Shepherd has shown that the category of bread and flour exports was the second most valuable export commodity for the thirteen colonies in 1768-1772.[8] Bread and flour exports comprised approximately 14 percent of the total value of all commodity exports in those years. In addition, they probably were the fastest growing of the major commodity exports, rising about 69 percent in terms of quantity shipped between 1768 and 1772. That the colonists were able to produce significant food surpluses despite the consumption demands of a rapidly growing population is one reason for believing, as most economic historians do, that substantial extensive growth was taking place. The question of intensive growth, meaning a growth in product per capita, is still an unsolved mystery though at least one researcher has educed

77

---

[6] Public Record Office, London, Customs 16/1.

[7] Under the head of Board of Trade Papers in the Colonial Office Catalog, Public Record Office, London, the Naval Office Lists cover the trade of the following colonies for the years given: Carolina, 1716-1719, 1721-1735, 1736-1767; Georgia, 1752-1767; Maryland, 1689-1702, 1751-1765; Massachusetts, 1752-1765; New England, 1686-1717; New Hampshire, 1723-1769; New Jersey, 1722-1764; New York, 1713-1765; Virginia, 1697-1706, 1725-1769.

[8] Shepherd, "Community Exports," p. 65.

fragmentary evidence which suggests that the eighteenth-century colonial Americans were experiencing improved living standards.[9] Many more narrow quantitative studies will have to be done before the question of intensive growth becomes amenable to empirical verification. The question of food supplies in the colonies is certainly an important one, for unless the colonists could feed their growing population at constant or rising per capita levels, the living standard of the population would have declined. The need for mass importation of foodstuffs in the early period of American economic development would probably have hindered both population growth and the increased specialization that marked the different paths of development followed by the various colonial regions. This study seeks to measure the agricultural self-sufficiency of the colonial economy in 1768-1772 and gives special attention to the interregional coastwise trade in certain basic foodstuffs—a trade which played a vital role in eliminating the shortages which existed in the New England colonies.

78

I

This research builds on the dissertation of Max George Schumacher who used Customs 16/1 to tabulate the net exports of particular foodstuffs by each colony.[10] Net exports refers to the excess of exports over any imports; negative net exports means that imports of that commodity exceeded any exports. If one assumes that any food surplus produced within a colony was marketed outside of the colony by water transport, that is, via coastwise or overseas shipping, then the actual surplus of foodstuffs can be approximated by the net export figure. Since land transportation at this time was both difficult and costly, it seems reasonably safe to assume that most of the marketed surpluses would have been carried by ship. Unrecorded intercolonial trade down rivers and over short stretches of land between colonies undoubtedly occurred. In addition, some of the actual surpluses probably were unable to reach markets economically due to their remoteness from the seacoast or suitable forms of river transportation to the sea. For these reasons

[9] George Rogers Taylor, "American Economic Growth Before 1840: An Exploratory Essay," THE JOURNAL OF ECONOMIC HISTORY, XXIV (Dec. 1964), pp. 427-44.
[10] Max George Schumacher, "The Northern Farmer and his Markets During the Late Colonial Period," (unpublished Ph.D. dissertation, University of California, 1948).

one should view the net export figure as a lower bound measure of the actual surpluses involved.

Schumacher was primarily concerned with examining the northern farmer's overseas markets and not with considering the deficit or surplus problem as such. Therefore he did not convert the individual commodity figures into values which could be added together for valuing total food surpluses and deficits. Similarly, he was not directly concerned with the size of the aggregate colonial food surpluses or deficits relative to consumption requirements.

A rich legacy of earlier economic historians working on the colonial period is the price information which they have made available. The studies comprising Arthur H. Cole's *Wholesale Commodity Prices in the United States, 1700-1861* were the basis for the conversion of the quantity figures into common units of value.[11] The monthly commodity prices were converted to a simple annual average and then to a weighted five-year price for 1768-1772.[12] In order to convert these current colony prices into a common sterling equivalent, the Boston, New York, Philadelphia, and Charleston prices were deflated by .75, .5625, .60, and .14, respectively.[13] The basis for this deflation into sterling was the rate at which the local currency could be exchanged for sterling. Thus all values in this paper are given in pounds sterling.

The specific commodities selected for valuing the food surpluses and deficits were bread, flour, wheat, corn, beef, and pork. It seems likely that grain and meat products constituted the fundamental source of nourishment for the average colonist throughout the American colonies. This is not to say that foods such as wild game, fish, rice, vegetables, cheese, and fruits were unimportant. It is probably true, however, that the average person derived a relatively small part of his diet from such foods in comparison to grain products, beef, and pork. Therefore this study is concerned with a subset of all foods that were available to the consumer. Any regional variation in diet that existed is also left out of account. Hereafter the bread, flour, wheat, corn, beef, and pork surplus or deficit is referred to as the *basic* surplus or deficit.

79

---

11 Arthur H. Cole, *Wholesale Commodity Prices in the United States, 1700-1861* (Cambridge: Harvard University Press, 1938), Statistical Supplement, pp. 57-64.
12 As monthly commodity data were not available, the calculation of a weighted average price was not possible.
13 Cole, Statistical Supplement, p. ix.

II

The average annual value of the grain and meat surpluses or deficits for each colony and commodity in 1768-1772 is given in Table 1. The table is in the familiar matrix form with the bottom row providing information on the value of the total average annual surplus for each commodity. The final basic surplus or deficit position of each colony is given in the last column of the table. The figures in brackets are deficit values.

Several interesting results emerge. Bread and flour, comprising approximately 63 percent of the basic surplus of £686,643, was by far the most important food surplus of the American colonies. By comparison, the Indian corn and beef and pork surpluses appear relatively small. It is evident that the colonists were processing the vast bulk of their wheat exports into flour, a procedure which would enhance the value and reduce freight costs. The extent to which grain, especially corn, was converted to meat is not known, although the feeding of grain to livestock may have been relatively unimportant in these times. Pennsylvania stands out as the leading surplus colony with nearly 48 percent of the aggregate basic surplus. By comparison, New York is much smaller and actually ranks behind Virginia and not much ahead of Maryland. The role played by grain in the tobacco colonies has tended to be overlooked in the literature.[14] All of the southern and middle colonies were surplus areas, but New England (excluding Connecticut) was a significant deficit region. Massachusetts, in particular, was consuming nearly £85,000 annually, and all of this was being imported from the other American colonies. Connecticut was the largest exporter of barreled meat and was also the largest exporter of livestock, for example, 4,375 horses, 2,582 cattle, and 7,105 head of sheep and hogs annually during 1768-1772.[15] No other American colony even came close to that performance. Most of the meat and livestock were shipped to the West Indies. Unless some of the animals were driven overland to markets in Rhode Island or Massachusetts, none apparently were sent to New England. Virginia was easily the leading surplus area for corn and was trailed distantly by Maryland and North Carolina. The upper South was also the leading exporter of loose wheat, with

[14] David Klingaman, "The Significance of Grain in the Development of the Tobacco Colonies," THE JOURNAL OF ECONOMIC HISTORY, XXIX (June 1969), pp. 268-78.
[15] Schumacher, p. 158.

TABLE 1

AVERAGE ANNUAL VALUE OF BASIC FOOD SURPLUSES AND DEFICITS IN THE AMERICAN COLONIES, 1768-1772
(Pounds Sterling)

	Bread[a] and Flour	Wheat	Corn	Beef[b] and Pork	Colony Totals
Maine	[3,002][c]	[25]	[1,216]	[223]	[4,466]
N. H.	[4,730]	[495]	[3,281]	[414]	[8,920]
Mass.	[42,516]	[9,595]	[24,637]	[8,103]	[84,851]
R. I.	[8,078]	[1,411]	[3,122]	283	[12,328]
Conn.	4,058	4,181	3,124	21,264	32,627
N. Y.	100,984	8,435	6,189	9,771	125,379
N. J.	2,366	[156]	406	[16]	2,600
Penn.	295,392	11,872	8,951	11,405	327,620
Del.	14,544	[23]	564	106	15,191
Md.	53,856	44,876	20,392	[165]	118,959
Va.	28,824	44,515	56,420	9,365	139,124
N. C.	1,010	1,202	14,439	11,610	28,261
S. C.	[4,058]	0	4,563	6,197	6,702
Ga.	[2,224]	0	1,276	1,693	745
Commodity Totals	436,426	103,376	84,068	62,773	686,643

81

Note: Boston prices were used in the calculations for Maine, New Hampshire, Massachusetts, and Rhode Island: 13.03 shillings per hundredweight of flour; 4.26 shillings per bushel of wheat; 2.63 shillings per bushel of corn; 42.92 shillings per barrel of beef or pork. New York prices were used in the calculations for Connecticut and New York: 10.79 shillings per hundredweight of flour; 3.51 shillings per bushel of wheat; 2.17 shillings per bushel of corn; 38.62 shillings per barrel of beef or pork. Philadelphia prices were used for New Jersey, Pennsylvania, Delaware, Maryland, Virginia, and North Carolina: 10.2 shillings per hundredweight of flour; 3.51 shillings per bushel of wheat; 1.94 shillings per bushel of corn; 39.85 shillings per barrel of beef or pork. Charleston prices were used for South Carolina and Georgia: 11.4 shillings per hundredweight of flour; 2.06 shillings per bushel of corn; 35.05 shillings per barrel of beef or pork. All prices are deflated to British pounds sterling.

a Customs 16/1 includes bread and flour in a single category. Flour probably made up a large proportion of bread and flour exports. See Arthur L. Jensen, *The Maritime Commerce of Colonial Philadelphia* (Madison, Wisconsin: The State Historical Society of Wisconsin, 1963), pp. 45-46, 60. Some kinds of bread were slightly cheaper than flour, but others were more expensive. In the table above, tons of bread and flour were valued as flour. The available quantity information does not differentiate among grades of flour.

b Customs 16/1 does not clearly distinguish between barrels of pork and beef. This makes pricing difficult since pork was considerably more valuable than was beef. It was assumed that half the imports and exports were beef, and the price used was the average of the beef and pork prices.

c The figures in brackets are deficits.

Sources: Max George Schumacher, "The Northern Farmer and His Markets During the Late Colonial Period," (unpublished Ph.D. dissertation, Department of History, University of California, 1948). Arthur H. Cole, *Wholesale Commodity Prices in the United States, 1700-1861* (Cambridge, Mass.: Harvard University Press, 1938).

Maryland and Virginia each exporting over £44,000 annually. Even bread and flour exports by the upper South were by no means trivial although here Pennsylvania and New York were the leading processors of wheat, the bulk of which was sold in southern Europe and the Wine Islands. When the important commodities of rice and fish are disregarded, the market value of the aggregate basic foods surplus was almost as great as the annual tobacco exports during 1768-1772, £686,000 compared to £766,000. If fish and rice are added to the basic surplus, the total average annual value comes to more than one million pounds sterling.[16]

82

III

So far we have been talking about the absolute size of the basic surplus and deficit for each colony, but if one is to gauge agricultural self-sufficiency, some reference will have to be made to food consumption. This is at best a crude process since actual consumption data for this period are lacking. Consumption estimates are necessary because a colony could have a relatively large absolute basic surplus and still be a trivial surplus colony in per capita terms if its population were also relatively large. Thus it becomes essential to attempt to estimate the per capita consumption requirements of the commodities forming the basic surplus. Adult consumption requirements were estimated at 2 hundredweight of flour, 11 bushels of corn, and 150 pounds of beef and pork (75 lbs. of each).[17] Children under the age of 16, who probably comprised

---

[16] See Shepherd and Walton, p. 258.

[17] The per capita flour consumption figure is near that used by Towne and Rasmussen for the 1800-30 period in their study of gross farm product in the nineteenth century. *Trends in the American Economy in the Nineteenth Century*, Studies in Income and Wealth, NBER, XXIV (Princeton: Princeton University Press, 1960), 294. They estimate 4.3 bushels of wheat per capita. Two cwt. of flour (224 lbs.) would convert to about 4.9 bushels of wheat per capita. This is based on 4½ bushels of wheat being equivalent to 196 pounds of flour. Percy W. Bidwell and John I. Falconer, *History of Agriculture in the Northern United States, 1620-1860* (New York: Peter Smith), p. 498. Applying estimates of per capita corn consumption to the colonial period is even more hazardous. Towne and Rasmussen estimate human per capita corn consumption in 1800-1840 at 4.4 bushels yearly. See p. 297 of their article. In 1839 average per capita consumption of corn by both humans and animals was approximately 22 bushels. See *Exports Domestic and Foreign, 1697 to 1789 Inclusive*, 48th Cong., 1st sess., House Misc. Doc. 49, Part 2 (Washington, D. C., 1884), p. 21; U.S. Bureau of the Census, *Historical Statistics of the United States, Colonial Times to 1957* (Washington, D. C., 1960), p. 297. It has also been estimated that slaves in Virginia not fed animal food consumed 15 bushels of corn annually. Kate Mason Rowland, "Merchants and Mills," *William and Mary Quarterly,*

about half of the population,[18] were allocated half of the adult requirements.[19] These basic annual per head consumption requirements had an average annual market value in Philadelphia wholesale prices of about £2.625 during 1768-1772.[20] There is, of course,

1st Ser., XI (Jan. 1903), 245-46. It seems unlikely that the practice of feeding corn to animals was as important in 1768-72 as it was in the first half of the nineteenth century when the ratio of total corn consumption to human corn consumption was roughly 5:1. If this ratio were only one-half as large in 1768-72, total per capita corn consumption could have been 11 bushels annually. This figure would be too low if human corn consumption were greater in 1768-72 than in the later period. Corn was an important food crop in the colonial period, especially in the South among the numerous small planters and slaves.

    With respect to beef and pork, Robert E. Gallman adjusted the Towne and Rasmusson figures of per capita production of pork, beef, and veal and concluded that it was about 230 pounds in 1860. This means that per capita consumption must have been less than 230 pounds per capita. Robert E. Gallman, "Self-Sufficiency in the Cotton Economy of the Antebellum South," *Agricultural History*, XLIV (Jan. 1970), 18. Kohlmeier assumed that in 1850 in southern Illinois and Indiana the per capita consumption of hogs was one per person. A. L. Kohlmeier, *The Old Northwest* (Bloomington, Ind.: The Principia Press, Inc., 1938), p. 95. The slaughter weight of hogs was probably about 140 to 150 pounds at this time. See Gallman, "Self-Sufficiency in the Cotton Economy," pp. 14-15. James T. Lemon estimated that in the agricultural area of southeastern Pennsylvania in 1740-90 the per capita beef and pork consumption was 150 pounds. James T. Lemon, "Household Consumption in Eighteenth-Century America and Its Relationship to Production and Trade: The Situation Among Farmers In Southeastern Pennsylvania," *Agricultural History*, XLI (Jan. 1967), 61. If the per capita beef and pork consumption were 224 pounds instead of the assumed 150 pounds, the aggregate colony percentage basic surplus would be 10.8 percent instead of 12.3 percent. The percentage basic surpluses and deficits are not very sensitive to errors in the estimated per capita quantities of the basic consumption requirements of grains and meat. They are, however, sensitive to errors in the per capita value of the basic surplus or deficit. Yet these are based on the net export, population, and the price data employed—all of which are probably as reliable as can be obtained. Manifestly, the per capita grain and meat consumption figures employed are at best a crude approximation to the correct ones. For estimates of colonial food consumption requirements which may be somewhat higher than those employed in this study, the reader should see Table Z, pp. 388-405 in *Historical Statistics*. Unfinished research by Lawrence A. Harper and Mrs. Marga Stone should eventually produce more accurate estimates of early American dietary standards.

  [18] The *First Census of the United States* has the white male population under 16 years of age as about 25 percent of the total population in 1790. See p. 8. If there were as many females as males and assuming the slave age distribution was the same as the white population, this would put half the population under 16 years of age.

  [19] Presumably older children consumed at a higher rate than half the adult ration whereas the more numerous younger children ate less than half the adult requirements. This procedure is employed by Gallman, "Self-Sufficiency in the Cotton Economy," p. 18. Gallman assigned half the meat ration for field hands to slaves under 15.

  [20] The figure of £2.625 was obtained as follows: 2 cwt. of flour at 20.4 shillings plus 11 bushels of corn at 21.34 shillings plus 150 lbs. of beef and pork at 26.7 shillings totals to 68.44 shillings or £3.42. Round this to £3½ to obtain the adult requirement value. This reduces to £2.625 when children are accounted for as consumers at one-half the adult rate.

a serious theoretical problem in valuing food consumption at the market price at which the commodities were sold. The fact is that much of the food crop was consumed on the farm and not sold. At the margin, if the alternative to consuming food was to sell it, then perhaps the foregone alternative value of the food consumed (the market price) is an approximation of the value of the food to those who consumed it.

The last column of Table 1 was divided by the corresponding colony population for 1770 to obtain the per capita value of the basic surplus or deficit for each colony. These results were then divided by £2.625 in order to obtain a crude estimate of the relative size of the surplus or deficit in comparison to consumption requirements.[21] These final results are the percentages given in Table 2; they represent the basic colony surplus or deficit as a proportion of total estimated consumption requirements for the colony.

For the colonies as a whole, it was estimated that the basic food surplus of £686,000 constituted approximately 12 percent of aggregate consumption requirements. This is clearly a sizeable surplus although perhaps less than one might have expected based on a casual scrutiny of the absolute value of the surpluses involved. If per capita incomes were stagnant during this period, it was not due to inability to produce beyond food consumption requirements. It would be interesting to know what the relative magnitude of the basic surplus was several decades earlier. If it were rising, it would be a modicum of support for the Taylor thesis that living standards were rising during the 65 years preceding the Revolution.[22] Using the naval lists, it would probably be feasible to calculate this for particular colonies.

On a colony and regional basis, Table 2 shows that the distribution of the percentage surpluses was quite uneven. As one would expect, the middle colonies (including Connecticut) led the way

---

[21] The fact that wholesale prices are used in calculating the £2.625 figure is not a source of error, since the surplus and deficit value (the numerator) is also in wholesale prices. However, the use of Philadelphia prices in employing the £2.625 figure for all regions of the colonies is a source of error since the surplus and deficit values are in regional prices. Alternative calculations show that this procedure does not affect the results by much. The main impact is to lower the percentage value of the New England deficit by approximately 15 percent.

[22] Taylor, "American Economic Growth Before 1840," p. 437. This scholar has speculated that between 1710 and 1775 the average annual rate of increase of real per capita income in the American colonies was slightly more than 1 percent per annum.

D. Klingaman

TABLE 2

AVERAGE ANNUAL PER CAPITA DEFICITS OR SURPLUSES OF
WHEAT, CORN, BEEF, AND PORK AS A PERCENTAGE
OF ESTIMATED CONSUMPTION REQUIREMENTS
BY COLONY, 1768-1772

Region Colony	Deficit[a] or Surplus
New England	[10.9]
Maine	[5.4]
New Hampshire	[5.4]
Massachusetts	[13.8]
Rhode Island	[8.1]
Middle Colonies	25.9
Connecticut	6.7
New York	29.3
New Jersey	0.8
Pennsylvania	52.0
Delaware	16.3
Upper South	15.1
Maryland	22.4
Virginia	11.8
Lower South	4.0
North Carolina	5.4
South Carolina	2.1
Georgia	1.2
Colonies	12.3

Note: Adult consumption requirements were estimated as 2 cwt. of flour, 11 bushels
of corn, and 150 pounds of beef or pork. Children under 16 (an estimated one
half of the population), were allotted one half the adult ration. In Philadelphia
wholesale prices, the per capita value was approximately £2.625 per annum.
[a] Figures in brackets are deficits.
Source: See Table 1. The colony population figures used in the calculations are for
1770 from U.S. Bureau of the Census, *Historical Statistics of the United
States, Colonial Times to 1957* (Washington, D. C.: G.P.O., 1960), p. 756.

with a basic surplus equal to nearly 26 percent of estimated basic consumption requirements. The percentage surplus in the upper South was substantial although less than three-fifths that of the middle colonies. The lower South had a relatively small percentage surplus, especially if North Carolina is excluded. It should be remembered, however, that rice is not included as part of the basic surplus, just as fish is omitted from consideration of the New England deficit. These regional dietary variations would make a difference in the actual regional food surplus or deficit. In New England the deficit as a percentage of the estimated requirements of grain and meat was approximately 11 percent although meat is relatively unimportant in the composition of the deficit. Massachusetts had a much higher basic deficit than did the rest of New England in both absolute and percentage terms. The food deficit in New England deserves some attention because it played an integral part in the burgeoning growth of the intercolonial trade and because the imports of foodstuffs were essential to the continued growth and development of the New England coastal towns.

IV

Most of the people in New England were self-sufficient pioneer farmers, but apparently the relatively rocky soil and the harsh climate were not conducive to the emergence of grain surpluses sufficient to sustain the growing population of the port towns. It may also be true that the cultivation of wheat in New England was curtailed after 1670 due to the persistence of the rust disease.[23] New England had probably been a net importer of foodstuffs since early in the eighteenth century and by the 1760's was dependent on external supply sources for her marginal requirements in corn, wheat, and meat. Data gleaned from the Massachusetts naval lists can be used to illuminate this intercolonial trade in foodstuffs. Unlike Customs 16/1, the naval lists make it possible to identify the specific sources of supply relied upon since they give the origin of all ships entering the colony. In addition, because the naval lists cover a broad period of time, it is feasible to approximate the growth of this food import trade over time. It may not be appropriate to generalize the results for Massachusetts to all of New England. Nevertheless, the average annual value of the basic New England food deficit was about £110,500 in 1768-1772, and over 75 percent of this basic deficit was attributable to Massachusetts.[24]

The average annual value of the coastwise import and export trade of Massachusetts amounted to at least £136,000 sterling in 1761-1765. More than 70 percent of this value consisted of imports, and approximately 85 percent of the total import value consisted of foodstuffs. The major coastwise exports in order of importance were rum, sugar, molasses, fish, and salt.[25]

23 Albert Bushnell Hart, *Commonwealth History of Massachusetts*, II (New York: The State History Co., 1928), p. 391.
24 See Table 1.
25 David C. Klingaman, "The Coastwise Trade of Colonial Massachusetts," Research Paper No. 51, Dept. of Economics, Ohio University. The study is based primarily on the Massachusetts Naval Office lists, which end in the year 1765.

TABLE 3
BASIC FOOD IMPORTS BY MASSACHUSETTS
1714-1717 and 1761-1765

Years	Grain[a] (bushels)	Flour[b] (barrels)	Beef and Pork (barrels)
Average Annual Imports, 1714-1717	2,100	102	142
Average Annual Imports, 1761-1765[c]	250,000	38,000	3,200

[a] The data source does not differentiate among the different kinds of grains which were mostly corn and wheat with a small amount of oats. In 1768-1772 about 80 percent of the bushels of corn and wheat imported consisted of corn. Rice is not included in this category (an annual average of 3,500 casks in 1761-1765 and none in 1714-1717).

[b] The flour imports include some bread valued as flour.

[c] These figures are rounded to the nearest thousands or hundreds.

Source: Massachusetts Naval Office Lists, Public Record Office, London, C.O. 5/848, C.O. 5/850, and C.O. 5/851.

87

The average annual imports of grain, flour, beef, and pork are given in Table 3 for the years 1714-1717 and 1761-1765. In the early period, the food imports were quite small, indicating that the colony was supplying most of its own needs. By the 1761-1765 period, food imports had increased enormously in every item although the growth may be somewhat overstated. Some of the ships which entered in the early period may have gone unrecorded by the naval officers, and it is known that a few of the ships contained cargoes which were not recorded by the naval officers in a manner which permitted quantification. This marked growth in imports of basic food supplies reflects the growing population in the coastal towns which needed larger quantities of foodstuffs but probably also reflects a change in the structure of employment in and around those towns. The seaboard inhabitants were becoming increasingly specialized in non-agricultural occupations. This rapid growth in the interregional trade between New England and the other colonies was significant because it enlarged the size of the market and facilitated the development of regional specialization which was already shaped by the overseas exchange of goods and services.

The identity of the colonies that supplied the Massachusetts market is given in Table 4. The relative importance of each colony in supplying a particular commodity is given by the percentages in that table. The upper South emerges as the principal supplier of corn and wheat, Pennsylvania as the dominant flour supplier, and North

TABLE 4
PERCENTAGES OF BASIC MASSACHUSETTS FOOD
IMPORTS FROM EACH COLONY, 1761-1765

Colony	Grain	Flour	Beef and Pork
South Carolina	1.4	0.0	18.4
North Carolina	16.5	0.0	55.1
Virginia	32.5	0.1	11.7
Maryland	46.4	4.5	6.1
Pennsylvania	3.0	92.3	6.8
New York	0.2	3.1	1.2
Georgia	0.0	0.0	0.7

Source: Public Record Office, C.O. 5/850 and C.O. 5/851.

Carolina as the most important meat supplier. It is interesting that New York was only a trivial supplier to the Massachusetts market. A casual inspection of the New York naval lists for 1763 and 1764 indicates that New York had a comparatively small coastwise trade business at this time. On the import side, rice from South Carolina predominated. Exports were diverse, were greater than imports, and centered around the sale of provisions. As New York had a large food surplus, it is not clear why so little was sent to the relatively near market in New England. The amount of trade between Massachusetts and North Carolina is also puzzling, since nearer supplies of meat were available in the middle colonies and in the upper South. Massachusetts was also importing substantial quantities of naval stores from North Carolina. Approximately 95 percent of the coastwise tar and turpentine imports and 75 percent of the coastwise pitch imports came from North Carolina. Thus it may have been economical for the merchants and ship captains to combine cargoes of meat and naval stores for trade between the two regions. But why did they not see fit to combine meat imports with the Philadelphia flour imports or meat imports with the upper South grain imports? Virginia, Maryland, and Pennsylvania were all large shippers of meat to the West Indies; yet these colonies claimed only approximately 25 percent of the Massachusetts market. Perhaps the quality of the North Carolina pork was more preferred by the New Englanders. This could also explain why Philadelphia flour was such an overwhelming choice of the New Englanders even though the upper South and New York had the capacity to satisfy easily the New England demand for flour. The price data from Cole for 1761-1765 may furnish a more satisfying motive for buying meat in the Carolinas and flour in Philadelphia.

Although North Carolina beef and pork prices are not available, the Charleston price of beef and pork was substantially lower than either the New York or Philadelphia price. Philadelphia flour prices were also slightly lower than those in New York;[26] we have no reliable prices for foodstuffs in the upper South. One suspects that the actual reasons for such trade patterns were more complex than those suggested above, and it illustrates how little we know about the flourishing intercolonial exchange of goods and services.

V

Economic historians have only a vague idea of what per capita income was during the colonial period.[27] The data base is simply insufficient to make a reasoned judgement concerning this matter. The question of income levels in colonial times is important historically because it concerns the economic welfare of over 2½ million persons on the eve of the Revolution. Political and social history is better understood when it is developed in the context of the level of material welfare experienced by the people who lived at the time. Perhaps the primary reason for the interest of economists in knowing the level of colonial per capita income is that it would establish an earlier benchmark for more comprehensive measurement of the long-run performance of the American economy. Information on colonial living standards would also be useful to development economists in appraising the relevance of the early American experience to the undeveloped countries of today. Given the need for this information and the improbability of ever estimating it directly through aggregation of production in certain sectors of the economy, researchers are probably justified in employing micro ap-

[26] These same relative price relationships also prevailed in the 1768-72 period although the price differentials in beef and pork between the lower South and the middle colonies appear to have narrowed appreciably. Any relative movement of colony exchange rates between 1761-65 and 1768-72 is not clear, hence the price comparisons among colonies is speculative.

[27] Several economists have conjectured about this question. Raymond W. Goldsmith, "Historical and Comparative Rates of Production, Productivity and Prices," Hearings before the Joint Economic Committee, 65th Cong., 1st Sess., Part 2, 1959, pp. 277-78. This is reprinted in Ralph Andreano, ed., *New Views on American Economic Development* (Cambridge: Schenkman Publishing Co., Inc., 1965). Also see p. 50 for Andreano's own remarks on the subject of growth rates. G. R. Taylor, "American Economic Growth Before 1840," pp. 427-37. Albert Fishlow, discussion of G. C. Bjork's article, THE JOURNAL OF ECONOMIC HISTORY, XXIV (Dec. 1964), 566.

proaches to income estimates for this period. This final section of the article is devoted to a crude approximation of what per capita income may have been, based on the value of food consumption requirements in the years 1768-1772.

It was estimated earlier that the average per head value of the basic consumption requirement in grain and meat was approximately £2.625 in Philadelphia wholesale prices in the years 1768-1772. In order to lessen any doubt that this estimate is too low and to allow for regional price variations and retail mark-ups, assume that this figure is inflated by one-third to £3½ per capita. This amount represents the average per head value of grains and meats consumed but excludes other food items which were consumed. It seems unlikely that less than half the value of the average person's food budget was composed of grain and meat—it was probably a good deal more than half. But if it were half, it would mean that the total per capita food consumed was about £7. Now if one knew what proportion of the average colonist's income was represented by the value of food consumption, it would be possible to approximate his per capita income. At present there is no way of knowing these percentage figures for the colonial period, but it is possible to guess what they may have been by observing the corresponding figures that exist today in some undeveloped countries. The percentage of disposable income spent on foodstuffs was calculated for the following six countries for various years in the 1953-1964 period: Equador, Honduras, Jamaica, Jordan, Panama, and Korea. The simple average percentage expenditure on foodstuffs out of disposable income was roughly 45 percent. The range was from 53 percent in Jordan to 37 percent in Jamaica.[28] Recent meager data are also available on rural farm per capita household expenditures on food as a percentage of per capita national private consumption expenditures for several countries. The average was about 48 percent for the following countries: United States, Japan, France, Italy, Norway, and Yugoslavia. The range was from slightly over

[28] United Nations, *Yearbook of National Accounts Statistics, 1965* (New York: U. N., 1966), pp. 482-83. Part D, Table No. 6, contains personal and percentage disposable income data. Scattered through pp. 3-423 in Part C are the country food consumption figures. The years used for Korea, Ecuador, Jamaica, and Panama were 1953, 1958, 1960, and 1964. For Honduras the years used were 1953, 1958, 1960, and 1963. In the case of Jordan it was 1959, 1960, and 1963. The percentage of disposable income spent on food was obtained for each country by averaging the data for the years. Then a simple six-country average was calculated.

TABLE 5
HYPOTHETICAL ESTIMATES OF COLONIAL PER CAPITA
INCOME, 1768-1772

Annual Value of Per Capita Meat and Grain Requirements[a]	Annual Value of Per Capita Total Food Requirements[b]	Percent of Income Spent on Foodstuff[c]	Resultant Income Per Capita[d]
£3 1/2	£4 1/2	70%	£6 1/2
3 1/2	5 1/2	60	9
3 1/2	6 1/2	50	13
3 1/2	7 1/2	40	19

[a] This is the £2.625 figure inflated by one-third to allow for any undervaluation or for a retail mark-up on the wholesale price.

[b] These figures are alternative per capita total food costs which include the £3 1/2 value of meat and grain consumed plus £1 to £4 more to allow for a broader diet that included other foodstuffs.

[c] These are alternative percentages of average per capita income applied toward consumption of all foods.

[d] The per capita income estimates were obtained by dividing the second column by the third column of the table. The figures are rounded to the nearest half pound sterling.

Sources: Consumption requirement estimates of meat and grain are those of footnote 17 valued in Philadelphia prices given in the note to Table 1. The proportions of income applied to food consumption are hypothetical, based on the discussion in the text and in footnotes 28 and 29.

55 percent for Central-North Italy to slightly below 37 percent for Norway.[29] It is surprising how comparable the two different sets of data are over both space and degree of development.

There is, of course, no way of knowing what the equivalent percentages were in colonial times. One is tempted to infer, however, that they were almost certainly between 40 and 70 percent. If the relevant percentage figures were 40 percent and assuming a total per capita food consumption value of £7, it would mean that per capita income was £17½. In Table 5 various combinations of data are used to set lower and upper bounds and two intermediate values for per capita income—the wide range is from £6½ per head to £19 per head. Food was relatively cheap in the colonies and the price data on consumables make the £7½ figure in the second column appear much too high. With respect to the £6½ per capita income figure in the last column, the 70 percent figure in the third column seems too high. Not a single developed or undeveloped

[29] United Nations, *Compendium of Social Statistics: 1967* (New York: U. N., 1968), pp. 245, 247. This gives data for American rural farm population in 1955, Japanese farm population in 1951-52, and French farm households in 1956. *Compendium of Social Statistics: 1963* (New York: U. N., 1963), pp. 201-02. This covers the Italian Central-North and South in 1953, Norway in 1954, and Yugoslavia in 1955.

country in the samples above had such a high percentage, even though the average per capita income in the first set of six undeveloped countries was not much above $200 per capita. In India, where per capita income is around $75 per head, working class families very seldom budget 70 percent of their total consumption expenditures for foodstuffs, and the average is probably below 60 percent.[30] Thus one is led to suspect that actual per capita income was more than £6½ and less than £19. How much more and how much less is an open question. Alice Hanson Jones has calculated a range of per capita income estimates for the American colonies. Inferring income from wealth estimates, she concluded that per head income was between £8.4 and £14.0 in 1774.[31] Manifestly, the congruity of her findings with those given above is striking.

It seems unnecessary to remind the reader that the results of this study are proffered as tentative approximations. This is particularly true of the last section concerning the per capita income estimates. It is hoped that other economic historians will check these unrefined income estimates through other micro-approaches which are more rigorous than the one employed here. If several such studies should lead to comparable results, it might be possible to resolve the question of colonial incomes to an acceptably reliable range of estimates. The problems involved in translating any such income estimates into current dollars that are meaningful for international and intertemporal comparisons are immense, but probably such an attempt should be made. The purpose of this paper was to measure approximately the agricultural self-sufficiency of the various colonial regions; the attempt to bracket per capita incomes was almost an incidental outcome.

DAVID KLINGAMAN, *Ohio University*

---

[30] Labor Bureau, *Indian Labor Statistics, 1968* (Delhi: Government of India Press, 1968), p. 148.

[31] Jones, p. 128, computed from Table 51.

Wealth Estimates for the New England Colonies about 1770

Introduction

THE purpose of my studies[1] is to estimate the total and per capita wealth of the thirteen colonies in the early 1770's and something of its composition and distribution. The estimates for New England presented here add another building block to the accumulating evidence that a rather high level of living was reached in the American colonies at the close of over 150 years of economic development. They also show that wealth was unequally distributed[2] among the population in this transitionally commercial era, well before the onset of industrialism. They yield quantitative evidence as well on size of wealth in relation to such characteristics of wealth

93

This research was supported by National Science Foundation Grant GS-2457, National Endowment for the Humanities Grant RO 258-70-4429 and, at an early stage, a grant-in-aid from the Council on Research in Economic History. Robert W. Fogel bears the onus of having encouraged the entire undertaking. Stephen E. Fienberg and F. Kinley Larntz, Jr. advised on sampling and other statistical procedures.

The following registers of Probate furnished copies of documents for the indicated county: John J. Costello, Essex; Walter Gilday, Plymouth; F. Joseph Donohue, Worcester. For Hampshire a microfilm was obtained through Juliette Tomlinson of the Connecticut Valley Historical Museum, with whom I was put in touch by Register of Probate Frank E. Tuitt, II. Connecticut document copies were obtained from the Connecticut State Library, where Frances Davenport was helpful.

Searches for age, occupation and other supplementary data were made by Harold S. Burt, John E. Miller, Mrs. Clinton Ober, Jimmie B. Parker, Mrs. Ralph L. Thresher.

I am indebted to colleagues, especially Theodore C. Bergstrom, John M. Murrin and Frederic Q. Raines, and students, the Computing Facilities and the Social Science Institute of Washington University; also to Chester McArthur Destler, Linda Hoffmaster, Donald L. Kemmerer, Stanley Lebergott, Glenn Weaver and many others who have answered queries or given criticism. The errors remain mine.

[1] Alice Hanson Jones, "Wealth Estimates for the American Middle Colonies, 1774," *Economic Development and Cultural Change*, XVIII, 4, Pt. 2 (July, 1970). This supplement may be ordered separately from the University of Chicago Press. It is referred to hereafter as *EDCC*. See also, Alice Hanson Jones, "La fortune privée en Pennsylvanie, New Jersey, Delaware, 1774," *Annales: Économies, Sociétés, Civilisations*, XXIV, 2 (Paris, France: Armand Colin, March-April, 1969), 235-49.

[2] Alice Hanson Jones, "Wealth Distribution in the American Middle Colonies in the Third Quarter of the Eighteenth Century," paper presented at annual meeting of the Organization of American Historians, New Orleans (April, 1971), mimeographed. Available at Economics Department, Washington University, St. Louis, Mo., 63130. Referred to hereafter as *OAH Paper*.

holders as their age and sex, occupations, urban or rural residence and testacy, that is whether or not they left a will at death.

The basic data come from probate inventories and from accounts of executors or administrators of 381 estates probated in 1774 in seven sample counties. These numbers may appear small to people not familiar with the theory of small samples and the refinements in their application developed in recent years by statisticians, but generalizations from them can be defended because of the sample design and the rigor with which it was executed. The 30 counties which existed in New England at that date were grouped into seven geographically contiguous strata, with each stratum or group of counties having an approximately equal number of then living potential wealth holders. One sample county was drawn at random to represent each stratum, its chance to be drawn being proportionate to its number of living potential wealth holders. Within the county chosen every estate probated in 1774 with surviving probate inventory was taken.[3] Appropriately combined, these inventories form an unbiased sample of all probate inventories made in 1774 in all 30 New England counties. The year 1774 was one when wholesale price indexes, measured either by the Warren and Pearson or the Bezanson indexes, were at about their average level of the preceding 10 years and had not yet reflected the wartime price increases which followed.

The probate inventories contain a detailed listing of wealth, valued on sworn oath by several, usually three, contemporary appraisers (often including a son or the widow) appointed by the court. They include "personal estate" or portable physical wealth as well as financial assets and claims; additionally, only in New England, they also value "real estate," that is, land and improvements thereon, and sometimes show a "list of debts" owed by the estate. In other cases, debts owed are found only in subsequent accounts filed with the court by the estate executor or administrator; in some they appear in reports of Insolvent Commissioners appointed, only in New England so far as I can learn, by the court. These documents are still found in county courthouses or state archives, both for people who left wills and for intestates who did

---

[3] With the exception of Essex, where I stopped with 102 cases at the letter P in an alphabetical listing of surnames, and in Hampshire where a few 1773 cases were included to bring the number over the minimum target of 25 cases.

not. For the latter, the court appointed an administrator to handle the assets, pay off the creditors and apportion the residue among heirs. Not only large estates were probated, but also very small ones, and ones which were insolvent by reason of debts greater than assets. That inventory valuations were realistic is indicated by their close agreement with amounts received at public vendue sales, often held in settling an estate. Probate documents do not tell age at death, and often not occupation, so genealogical search for this information for each decedent case was required.

Wealth estimates at two levels for the living are derived from the sample data. First, the estimates for the "probate-type" living potential wealth holders are firmly based on age-adjusted data from the probated decedents in the sample which represents all New England. For these I can state the confidence interval. Second, the more glamorous, but necessarily more tenuous end product, estimates of wealth of all the living free population in New England, are derived from the foregoing after several additional adjustments described briefly later on and more fully in an appendix.[4] No precise statistical measure of confidence can be given for these wider estimates since they involve more than drawing a sample from a larger population. Rather the confidence placed in them must hinge on the confidence in the underlying sample for the "probate-type" together with the acceptability of my assumptions regarding the wealth of the "nonprobate-type" living. The combined estimates pertain to all living, free adult, potential wealth holders who I consider comprised all the free men and 10 percent of the free women, mostly widows and a few single women who in New England held property in their own right. Since wealth held by others, indentured servants, slaves, minors and most women, was very small or negligible, we may infer that this wealth in aggregate was also essentially that of the total population.

I sketch some of my major results in skeleton form, and suggest possible revisions which they might imply for some conventional literary interpretations of the economic structure of the colonies. The framework can be fleshed out with additional details which I hope to present at a later date.

[4] Appendix available at Economics Department, Washington University, St. Louis, Mo. 63130.

High Level of Living Implied by High Physical Wealth

For New England, my provisional estimate for the total living population is a per capita figure for physical wealth (excluding all financial assets and also excluding the value of servants and slaves[5]) of a little over £36 sterling[6] in 1774; that I calculate to be the equivalent of $933 in dollars of 1969 purchasing power (see Table 1). If we eliminate the non-free population, as well as the children and women as holders of little or no wealth, the same private wealth averaged almost $4,500 per free man in dollars of our day, £174 in sterling or £226 in the local pounds of Connecticut or Massachusetts. Looking at free adult, potential wealth holders (all the free men plus 10 percent of free women) the figure is a bit lower, £157 sterling or around $4,045 in 1969 dollars. Except for households containing several adult males, or widows with adult male sons still present, and the very few single women who probably lived in the households of relatives, the potential wealth holders may be thought of as roughly equivalent to heads of households.

96

Neither financial assets nor financial liabilities are included in these figures for physical wealth, but I shall use them to compute net worth, to be presented at a later date. Physical wealth is the figure that interests us for an estimate of real wealth of the population as a whole, since individual financial claims from and to debtors tend to cancel out. Metal coin is the only part of financial wealth which conceptually might desirably be included in physical wealth, and I am unable to provide that figure because the probate inventories usually stated merely "cash," for example "cash in house" or "cash in purse," without specifying whether it was in paper or coin. In watching for specific mention of coin, I rarely found this item.[7] Coin specified as such represents a tiny fraction of "cash," which latter is shown as a separate item in Table 2 should anyone desire to approximate a physical wealth figure including coin. The

[5] Inclusion of servants and slaves as wealth would increase the figure for New England by one-half of one percent to £36.8 sterling or $948 in 1969 dollars.
[6] £1 sterling = 1.33 local pound of Massachusetts or Connecticut and was the equivalent in purchasing power of $25.77 in 1969. £1 of Massachusetts or Connecticut = £0.75 sterling and was the equivalent in purchasing power of $19.33 in 1969. See *EDCC*, Table 48, Price Trends 1774-1967, pp. 124-26; *OAH Paper*, Table 3, Price Trends 1774-1969, p. 2.
[7] In the Middle Colonies such entries appeared only in one-tenth of 1 percent of the inventories; the average for the entire sample was less than one-half local pound and less than 0.05 percent of gross portable wealth.

TABLE 1

LIVING POPULATION AND TOTAL PRIVATE PHYSICAL WEALTH[a]
PER HEAD NEW ENGLAND COLONIES, 1774

		Estimated Number (1)	Wealth per Head, in Pounds Sterling and decimals thereof		
			Including Cash and Servants and Slaves (2)	Excluding Cash Including Servants and Slaves (3)	Excluding Cash and Servants and Slaves[d] (4)
I.	Population	606,596	36.8	36.4	36.2
II.	Free population	580,268	38.5	38.1	37.9
	A. Free adults	261,786	84.7	83.8	83.4
	1. Free adult, potential wealth holders	138,923	159.6	157.9	157.2
	a. Men	125,255	177.0	175.1	174.4
	b. Women[b]	13,668	—	—	—
	c. Probate type	45,428	—	—	—
	d. Nonprobate type	93,495	—	—	—
III.	Nonfree adults[c]	11,926	—	—	—
IV.	Adults, free plus nonfree	273,712	81.0	80.1	79.8
	A. Men, free plus nonfree	130,860	169.4	167.6	166.9

[a] Nonprobate type wealth assumed to be one-half that of probate types.
[b] Ten percent of free women. Includes chiefly widows, a few single women.
[c] Two percent of white adults and 91 percent of black adults.
[d] In dollars of 1969 purchasing power, the corresponding figures are:

		New England	Middle Colonies
I.	Population	$ 933	$1,093
II.	Free Population	977	1,180
	A. Free Adults	2,149	2,742
	1. a. Free Men	4,494	5,316
III.	Adults, free plus nonfree	2,056	2,538

Note: Corresponding estimates for the Middle Colonies appear in *EDCC* Table 44, p. 118. A revision since that printing, using Larntz' county weights, changes the Middle Colony number of free adult probate-type potential wealth holders to 70,724 and of nonprobate type to 29,169.
Source: See appendix cited in fn. 4.

paper money was mostly the issue of respective colonial provincial governments and was the printed promise to pay out of future tax revenue. From a standpoint of net worth distribution among persons, it is reasonable to include such paper money, since it represented that private person's claims upon future taxes, not cancelling claims upon present wealth. However, its value was certainly not a physical magnitude, and I have accordingly omitted cash as well as all other financial assets from my calculations of size distribution of

TABLE 2

COMPONENTS OF PRIVATE PHYSICAL WEALTH,[a] AND CASH PER PROBATE-TYPE LIVING, FREE ADULT AND LIVING FREE ADULT POTENTIAL WEALTH HOLDER, NEW ENGLAND, MIDDLE COLONIES, 1774

	Pounds Sterling, 1774				1969 Dollars			
	All Living		Probate-type Living		All Living		Probate-type Living	
	New Eng. (1)	Mid. Col. (2)	New Eng. (3)	Mid. Col. (4)	New Eng. (5)	Mid. Col. (6)	New Eng. (7)	Mid. Col. (8)
I. Total Physical Wealth[b]	157	189	238	259	4,046	4,871	6,133	6,674
A. Land (real estate)	112	123	169	169	2,886	3,170	4,355	4,355
B. Portable Physical Wealth,[c] Total	46	69	69	95	1,185	1,778	1,778	2,448
1. Servants and Slaves	0.7	3.9	1.1	5.4	18	101	28	139
2. Producer Durables[d]	19.3	37.0	29.0	50.7	497	953	747	1,307
3. Producer Perishables	2.5	9.3	3.7	12.8	64	240	95	330
4. Consumer Durables	19.5	13.8	27.9	18.9	503	355	719	487
5. Consumer Perishables	1.0	1.2	1.4	1.6	28	31	36	41
6. Business Inventories[e]	3.7	4.1	5.5	5.6	95	108	142	144
II. Cash	1.8	4.8	2.7	6.5	46	124	70	168

[a] Average wealth of non-probate types assumed to be one-half that of probate types for New England. See appendix cited in fn. 4.
[b] Excluding cash and servants and slaves.
[c] Excluding cash; includes servants and slaves.
[d] Includes livestock and durable equipment and goods.
[e] Other than farm business.

Source: Sample of probate inventories with adjustments by author. Data for Middle Colonies from EDCC.

physical wealth shown in Table 6. In Table 1, when cash of all kinds, both coin and paper, is included, the total is greater by about 1 percent, not a major magnitude.

Inclusion of values for servants and slaves is appropriate with respect to identifying the wealth of any particular individual, studying distribution of wealth in a conventional sense, and considering wealth in a legal sense. In an economic sense, however, so far as the total economy is concerned, there seems no valid reason for including human capital which is owned by another and excluding human capital which is self-owned. It is not within the range of this study to undertake valuation of the self-owned capital; accordingly I present some estimates excluding the value of servants and slaves in Table 1, though I include it in Table 6.

99

The case for not including the value of an indentured servant in the real or physical wealth of the country is further indicated by the fact that the claim represented only a part of the servant's value as human capital, especially if the term of servitude had only a short remaining time to run. Indeed the indentured servant relation may be looked upon as financial. The "owner" had a financial claim which was to be repaid in services. The indentured servant was a user of consumer credit—travel now, pay later. When value of servants and slaves are excluded, the per capita total wealth figure for New England is reduced about ½ of 1 percent, as can be seen from Tables 1 and 2.

The average, either way, of close to $4,500 per free man is surely a not inconsiderable sum today, and I submit implies a higher level of living than that of the average free man in England or Europe at that time. The level was probably the highest achieved for the great bulk of the population in any country up to that time. A number of indications, in addition to my sample data, support the belief that average American colonists lived better than their counterparts in Europe by the third quarter of the eighteenth century.[8] High wealth would go hand in hand with such good living.

---

[8] See citations and discussion in *EDCC*, pp. 129-32. Raymond Goldsmith calls to my attention that it might be argued from the well known income estimates of Gregory King in 1688 and Arthur Young in 1770 for England that average wealth in England was higher than that indicated by my colonial figures. Yet, the problem remains that the variance was probably much greater in England (King shows over half the population running an annual deficit), so that higher average wealth in England could still be compatible with my estimates of a relatively higher level of living for a large bulk of the colonial population.

The $933 per capita for New England is somewhat lower than the corresponding figure $1,093 I found for the Middle Colonies. The approximate $160 difference in today's terms, a little over £6 sterling then, is not statistically significant, given the sample sizes on which the underlying probate data are based. The true figures may lie somewhere around $1,000 or £39 sterling for both regions. When tabulation of data already gathered for the South, and perhaps also for New York (where there are especially severe data gap problems) are completed, we may be better able to see clearly to what extent we had significant regional differences in size of wealth in 1774.

100

The figures I find for New England and the Middle Colonies seem economically high as compared with likely wealth in Europe at that time and in some developing countries today. They tend to refute the idea that the colonies were economically exploited, to the disadvantage of the inhabitants, by the mother country Britain. My belief is that rather than being exploited, the colonists were participating, within the military protection, special preferential shipping, and other privileges of the British empire, in the increasing fruits of expanding commercial horizons and growing market demand in Europe for colonial products. For New England these products included among other things the building of ships and furnishing of shipping services, as well as the sale of fish and fish products, timber, potash, furs and to a lesser extent than in some other regions, of agricultural products. These products did not have to go directly to England for the New England colonies to benefit; they profited as well from the exchange with the West Indies, the African trade and the coastal trade, all of which to some extent were stimulated by or interdependent with trade with Europe, particularly England.

Comparison with Wealth in 1966 and Inferred Economic Growth Rates

The per capita $933 figure for New England compares with an estimated private physical wealth per capita in the United States in 1966 of $11,936 expressed in 1969 dollars. Corresponding figures (in preliminary 1967 dollars) were presented in *EDCC*[9] with compound annual rates of growth between the various dates. The differ-

[9] *EDCC*, pp. 128, 135-40. The 1966 figure was expressed there as $11,032 and the 1805 one as $926 in terms of preliminary 1967 dollars.

ence between the 1774 average for New England and that for the
Middle Colonies is small enough that the growth rates presented
there, from an average of around $1,000, can be considered also
applicable to New England. The eleven-fold increase over the near
two centuries to 1966 in real physical wealth indicates an average
annual compound rate of growth per capita of 1.26 percent per
year. However, the relatively high absolute level of wealth I find
for 1774, as compared with data we have from Samuel Blodget[10] for
1805, which yields $1,014 per capita for that date in 1969 dollars,
suggests that there might have been little or no advance in real
wealth per head during wartime and the uncertain years of the first   *101*
decade or so after establishment of a federal government. Such a
hypothesis supports the possibility that a higher rate of growth
came after that date, as Raymond Goldsmith has speculated,[11]
rather than that slow fairly steady increments may have occurred
from the mid- or earlier eighteenth century on to the mid-nineteenth century as Paul David[12] suggests. Growth between 1805 and
1966 was at an average rate of something like 1.55 percent per year.
However, for intervening shorter periods, especially 1850 to 1900
it attained rates as high as 1.90, and from 1929 to 1966, a period
which included the Great Depression and World War II as well as
the Korean War, it fell to 1.09. The tentative nature of the 1805
figure, relying as it does on one contemporary, although careful,
observer, does not foreclose the question of when acceleration in
growth rates may have been significantly resumed. If another
study, parallel to mine, could be replicated for a date early in the
1800's we would have a valuable additional check.

Per capita figures of wealth represent the accumulated savings
from past production, certainly for the reproducible portions such
as portable wealth and buildings and quite possibly for much of the
value attached to developed land, regardless of the conditions under

[10] Samuel Blodget, *Economica: A Statistical Manual for the U.S.A.* (Washington,
D.C., 1806).
[11] Raymond W. Goldsmith, *Historical and Comparative Rates of Production, Pro-
ductivity and Prices.* Hearings before the Joint Economic Committee, 86th Congress,
1st session, 2, April 7, 1959 (Washington, D.C.: Government Printing Office, 1959).
See also George R. Taylor, "American Economic Growth before 1840: An Exploratory
Essay," THE JOURNAL OF ECONOMIC HISTORY, XXIV, 4 (Dec., 1964), 427-44.
[12] Paul A. David, "The Growth of Real Product in the United States before 1840:
New Evidence and Controlled Conjectures," THE JOURNAL OF ECONOMIC HISTORY,
XXVII, 2 (June, 1967), 151-97.

which the wealth was produced. Though our absolute increase in real wealth over two centuries has been enormous, some question may be permitted as to whether our measures of quantity capture some important qualitative differences. It is becoming increasingly clear, as problems of pollution and urban congestion arise, that some negative items of private cost and of social cost might be subtracted from our present day measures of "real" product from which our wealth is now accumulating. Or conversely, perhaps some pluses for some of these items should be awarded to the American colonists and perhaps to some presently developing countries as well. Some important ways in which colonists may have had qualitative advantages over us may be enumerated in the following over-simplified list: abundance of open space with plenty of wild birds, other game and fish, many choices of areas for picnicking, skating and other simple forms of outdoor recreation; good water from wells or streams, fresh air; sturdy homespun cloth, hand-tailored garments, hand-made shoes; slower tempo or pace of work; a wide variety of tasks performed in the household, garden and fields by men, women and children which created an economic unit of the family and brought daily cooperative association of household members, totally different from today's dichotomy between activities on the job or at school and at home.

102

Composition of Physical Wealth

Further insight into the probable consumption levels and production functions is afforded by taking a look at the composition of wealth (Tables 2 and 3). For wealth classified according to some categories useful in economic analysis, we find that the wealth of 1774 was, in general outlines, surprisingly like that for the United States in 1966. Real estate (land and structures) formed close to the same percentage of wealth, 70 percent in New England, 63 in the Middle Colonies and 67 percent of national physical United States wealth in 1966. (However, the latter figure includes public and other than residential, business or agricultural land and structures; these were of negligible quantity in 1774 and are not included in my private wealth estimates and are excluded from the figure I have presented of $11,936 private per capita wealth in 1966.)

There were of course no servants or slaves in 1966, but these

TABLE 3
COMPARISON OF STRUCTURE OF PHYSICAL WEALTH,
NEW ENGLAND, MIDDLE COLONIES, 1774;
UNITED STATES, 1966

		Percentage	
		Private Physical Wealth 1774	
Type of Asset	National Wealth United States 1966[a]	New En- gland[b]	Middle Col- onies[c]
Total Physical Wealth including Cash	n.a.	100.0	100.0
Total National Wealth	100.0	n.a.	n.a.
Residential structures	25.5	n.a.	n.a.
Business structures	13.2	n.a.	n.a.
Agricultural land	5.2	n.a.	n.a.
Business land	3.7	n.a.	n.a.
Residential land	4.8	52.4	n.a.	n.a.
Public and other structures	12.3	n.a.	n.a.
Public and other land	2.2	14.5	n.a.	n.a.
Land (real estate)	—	70.3	62.5
Indentured servants and slaves	—	0.4	2.0
Producer durables	11.7	12.1	18.7
Producer perishables	—	1.6	4.7
Consumer durables	11.5	11.6	7.0
Consumer perishables	—	0.6	0.6
Business inventories	7.3	2.3	2.1
Cash	—	1.1	2.4
Monetary metals	0.6	n.a.	n.a.
Net foreign assets	1.9	n.a.	n.a.

Source:

[a] U.S. Bureau of the Census, *Statistical Abstract of the United States, 1970* (91st ed.; Washington, D.C.: G.P.O., 1970), p. 334, table 513, which incorrectly dates the table 1967 preliminary. It is based on estimates in Raymond W. Goldsmith and Robert E. Lipsey, *Studies in the National Balance Sheet of the United States*, I (Princeton: Princeton University Press, 1963) table 1, extended to 1966, preliminary, by John W. Kendrick in *Finance* Magazine, LXXXIV (Jan., 1967) 10-13, 34, table 3.

[b] Author's rigorous sample of decedents, with age and other adjustments to approximate wealth of living. See appendix cited in fn. 4.

[c] *EDCC*, Table 45, p. 119. Computed using item "III. Physical Wealth Including Cash" = 100.0 percent.

accounted for less than half of 1 percent of the New England 1774 total. Producer durables and consumer durables were close, each running around 11 to 12 percent for New England colonists and for the United States in 1966, though the producer durable figure was somewhat higher for the Middle Colonies, where livestock was an important part of that total. Business inventories (for business other than farm) were substantially greater in 1966, hardly a

surprise given our tremendous industrial development. They were
partially offset, however, in 1774 by stores of producer perishables
and consumer perishables in households, for which there are no corresponding figures in 1966. In a sense, the modern equivalents of the
stores of dried foods, liquors, cloth, yarn, firewood, candles and so
forth which we find in households in 1774 are the business inventories of processors, wholesalers or retailers today. Monetary metals
in 1966 were greater than the unknown but small portion of specie
or coin in the colonial "cash" figure. I have no figure for the colonists
comparable to the 2 percent held in "net foreign assets" in 1966. Perhaps for the colonies this was a negative figure, represented by European claims to physical assets, such as ships or merchants' goods here.
To the extent that debts owed by the colonists included obligations
due overseas, some of it will appear as part of the data on financial
liabilities owed, not yet available for New England at the time
this paper was prepared.

104

The similarity in general profile of wealth in 1774 and in 1966,
however, belies the great change over the years in the nature of
individual items which make up the several major wealth categories. The 1774 content reflects an economy which ranged from
substantial segments of subsistence production to commercial agriculture and fishing, artisans' production, services of taverns and
inns, teachers, doctors, lawyers, and some rather sophisticated
commercial operations by merchants who engaged in a variety of
local buying, selling and financing services and overseas shipping.
The 1966 content reflects the highly intertwined industrial, agricultural and commercial economy which undergirds our "affluent
society."

In 1774 the private structures included no skyscrapers nor as-
sembly-line factories, but besides houses, barns and the like on
farms, there were shipyards, warehouses, wharves, fish houses, mills,
blacksmith shops, inns and taverns, bakeries and artisans' or other
shops, often in a part of the dwelling house. Producer durables
comprised no steel furnaces nor tractors, but there were forges,
schooners and other boats, fishing equipment, horses and livestock,
wagons and sleds, harness, plows, harrows, hilling hoes and other
"utensils of husbandry," mauls and wedges, irons of various sorts,
lumber, artisan's tools, surveying instruments, guns, spinning wheels,
looms, wool cards, wool cloth, leather, apple presses, sacks, barrels,

scales, soap kettles and so on. No automobiles, refrigerators, nor tele-
visions were in the 1774 consumer durables, but I found an occasional riding chaise or carriage, often books, especially a "large
Bible," occasionally a painting; apparel and household furnishings
were almost always included, some enumerated as to garments of
sturdy homespun linen or wool, leather garments, occasional ones of
velvet or silk, wool great coats, worsted stockings, beaver hats, gold
watches, silver shoe buckles and sleeve buttons, beds and their
accompaniments, feather beds, curtains, bolsters, pillows, furniture
from "old pine table" to "oval mahogany tea table," box irons,
grates, sieves, riddles, pot hooks, pitchers, basons, cups, plates,
glassware, china ware, pewter, "plate" or silverware, lacquer ware,
tea boxes, wooden ware and so on. Consumer perishables included
no canned nor frozen foods but honey, sugar of several kinds, cider,
rum, coffee, tea, soap, meal, firewood, candles, dried or salted meat
and fish, and cheese. I placed crops in producer perishables, as well
as tallow, grease, oil, salt, sand, lime, powder and shot, materials for
making cloth and bedding such as yarn, thread, feathers. Many of
the wealth items were the product of the household; others were
purchased from craftsmen, peddlers, shopkeepers or merchants who
offered a variety of imported items, especially when a schooner had
just come in.

105

The richness of detail in the probate inventories, with the strong
implications I find therein for interpreting the level of living as well
as the production functions of the economy, is barely suggested by
the foregoing list.[13] It indicates, however, some of the fine decisions required as to whether a durable item was more used for further production and hence should be classed a producer durable, or
a consumer good used chiefly or only for final consumption. Illus-
trations are "big iron kettle," harness, lantern, and a "slay." The
problem was compounded when, as happened fairly often, the
inventory gave a single valuation for a lumped group of specified
items, some belonging to one and some to another wealth category.[14] Though we strove for consistency, inadvertent differences

---

[13] An item classification code, which runs to over 50 mimeographed pages, is
available on request to the author.
[14] In New England we assigned the total value for a lumped group of items, to
the category containing the item of presumably greatest value in the mixture.

in classifying may explain some of the apparent difference between producer and consumer durables for New England and the Middle Colonies. Larger producer durables in the Middle Colonies are reasonable in view of the large component of livestock on the relatively more fertile farms there, but perhaps producer durables are somewhat overstated there, or conversely understated for New England. If so, some portion of the New England consumer durables might be shifted and added to the producer durables.[15]

106 An idea of the difference in wealth estimates created by incorporating the wealth of nonprobates, people whose estates would not be probated when they died, can be gained by examining Table 2. The figures for the probate-type living (columns 3, 4, 7, 8), approximately one-third of potential wealth holders in New England, have been pulled down in columns 1, 2, 5, and 6 by the effect of our inclusion of lower wealth estimates for the nonprobate types. The latter, whom I awkwardly dub the "nonprobate-type" living, may comprise as many as two-thirds of the potential wealth holders in New England, whereas they comprised only 29 percent in the Middle Colonies. Our present knowledge of the composition of wealth of people who left no probate inventories is too limited to justify altering the relative numbers in Table 2. We must, however, accomodate these people about whose wealth we know little if we are to approach defensible estimates for the total living population; this is true not only for their average (mean) wealth, but also for its size distribution. These matters are considered further later in this article.

Reliability of Estimates

Estimates for the probate-type living (Table 2, columns 3, 4, 7, 8) approach the true figures, within the range of sampling error,[16]

---

[15] Correction would be a time-consuming matter of restudying and rejudging the proper classification of each entry, and perhaps making more allocations of lumped values.

[16] The size of the decedent samples in New England and in the Middle Colonies justifies the use of the central limit theorem and the expectation that successive sample means would be approximately normally distributed. The difference between average physical wealth for the age-adjusted probated decedents in the two regional samples cannot be said to be statistically significant at the .95 level of confidence, but it is statistically significant at the .64 level of confidence; that is, the null hypothesis can be rejected at the latter level. A summary of the relevant numbers for

for all New England. This is so because the figures come directly
from the probated inventories and related documents for essentially
all estates probated in 1774 in an unbiased sample of counties, with
an age adjustment for the disproportionate numbers of older persons found among the dying. In view of the sample design, it is
an incorrect inference that the two Connecticut counties represent
only Connecticut, or the five Massachusetts counties only Massachusetts. Rather each county in the sample represents a group of
geographically contiguous counties, some of which were in adjoin-
ing provinces. Our basic sample thus approximates the results we
would have obtained if we could have studied all inventories probated in 1774 in all 30 counties.

107

According to the sample design, each sample county represents
an equal number of then living potential wealth holders in the
stratum or group of counties from which it was drawn. Although
the numbers of inventories filed in 1774 in each sample county
were not the same, we used essentially all of them to take full
advantage of such data as exists. Yet we were able to preserve the
unbiased character of the combined county results by the method of
data processing. This insured that the average or other statistic
from each county's data made the same proportionate or equal relative contribution to the overall average or appropriate statistic.
The essence is set forth in Table 5 and further details are available

the mean of the age-adjusted decedent sample in each of the two regions is given
below. S. D. = Standard Deviation.

	Mean	S. D.	95 percent Confidence Interval
New England (Local Pounds)	317	20.3	(277, 357)
(Sterling)	238	15.2	(208, 268)
Middle Colonies (Local Pounds)	441	27.9	(386, 496)
(Sterling)	259	16.4	(227, 292)

The 95 percent confidence interval for the difference between the means for New
England and the Middle Colonies (Sterling) is (−22, 66).
A larger sample size would, of course, decrease the width of the confidence interval and provide more accurate estimates for the age-adjusted probate-type living
samples. In general, to double the precision, that is, to halve the width of the confidence interval, a sample approximately four times as large as the present one would
be required. Since I have used all the 1774 cases in all the sample counties except
Essex, more cases could have been obtained only by adding more years or going
to additional counties.
Another method of cutting variability would involve sampling every county, but
costs precluded this alternative.

in the appendix. The method used means the larger numbers of cases obtained for Suffolk and Essex are not permitted to influence unduly the results which might push the overall New England wealth figure too high, and the smaller numbers of cases from some more rural counties exert their proper influence as representatives of wealth holders in not only their own but other rural counties near them. Hence, we can claim the results are an unbiased estimate of wealth of the probate-type living (after the age adjustment discussed hereafter) in all 30 New England counties.

108   No precise statistical measure can be given of the confidence interval for the estimates for all living potential wealth holders, after we have incorporated estimates for the nonprobate types as well as the probate types, since the combined estimates involve more than the drawing of a sample from a larger population, and adjustment to living age structure. Hence the confidence placed in the combined estimates must hinge upon the confidence in the firmer underlying sample data for the probate-type living, plus the acceptability of our assumptions regarding the most probable wealth of the nonprobate types. The wealth of the nonprobates will be discussed further, after brief discussion of the essential age correction which moves the sample results from representing wealth of people who died to that of the living probate types.

Age Correction to Reach Estimates for Probate-type Living

If we wish to infer wealth of the living, the necessity for age correction of probate data becomes apparent from inspection of Table 4. Not only are a cross-section of the dying found too heavily in the older age brackets, as compared with an age distribution of the living, but older persons accumulated more wealth; this was true then as it is today. The older people had approximately ten times the average land value, over ten times the financial assets, and over three times as much portable physical wealth as the youngest group.[17] To ignore this systematic difference in wealth by age would yield too high a wealth estimate for the living; hence an age correction is mandatory. Such correction has been made

---

[17] The number of cases was smallest and hence the averages for the youngest group are subject to a wider range of sampling error; yet even within the small sample, the consistency of the pattern of rising wealth with age seems undeniable. Similar results were found for the Middle Colonies.

TABLE 4
AGE AND WEALTH, NEW ENGLAND, 1774

Item	All Ages	21-25 (1)	26-44 (2)	45 and over (3)	Age not de-termined (4)
			Age class[a]		
			Percentage		
Probated Decedents in 7 Counties:[b]					
Ages as found	100.0	3.3	29.5	60.2	7.0
Age class (4) allocated[c]	100.0	3.6	31.7	64.7	—
Living, Free Adult, Potential Wealth Holders in New England[d]	100.0	21.2	45.4	33.4	—
		Overall Wealth held by Sample Decedents (average[b] in pounds sterling and decimals)			
I. Total physical wealth	383.5	75.5	280.8	486.7	—
A. Land (real estate)	284.7	39.7	188.6	372.3	—
B. Portable physical wealth	98.8	35.8	92.2	114.4	—
II. Financial Assets, including "Cash"	69.0	7.7	50.0	87.9	—

109

Note: For corresponding data for Middle Colonies, see *EDCC*, Table 34, p. 94 and *OAH Paper*, Table 5.

[a] Class intervals as used in the 1800 Census, except I used half of census class 16-25 for my age class 1. See *EDCC*, fn. 69, p. 114.

[b] Each county contributed equally to the 7-county percentages and averages.

[c] Assumes that if age unknowns could have been determined, they would have been distributed by age as were those decedents whose age was found.

[d] Based on age proportions as found for 1800 Census, with slight adjustment for children between 1774 and 1800. See *EDCC*, p. 111.

Source: Decedent data from author's rigorous sample of probate inventories; their ages determined by research of genealogists named on p. 98. Data for living, free adult, potential wealth holders from population figures in 1800 Census for all New England, with adjustments by author to move date to 1774 and to remove children and 90 percent of women. See appendix cited in fn. 4.

in studies of twentieth-century wealth,[18] but so far as I am aware, mine is the first to attempt the correction for the colonial inventories. This is handled by restructuring (weighting)[19] the inventory data, using the age distribution of the living for relative proportions, rather than that of the dying probates. All we need assume is that

[18] See citations in *OAH Paper*.

[19] Mechanically, to minimize operations, these weights and the weights required to keep the county contributions equal are combined into a single factor for each decedent.

when the living in the indicated age brackets died and their estates came to be probated, it is reasonable that they might have held wealth similar to that held by the probates who died at the corresponding age. Treating their wealth as having been like that of the sampled probated decedents in the same age class, I call such then-living people the "probate-type" living, free adult potential wealth holders. At least one-third, and perhaps more, of all living potential wealth holders in New England may have been expected to have their estates probated at death, and hence to be represented by my relatively firm, age-adjusted, unbiased sample of inventories. The reason the figure is not larger becomes apparent when we consider the problem raised by the nonprobate types.

Nonprobate-type Living, Free Adult, Potential Wealth Holders

That there were a substantial number of then-living people whose wealth is not represented by the probate inventories in the sample is undeniable. The proof is that the numbers of probate cases do not tally with numbers of deaths of adults. Probable deaths[20] (in one year of living, free adult, potential wealth holders) in the sample counties exceed the total numbers of cases I found probated there (both in my sample plus additional cases of probated deaths for which inventories either were not taken or have not survived). For one who prefers simplicity and little work, it would be much pleasanter to sweep these difficulties under the rug. But, to move on to a defensible estimate of wealth of all the living, we are inexorably driven to ask: (1) what proportion of then-living potential wealth holders were of this "nonprobate type" and (2) what might their wealth most probably have been (a) on average, and (b) how might it most probably have been distributed among them, that is how many of them were poor, how many of medium or high wealth?

On the first question I found varying figures by county, lowest in Suffolk, highest in Hampshire and Worcester with an average for

---

[20] Since the preferred figure of number of adult deaths which actually occurred is unknown, numbers of probable deaths were approximated, using the same death rates for adult age classes as I used for the Middle Colonies for this purpose. As additional data become available, it is possible that these death rates will be revised downward, hence reducing somewhat my estimated proportion of nonprobate types in the living population. This is one reason why I term my present estimates provisional.

all 7 sample counties of 67.3 percent of potential wealth holder deaths not accounted for by probate cases; this figure, applied to living potential wealth holders, tells us that 67.3 percent is the estimated proportion of "nonprobate types" among them. This leaves a balance among the living wealth holders, of 32.7 percent "probate types." The 67.3[21] is much higher than the average of 29.2 I found for the Middle Colonies, which I used to calculate the wealth distributions presented in the *OAH Paper*.

On the second question, since nonprobates' dying counterparts left no records, we can only infer their wealth from consideration of the probable reasons for an estate's not being probated. We can be sure these reasons did not include estate or inheritance taxes which were nonexistent in 1774, and reasonably sure that costs of probate which I observed to be small though not negligible, were probably not a significant deterrent. One obvious reason was that there was no wealth or so little as not to justify the bother; this would be true of the drifters and ne'er-do-wells, the infirm, the young who had not accumulated anything, the old who had already transferred all assets to their children, and any other reasons for not possessing wealth; surely there were considerable numbers of these. But also, it seems reasonable that for many others of middle and all the way to high wealth, their families or agents found it unnecessary to incur the costs and inconvenience of travel by horse or boat to the county seat and simply made an informal distribution of assets among heirs. This would seem acceptable when there were no creditors or heirs demanding an accounting, and if it were not desired to sell the land[22] in order to settle the estate.

Striking something of a balance among these reasons, I assumed for the Middle Colonies that the estimated 29 percent of nonprobate-

111

21 The 67.3 figure could also be revised downward if a re-check of some counties would show that we overlooked counting some of the 1774 probate cases. As the records were kept in differing ways in various counties, some with good and some with poor or no indexes, it is difficult to be sure exactly how many probate cases were filed in a given year and hence to make consistent counts from county to county. Sometimes a case of administration granted, or probate inventory filed turns out, after genealogical search, to pertain to a person dead several or even many years earlier, and hence such case should not be counted. Such a re-check is in process in Essex County, and if justified there, may be made for other counties. This possibility is a second reason for terming my present estimates provisional.

22 To pass on legal title to land in New England, probate was required, and this is the reason that sometimes, many years after death, a probate inventory was filed, at a time when it was desired to convey the land to a new owner who required a legal title. Land, apparently at least, sometimes descended to heirs informally and was sometimes purchased informally without legal title.

type living potential wealth holders might have held an average wealth equal to one-quarter the average (weighted mean) held by the probate-type livings. But in New England, with such a large fraction as possibly 67.3 percent of livings being of the nonprobate-type, I find the one-quarter assumption too low to be convincing

TABLE 5

KEY TO INTERPRETATION OF DATA AS PRESENTED FOR VARIOUS POPULATION GROUPS

Line (1)	Results Presented for (2)	Assumptions, Weights Used (3)	Notation for Weights (4)
1	Probated Decedents in all New England, or in named counties	Not adjusted to age of living. Each decedent within the county contributes an equal portion to the county total or average. Average data from each sample county is given equal one-seventh weight to reach a total for New England. When presented for fewer than seven counties, then each county included contributes an equal portion to the weighted total.	c
2	Probate-type Living, Free Adult, Potential Wealth Holders in all New England, or in named county or subgroup of counties	Adjusted to age of living. Each decedent within the county contributes his proper age-adjusted proportion to the county total or average. Average data from each sample county is given equal one-seventh weight to reach a total for New England. When presented for fewer than seven counties, then each county included contributes an equal portion to the weighted total.	w
3	All Living, Free Adult, Potential Wealth Holders in all New England, or in named county or subgroup of counties	Combination of "Probate-type Living" (line 2) given 32.7 percent of total weight and "Nonprobate-type Living" given 67.3 percent of total weight. Wealth of nonprobate types is assumed to average:	
		a. A(one-fourth): One-fourth that of probate types, and distribution to be as in assumption A	w° ¼
		b. A(one-half): One-half that of probate types, and distribution to be as in assumption A	w° ½
		c. B(one-fourth): One-fourth that of probate types, and distribution to be as in assumption B	w°° ¼
		d. B(one-half): One-half that of probate types, and distribution to be as in assumption B	w°° ½

Note: For mathematical statement of derivation of weights, see appendix cited in fn. 4.

Source: Author's sample of decedents. See appendix cited in fn. 4.

and advance an alternative assumption that it might have been as high as one-half.

I had hoped that outside data such as tax lists might be a source to improve my nonprobate wealth estimate. But in an experiment for Philadelphia County, reported in the *OAH Paper* (pp. 31-34), I found a very poor correlation between taxed wealth and probate wealth for identical persons, with differences going erratically in both directions, which leads me to have serious doubts about usefulness of tax lists for estimates of probable nonprobate wealth.

The £157 physical wealth per wealth holder in Table 2 and the £36 per capita in Table 1 use the assumption one-half for the non-probates and the sample mean for the probate types; the two values are combined with respective weights of 67.3 and 32.7, as indicated in Table 5. If we wish, however, to say something not just about average but about size distribution of wealth among the entire wealth-holding population, we must further assume how those nonprobate-type livings who held the one-half (or one-quarter) average wealth were distributed. In my *OAH Paper* and in un-published graphs of data in Table 6 I present Lorenz curves on two alternate assumptions as to size distribution. Assumption A is that the nonprobate-type livings were distributed as were the probate types at the lower end of a distribution of the probate types, moving from bottom upward to that point where their average wealth is one-half (or one-quarter) the wealth of all the probate types. (See *EDCC*, pp. 121 and 112-18, and appendix to this paper.) Assumption B may be somewhat more realistic, in assigning a large proportion of the nonprobate types to the lowest decile of a probate-type dis-tribution, and some but diminishing proportions to all of the higher deciles, all within the constraint that their overall wealth shall average one-half (or one-quarter) that of the probate types. We could also make a third assumption C which would be more in accord with Jackson Main's judgment that perhaps a more sub-stantial proportion of nonprobates than under assumption B had high wealth. This would still further increase the inequality of the Lorenz curves (indicated by the Gini coefficients of concentra-tion in Table 6) for the varying assumptions. The firmer data for the probate types only are also shown. Obviously the nonprobate as-sumptions are more speculative and I would welcome suggestions for improving them.

The effects of the varying assumptions as to size and distribution

TABLE 6
DISTRIBUTION OF "WEALTH," 1774, 1860

Date and Population Group or Item	Mean Wealth in		Cumulative Proportion of Wealth held by					Gini Co-efficient
	1969 Dollars	1774 Local Pounds	Poorest			Richest		
			10 Per-cent	20 Per-cent	50 Per-cent	20 Per-cent	10 Per-cent	
Decile No., from poorest to richest			1	2	5	9	10	
I. Probate-type Living, Free Adult Potential Wealth Holders								
New England	$6,133	£317.3	0.3	1.0	11.0	59.7	40.4	.58
Middle Colonies	6,609	434.2	0.5	1.9	22.9	47.1	32.0	.43
II. 1774 All Living, Free Adult Potential Wealth Holders, using assumption B for nonprobates:								
New England: 1. (B-½)	4,075	210.8	0.3	1.0	7.9	66.1	47.3	.64
2. (B-¼)	3,039	157.2	0.5	1.4	7.9	60.2	31.7	.71
III. 1774 All Living, Free Adult Potential Wealth Holders, using assumption A for nonprobates:								
New England: 1. (A-½)	4,090	211.6	0.4	1.5	12.7	55.7	37.2	.55
2. (A-¼)	3,045	157.5	0.4	1.4	10.1	64.0	49.1	.62
Middle Colonies (A-¼)	5,151	338.4	0.4	1.4	13.6	53.3	35.7	.51
IV. 1860, U.S., Free Families								
(Gallman's A distribution)	14,931	$3,000ª	0	0	0	88	71	.82
(Gallman's B distribution)	—	—	0	0	0	88	72	—

Note: For lines I, II and III: "Wealth" means "Total Physical Wealth." It includes land ("real estate"), slaves, clothing and other portable physical wealth; it excludes cash and financial assets. For line IV: "Wealth" means "Personally Held Wealth" as defined in the 1860 Census. It includes "real estate," "personal property" if valued over $100, "intangible assets"; it excludes clothing.

ª Round number suggested orally by Professor Gallman in 1860 dollars, of which I calculate $3.05 to be the equivalent in purchasing power of a 1774 local pound in the Middle Colonies and $3.88 in New England.

Source: Lines I and III for Middle Colonies: OAH Paper, Tables 14 and 14A. Line IV: R. E. Gallman, "Trends in the Size Distribution of Wealth in the Nineteenth Century: Some Speculations," in Lee Soltow, ed., Six Papers on the Size Distribution of Wealth and Income. NBER Conference on Research in Income and Wealth, Studies in Income and Wealth, XXXIII (New York: Columbia University Press, 1969), 6.

of nonprobate wealth, viewed graphically, are not as different as one might expect. The general conclusion emerges that there was substantial inequality of wealth, certainly among probate types, which inequality almost certainly should be increased when we make our best allowance for the nonprobate types. For all the free adult, potential wealth holders, using assumption A (one-half), I find that the richest 10 percent may have held about 47 percent of the total physical wealth, the bottom 20 percent only 1 percent, and the bottom half or 50 percent only 8 percent. The Gini coefficient[23] of wealth concentration for that distribution is .64 percent, implying rather high departure from equality of wealth distribution. It may be pointed out that perfect equality of wealth for persons of all ages is hardly to be expected even if there were equal distribution among families (defined to include persons of several generations, which we may call vertically extended families). If individuals in certain age groups, for example those aged 45 years and more, have larger wealth than others, it will appear that wealth is unequally distributed, even though among the vertically extended families it could be equally distributed. Such apparent inequality of wealth distribution may prevail because a person accumulates wealth as his age progresses, and also because the old on the whole tend to leave their wealth to the middle aged and not to the young.

115

If we were to add at the bottom end of these distributions the indentured servants and slaves as essentially holders of no wealth (and subtract the value of servants and slaves as wealth, which in New England would make a scarcely perceptible difference) we would, of course, further increase the inequality. Since I estimate this would add about 4 percent more wealth holders in New England, but 7 percent in the Middle Colonies, the change would be greater for the Middle Colonies and would therefore slightly reduce the regional inequality difference.

Size Distribution—Inequality, Regional Comparison

Despite a wider range (see Table 7) from low to high in the probate-type living sample for the Middle Colonies physical wealth was more unequally distributed in New England, judged by the proportions of wealth held by each tenth of the wealth holders (Table

---

[23] The greater the Gini coefficient, the greater the wealth inequality. Its range is from 0, if everyone had equal wealth to 1 for maximum inequality if one person had all the wealth.

6). For probate-type livings (my sample, age adjusted and hence the figures about which I am most confident) when graphed in the familiar Lorenz curve, the New England curve is further bowed out from the 45 degree line of perfect equality. Its Gini coefficient is higher, .58 as compared with .43 for the Middle Colonies.[24] Forty percent of the physical wealth was held by the upper 10 percent, against 32 percent in the Middle Colonies; for the poorest 20 percent the figures were respectively 1 percent and 2 percent.

Size Distribution—Inequality, Comparison over Time

116

My finding of inequalities in the Middle Colonies and New England in 1774 reinforce recent questioning of the long widely-held assumption that wealth inequalities were fairly small before the nineteenth century and were then sharply increased by industrialization. Besides the work of James Henretta, I am thinking of work by Jackson Main, Aubrey Land, James Lemon, Gary Nash, Robert Doherty and Michael Katz. My belief is that wealth inequality probably did increase in the nineteenth century as compared with the late eighteenth, though perhaps not to the extent that some have suggested, and diminished by a century later, to a degree somewhat, but perhaps not extremely greater than that for New England in 1774.

My Gini coefficients are substantially below the figure of .82 found by Robert Gallman[25] for a preliminary subsample of the 1860 census returns, shown in Table 6 which show zero wealth for the bottom five deciles of free families. (I shall argue elsewhere that at least some wealth should be attributed to most, if not all, of those lower-end-of-the-distribution families in 1860, but unless unreasonably large sums were added, this would apparently not very greatly alter his results.) My figures are surprisingly close to a figure of .76 for

---

[24] For the Middle Colonies, the distribution of net worth was more skewed than that for physical wealth, with a Gini coefficient of .50 for the probate types and .54 or .57 for all living free adult potential wealth holders. For Philadelphia County alone, using assumption B (one-fourth) for nonprobates' wealth, it was the most skewed of all, with a Gini coefficient of .68. Taxed wealth in Philadelphia County was even more highly skewed with a Gini coefficient of .83. Supporting tables and graphs appear in the *OAH Paper*. The net worth distribution is not yet available for New England, but I anticipate that it will be more unequal than that for physical wealth.

[25] R. E. Gallman, "Trends in the Size Distribution of Wealth in the Nineteenth Century: Some Speculations," in Lee Soltow, ed., *Six Papers on the Size Distribution of Income and Wealth*, NBER Conference on Research in Income & Wealth, Studies in Income and Wealth, 33 (New York and London: Columbia University Press, 1969), pp. xiii, 6.

data for "wealth" from a Federal Reserve Board survey for the
United States at the end of 1962.[26] Between the latter two dates, of
course, we have witnessed imposition of the income tax, great increase in inheritance and estate taxes, as well as substantial increases
in transfer payments as in the form of social security, which all
tend in the direction of decreasing wealth inequality.

Size Distribution of Wealth—Range Among Probates

My data indicate wide spread from low to highest wealth in New
England on the eve of the American Revolution. Physical wealth[27]
ranged from essentially nothing but the clothes on their backs for
the relatively small servant and slave fraction[28] of the population
and about $93 for the poorest probated wealth holder in my sample,
a widow in Worcester County whose age I could not determine, to
about $108,000 expressed in 1969 dollars[29] for the richest probate
I drew, Thomas Gerry, merchant in Marblehead, who died aged
72. These compare with an even wider range for the Middle
Colonies from $98 for the poorest probate, a Philadelphia shoe-
maker, to approximately $216,000 or twice Gerry's wealth, for the
richest, also a merchant, one Samuel Neave of Philadelphia.

Besides Gerry, two others of the richest were of Essex County and
six of Suffolk, both counties with significant urban population. However, five of the eleven poorest also came from these counties. No
women appear among the eleven richest, though one "gentlewoman," Kathran Upham, was the richest Worcester County probate. All of the richest were 35 years or older. Of the eleven poorest,
despite the small proportion of women in the total sample, nearly
half were women, none of whom owned land. The eleven poorest
also included two mariners, a fisherman, two farmers and one
tailor, aged 27. The importance of the sea and shipping in the
formation of New England's wealth is suggested by the three captains in the list of richest (one of these both a "merchant" and a

117

---

    [26] D. S. Projector and G. S. Weiss, *Survey of Financial Characteristics of Con-
sumers* (Washington: Board of Governors of Federal Reserve System, 1966), p. 30.
    [27] The value of servants and slaves is included in physical wealth for this com-
parison; cash and all other financial assets are excluded.
    [28] I estimate at over 4 percent for New England and over 7 percent for the Middle
Colonies the proportion which servants and slaves formed of all adults, in 1774.
    [29] Values are stated in local money in the inventories. In Massachusetts pounds,
the figure for the widow is £4.8, for Gerry £5,584; in Pennsylvania pounds, the
shoemaker had £6.5, Neave £14,176. Reduced to equivalent pounds sterling the
figures are: widow £3.5, Gerry £4,188, shoemaker £3.9, Neave 8,335.

TABLE 7

THE RICHEST AND POOREST DECEDENTS: THEIR OCCUPATION, AGE, RESIDENCE

Name	Occupation	Total Physical Wealth (local £)	Age	Place
Eleven Richest in Seven County Sample				
Thomas Gerry	Merchant	5,584.2	72	Marblehead, Essex Co.
William White	Esquire	5,507.9	58	Boston, Suffolk
Andrew Oliver	Esquire	3,887.6	67	Boston, Suffolk
Humphrey Devereaux, Jr.	Physician	3,003.5	42	Marblehead, Essex
Thomas Grey	Shopkeeper	2,901.5	53	Boston, Suffolk
Enoch Witten	Yeoman/Cooper	2,467.5	75	Hingham, Suffolk
Samuel Tilden	Yeoman	2,460.4	55+	Marshfield, Plymouth
Thomas Clark, 3rd	Captain	2,346.9	75	Milford, New Haven
Edward Bridge	Gentleman	1,915.1	35	Roxbury, Suffolk
Jonathan Orne	Merchant/Captain	1,708.6	51	Salem, Essex
Barnabas Binney	Captain	1,637.9	51	Boston, Suffolk
Richest in Each County in Sample not Shown above				
John Hart	Officer and Landowner	1,322.8	59	Cornwall, Litchfield
Josiah Dickinson	Yeoman/Hatter	796.5	48	Hadley, Hampshire
Kathran Upham	Gentlewoman	876.6	57	Brookfield, Worcester
Eleven Poorest in Seven County Sample				
Anne Haskell	Widow	4.8	(Cl. 4)	Brookfield, Worcester
Sarah Cole	Singlewoman	4.9	19	Waterbury, New Haven
Jabez Dodge	Yeoman	5.1	88	Shrewsbury, Worcester
Isaac Herault	Tailor	5.2	(Cl. 4)	Boston, Suffolk
Seth Nickerson	Mariner	5.4	27	Plymouth, Plymouth
Mehitabel Burpe	Singlewoman	5.4	24	Rowley, Essex
Sarah Leonard	Widow	6.1	89	Springfield, Hampshire
Edmund Perkins	Husbandman/Chairman	6.2	40	Boston, Suffolk
George Hyter	Fisherman	7.5	36+	Marblehead, Essex
Mary Dwinell	Widow	9.1	90+	Topsfield, Essex
John Nickerson	Mariner	9.7	45+	Scituate, Plymouth

"captain"). The role of land ownership is also indicated by the three esquires or gentlemen and two yeomen. Also Humphrey Devereaux, the physician of Marblehead, held extensive property and collected rents.

From earlier discussion on the thinness of our knowledge regarding nonprobates, it will be understood why my remarks on specific range of wealth are confined to probates. For the same reason, for comparisons of wealth by place, occupation, sex, or testacy we do better to examine data only for the probate-type living, that is the sample decedents, with correction to the age structure of the living. *119*

Wealth by County

The main function, for this study, of data from the sample counties is to contribute their share to the total New England estimate, but since they must be tabulated separately, I present them so the reader will have an opportunity to study the parts and because the county figures are of interest in their own right.

I will just point out that the highest wealth was found in Suffolk County which includes Boston, and rural Plymouth, with large values in land, came second. The counties are ordered in Table 8 by size of total physical wealth. Consumer durables were highest in Suffolk County, as were business inventories and slaves. Producer durables, perhaps reflecting fewer farmers and lesser livestock, were the lowest there among the counties.

Urban-Rural Residence and Wealth

Though urban counties show generally high wealth, I did not find significantly higher physical wealth held by urban individuals. Urban dwellers formed 25 percent of the probate-type livings, that is the decedent sample, age-adjusted, a higher proportion than I found in the Middle Colonies where Philadelphia furnished almost all the urban cases. Urban inventories came from Boston, Salem, and additionally some from such places as Marblehead, Ipswich, Newburyport, Gloucester, Bridgewater, Middleborough and Scituate, unless the occupation[30] was a clearly rural one, as yeoman. Grouping the urban cases into low, middle and high physical wealth classes, no pronounced higher urban wealth was evident, the re-

[30] Since "town" in New England comprised a wide area, similar to a township in some other regions, "town" population is not a clear guide to whether places within the "town" were urban or rural, and occupations were used for marginal decisions.

TABLE 8

SIZE AND COMPOSITION OF PHYSICAL WEALTH, PROBATE-TYPE LIVING FREE ADULT POTENTIAL WEALTH HOLDERS, ALL NEW ENGLAND AND BY COUNTY, 1774

Item, Kind of Wealth	All New England (1)	Suffolk (2)	Plymouth (3)	Essex (4)	Worces-ter (5)	Hamp-shire (6)	New Haven (7)	Litch-field (8)
Number of cases in sample	381	100	35ᵃ	102	49	27	31	37
Est. No. Probate-type Liv. Fr. Ad. Pot. W. Holders	45,428							
	Average Value per P.T.L.F.A. Wealth Holder in Pounds Sterling and decimals thereof							
I. Tot. physical wealth incl. cash	240.6	324.3	271.3	270.6	241.7	212.9	189.8	174.0
II. Tot. physical wealth excl. cash	238.0	321.1	267.7	266.6	240.8	207.7	188.8	173.1
A. Land (real estate)	169.1	218.1	203.6	187.7	172.0	143.4	139.1	120.3
B. Portable physical wealth, total	68.8	103.0	64.1	79.0	68.9	64.3	49.7	52.8
C. Cash	2.7	3.3	3.5	3.9	0.9	5.2	1.0	0.9
	Percentage							
III. Tot. physical wealth excl. cash	100.0	100.0	100.0	100.0	100.0	100.0	100.0	100.0
A. Land (real estate)	70.9	67.9	75.5	70.4	71.5	69.1	73.7	69.5
B. Portable physical wealth, total	29.1	32.1	24.5	29.6	28.5	30.9	26.3	30.5
1. Producer capital, total	16.7	15.0	13.0	16.0	19.7	20.1	14.3	20.0
a. Servants and Slaves	0.5	1.3	0.0	0.3	0.1	0.3	1.0	0.0
b. Durable, incl. livestock	12.3	6.8	11.8	9.5	17.0	16.3	12.0	16.5
c. Perishable	1.6	0.6	1.2	1.2	0.9	3.5	1.0	3.5
d. Business inventoriesᵇ	2.3	6.3	0.1	5.0	1.7	0.0	0.4	0.0
2. Consumer goods, total	12.4	17.0	11.4	13.6	8.8	10.9	12.1	10.5
a. Durable	11.8	16.5	10.6	13.1	8.1	10.5	11.4	10.1
b. Perishable	0.6	0.6	0.8	0.5	0.8	0.4	0.6	0.5

Note: Components may not add to totals due to rounding.
ᵃ Of which three had only a total wealth figure, with no details stated.
ᵇ Other than farm business.
Source: Author's sample of decedents, with adjustments outlined in appendix cited in fn. 4.

spective figures for urban, rural being: low wealth 29, 28 percent of cases; middle 45, 48; high 26, 24 percent. When we include financial assets and use net worth, not yet available, the urban wealth may appear higher.

Occupation and Wealth

Among the probate-type living wealth holders I found 14 percent merchants, captains, professional, official, esquire, gentleman or gentlewoman; at least one gentleman-farmer is included here and perhaps other esquires and gentlemen were also farmers. Fifty-four percent were clearly farmers or yeomen, some with side occupations, 2 percent fishermen, 7 percent laborers and mariners (not captain), 15 percent shopkeepers or artisans, and 8 percent widows, single-women or males whose occupation I could not determine. In terms of their respective percentages falling in high, middle, low physical wealth classes, the following wealth hierarchy emerges:

Richest: Merchants, captains, professional, official, gentleman, esquire, with 9, 40, and 51 percent respectively in low, middle and high wealth class; farmers with 22, 52, and 26 percent respectively; shopkeepers and artisans, with 38, 44, and 18 percent respectively; laborers and mariners, 35, 65, and none in highest wealth class; fishermen, 79, 21, and none in highest wealth class.

Poorest: Widows, singlewomen, males of unspecified occupation, 79, 18, and 3 percent respectively.

Sex and Wealth

By sex, the story is clear. The women (mostly widows and a few singlewomen) had far lower wealth on average than the men, though there were some rich women. Eight percent of the sample (using county weights) were women. Age-adjusted, women formed six percent (men 94 percent) of probate-type living adult potential wealth holders, and they fell much more preponderantly than men in the lower wealth classes. This is partly because widows usually did not receive the land, which went directly to their sons. Occasionally a daughter was left a bequest of land by her father and some of the singlewomen for whom probate inventories were found had some real estate as well as personal.

Testacy and Wealth

In the age-adjusted decedent sample (probate-type living) 75 percent were intestate (left no will), while 25 percent, fewer than in the Middle Colonies, left wills. Testates fell preponderantly into the two higher wealth classes; intestates proportionately more in middle and lower physical wealth class. This corresponds with the Middle Colonies, where average wealth of intestates was somewhat, but not strikingly, below that of testates.

ALICE HANSON JONES, *Washington University*

122

Trade, Distribution, and
Economic Growth in Colonial America

THE purpose of this paper is to present some of the findings and contentions of our forthcoming study[1] of shipping, distribution, and overseas trade in colonial America from the middle of the seventeenth century to the American Revolution, with emphasis upon the later years. In order to provide an explanation of the contribution of overseas trade to colonial growth, we begin the study 123 by proposing a simple theoretical framework for viewing economic development in the colonies. Then, to provide some perspective for the study, we examine the long-term trends in output, population, and overseas trade (subject to fairly severe data limitations, which allow us to make only tentative statements about these long-term trends, and which largely limit us to the eighteenth century). Next we examine the costs of shipping and distributing commodities in overseas trade and show that these costs declined over the long run. The increased productivity in shipping is explicitly measured, and the sources of these advances analyzed. Finally, a balance-of-payments study is presented for 1768 through 1772, the only years in the colonial period for which we have statistics of all legal overseas trade.

From the results of our study, we wish to argue here that overseas trade was an important part of the market sector and of overall economic activity in the colonies, and that it was the growth of the market sector which was mainly responsible for the growth in productivity that occurred in the colonial economy. The sources of increased productivity were primarily increased specialization stemming from increased production for markets, and improvements in shipping and other activities associated with distribution. It is this last source of growth which we particularly wish to emphasize. The evidence strongly suggests that the costs of distribution relative to the costs of production[2] were large. Consequently productivity

---

[1] *Shipping, Maritime Trade, and the Economic Development of Colonial North America* (Cambridge: Cambridge University Press, forthcoming 1972).

[2] By distribution we mean activities associated with transporting and distributing commodities from producers to consumers, and by production we mean activities associated with the physical production of commodities within limited geographical areas.

advances in distribution services could have affected overall average productivity and per capita output significantly, even with little or no increased productivity in activities associated with production. We suggest that these types of improvements—increased specialization and those observed in distribution—dominated earlier American productivity growth. This growth, in turn, contributed to an increasing output per capita, which the evidence suggests was positive although low when compared with post-1840 rates of growth.

In part I we present the evidence pertaining to magnitudes and patterns of colonial overseas trade. Because this is done on a regional basis, an examination of regional differences is possible. In part II we develop a brief version of the model underlying our analysis of improvements in distribution, and then present evidence pertaining to the magnitudes of the costs of distribution followed by our explanation of the decline of these costs over time. Finally, in part III we briefly state the significance of our findings for interpreting early American growth and development.

124

I

It is apparent that population grew more rapidly than exports to Great Britain during the eighteenth century. The annual average per capita values of exports (computed for five-year periods) to Britain fluctuate, but they do exhibit a downward trend. When exports to southern Europe and the West Indies are added to exports to Britain, however, the resulting annual average per capita commodity export values indicate no clear trend:[3]

	to Great Britain	to all areas
1698-1702	£ 1.2	—
1708-1712	1.0	—
1718-1722	1.1	£ 1.4
1728-1732	1.0	1.3
1738-1742	0.9	1.1
1748-1752	0.8	1.1
1758-1762	0.7	0.9
1768-1772	0.7	1.3

[3] The values for Great Britain are based upon the English official values (U.S. Bureau of the Census, *Historical Statistics of the United States, Colonial Times to 1957* [Washington, D.C.: U.S. Government Printing Office, 1960], p. 757) plus the Scottish official values for 1758-1762 (London, Public Record Office, Customs 14). Exports to Scotland for the earlier periods have been based upon tobacco exports to there (*Historical Statistics*, p. 766). Exports for 1768-1772 have been estimated from data in the American customs records (London, Public Record Office, Customs 16/1).

Thus the increased export earnings from the southern European and West Indian trades tended to offset the decline (relative to population) of exports to Britain.

Was overseas trade of declining relative importance to the colonies during the eighteenth century? If per capita colonial output did not rise, then no such conclusion is justified. But if per capita output rose, as has been suggested by Robert Gallman,[4] then overseas trade was a declining proportion of total economic activity over the century. If per capita output rose from levels of £8-9 at the beginning of the century to £11-12½ by the 1770's,[5] then commodity exports as a percentage of total output declined from somewhere around 14 to 18 percent at the beginning of the century to 11-12 percent by the Revolution. When invisible earnings for 1768-1772[6] are added to earnings from commodity exports, then earnings from overseas trade approached 14 to 15 percent of total output. If invisible earnings were the same proportion of commodity trade at the beginning of the eighteenth century as they were during 1768-1772, then total earnings from overseas trade would have been around 18-22 percent of total output.[7] Despite the imprecision of these estimates, the conclusion is inescapable that the proportion of colonial economic activity devoted to production for overseas markets was relatively large at the beginning of the eighteenth century, and, although it declined over the century, it remained a substantial portion of total output.

It appears, however, that not all of the colonies shared in this overseas trade to an equal degree. In fact, the evidence suggests that overseas trade was of greatly varying importance to different

---

[4] Robert E. Gallman, "The Pace and Pattern of American Economic Growth," in Davis, Easterlin, Parker, *et al.*, *American Economic Growth: An Economist's History of the United States* (New York: Harper & Row, 1972). Gallman's estimates are supported by probable ranges of per capita output developed by Alice Hanson Jones, "Wealth Estimates for the American Middle Colonies, 1774," *Economic Development and Cultural Change*, XVIII, 4, Supplement (July, 1970), p. 129; and David Klingaman, "Food Surpluses and Deficits in the American Colonies, 1768-1772," THE JOURNAL OF ECONOMIC HISTORY, XXXI, 3 (Sept., 1971), 553-69. Gallman's estimates are based partly upon Mrs. Jones' wealth estimates.

[5] Gallman, "The Pace and Pattern . . . ." These estimates imply an annual growth rate of per capita output of less than one-half of 1 percent.

[6] James F. Shepherd and Gary M. Walton, "Estimates of 'Invisible' Earnings in the Balance of Payments of the British North American Colonies, 1768-1772," THE JOURNAL OF ECONOMIC HISTORY, XXIX, 2 (June, 1969), 230-63.

[7] Such percentages for the early eighteenth century, however, may overstate the proportion overseas trade formed of total output because levels of per capita output may have been greater, or, as was likely the case, because invisible earnings were not as large relative to commodity trade at the beginning of the century.

regions and colonies by the late colonial period. Trade with overseas areas depended upon such factors as geographical differences in costs of production (which in turn depended upon a colony's particular resource endowments), transportation costs, and other costs of distribution, on the supply side; and, upon demand in overseas markets for colonial products, and demand in the colonies for imported goods, on the demand side. These factors gave rise to various patterns of regional specialization in the colonies, and, in general, these patterns reflected the comparative advantages held by the colonies in the production of various primary products. Newfoundland and Nova Scotia were exporting dried and pickled fish and whale oil; Quebec exported wheat and furs; New Hampshire's exports were mainly forest products; Massachusetts sold forest products, fish, and shipping and mercantile services to overseas areas; Connecticut, Rhode Island, and the middle colonies exported primarily foodstuffs, especially grains and grain products from New York and Pennsylvania, and invisible earnings were important to the latter two colonies; the exports of the upper south were dominated by tobacco although wheat was of increasing importance in the later colonial period; naval stores came from the sandy pine forests of North Carolina along with some foodstuffs; rice, indigo, and deerskins from the back country were produced for export in South Carolina and Georgia; and, finally, the beginnings of rice and indigo exports were seen in Florida, which was only just beginning to be settled by the late colonial period.

126

This general description of the patterns of regional specialization, however, lends little insight into the *degree* of such specialization in the various colonies. Per capita exports by colony can be estimated from the data underlying our estimates of exports for the period 1768-1772, and from the estimates of colonial population.[8] These estimates are presented in Table 1, and, perhaps not surprisingly, the per capita value of commodity exports from New England was relatively low, somewhat higher from the middle colonies, and highest from the southern colonies.

Within each region, however, there were large variations (with the exception of the upper south). New Jersey and North Carolina, for example, stand out as having had exceptionally low exports relative to their population.[9] It would also seem that plantation

[8] *Historical Statistics*, p. 756.
[9] This result must be qualified to the extent their products were exported from

agriculture (if its existence can be indicated by a sizable slave labor force) was not necessarily correlated with a heavy concentration of production for export markets, because at this time 35 percent of North Carolina's population was black.

The other southern colonies, as noted above, did have relatively high per capita exports, but still there are noticeable differences. For example, per capita exports from South Carolina and Georgia were exceptionally high, and if one views these exports relative to only the white population, this tendency is even more pronounced. Such a view is legitimate because the slave population's claim against output was essentially for a subsistence level of income. An examination of the coastal trade for this period shows that the southern colonies were self-sufficient in the production of food-stuffs,[10] so a large portion of this subsistence income must have been produced within each colony. For practical purposes, therefore, export earnings can be viewed as accruing to the free population. On this basis (as in Table 1), South Carolina, whose population was less than 40 percent white in 1770, appears to have been heavily engaged in plantation agriculture for export (mainly rice and indigo). Indeed, export earnings per white resident come to more than three-quarters of the above conjectural estimate of per capita output for the late colonial period.

Based upon these estimates, Newfoundland appears to have been the colony most heavily oriented to producing for overseas markets.[11] Perhaps this is not so surprising; cod fishing was virtually Newfoundland's sole economic activity, and most foodstuffs and other necessities had to be imported. Exports from Newfoundland consisted mostly of dried cod to southern Europe—82 percent of

other colonies, as was, to some degree, the case (some North Carolina tobacco was said to have been exported from Virginia, and some commodities produced in east and west New Jersey were exported through New York and Philadelphia, respectively).

[10] See Klingaman, "Food Surpluses . . ."; and James F. Shepherd and Samuel H. Williamson, "The Coastal Trade of the British North American Colonies, 1768-1772," paper presented to the Conference on the Application of Economic Theory and Quantitative Techniques to Problems of Economic History, University of Wisconsin, Madison, Wisconsin, April 30, 1971.

[11] The estimate for Newfoundland must be qualified because the recorded exports may have included the catch of the west country fishermen from Britain in addition to that of the resident population. There is no way of knowing for certain (the source gives no indication), but probably the British catch was included because the cod were dried ashore. On the other hand, the source did state that these were exports from St. Johns only; therefore, total exports from Newfoundland may have been even greater.

TABLE 1
AVERAGE ANNUAL COMMODITY EXPORTS OF THE BRITISH
NORTH AMERICAN COLONIES, BY COLONY AND REGION,
1768-1772

	Total[a]	Per Capita[b]	Per White Resident
Newfoundland	£ 131,000	£ 11.5	—
Quebec	67,000	0.9	—
Nova Scotia	10,000	0.5	—
Northern Colonies	£ 208,000	2.0	—
New Hampshire	£ 47,000	0.7	£ 0.7
Massachusetts	265,000	1.0	1.0
Rhode Island	83,000	1.4	1.5
Connecticut	94,000	0.5	0.5
New England	£ 489,000	0.8	0.9
New York	£ 191,000	1.2	1.3
New Jersey	2,000	0.0	0.0
Pennsylvania	361,000	1.5	1.5
Delaware	18,000	0.5	0.5
Middle Colonies	£ 572,000	1.0	1.1
Maryland	£ 398,000	2.0	2.9
Virginia	783,000	1.8	3.0
Upper South	£ 1,181,000	1.8	3.0
North Carolina	£ 76,000	0.4	0.6
South Carolina	463,000	3.7	9.5
Georgia	75,000	3.2	5.9
Lower South	£ 614,000	1.8	3.2
Total, above colonies	£ 3,064,000	1.4	—

128

[a] The total value of exports from each of the thirteen colonies and Nova Scotia was estimated in the same manner as exports from each region in the source. Because this method would have understated exports from Quebec, those commodities in the source for which values were computed were added to the estimated value of fur exports from Quebec in 1770 of £ 28,433 (*Historical Statistics*, p. 762). Also, because exports from Newfoundland were primarily codfish, the estimate of total exports from there was based only upon those commodities for which values were computed in the source.

[b] Population estimates for Newfoundland, Quebec, and Nova Scotia were based upon statements about early Canadian population found in Dominion Bureau of Statistics, Canada, *Seventh Census of Canada, 1931* (Ottawa, 1936), I, pp. 133-53. Newfoundland was said to have had 11,418 British residents in 1770 (*ibid.*, p. 143). The populations of Quebec and Nova Scotia circa 1770 were assumed to have been 72,500 and 21,000, respectively, in order that the total population for the three colonies approximate 105,000 (see *ibid.*, p. 100).

Source: Based on the detailed estimates by James F. Shepherd, "Commodity Exports from the British North American Colonies to Overseas Areas, 1768-1772: Magnitudes and Patterns of Trade," *Explorations in Economic History*, VIII, 1 (Fall, 1970), 5-76.

TABLE 2
THE SHARE OF EACH REGION'S COMMODITY EXPORTS TO
EACH OVERSEAS AREA, 1768-1772 (in percentages)

	Great Britain & Ireland	Southern Europe	West Indies	Africa
Northern Colonies	22	71	7	0
New England	18	14	64	4
Middle Colonies	23	33	44	0
Upper South	83	9	8	0
Lower South	72	9	19	0
Flor., Ba., & Ber.	88	0	12	0
Total	56	18	26	1

Source: These percentages are an average of the five years, 1768-1772, and are derived *129*
from estimates of commodity trade in James F. Shepherd and Gary M.
Walton, *Shipping, Maritime Trade, and the Economic Development of
Colonial North America* (Cambridge: Cambridge University Press, forthcoming 1972).

all exports from there during this period went directly to southern
European markets. Alternatively, Quebec, even with its fur trade,
was below the average for all the colonies.

These estimates provide a rough indication of the degree of
production for markets relative to subsistence production in the
colonies. Because trade took place among the colonies and within
each colony, as well as with overseas areas, these estimates represent
only a lower bound to the ratio of market production to total output. Whether production for markets was less in colonies such as
North Carolina and New Jersey depends, of course, upon the
magnitudes of their intercolonial and intracolonial trade. Although
there is little information about the magnitude of trade within
each colony, the evidence pertaining to the coastal trade indicates
that the value of all commodities exchanged in that trade amounted
to about 25 percent of the value of commodity exports to all overseas areas for 1768-1772;[12] and that the more important commercial
colonies like Massachusetts, New York, and Pennsylvania participated more in the coastal trade than such colonies as New Jersey
and North Carolina. It would appear, therefore, that in some
colonies (like New Jersey and North Carolina) subsistence production was a significantly larger proportion of total output than
in other colonies in which production for overseas markets comprised a large proportion of total output (South Carolina and Newfoundland are the outstanding examples).

[12] Shepherd and Williamson.

TABLE 3

THE SHARE OF EACH REGION'S COMMODITY IMPORTS FROM
EACH OVERSEAS AREA, 1768-1772 (in percentages)

	Great Britain & Ireland	Southern Europe	West Indies	Africa
Northern Colonies	95	2	3	0
New England	66	2	32	0
Middle Colonies	76	3	21	0
Upper South	89	1	10	0
Lower South	86	1	13	0
Flor., Ba., & Ber.	87	2	11	0
Total	80	2	18	0

130   Source: See Table 2.

Our estimates of trade also clearly show the relative importance
of each overseas area as a trading partner with each colonial region.
Table 2 shows in percentage terms the importance of each overseas
area as a market for each region's commodity exports. Table 3
shows the importance of each overseas area as a source of each
region's commodity imports.[13] Southern Europe was by far the
most important export market of the northern colonies, rivaling the
importance of the West Indies as a market for New England exports.
No single overseas area greatly dominated the export trade of the
middle colonies, but for the regions south of Pennsylvania, Great
Britain was by far the most important market. However, a substantial proportion of these southern exports were ultimately reex-
ported from Great Britain to other European countries. For instance,
over 90 percent of the tobacco imported into Great Britain in 1768-
1772[14] was re-exported. Of the total value of commodity exports,
56 percent went to Great Britain and Ireland, 18 percent to
southern Europe, 26 percent to the West Indies, and less than 1
percent to Africa. It is clear from Table 3 that Great Britain over-
whelmingly dominated the import trade to all regions, although the
import trade from the West Indies was not insignificant, especially
to New England and the middle colonies. The values of commodity
imports from Africa and southern Europe were a very small part
of total imports.

An alternative perspective is to view the importance of each region's trade compared to total trade with each overseas area. Table

[13] These figures do not necessarily reflect the origin of the imports (or final desti-
nation of the exports) because most goods not of British or West Indian origin were
channelled through Great Britain to the colonies.

[14] *Historical Statistics*, p. 766.

TABLE 4
REGIONAL SHARES OF TOTAL COMMODITY EXPORTS TO
EACH OVERSEAS AREA, 1768-1772 (in percentages)

	Great Britain & Ireland	Southern Europe	West Indies	Africa	All Overseas Areas
Northern Colonies	2	25	2	0	6
New England	5	12	39	93	16
Middle Colonies	8	34	32	5	19
Upper South	57	19	13	0	39
Lower South	26	10	14	2	20
Flor., Ba., & Ber.	1	0	0	0	1

Source: See Table 2.

4 shows in percentage terms each region's share of total commodity
exports to each overseas area. Table 5 shows each region's share of
total imports from each overseas area. The southern regions dominated the export trade to Great Britain and Ireland with 57 percent
of all exports to Great Britain coming from the upper south and
26 percent coming from the lower south. In the export trade to
southern Europe, the middle colonies were the most important
(34 percent of the total), but the northern colonies held a significant share of this trade (25 percent). New England and the middle
colonies together dominated the export trade to the West Indies, and
New England overshadowed all others in the African trade. Out
of the total commodity export trade to all areas, 60 percent came
from the southern regions and 40 percent came from the colonies
to the north of Maryland.

The percentage of total colonial imports to each region from
each overseas area was relatively evenly balanced, especially in

TABLE 5
REGIONAL SHARES OF TOTAL COMMODITY IMPORTS FROM
EACH OVERSEAS AREA, 1768-1772 (in percentages)

	Great Britain & Ireland	Southern Europe	West Indies	Africa	All Overseas Areas
Northern Colonies	10	10	1	—	8
New England	20	23	43	—	24
Middle Colonies	26	42	32	—	28
Upper South	29	14	14	—	26
Lower South	13	9	9	—	12
Flor., Ba., & Ber.	2	2	1	—	2

Source: See Table 2.

the import trade from Great Britain (and from all areas combined). However, in the trade from southern Europe and the West Indies, the middle colonies and New England took the largest shares of imports from these areas, and there was a substantial redistribution of these imports in the coastal trade.[15]

132 It should be stressed that the above percentages show the relative importance of overseas markets and regions only in terms of commodities traded. When the sales of ships, the sales of shipping and other merchandizing services, and the slave trade are considered, the picture does change. Specifically, with regard to the export trade, the West Indies market appears to have been even more important to the thirteen colonies, and especially to the middle colonies and New England. Moreover, the degree of dominance of the southern regions in the export trade also changes when ship sales and especially invisible earnings are included, making the northern and southern regions more evenly balanced from the viewpoint of foreign exchange earnings. This has an equalizing effect on per capita as well as total foreign exchange earnings of the major colonial regions. This clearly illustrates the importance of invisible earnings to the development of the colonies. Not only did such earnings offset over three-fifths of the estimated overall deficit incurred from commodity trade for 1768-1772,[16] but they point out the growth and importance of shipping and commercial activities carried on by colonists themselves. This growth of a resident commercial sector undoubtedly had important implications for later development, and almost certainly it differentiates the development of the North American colonies from other colonial areas, such as Brazil and the regions colonized by the Spanish in North and South America.

After considering all items in the current account of the colonial balance of payments, our more detailed estimates for 1768-1772 together with those based on less complete evidence from the rest of the eighteenth century suggest that only very small deficits, if any, remained for the thirteen colonies. Consequently, we argue that foreign borrowing was not important to these colonies in the

---

[15] Shepherd and Williamson.
[16] Shepherd and Walton, "Estimates of 'Invisible' Earnings . . . ." A large source of additional earnings was the civil and defense expenditures of the British government in the colonies. These more than offset expenditures of foreign exchange on slaves and indentured servants, which were not included in the above discussion of commodity trade.

eighteenth century, and that capital accumulation was due to domestic rather than to foreign saving.[17] Foreign trade was important in other respects, however, and it is to an examination of this contention that we now turn.

II

The above estimates of per capita exports indicate that overseas trade grew at about the same high rate as population over the first three-quarters of the eighteenth century, and that this trade very likely was a significant part cf total output. Viewed analytically, changes in the value of this trade with overseas areas could come from either changes in demand in overseas markets or from changes in supply in the colonies. The growth of demand for colonial goods was certainly a major force of trade expansion; our attention here, however, is directed to changes that occurred on the supply side.

Consider the situation illustrated in Figure 1. Given the demand curve, D_{CIF}, in the overseas market, a shift of the supply curve, S_{CIF} to $\hat{S}_{CIF}$, would lower prices to overseas consumers and result in increased quantities purchased. This shift could stem from a reduction in the costs of the production in the colonies, indicated by the shift of S_{FOB} to $\hat{S}_{FOB}$, with distribution costs of AB ($= CF$) remaining unchanged. Alternatively the shift to $\hat{S}_{CIF}$ could be the result of falling distribution costs (with production costs, denoted by S_{FOB}, remaining unchanged) between the colonies and overseas markets (from AB to CE in Figure 1).

If the reduction in the costs of distribution represented long-run productivity advances, the gains to colonists can be approximately measured by the area $\overline{P}_2 EB\overline{P}_1$. The gains to overseas consumers can be roughly estimated by the area P_1ACP_2. The question to which we now turn is how significant were the costs of distribution and how important might have been the improvements in distribution that occurred. In terms of Figure 1, what proportion of P_1 was due to AB (distribution costs) at specific dates in time, and how significant was the decline in AB over the period?

The importance of distribution costs in the price of delivered goods varied significantly, of course, among commodities. They were generally a larger percentage of the value of low-valued,

133

---

[17] This contention is examined for 1768-1772 in detail in *ibid.*

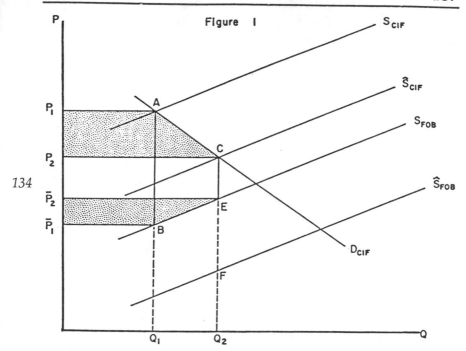

Figure I

134

high-bulk items, which were representative of most colonial exports, and a smaller percentage of expensive low-bulk wares, such as imported manufactures from Britain. Colonial merchants' accounts provide some evidence on the numerous explicit charges incurred in trade. From Table 6 we see that the explicit distribution charges on pitch—a fairly representative colonial export—amounted to more than one-half the value of gross sales.[18] In the late colonial period similar charges on wheat and flour were somewhat lower, being approximately one-quarter of gross sales. From the accounts of the same firm (Wallace, Davidson, and Johnson of Annapolis), we find that various charges (exclusive of English duty) averaged 64 percent of the net proceeds received by the colonial consignee of tobacco, or about 40 percent of gross sales.[19]

[18] The comparison of the explicit distribution charges on pitch in Table 6 to gross sales understates the importance of distribution costs in that the charges do not reflect the complete difference between a colonial planter's selling price and the price paid by a British or European merchant. The net proceeds include some inventory, packaging, insurance, and transport costs, as well as a return to the colonial merchant for his services and assumption of risk.
[19] Tobacco Sales Book, Wallace, Davidson, and Johnson, Maryland Hall of Records, Annapolis, Maryland.

TABLE 6
ACCOUNTS OF SALES, CHARGES, AND NET PROCEEDS ON
252 BARRELS OF PITCH SOLD IN LONDON, 1775

	£	s.	d.
Gross sales	203	9	6
Freight	71	17	6
Primage	2	1	8
Pierage	1	3	5
Duty	11	9	0
Sufferance and Duplicate	0	3	6
Landwaiters and Weighers	1	10	0
Oath	0	1	0
Weighers and Henekens	0	2	0
Post entry on 2 barrels	0	3	0
Land Surveyors for certificate	1	5	0
Passing certificate in the custom house	1	1	0
Clerk at the Navy office	0	2	6
Heneken for Wharfage	4	4	0
¼ discount allowed as per agreement and custom	2	10	10
Brokerage for attendance at weighing and making entries at 1%	2	6	0
Commission on gross sales at 2½%	5	1	8
Total charges	105	2	1
Net Proceeds	98	7	5

Source: Account and Invoice Book, Wallace, Davidson, and Johnson, Maryland Hall
of Records, Annapolis, Maryland.

These measures clearly indicate that distribution costs were a significant portion of the value of colonial goods traded in overseas markets on the eve of the American Revolution. Additional evidence indicates that distribution costs were even higher relative to the costs of production in earlier periods. For example, Nettels states: "Reports from New England stated that the price of English goods there was between 150 and 225 percent higher than in England; while at New York it was commonly said that foreign goods at twice their English prices were considered cheap."[20] Probably such statements referred to the retail prices of English goods in the colonial currency, which would have included the exchange differential between New England currencies and sterling, as well as the mark-up of the colonial merchant. Adjusting for the exchange differential,[21] this would mean that colonial prices were

[20] Curtis P. Nettels, "England's Trade with New England and New York, 1685-1720," *Publications of the Colonial Society of Massachusetts*, XXVIII (Feb. 1933), p. 326.

[21] Around the turn of the eighteenth century, 137 pounds in Massachusetts currency would buy 100 pounds sterling; see Curtis P. Nettels, *The Money Supply of the American Colonies before 1720* (New York: Augustus M. Kelly, 1964 [1934]), p. 181.

80 to 140 percent higher than the cost of the same goods in England. J. H. Soltow has said that Scottish traders in Virginia priced goods which cost £100 sterling in Britain at £175 in Virginia currency during the late colonial period (this included an exchange differential of between 15 to 25 percent as well as freight and other charges).[22] Adjusting for exchange differentials, this would suggest that British goods were selling from 40 to 50 percent higher in Virginia than their cost in Britain. Evidence from a Philadelphia merchant's accounts suggests that from 1748 to 1750 he was selling British goods in Pennsylvania currency for 2½ to 3 times (the average probably being closer to 3) their sterling cost to him.[23] Again adjusting for the exchange differential, this suggests that he was selling British goods from 45 to 75 percent higher than their cost in Britain. If the statements about the earlier eighteenth century are correct, the evidence suggests that the distribution costs from the British manufacturer to the colonial consumer declined significantly during the century.

136

Additional supporting evidence is available on tobacco, the major colonial export. For instance, in 1737 charges on a hogshead of tobacco (similar to those given in the accounts of Wallace, Davidson, and Johnson) were 75 percent or more of its cost in the colonies[24] (as compared with 64 percent in our example from 1774). Admittedly, these are isolated examples; but it is possible to view systematically an overall trend in the costs of distribution for tobacco by comparing tobacco prices in Philadelphia with those in Amsterdam. By the use of exchange rates and prices given in the sources to Figure 2, we have converted Philadelphia and Amsterdam prices to English sterling price equivalents for Virginia leaf tobacco.[25] Figure 2 shows the differences between Amsterdam and

[22] J. H. Soltow, "Scottish Traders in Virginia, 1750-1775," *The Economic History Review,* Second Series, XII, 1 (Aug. 1959), 93.

[23] Samuel Powel, Jr., Invoice and Day Book, 1748-1750, The Historical Society of Pennsylvania, Philadelphia, Pennsylvania.

[24] Lewis C. Gray, *History of Agriculture in the Southern United States to 1860* (Washington, D.C.: Carnegie Institute of Washington, 1933), I, p. 224. Gray's example was for a hogshead of 790 pounds, which would have been worth probably not more than 1½ d. per pound in the colonies. If the average price was lower, distribution costs as a percentage of colonial value would have been greater than 75 percent.

[25] Philadelphia prices of leaf tobacco and exchange rates between Pennsylvania currency and English sterling are given in Anne Bezanson, *et al., Prices in Colonial Pennsylvania* (Philadelphia: University of Pennsylvania Press, 1935), pp. 422 and 432, respectively. Amsterdam prices of Virginia leaf tobacco are given in N. W. Posthumus, *Inquiry into the History of Prices in Holland,* (Leiden: E. J. Brill, 1946),

FIGURE 2
A Comparison of Amsterdam and Philadelphia Tobacco Prices, 1720-72

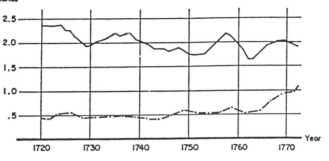

Source: N. W. Posthumus, *Inquiry Into the History of Prices in Holland* (Leiden:
E. J. Brill, 1946), I, pp. 202-203 and 597-602; and Anne Benzanson, *et al.*,
Prices in Colonial Pennsylvania (Philadelphia: University of Pennsylvania
Press, 1935), pp. 422 and 432. (See Footnote 25.)

Philadelphia prices, and clearly depicts a convergence of tobacco
prices between these areas. For each five-year period, the average
difference between the Amsterdam and Philadelphia prices as a
percentage of the Amsterdam price was:

1720-4	82%	1745-9	76%
1725-9	76	1750-4	67
1730-4	82	1755-9	72
1735-9	77	1760-4	70
1740-4	77	1765-9	65
		1770-4	51

This evidence clearly indicates that substantial improvements in
distribution occurred in the tobacco trade during the eighteenth
century.

Supporting evidence on the reduction in the costs of ocean transport, an important part of distribution costs, has been given elsewhere by Walton.[26] From that evidence, and from further sup-

I, pp. 202-03. Rates of exchange between schellingen and English sterling are given
in *ibid.*, pp. 597-602, for the years 1722-72; 20 schellingen equalled 6 guilden (*ibid.*,
p. LIV).

[26] Gary M. Walton, "Sources of Productivity Change in American Colonial Shipping, 1675-1775," *The Economic History Review*, Second Series, XX, 1 (April, 1967),
67-78; Walton, "A Measure of Productivity Change in American Colonial Shipping,"
The Economic History Review, Second Series, XXI, 2 (Aug. 1968), 268-82; and
Walton, "Obstacles to Technical Diffusion in Colonial Shipping, 1675-1775," *Explorations in Economic History*, VIII, 2 (Winter, 1970-71), 123-40.

porting evidence in the larger study, it appears that within the commercial sector, in general, and clearly in the shipping industry, in particular, improvements came from a variety of sources associated with the reduction of risks, increased information about markets, increased knowledge about doing business in these markets, and improvements in business organization. It is difficult to over-emphasize the importance of the growing security of trade. The mere growth of population had an important influence on the level of risks and possibilities due to the market. For instance, as settlement increased and trade expanded, the gains from better law enforcement, like that of removing pirates from the seas (and using international diplomacy to reduce privateering and the issues of letters of marque) came to exceed the costs of these actions, and it ultimately paid to use specialized naval facilities to eliminate piracy. Also, the growth of trade itself had important feedback effects, which lowered the costs of distribution and led to further expansion of trade. Information costs and the risks associated with trade were reduced as trade increased and commercial centers were established. Two examples may prove useful to describe the effects of these changes. First, in the Carribean trade, colonial shippers had to undertake a great deal of search and undergo an immense amount of petty detail in the process of exchange. Colonial goods had to be sold and return cargoes acquired at the best possible prices. To find the best markets (for delivery and purchase) required much search, and then there were the problems of quality variation, credit, media of exchange, currencies of fluctuating value, as well as others which had to be settled. The strengthening of commercial ties as trade developed reduced these problems. Second, in the Chesapeake trade, we have a fairly clear account of numerous changes that lowered the marketing costs of tobacco. As the production and trade of tobacco increased, it became profitable to establish centrally located warehouses for the storage of tobacco. This reduced the costs of search and lowered port and inventory times. Also, certificates of tobacco deposits came to be used as a medium of exchange, and this led to inspection systems which permitted quality control of tobacco. These and other improvements, such as productivity advances in the packaging of tobacco, permitted a marked reduction in the difference between the price of tobacco in the colonies and in Europe. As stated above, the price of Virginia leaf tobacco in Amsterdam was nearly four times the Philadelphia

138

price in the early eighteenth century, but by 1770 it was only about twice as high as in Philadelphia. It was these and similar improvements that played such an important role in the commercial growth of the period. By comparison, the qualitative evidence pertaining to technological change suggests that it was an unimportant aspect of this development.[27]

III

Our hope is that this and the larger study will add significantly to an understanding of American colonial economic development, and *139* to the nexus between the external relations of the colonies and this development. Our estimates make clear not only the patterns, but also the magnitudes of colonial overseas trade. Important conclusions, such as the unimportance of foreign investment (in the eighteenth century), and the importance of invisible earnings and the development of a resident commercial sector, emerge from these estimates. These estimates also show that production for overseas markets was an important part of overall economic activity.

We conclude that this development and growth of a market economy in the colonies held important consequences for increased productivity for economic activity in the colonies. Not only did the growth of market trade promote specialization of production for markets, but improvements in transportation and distribution were

---

[27] We do not mean to imply that no other factors contributed to economic growth in the colonies. A growing stock of capital was undoubtedly an important source of growth, but our concern here has been with possible sources of productivity increase. With regard to productivity, one might wonder about the contribution of increasing specialization in view of the above estimates of per capita exports, which were roughly stable over the first 75 years of the eighteenth century (without additional information about the extent of market trade, and knowledge of the production functions for colonial products, it is impossible to say anything more). We do think, nevertheless, that the evidence supports our contention that improvements in distribution made an important contribution to growth. Take, for instance, a *hypothetical* example (and we stress hypothetical). Suppose the annual average rate of growth of per capita output from 1700 to 1775 was one-half of 1 percent, and that about 25 percent of output was produced for markets. Then the required annual rate of growth in market output per capita that would have been necessary to produce this rate of growth (of per capita output) would have been 2 percent (neglecting the complexities of compound rates and assuming increased productivity occurred only in activities associated with production for markets). If one-half of this 2 percent increase in per capita market output was due to an increasing stock of capital, and one-half to increasing productivity, it seems entirely possible to us that the major share of this hypothetical 1 percent rate of growth of per capita market output (due to increasing productivity) came from improvements in distribution.

themselves a very important source of increased productivity. These increases of productivity in shipping and other activities associated with distribution clearly indicate economic growth was occurring in the colonies, however slowly. Finally, we hope that from this others will be encouraged to do further research into distributional activities, especially those other than shipping which have been relatively neglected by economic historians as a source of growth.

JAMES F. SHEPHERD, *Whitman College*
GARY M. WALTON, *Indiana University*

The Transformation of Urban Politics 1700-1765

GARY B. NASH

T HAT colonial politics were highly factional and unstable is a familiar theme in early American history. Like pieces of colored glass in kaleidoscopic arrangement, it is said, factions came and went, shifting with time, place, circumstances, and the personalities of leaders. But rarely, according to the historical studies of recent decades, did these groupings develop the organizational machinery, the coherence, the continuity, or the political sophistication of the political parties which emerged in the aftermath of the American Revolution.[1]

Historians have attempted primarily to unravel the legislative history of these factional struggles, especially as they pitted representative assemblies against royal or proprietary governors and officeholders, and to invest these contests with either economic or ideological significance. Thus scholars know a great deal about struggles over parliamentary privileges, the power of the purse, and control of the courts. Historians have passed through almost a century of argument which has cyclically explained political contention as a clashing of rival social and economic groups or, alternatively, as a Whiggish struggle against prerogative government. But for all of this investigation, little is known about the actual practice and style of electoral politics in the first two thirds of the eighteenth century.

By taking political factionalism as given, playing down the issues dividing factions, and shifting the analysis from the motivations of political groups, it is possible to focus on the practice of factional politics and on the kind of political ethos or culture which was emerging in the period before 1765. An examination of three cities which would become instrumental in

Gary B. Nash is professor of history in the University of California, Los Angeles.

[1] Bernard Bailyn, *The Origins of American Politics* (New York, 1968); Jack P. Greene, "Changing Interpretations of Early American Politics," Ray A. Billington, ed., *The Reinterpretation of Early American History: Essays in honor of John Edwin Pomfret* (New York, 1968), 151-84.

the coming of the Revolution—Boston, New York, and Philadelphia—
yields compelling evidence that in the six decades before the Stamp Act
crisis a "radical" mode of politics was evolving in the urban centers of colonial life.[2] This "transformation" involved activation of previously quiescent lower-class elements; the organization of political clubs, caucuses, and
tickets; the employment of political literature and inflammatory rhetoric as
never before; the involvement of the clergy and the churches in politics; and
the organization of mobs and violence for political purposes. Although
many of these innovations were managed by and for political élites and not
intended to democratize colonial political life, the effect was to broaden the
spectrum of individuals actively involved in public affairs and to produce a
political culture that was far from deferential, increasingly anti-authoritar-
ian, occasionally violent, and often destructive of the very values which the
political élite wished to preserve.

At election time in 1726, a prominent Quaker merchant in Philadelphia
wrote an English friend that "we have our Mobs, Bonfires, Gunns, Huzzas
. . . Itinerations and processions too—Trains made up (as 'tis said) not of
the Wise, the Rich or the Learned, for the Gentleman while he was Gov-
ernour took care to discard all Such. . . ."[3] In this description Isaac Norris
expressed his dismay that Governor William Keith, who no longer felt
obliged to serve the interests of his employer, the widow of William Penn,
had cultivated the support of a stratum of society that the "wise, Rich and
Learned" believed had no place in the political process. Since 1723, in fact,
Keith had been mobilizing support among lower-class workingmen in Philadelphia and newly arrived German and Scotch-Irish immigrants.

Elitist politicians and proprietary supporters complained bitterly of "Sir
William's town Mob" and the governor's "sinister army," lamented that
elections were "mobbish and carried by a levelling spirit," and charged that
the "common People both in town & Country" were "blown up even to a
degree of madness."[4] Of the 1726 elections Norris wrote that Keith had

---

[2] Eighteenth-century writers employed the term "radical" only infrequently; and when
they did, they meant "root" or "basic." Thus Samuel Davies looked for an "*outpouring of
the Spirit*" as the "grand, radical, all-comprehensive blessing" in 1757; and "Plain Dealer,"
writing from Philadelphia in 1764, asserted that the cause of Pennsylvania's troubles "is
radical, interwoven in the Constitution, and so become of the very Nature of Proprietary
Governments." See Alan Heimert, *Religion and the American Mind from the Great Awakening to the Revolution* (Cambridge, Mass., 1966), 13; [Hugh Williamson], *Plain Dealer*
#2 (Philadelphia, 1764), 7. The term is used here to mean not only basic but also basic in
its tendency to shift power downward in a society where politics had heretofore been corporate and élitist in nature.

[3] Isaac Norris to Jonathan Scarth, Oct. 21, 1726, Letter Book, 1716-1730, Isaac Norris
Papers (Historical Society of Pennsylvania, Philadelphia).

[4] Thomas Wendel, "The Keith-Lloyd Alliance: Factional and Coalition Politics in Colonial
Pennsylvania," *Pennsylvania Magazine of History and Biography*, XCII (July 1968), 298,
296n, 301.

"perambulated" the city, "Popping into ye dramshops tiff & alehouses where he would find a great number of modern statesmen & some patriots settling affairs, cursing some, praising others, contriving laws & swearing they will have them enacted *cum multis aegis*." Worse still, Keith's electoral victory was celebrated by an exuberant procession, "mostly made of Rabble Butchers porters & Tagrags—thus triumphantly has he made his Gradations Downward from a Government to an Equal with Every plain Country Member."[5]

Keith's attempt to build a broader political base in order to gain control of an assembly dominated by Quakers was not the first attempt in Philadelphia to develop new sources of political support to defeat an entrenched opponent. Two decades before, David Lloyd had accomplished a substantial shift of political power by expanding the politically relevant strata of Pennsylvania society and activating a part of the community that had played an insignificant role in politics. Though his real goal was to shield Pennsylvania from proprietary authority, not to shift the center of political gravity downward, Lloyd found that—given the power of the proprietary group—it was mandatory to establish a new base of political support.[6]

This technique of mobilizing the politically inert became increasingly more important to eighteenth-century political life. For the Pennsylvania Quakers, who had overcome earlier disunity and formed a strong anti-proprietary party, the problem was how to maintain influence in a society where they were fast becoming a minority. For the proprietary party, the problem was how to develop popular sources of support in order to overcome Quaker domination of the assembly. Thus both factions, led by men of high position and reputation, nervously began to eye the Germans who were streaming into the colony after 1715. Neither the Quaker-dominated anti-proprietary or "Assembly" party nor the Anglican-based proprietary party welcomed the inundation of German immigrants who were regarded by Englishmen of both groups as crude, alien, and too numerous. But both factions cultivated their support. That the Quakers continued to control the assembly throughout the half-century preceding the Revolution, despite their fading numerical importance, was attributable largely to their success in politicizing the Germans, who were more interested in farming than leg-

143

---

[5] Norris to Scarth, Oct. 21, 1728, Letter Book, 1716-1730, Norris Papers. Eight years later, commenting on the residual effects of William Keith's politics, Norris would write with displeasure that the "usual care was taken to bring in Crowds of Journeymen & such like in opposition." Norris to his son, Oct. 2, 1734, Copy Book of Letters, 1730-1735, *ibid.*

[6] Gary B. Nash, *Quakers and Politics, Pennsylvania, 1681-1726* (Princeton, 1968), 294-99.

islative assemblies but found themselves dragged into the thicket of politics.[7]

With even greater misgivings, the proprietary party courted the German community, which by the 1750s represented about 40 percent of the population in Pennsylvania. In private discourse and correspondence its leaders continued to regard the Germans as "an uncultivated Race" of uncouth peasants, incapable, as one put it, "of using their own Judgment in matters of Government. . . ."[8] But political requirements conquered social and ethnic reservations, and, while proprietary leaders could describe the Germans in 1750 as "more licentious and impotent of a just government than any others" and "a body of ignorant, proud stubborn Clowns," they worked hard to split the German vote, as they had been doing since about 1740.[9] This drive for German support yielded only meager rewards in the political battles of the mid-1750s, but by 1764 the proprietary campaign was crowned with success. Benjamin Franklin and Joseph Galloway attributed their loss in the hotly contested election of that year to the "Dutch vote" which had swung against them.[10] Proprietary leaders would have preferred to exert political leverage from power bases where men were appointed out of regard for their background, accomplishments, and standing in the community—the council, city corporation, College of Philadelphia, hospital, and Library Company.[11] But gradually—and reluctantly—proprietary politicians learned to seek support from groups which they would have preferred

144

(margin: 144)

---

[7] Arthur D. Graeff, *The Relations Between The Pennsylvania Germans and The British Authorities (1750-1776)* (Philadelphia, 1939); Dietmar Rothermund, *The Layman's Progress: Religious and Political Experience in Colonial Pennsylvania, 1740-1770* (Philadelphia, 1961); Glenn Weaver, "Benjamin Franklin and the Pennsylvania Germans," *William and Mary Quarterly*, XIV (Oct. 1957), 536-59; John J. Zimmerman, "Benjamin Franklin and the Quaker Party, 1755-1756," *ibid.*, XVII (July 1960), 291-313.

[8] Graeff, *Pennsylvania Germans*, 61-63.

[9] James Hamilton to Thomas Penn, Nov. 8, 1750, Official Correspondence, V, 88, Penn Family Papers (Historical Society of Pennsylvania, Philadelphia); [William Smith], *A Brief State of the Province of Pennsylvania, in which the Conduct of their Assemblies for several Years past is impartially examined, and the true Cause of the continual Encroachments of the French displayed, more especially the secret Design of their late unwarrantable Invasion and Settlement upon the River Ohio. To which is annexed . . .* (London, 1755), 40. By 1764 William Smith would be defending the "industrious Germans" from what he claimed were Benjamin Franklin's reference to them—after they defected from Franklin's party in large numbers—as "a wretched rabble." Leonard W. Labaree and others, eds., *The Papers of Benjamin Franklin* (16 vols., New Haven, 1959-   ), XI, 505. The attempts of the proprietary party to recruit the German vote in the early 1740s can be followed in the letters of the party leaders, James Allen and Richard Peters, to John Penn and Thomas Penn, Official Correspondence, III, Penn Family Papers.

[10] Labaree and others, eds., *Papers of Benjamin Franklin*, XI, 397; Weaver, "Franklin and the Pennsylvania Germans," 550.

[11] G. B. Warden, "The Proprietary Group in Pennsylvania, 1754-1764," *William and Mary Quarterly*, XXI (July 1964), 367-89.

to regard as inadmissible to political life. The problem of challenging the legislative strength of their opponents could not otherwise be solved.

Just as members of the proprietary party learned to overcome their scruples with regard to involving Germans in the political process, they learned to swallow reservations about soliciting the support of lower-class mechanics and laborers. Galloway, a Quaker party stalwart, took great delight in pointing out that the "Gentlemen of the best fortune" in the proprietary party, who in their public statements spoke for hierarchy and order in all affairs, "thought it not mean or dishonourable to enter the Houses of the Lowest Mechanics to solicit their Opposition" to the Militia Act of 1756.[12] By 1764 these artisans would become all-important in the attempts of the proprietary party to defeat their opponents.

In New York a similar process was taking place, although attempts to mobilize a broad-based electorate were not as continuous. Jacob Leisler was perhaps the first to seek support among those whom by traditional thinking were better left outside the political arena. Leisler also relied upon the support of the Dutch who would continue to play a crucial role in electoral politics throughout the pre-Revolutionary period. Unlike the Germans in Philadelphia, however, the Dutch were well represented at all levels of the social structure and were well integrated into the social and economic fabric of New York City at the beginning of the eighteenth century.

Only a few years after Keith so effectively organized the artisanry of Philadelphia, the fires of political contention in New York, banked briefly after the Leislerian era by the adroit management of Governor Robert Hunter, grew hot enough to convince upper-class leaders that they must delve to deeper strata in society to develop political support. The heavy-handed aggrandizement of power by Governor William Cosby and a decisive defeat in the assembly elections of 1727 were enough to convince the Morris party that they must play the game of tavern politics if they hoped to prevail. The city elections of 1733 and 1734, which among other things led to the trial of John Peter Zenger for seditious libel, reflected this new appeal to workingmen and the Dutch in the city.[13] That both sides could play the same game is evident in the attempts of Stephen De Lancey and Francis Harrison, members of the governor's inner circle, to carry the aldermanic election in the South Ward in 1734 by sending a troop of English

[margin note] 145

---

[12] [Joseph Galloway], *A True and Impartial State of the Province of Pennsylvania: Containing an Exact Account of the Nature of Its Government, the Power of its Proprietaries, and Their Governors . . . also the Rights and Privileges of the Assembly and People . . .* (Philadelphia, 1759), 61.

[13] Stanley N. Katz, *Newcastle's New York: Anglo-American Politics, 1732-1753* (Cambridge, Mass., 1968), 68-70, 83-85; Bailyn, *Origins of American Politics,* 108-11.

soldiers from Fort George to the polls; and in the remarkable invitations of
Governor Cosby himself, as Cadwallader Colden noted indignantly, to
"many of low rank to dine with him such as had never pretended or expected so much respect."[14] These attempts at political mobilization were
carried even further in 1737, if Colden can be believed. Describing the municipal elections he wrote: "The sick, the lame, and the blind were all carried to vote. They were carried out of Prison and out of the poor house to
vote. Such a struggle I never saw and such a hurra[h]ing that above one
half of the men in town are so hoarse that they cannot speak this day. The
pole lasted from half an hour after nine in the morning till past nine at
night."[15]

The ambition and energy of the De Lancey brothers, Stephen and Oliver,
pushed the process a step further during the next decade. In their hatred of
Governor George Clinton, who held office in New York from 1743 to
1753, the De Lanceys carefully cultivated the support of the large mechanic
population in the city—an attempt, as Clinton complained, "to overturn his
Majesty's Government by wresting the Power out of the Hands of His Officers, and placing it in a popular faction."[16] To the imperious Colden the
sight of rich assembly candidates courting workingmen conjured up the re-
membrance that "true roman virtue was allmost totally extinguished before
their great or rich men went about to court the common people for their
votes." Colden hoped the "lower rank" in New York would not become "so
low & weak as to take it as favour to be call'd by their names by rich men &
to be shook by the hand," as had happened centuries ago while the Roman
Empire was crumbling.[17]

Charges by élitists such as Colden and Clinton that opponents were attempting to rule by "meer popular influence" or were attempting "to insti-
gate the passions of the lowest rank of people to the most wicked purposes"
must be approached with caution.[18] But analysis of the three assembly
elections of the 1760s indicates that the work of politicizing the laboring
class had proceeded far enough to make it all but impossible to win elec-

[14] Nicholas Varga, "New York Politics and Government in the Mid-Eighteenth Century,"
(doctoral dissertation, Fordham University, 1960), 397; *The Letters and Papers of Cadwallader Colden* (9 vols., New York, 1918-1937), IX, 298.

[15] *Letters and Papers of Cadwallader Colden*, II, 179 (punctuation added).

[16] Quoted in Katz, *Newcastle's New York*, 175.

[17] *Letters and Papers of Cadwallader Colden*, IV, 214, III, 313-14, 318-19.

[18] *Ibid.*, III, 390, 319. In 1740 Clinton accused Oliver De Lancey of working "openly and
in all companyes, and among the lower rank of people" to defeat the governor's friends.
Clinton to Duke of Bedford, June 12, 1750, in John R. Brodhead and others, eds., *Documents Relative to the Colonial History of the State of New York* (15 vols., Albany, 1853-
1887), VI, 571.

toral contests without the support not only of the skilled artificers, who often owned considerable property, but also the unskilled laborers, cartmen, mariners, and boatmen.[19] It is also important to note that the factional fighting that went on from the late 1720s through the 1760s sent all leaders scurrying after the Dutch vote. The Morris party did its best to cultivate the Dutch at the beginning of this period, as did the De Lancey faction at mid-century.[20] In the mid-1750s when New York was inflamed by the controversy over King's College, both sides recognized that the support of the Dutch was crucial and exhausted all means to obtain it. The inability of William Livingston and his partisans to win a large part of the Dutch vote explains more than anything else the shattered hopes of the Presbyterian faction in its attempt to prevent the Anglicans from obtaining a charter for the college.[21] The effect of this competition for Dutch support was to split an ethnic bloc which early in the century had been virtually unified at the polls.[22]

147

In Boston the process of activating the inactive proceeded along some-

[19] Roger J. Champagne, "Liberty Boys and Mechanics of New York City, 1764-1774," Labor History, 8 (Spring 1967), 124-31; Milton M. Klein, "Democracy and Politics in Colonial New York," New York History, XL (July 1959), 238-39; Milton M. Klein, "Politics and Personalities in Colonial New York," ibid., XLVII (Jan. 1966), 5-10.

[20] Katz, Newcastle's New York, 84; Milton M. Klein, "The American Whig: William Livingston of New York" (doctoral dissertation, Columbia University, 1954), 450. Historians have neglected the role of the Dutch in New York City politics, although they comprised about 35 percent of the electorate in the 1760s.

[21] Klein, "American Whig," 402. See also Beverly McAnear, "American Imprints Concerning King's College," Papers of the Bibliographic Society of America, 44 (Fourth Quarter 1950), 315.

[22] The extent to which ethnic bloc voting broke down in the eighteenth century is dramatically apparent in a comparison of surnames on the 1701 and 1761 poll lists that give the names of the electors for each candidate. All the percentages are higher on the 1761 breakdown because voters were choosing four representatives from a slate of six candidates whereas in the 1701 election (three wards only) voters were choosing one of two candidates. For the 1701 list, see Minutes of the Common Council of the City of New York, 1675-1776 (8 vols., New York, 1905), II, 163-78. For the 1761 list, see A Copy of the Poll List of the Election for Representatives for the City and County of New York which election began on Monday the 23rd day of January and ended on Friday the 27th day of the same month in the year of our Lord . . . . (New York, 1880). The author is indebted to Joyce Goodfriend for an analysis of surnames.

	1701 Percentage of		1761 Percentage of	
	English Vote	Dutch Vote	English Vote	Dutch Vote
Candidate 1	73.7	11.5	83.1	85.0
Candidate 2	93.2	13.5	72.1	73.4
Candidate 3	94.1	24.4	59.0	76.1
Candidate 4	26.3	88.5	68.3	57.9
Candidate 5	6.8	86.5	60.4	55.7
Candidate 6	5.9	75.6	55.4	54.3

what different lines but in the same direction. Unlike Philadelphia and New York, Boston had a population that was ethnically homogeneous. Throughout the colonial period factional leaders appealed for the support of a mass of English voters only lightly sprinkled with Scotch and Irish. Boston was also different in that ever since an armed crowd had mysteriously gathered in April 1689 to command the streets of Boston and force Edmund Andros into exile, its citizens, at all levels of society, had been far less quiescent than their counterparts in other urban centers. This may be partially explained by the effect on the political life of the city which the town meeting fostered.[23] In Boston, as in no other city, open debate was heard and decisions were made by majority vote on many issues, ranging from passing a bylaw "to prevent playing football in the streets" to voting £10 to Susana Striker for a kidney stone operation for her son, to taxing inhabitants for the erection of public buildings, poor relief, school teachers' salaries, and other expenses.[24] And whereas in New York and Philadelphia only a small number of municipal officers were elected, in Boston the voters installed not only selectmen, sheriffs, assessors, and constables, but surveyors of hemp, informers about deer, purchasers of grain, haywards, town criers, measurers of salt, scavengers, viewers of shingles, sheepreeves, hogreeves, sealers of leather, fenceviewers, firewards, cullers of stave hoops, auditors, and others.[25]

Thus in terms of a politically minded and active lower rank, Boston had already developed by the early eighteenth century what other urban centers haltingly and sporadically moved toward in the half century before 1765. Governor Cosby of New York pointed up this difference in 1735 when he charged the Morris faction, which was working the streets of New York to stir up opposition, with copying "the example and spirit of the Boston people."[26]

But if the clay with which leaders of political factions worked was of a somewhat different consistency in Boston, the problems of delving deeper in society to insure political victory was essentially the same. Thus the "soft money" faction led by Elisha Cooke, Oliver Noyes, Thomas Cushing, and William Clark "turned to the people as the only possible base of political

[23] See G. B. Warden, *Boston, 1689-1776* (Boston, 1970), 28-33.
[24] William H. Whitmore and others, eds., *Reports of the Record Commissioners of Boston* (39 vols., Boston, 1880-1902), VIII, 12, 23, XII, *passim.*
[25] In New York annual elections were held for the aldermen and assistants of the municipal corporation and for assessors, collectors, and constables. In Philadelphia the municipal corporation was self-perpetuating, but sheriffs, commissioners, assessors, and coroners were elected annually.
[26] Katz, *Newcastle's New York*, 83-84.

strength in Boston and took it upon [themselves] to organize politics and elections in the town with unprecedented vigor and attention" in the 1720s.[27] In the following decade, when a series of economic issues in Boston came to a head, and in the 1740s, when the second currency crisis ripened, exceptional measures were again taken to call upon those not included in the ranks of respectability. "Interested Men," complained Peter Oliver in 1749, had "set the Canaille to insult" Thomas Hutchinson for his leadership of the conservative fiscal movement.[28] In this way political leaders recruited the support of lower-class artisans and mechanics whose bodies provided a new kind of political power, as demonstrated in three mob actions of the 1740s in Boston directed by men of stature in the community, and whose votes provided the margin of victory in the increasingly frequent contested elections.[29]

To engage in political mobilization, factional leaders found they had to pursue a course which ran against the grain of their social philosophy. Given the widely shared belief in maintaining rank and order in all human affairs and the rationalist view that only the cultivation of the mind raised man above his naturally depraved state, it was to be expected that the gentility would look upon courting the favor of "the lesser sorts" or involving them in politics as a reckless policy containing the seeds of anarchy. To activate the multitude was to energize precisely that part of society which was ruled by passion—the baser impulses in human nature—rather than by reason. The letters and reports of leaders in Boston, New York, and Philadelphia are filled with allusions to "the rabble," "the unthinking multitude," and the dangers of exciting "the passions" of the populace. Although these fears resonated most strongly in conservative quarters, they were shared by popular leaders such as Livingston and Franklin, who were also concerned

149

[27] Warden, *Boston*, 92.

[28] Douglas Adair and John A. Schutz, eds., *Peter Oliver's Origin & Progress of the American Rebellion: A Tory View* (San Marino, Cal., 1961), 32.

[29] Eighteenth-century elections were by no means always contested. One measure of politicization is the frequency of contested elections. A few preliminary statistics for Boston may be illustrative. Defining a contested election as one in which the candidate was opposed and lost at least 25 percent of the vote, one can trace a rise in oppositional politics from the 1720s (when voting statistics for General Court elections are first regularly available) through the 1750s.

Boston Election Contests

Decade	Number of Contested Seats
1720–1729	14/45 (31.1%)
1730–1739	23/48 (47.9%)
1740–1749	25/45 (55.0%)
1750–1759	24/40 (60.0%)

with preserving social hierarchy and respect for authority. It was more difficult, of course, for those with a more rigid and authoritarian outlook to
reconcile the eighteenth-century rationalist philosophy with the necessity of
campaigning for votes and adopting the techniques of popular politics. But
when political necessity called, they too learned to set aside ingrained social
principles. The best that could be hoped for was that somehow the support
of unassimilated or lower-class elements could be engaged without altering
the structure of values by which such groups deferred to élitist politicians.
Men at the top had embarked upon a radical course of political recruitment
while hoping that these stratagems would not have radical effects.

150   Because all factions felt the necessity of broadening the political base, the
dynamics of politics changed markedly. In a society in which the people at
large acquiesced in the rule of the upper stratum, and in which social, economic, and political leadership were regarded as indivisible, political decisions could be made quietly and privately. Elites would be held in check, of
course, by periodic tests of confidence administered by the propertied part
of the community. But when the upper layer of society split into competing
factions, which were obliged to recruit the support of those previously inert
or outside the political process, then politics became open, abusive in tone,
and sometimes violent.

New techniques of political organization were required. Men began to
form political "tickets," as happened in Pennsylvania as early as 1705, in
Boston at the end of the 1720s, and in New York probably in the 1730s.
Leaders of the more conservative factions usually resisted this move in the
direction of popular politics. Philadelphia conservatives James Logan and
Norris, for example, decried the use of tickets that obliged the voter to
"have eight men crammed down his throat at once."[30] The use of tickets
was also accompanied by written balloting and the introduction of the caucus—closed at first—to nominate a slate of candidates. Thus Quaker leaders in the 1720s loudly declaimed Keith's "Electing-Club" in Philadelphia.[31]
But within a few decades the anti-Quaker proprietary leaders would be
complaining bitterly that the Quakers used their yearly meeting, which met
during the week before assembly elections, as a political caucus—a practice
condemned in 1755 as "the finest Scheme that could possibly be projected
for conducting political Intrigues, under the Mask of Religion."[32] Yielding

[30] Edward Armstrong, ed., *The Correspondence between William Penn and James Logan*
(2 vols., Philadelphia, 1870-1872), II, 188, 336, 427.
[31] Norris to Joseph Pike, Oct. 28, 1728, Letter Book, 1716-1730, Norris Papers; *A Modest
Apology for the Eight Members* ... (Philadelphia, 1728).
[32] [William Smith], *A Brief State*, 26; Peters to Thomas Penn, Aug. 25, Nov. 17, 1742,
Letter Book, 1737-1750, Richard Peters Papers (Historical Society of Pennsylvania, Philadelphia).

to the realities of political life, the proprietary leaders in 1756 adopted the tactics of their opponents and even outdid the Quaker party by calling for open rather than private caucuses. A notice in the *Pennsylvania Gazette* summoned the electorate to the Philadelphia Academy for an open-air, on-the-spot primary election. Ideological consistency was abandoned as Quaker party writers condemned the innovation in the next issue of the newspaper, only to be attacked by the aristocratic proprietary spokesman who defended the rights of the freeholders "to meet in a peaceable Manner to chuse their Representatives."[33] Seeing a chance for electoral success in the Quaker opposition to war appropriations, the proprietary leaders put scruples aside and resorted to tactics that heretofore had offended their sense of political propriety.

151

In Boston popular politics came under the control of perhaps the best organized caucus in the English colonial world. So far as the limited evidence indicates, the Boston caucus was organized about 1719 and functioned intermittently for about four decades before splitting into the North End Caucus and South End Caucus. The Boston caucus nominated candidates for the city's four seats in the General Court and proposed selectmen and other town officials at the annual elections. Operating in the taverns, it perfected a network of political influence through affiliations with the independent fire companies, the Merchants' Club, and other social organizations.[34]

In New York the devices of popular politics were less in evidence than in Philadelphia or Boston because New York did not have annual assembly elections and employed viva-voce voting rather than the written ballot. Though a secret balloting law had been "long desired by . . . Friends to Liberty in this City," according to a political writer a few years before the Revolution, such a law had never passed.[35] Nonetheless, popular politics took a long stride forward in 1739 with the replacement of the private nomination of assembly candidates by public nominating meetings. As Carl Becker noted half a century ago, this change constituted a recognition on the part of political leaders that "great numbers constituted as good a political asset as great names."[36] The origins of this innovation may be traced

---

[33] *Pennsylvania Gazette*, Sept. 12, 19, 1756. See also William R. Steckel, "Pietist in Colonial Pennsylvania: Christopher Sauer, Printer, 1738-1758" (doctoral dissertation, Stanford University, 1949), 233-44.

[34] G. B. Warden, "The Caucus and Democracy in Colonial Boston," *New England Quarterly*, XLIII (March 1970), 19-33.

[35] New York *Gazette*, Jan. 8, 1770; Bernard Friedman, "The New York Assembly Elections of 1768 and 1769: The Disruption of Family Politics," *New York History*, XLVI (Jan. 1965), 17-18.

[36] Carl L. Becker, "The History of Political Parties in the Province of New York, 1760-1776," *Bulletin of the University of Wisconsin*, II (1909-1910), 18.

back to the work of the Morris-Alexander-Smith coalition against Governor Cosby in the early 1730s, although the first solid evidence of the open caucus is found in 1739 when the New York *Gazette* reported that "a great number of the freeholders and freemen of the . . . city have agreed and resolved to choose the following persons to represent them. . . ."[37]

An even more significant element in transforming positions from a private to a public affair was the use of the press. Although the political press had been used extensively in seventeenth-century England, it was not widely employed in colonial politics until the 1720s. Before that an occasional pamphlet had directed the attention of the public to a controversial issue. But such early polemical efforts as Joseph Palmer, *The Present State of New England* (Boston, 1689), or Thomas Lloyd, *A Seasonable Advertisement to the Freemen of this Province* . . . (Philadelphia, 1689), were beamed at the General Court or the assembly, though their authors probably hoped also to cultivate the support of the populace at large. "Campaign literature"—direct appeals to the freemen at election time—was rare in Boston before 1710, in Philadelphia before 1720, and in New York before 1730. But as issues became more heated and politicians discovered the need to reach a wider audience, the resort to the press became a fixed part of political culture. In Philadelphia, for example, where only five pieces of political literature had appeared in the first quarter of the century, the public was bombarded with forty-six pamphlets and broadsides between 1725 and 1728. Bostonians in 1721 and 1722 could spend their evenings in tavern discussions of any of the twenty-eight argumentative tracts on the currency crisis that appeared in those years. In New York, where the political press was somewhat more restrained in the pre-Revolutionary period than in Boston or Philadelphia, the Morris-Cosby struggle for power brought twenty-seven pamphlets from the presses between 1732 and 1734, when only an occasional piece had appeared before.[38]

By the 1740s the printed word had become an indispensable part of campaigning. In every contested election pamphleteers industriously alerted the public to the awful consequences that would attend a victory by the other

---

[37] Quoted in Carl L. Becker, "Nominations in Colonial New York," *American Historical Review*, VI (Jan. 1901), 272. Another important aspect of popular politics was the proliferation of clubs which became both social and political organisms. These operated in all the cities from early in the eighteenth century and seem to have increased rapidly in the third quarter of the century. By the 1750s cultural and civic groups such as Franklin's Junto in Philadelphia, the Library Society in New York, and fire companies in all cities had also been highly politicized, much to the dismay of some of their founders.

[38] The pamphlets were identified in Charles Evans, *American Bibliography* (14 vols., Chicago and Worcester, Mass., 1903-1959); and Clifford K. Shipton and James E. Mooney, *National Index of American Imprints Through 1800: The Short-Title Evans* (2 vols. [Worcester, Mass.], 1969).

side. When the excise bill was under consideration in 1754, seventeen pamphlets appeared in the streets of Boston to rally public support against it.[39] The King's College controversy in New York kept the city's two printers busy with the publication of several dozen efforts.[40] In Philadelphia the Paxton Massacre was argued pro-and-con in at least twenty-eight pamphlets, and in the election contest that followed in the fall of 1764 no less than forty-four pamphlets and broadsides were published, many with German editions.[41] A rise in polemical literature and election appeals is also evident in colonial newspapers which were increasing in number in the eighteenth century.[42]

This increase in the use of the press had important implications, not merely because of the quantity of political literature but also because the pamphlets and newspaper creeds were intended to make politics everyone's concern. The new political literature was distributed without reference to social standing or economic position and "accustomed people of all classes, but especially of the middling and lower estates, to the examination and discussion of controversial issues of all sorts."[43] Thus, those whom even the most conservative politicians would not have formally admitted to the political arena were drawn into it informally.

The anguished cries of politicians about the dangerous effects of this new

153

[39] Paul S. Boyer, "Borrowed Rhetoric: The Massachusetts Excise Controversy of 1754," *William and Mary Quarterly*, XXI (July 1964), 328-51.

[40] See McAnear, "American Imprints Concerning King's College," 301-39.

[41] Many, although by no means all, of the pamphlets are reprinted in John R. Dunbar, ed., *The Paxton Papers* (The Hague, 1957), or discussed in J. Philip Gleason, "A Scurrilous Colonial Election and Franklin's Reputation," *William and Mary Quarterly*, XVIII (Jan. 1961), 68-84.

[42] The sheer bulk of this literature grew rapidly in the second quarter of the century, though tapering off in New York and Boston thereafter. Election day sermons are not included in the figures for Boston.

Number of Pamphlets

Decade	Boston	New York	Philadelphia
1695–1704	6	5	2
1705–1714	12	3	2
1715–1724	40	0	2
1725–1734	28	32	43
1735–1744	37	13	15
1745–1754	38	26	15
1755–1764	26	19	109

[43] Carl Bridenbaugh, "The Press and the Book in Eighteenth—Century Philadelphia," *Pennsylvania Magazine of History and Biography*, LXV (Jan. 1941), 5. Although it is difficult to determine precisely who read—or was affected by—this literature, it is clear that for a few pounds an interested politician could supply every eligible voter in a city such as Philadelphia with a copy of an election polemic. One to three thousand copies of election pamphlets such as these were often printed in Philadelphia. Of equal significance, election pamphlets and broadsides were commonly read aloud at the polls.

polemical literature give a clue to the ambivalent feelings which the élite held in regard to the use of the press. An optimist like Franklin looked upon fiery pamphlets and newspaper fusillades as instruments "to prepare the Minds of the Publick,"[44] but most men assumed that man easily succumbed to his basest instincts and that the unthinking multitude, which included a vast majority of the population, was moved by passion rather than reason. Guided by these views, most leaders could not help but look upon exhortatory literature as a threat to the social order. Conservative politicians frequently attacked what they called irresponsible attempts "to inflame the minds of the people" or "to breed and nourish Discontent, and to foment Faction and Sedition."[45] And yet by the 1750s, and often before, even the most conservative leader could not resist the resort to the press, even though it might contradict his social philosophy. Men such as James De Lancey, who earlier had lamented its use, were eagerly employing the press by mid-century. Their opponents could only shake their heads in dismay—charging that attempts were being made to propagate "Clamour & Slander" and to turn the heads of "ignorant people & others who are not well acquainted with the publick affairs"—and then take up the pen themselves.[46] In Philadelphia it was the proprietary party, espousing social conservatism and constantly warning about the anarchic and levelling designs of Quaker politicians, that raised the art of pamphleteering to new levels of sophistication in the 1750s. No one in Philadelphia could quite match the imperious William Smith for statements about the necessity of the ordered, deferential society; but no one did more to make the abusive pamphlet a part of the eighteenth-century political arsenal.[47]

Given this increasing reliance upon the press, it was inevitable that the professional pamphleteer would emerge as a new figure in politics. Isaac

154

[44] Labaree and others, *The Papers of Benjamin Franklin*, VII, 374. Franklin came close to changing his mind concerning the beneficial effects of the political press when he became the target of a savage pamphlet offensive in 1764.

[45] For example, see *A View of the Calumnies lately spread in some Scurrilous Prints against the Government of Pennsylvania* (Philadelphia, 1729).

[46] James De Lancey, *The Charge of the Honourable James De Lancey, Esqr. Chief Justice of the Province of New-York, To the Gentlemen of the Grand-Jury for the City and County of New-York, on Tuesday the 15th of October, 1734* (New York, 1733); James De Lancey, *The Charge of the Honourable James De Lancey Esq; Chief Justice of the Province of New-York, to the Gentlemen of the Grand-Jury for the City and County of New-York, on Tuesday the 15th Day of January, Annoq; Domini. 1733* (New York, 1734); *Letters and Papers of Cadwallader Colden*, IV, 122, 161.

[47] Writing to the proprietor in 1755, Smith confessed that "The Appeal to the public was against my Judgment." Another proprietary leader, Peters, had written earlier that "I never knew any good come to the honest & right side of the Question in the Province by Publick Papers." See Paul A. W. Wallace, *Conrad Weiser, 1696-1760, Friend of Colonist and Mohawk* (Philadelphia, 1945), 115.

Hunt, David James Dove, and Hugh Williamson of Philadelphia were only three of a group of political writers who earned their pay by devising new ways of touching the fears and aspirations of the electorate through deception, innuendo, and scurrility. The professional pamphleteer, in the hire of élitist politicians, symbolized the contradiction between the new political stratagems and the old social outlook.[48]

Not only a quantitative leap in political literature but also an escalation of rhetoric made the use of the press a particularly important part of the new politics. As political literature became institutionalized, the quality of language and the modes of argumentation changed markedly. In the early eighteenth century pamphleteers exercised restraint, appealing to the public judgment and the "best interest of the country." Perhaps mindful of the revolutionary potential of the printed word, authors couched their arguments in legalistic terms. For example, in Boston, during the exchange of pamphlets on the currency crisis in 1714, hundreds of pages were offered to the public, but readers encountered nothing more virulent than charges that the opposition view was "strange and Unaccountable," "intolerable," "unreasonable and unjust," or that writers on the other side were guilty of "bold and wilful Misrepresentation." But by 1754 the anti-excise pamphleteers were raising images in the public mind of "Little pestilent Creature[s]," "dirty miscreants," and unspeakably horrible creatures ready to "cram [their] . . . merciless and insatiable Maw[s] with our very Blood, and bones, and Vitals" while making sexual advances on wives and daughters.[49] In Philadelphia, Keith's political campaigns in the 1720s introduced a genre of literature that for the first time directly attacked men of wealth and learning. "According to my experience," wrote David Lloyd, "a mean Man, of small Interest, devoted to the faithful Discharge of his Trust and Duty to the Government, may do more good to the State than a Richer or more Learned Man, who by his ill Temper and aspiring Mind becomes an opposer of the Constitution by which he should act."[50] This was egalitarian rhetoric which inverted the social pyramid by rejecting the traditional notion that the maintenance of social order and political stability depended on vesting power in men of education and high status.

But this kind of language was a model of restraint compared to mid-century political vitriol. In newspapers and pamphlets, contending élites

155

[48] Almost nothing has been written on the professional pamphlet writers of the colonial period, many of whom seem to have been schoolteachers. For a sketch of David James Dove, which indicates how willingly he changed sides in the factional struggles in Pennsylvania, see Joseph Jackson, "A Philadelphia Schoolmaster of the Eighteenth Century," *Pennsylvania Magazine of History and Biography*, XXXV (No. 3, 1911), 315-32.

[49] Boyer, "Borrowed Rhetoric: The Massachusetts Excise Controversy of 1754," 341-44.

[50] *A Vindication of the Legislative Power* (Philadelphia, 1725).

hurled insults at each other and charged their opponents, to cite one example from Philadelphia, with "Inveterate Calumny, foul-mouthed Aspersion, shameless Falsehood, and insatiate Malice. . . ."[51] New York also witnessed a change in rhetorical style as pamphleteers substituted slander and vituperation for reasoned discourse. The Anglican clergy was left no semblance of integrity in the attacks of the Livingston faction during the King's College controversy. In phrases that made Zenger's New York *Journal* seem polite by comparison, readers were told of the "ghastly juggling . . . and insatiate Lust of Power" of the Anglican clergymen and learned of "our intended Vassalage," the "Seduction of Priest-craft," and "clerical Rubbish and Villainy."[52]

In effect, the conservatives' worst fears concerning the use of the press were being confirmed as the tactics of printed political discourse changed from attacking the legality or wisdom of the opposition's policies or pleading for the election of public-minded men to assailing the character and motives of those on the other side. The effect of the new political rhetoric was self-intensifying as each increase in the brutality of language brought an equivalent or greater response from the opposition. Gradually the public was taught to suspect not simply the wisdom or constitutional right of one side or the other, but the motives, morality, and even sanity of its leaders. The very high-placed individuals to whom the rank-and-file were supposed to defer were being exposed as the most corrupt and loathsome members of society.

In mob activity and threats of violence the radicalization of politics can be seen in its most dramatic though not its most significant form. It is well to make a distinction between spontaneous disorders expressive of deeply felt lower-class grievances and mob activity arranged and directed by political leaders to serve their own purposes. A connection existed between the two kinds of activity since political élites, witnessing random lower-class disorder, did not fail to note the effectiveness of collective force; and lower-class elements, encouraged or even rewarded by political leaders for participating in riotous activity, undoubtedly lost some of their awe and reverence for duly constituted authority, gaining a new sense of their own power.[53]

Mobs expressing class grievances were less common in the colonial cities

[51] *Pennsylvania Journal*, April 22, 1756. The charges were made against Smith in return for "the Vomitings of this infamous Hireling" whose attacks on Franklin "betoken that Redundancy of Rancour, and Rottiness of Heart which render him the most despicable of his Species." *Ibid.*

[52] Thomas Gordon, *The Craftsman* (New York, 1753), iii-xiii, xxv, xxvi.

[53] Pauline Maier has shown that the pre-Revolutionary mob was usually anti-imperial or designed to extend rather than attack authority. See Pauline Maier, "Popular Uprisings and Civil Authority in Eighteenth-Century America," *William and Mary Quarterly*, XXVII

than in rural areas, where land disputes and Indian policy were major sources of conflict throughout the eighteenth century.[54] The food rioting that was a persistent factor in the history of European cities of this period was almost unknown in Boston, New York, and Philadelphia.[55] Far more common was the sporadic violence directed at individuals identified with unpopular causes. Cotton Mather, who went unappreciated by a large part of Boston's population throughout his lifetime of religious and political eminence, had his house fire-bombed in 1721.[56] In 1749 Thomas Hutchinson, long identified with hard-money policies, watched ruefully as his house burned to the cheers of the mob while the fire company responded with a suspicious lack of speed.[57] James Logan and his wife spent a night under the bed when the mob bombarded their stately house with stones, convincing Logan that law and order in Philadelphia was as shattered as his window panes.[58] This kind of violence, along with unofficially sanctioned riots such as the annual Pope's Day battles between North End and South End in Boston, reflected the general abrasiveness of life in the eighteenth century and the frailty of law enforcement in the cities.[59]

Far more significant was violence inspired and controlled by the élite. This was often directed at imperial officers charged with carrying out unpopular trade or military policies. Thus Boston was more or less in the hands of the mob for three days in 1747, after the commander of the British fleet in the harbor ordered his press gang to make a nocturnal sweep through the streets. The mob, wrote Governor William Shirley, "was se-

157

(Jan. 1970), 3-35. But she has ignored the role of the mob in provincial politics and, by focusing exclusively on the quasi-legal activity of mobs, overstates the acceptance of mob activity.

[54] There are few parallels in the history of the colonial cities to the forays of the White Pine rebels in Massachusetts, the land rioters in New York and New Jersey in the 1740s, and the Paxton Boys in Pennsylvania. For accounts of these movements, see Joseph J. Malone, *Pine Trees and Politics, The Naval Stores and Forest Policy in Colonial New England, 1691-1775* .(Plymouth, England, 1964); Irving Mark, *Agrarian Conflicts in Colonial New York, 1711-1775* (New York, 1940); Donald L. Kemmerer, *Path to Freedom: The Struggle for Self-Government in New Jersey, 1703-1776* (Princeton, 1940); Theodore Thayer, *Pennsylvania Politics and the Growth of Democracy, 1740-1776* (Philadelphia, 1953); and Brooke Hindle, "The March of the Paxton Boys," *William and Mary Quarterly*, III (Oct. 1946), 461-86.

[55] For a comparative view of the mob, see Gordon S. Wood, "A Note on Mobs in the American Revolution," *William and Mary Quarterly*, XXIII (Oct. 1966), 635-42; and William A. Smith, "Anglo-American Society and the Mob, 1740-1775" (doctoral dissertation, Claremont Graduate School, 1965).

[56] *The Diary of Cotton Mather, 1709-1724*, Massachusetts Historical Society Collections (8 vols., Boston, 1900-1912), VIII, 657-58.

[57] Warden, *Boston*, 140.

[58] James Logan to James Alexander, Oct. 23, 1749, Letter Book, 1748-1750, James Logan Papers (Library Company of Philadelphia).

[59] R. S. Longley, "Mob Activities in Revolutionary Massachusetts," *New England Quarterly*, VI (March 1933), 102-03.

cretly Contenanc'd and encourag'd by some ill minded Inhabitants and Persons of Influence in the Town. . . . ."[60] The garrisoning of troops in New York City led to "constant violence" and the efforts of crown officials to block illegal trade with the enemy was forcibly resisted in 1759 by the city's merchants who employed waterfront mobs to do their work.[61] But mobs were also used in internal political struggles that did not involve imperial policy. In Boston in the 1730s, when the issue of a public market dominated municipal politics, a band of night raiders sawed through the supports of the market houses in the North End and later demolished another building. When Governor Jonathan Belcher vowed to see justice done, letters circulated in the town claiming that 500 men stood ready to oppose with force any attempt to intervene in the case.[62] In Philadelphia, Keith's "town mob," as his detractors called it, was sufficiently enlivened by their election victory in 1726 to burn the pillory and stocks—the symbols of authority and social control.[63] Two years later a dispute over a vacant assembly seat led to a campaign of intimidation and assault on Quaker members of the assembly by Keith's partisans. The Quakers complained that such "Indecensies [were] used towards the Members of Assembly attending the Service of the Country in *Philadelphia*, by rude and disorderly Persons," that it was unsafe to meet any longer in Philadelphia.[64] When the assembly met in the following spring, it faced an incipient insurrection. Keith's mob, according to James Logan, was to apply "first to the Assembly and then storm the Government," knocking heads, plundering estates, and putting houses to the torch, if necessary, to get what it wanted.[65] Only the hasty passage of an act authorizing the death penalty for riot and insurrection seems to have averted violence.

158

[60] Maier, "Popular Uprisings," 4-15; Charles H. Lincoln, ed., *The Correspondence of William Shirley: Governor of Massachusetts and Military Commander in America, 1731-1760* (2 vols., New York, 1912), I, 406.

[61] Julius Goebel, Jr., and T. Raymond Naughton, *Law Enforcement in Colonial New York: A Study in Criminal Procedure (1664-1776)* (New York, 1944), 194; Milton M. Klein, "The Rise of the New York Bar: The Legal Career of William Livingston," *William and Mary Quarterly*, XV (July 1958), 348.

[62] Warden, *Boston*, 121-24; Carl Bridenbaugh, *Cities in the Wilderness: The First Century of Urban Life in America, 1625-1742* (New York, 1938), 352.

[63] Patrick Gordon to John Penn, Oct. 17, 1726, Official Correspondence, I, Penn Family Papers.

[64] Gertrude MacKinney, ed., *Votes and Proceedings of the House of Representatives of the Province of Pennsylvania, Pennsylvania Archives* (Eighth Series) (8 vols., Harrisburg, Pa., 1931-1935), III, 1908. See also *The Proceedings of some Members of Assembly, at Philadelphia*, April 1728 vindicated from the unfair *Reasoning* and unjust *Insinuations* of a certain *Remarker* (Philadelphia, 1728).

[65] Logan to John, Richard, and Thomas Penn, April 24, 1729, Official Correspondence, II, 55, Penn Family Papers.

In 1742 Philadelphia was ·shaken by a bloody election day riot. It is a prime example of the élite's willingness to employ the mob.[66] Even before election day, rumors circulated that the Quaker party intended to maintain its majority in the assembly by steering unnaturalized Germans to the polls and that the proprietary party meant to thwart this attempt by engaging a pack of toughs. The rumors'had substance. When the leaders of the two political factions could not agree on procedures for supervising the election, heated words and curses were exchanged; and seventy sailors wielding clubs and shouting "down with the plain Coats & broad Brims" waded into the Quaker crowd assembled before the courthouse.[67] When the Quaker leaders retreated inside, the sailors filled the air with a hailstorm of bricks. A counterattack was launched by Germans and younger Quakers, who momentarily forgot their pacifist principles. "Blood flew plentifully around," the proprietary secretary reported.[68] Conducting investigations later, the Quaker assembly concluded that the riot had been engineered by the leaders of the proprietary party. Though some historians have disputed this, two of the proprietor's chief officials in Pennsylvania privately admitted as much.[69]

159

Although mob violence was probably not nearly so widespread in the colonial cities as in London, the leaders of all factions were sensitive to the power that the mob possessed. Few colonial leaders wanted to democratize society or shift political power downward in the social order. But locked in competition with other upper-class groups, they found it necessary to expand the politically relevant sector of society by encouraging the common people to participate in direct political action.

It would be a mistake to believe that political mobs were passive instruments manipulated by the élite. Though lower-class economic and social grievances only rarely achieved ideological expression in this period, the men who worked by night in Boston or Philadelphia surely gained a new sense of their own power. The urban artisan or laborer discovered that he was not only a useful but also often an essential part of politics. As early as 1729, James Logan sensed the implications of deploying "the multitudes."

[66] For two interpretations of the riot, see Norman S. Cohen, "The Philadelphia Election Riot of 1742," *Pennsylvania Magazine of History and Biography*, XCII (July 1968), 306-19; and William T. Parsons, "The Bloody Election of 1742," *Pennsylvania History*, XXXVI (July 1969), 290-306.
[67] Richard Hockley to Thomas Penn, Nov. 1, 1742, Official Correspondence, III, Penn Family Papers.
[68] Peters to the Proprietors, Nov. 17, 1742, Letter Book, 1737-1750, Peters Papers.
[69] Hockley to Thomas Penn, Nov. 1 and Nov. 18, 1742, Official Correspondence, III, 241-43, Penn Family Papers; Peters to Thomas Penn, Nov. 17, 1742, Letter Book, 1737-1750, Peters Papers.

"Sir William Keith," he wrote, "was so mad, as well as wicked, most industriously to sett up the lowest part of the People; through a vain expectation that he should always be able to steer and influence them as his own Will. But he weakly forgot how soon the minds of such People are changed by any new Accident and how licentious force, when the Awe of Government . . . is thrown off, has been turned against those who first taught them to throw it off."[70]

Another important facet of the "new politics" of the pre-Revolutionary decades was the growing involvement of religious leaders in politics, something nearly all leaders deplored but nonetheless exploited. Of course religious leaders had never been isolated from political life in the early history of the colonies; but such efforts as they made to influence public affairs were usually conducted discreetly and privately. When clergymen published pamphlets on political subjects, they did so anonymously. The common assumption that it was inappropriate for clergymen to mix religion and politics was clearly articulated in 1722 when Cotton Mather and John Wise were exposed as two of the principal controversialists in the heated currency debate in Massachusetts. "Some of our Ecclesiasticks of late," wrote an anonymous pamphleteer, "have been guilty of too officious a meddling with State Affairs. To see a Clergy-man (Commedian-like) stand belabouring his Cushion and intermixing his Harrangue with THUNDER-BOLTS, while entertaining his peaceable Congregation with things whereof he is . . . Ignorant . . . how ridiculous is the Sight and the Sound."[71] Such attacks on clerical involvement in politics would continue throughout the pre-Revolutionary period. But by mid-century church leaders were beginning to shed their anonymity and to defend their right to engage in "preaching politics," as Jonathan Mayhew put it in Boston in 1750.[72]

To some extent this politicization of the clergy can be attributed to the Great Awakening, for amidst the evangelical fervor of the early 1740s "religious controversies and political problems were blended in a unique pattern of interaction."[73] But perhaps more important was the fact that by the 1740s the fires of political contention were growing hotter, impelling factional leaders to enlist the services of religious leaders. In Philadelphia, the issue of war and defense appropriations in 1748, not the Great Awakening, brought the first full-scale exchange on a secular question between oppos-

[70] Logan to John, Richard, and Thomas Penn, April 24, 1729, Official Correspondence, II, 55, Penn Family Papers.
[71] Andrew McF. Davis, *Colonial Currency Reprints, 1682-1751* (4 vols., Boston, 1910-1911), II, 134.
[72] Quoted in Heimert, *Religion and the American Mind*, 15.
[73] Rothermund, *Layman's Progress*, 82.

ing denominational spokesman. In a dozen signed pamphlets Presbyterian and Quaker leaders such as Gilbert Tennent and Samuel Smith carried out a public dialogue on the necessity of military defense—a battle of words that thrust the clergy into the political arena.[14]

No more dramatic representation of a politicized clergy can be imagined than the jailing of the Anglican ecclesiastic William Smith by the Pennsylvania assembly in 1758. Writing anonymously, Smith had published two open-handed attacks on the Quaker party in 1755 and 1756 as part of the proprietary party's offensive against the Quaker-dominated assembly. He continued his assaults in 1757 and 1758 in the *American Magazine* and the *Pennsylvania Journal*. Determined to halt these attacks, the assembly charged Smith and one of his fellow writers with libel. During the course of a long trial and subsequent appeals to England, Smith carried out his duties and political ambitions from the Philadelphia jail.[15]

161

The clergy's increasing involvement in politics had a second dimension which was closely related to the Great Awakening. One of the side effects of the revivalist movement was an expansion of political consciousness within the lower reaches of society. The average city dweller developed a new feeling of autonomy and importance as he partook of mass revivals, assummed a new power in ecclesiastical affairs, and was encouraged repeatedly from the pulpit to adopt an attitude of skepticism toward dogma and authority. Doctrinal controversy and attacks on religious and secular leaders became ritualized and accepted in the 1740s.[16] It was precisely this that caused high-placed individuals to charge revivalists with preaching levelism and anarchy. "It is . . . an exceedingly difficult gloomy time with us . . . ," wrote Charles Chauncey from Boston; "Such an enthusiastic, factious, censorious Spirit was never known here. . . . Every low-bred, illiterate Person can resolve Cases of Conscience and settle the most difficult

---

[14] The debate can be followed in a series of pamphlets published in 1748. See, for example, William Currie, *A Treatise on the Lawfulness of Defensive War* (Philadelphia, 1748); Gilbert Tennent, *The Late Association for Defence, Encourag'd, or the Lawfulness of a Defensive War* (Philadelphia, 1748); and John Smith, *The Doctrine of Christianity, As Held by the People Called Quakers, Vindicated: In Answer to Gilbert Tennent's Sermon on the Lawfulness of War* (Philadelphia, 1748).

[15] William Renwick Riddell, "Libel on the Assembly: a Prerevolutionary Episode," *Pennsylvania Magazine of History and Biography*, LII (No. 2, 3, 4, 1928), 176-92, 249-79, 342-60; William S. Hanna, *Benjamin Franklin and Pennsylvania Politics* (Stanford, 1964), 134-37; Leonard W. Levy, *Freedom of Speech and Press in Early American History: Legacy of Suppression* (New York, 1963), 53-61.

[16] Rothermund, *Layman's Progress*, 55-60, 81-82; Heimert, *Religion and the American Mind*, 27-58, 239-93. The process was not confined to the cities. See Richard L. Bushman, *From Puritan to Yankee: Character and the Social Order in Connecticut, 1690-1765* (Cambridge, Mass., 1967).

Points of Divinity better than the most learned Divines."[77] Such charges
were heard repeatedly during the Great Awakening, revealing the apprehension of those who trembled to see the "unthinking multitude" invested
with a new dignity and importance. Nor could the passing of the Great
Awakening reverse the tide, for this new sense of power did not atrophy
with the decline of religious enthusiasm, but remained as a permanent part
of the social outlook of the middle and lower strata of society.

The October 1764 elections in Philadelphia provide an opportunity to
observe in microcosm all of the radicalizing tendencies of the previous
three-quarters of a century. The city had already been badly shaken by the
Paxton Boys, who descended on the capital to press demands for frontier
defense and to take the lives of a group of Christian Indians, who were
being sheltered by the government in barracks at Philadelphia. This exercise in vigilante government led to a Quaker-Presbyterian pamphlet war.
Against this background the Quaker party decided to organize the October
assembly elections around a campaign to replace proprietary with royal government.[78]

By the spring of 1764 the move to place Pennsylvania under royal government was underway, and political leaders in both camps were vying for
popular support. Proprietary aristocrats, suppressing their contempt for the
urban working class, made strenuous efforts to recruit artisan support and,
for the first time, placed three ethnic candidates—two Germans and one
Scotch-Irish—on their eight-man assembly slate. "The design," wrote a
party organizer, "is by putting in two Germans to draw such a Party of
them as will turn the scale in our Favor. . . ."[79] The success of these
efforts can be measured by the conversion to the proprietary cause of Carl
Wrangel and Henry Muhlenberg, the Lutheran church leaders in Philadelphia, and Christopher Sauer, Jr., and Heinrich Miller, the German printers.
By the end of the summer all of these men were writing or translating anti-
Quaker pamphlets for distribution in the German community.[80]

[77] John C. Miller, "Religion, Finance and Democracy in Massachusetts," *New England
Quarterly*, 6 (1933), 52-53.
[78] Hindle, "The March of the Paxton Boys," 461-86; Hanna, *Benjamin Franklin and
Pennsylvania Politics*, 154-68; James H. Hutson, "The Campaign to Make Pennsylvania a
Royal Province, 1764-1770," *Pennsylvania Magazine of History and Biography*, XCIV (Oct.
1970), 427-63, XCV (Jan. 1971), 28-49.
[79] Samuel Purviance, Jr., to James Burd, Sept. 10, 1764, Vol. I, Shippen Family Papers
(Historical Society of Pennsylvania, Philadelphia). James Pemberton, a Quaker leader,
wrote that the proprietary leaders engaged in "unwearied Endeavors . . . to prejudice the
minds of the lower class of the people" against Franklin. James Pemberton to John Fother-
gill, Oct. 11, 1764, James Pemberton Papers (Historical Society of Pennsylvania, Philadelphia).
[80] Hutson, "Campaign to Make Pennsylvania a Royal Province," 452; Theodore Tappert
and John W. Doberstein, trans. and eds., *The Journals of Henry Melchoir Muhlenberg*
(3 vols., Philadelphia, 1942-1945), II, 91, 99-102, 106-07, 123.

The efforts of the proprietary party to search in the lower social strata for support drove Franklin and the assembly party to even greater lengths. In early April, Franklin called a mass meeting and sent messengers house-to-house to turn out the largest possible audience. The featured speaker was Galloway, who delivered an "inflammatory harangue" about the evils of proprietary government.[81] This was the opening shot in a campaign to gather signatures on a petition pleading for the institution of royal government. In the concerted drive to obtain signatures, according to one critic, "Taverns were engag'd, [and] many of the poorer and more dependent kind of labouring people in town were invited thither by night, the fear of being turn'd out of business and the eloquence of the punch bowl prevailed on many to sign. . . ."[82] The town was saturated with polemical literature, including 3,000 copies of the assembly's biting message to the proprietor and their resolves for obtaining royal government. Franklin and Galloway published pamphlets designed to stir unrest with proprietary government, and Quakers, according to one observer, went door-to-door in pairs soliciting signatures for the royal government petition.[83] John Penn, the nephew of the proprietor, was shocked that Franklin's party went "into all the houses in Town without distinction," and "by the assistance of Punch and Beer" were able to procure the signatures of "some of the lowest sort of people" in the city.[84]

163

It was only a matter of time before the proprietary party, using fire to fight fire, circulated a counter-petition and far outstripped the efforts of Franklin and Galloway to involve the populace in politics. Everyone in Philadelphia, regardless of religion, class, or ideological predisposition, found himself being courted by the leaders of the two political factions.[85] Never in Pennsylvania's history had the few needed the many so much.

As the battle thickened, pamphleteers reached new pinnacles of abusiveness and scurrility. Franklin was reviled as an intellectual charlatan who begged and bought honorary degrees, a corrupt politician intimately acquainted "with every Zig Zag Machination," a grasping, conniving, egotistical climber, and a lecherous old man who promoted royal government only for the purpose of installing himself in the governor's chair.[86] His

---

[81] John Penn to Thomas Penn, May 5, 1764, Official Correspondence, IX, 220, Penn Family Papers; John Dickinson, *A Reply to a Piece called the Speech of Joseph Galloway, Esquire* (Philadelphia, 1764), 32-33.

[82] Dunbar, ed., *Paxton Papers*, 369; Hutson, "Campaign to Make Pennsylvania a Royal Province," 437-52.

[83] William Bingham to John Gibson, May 4, 1764, Shippen Papers.

[84] John Penn to Thomas Penn, May 5, 1764, Official Correspondence, IX, 220, Penn Family Papers.

[85] Autograph Petitions, 1681-1764, Penn Family Papers.

[86] Labaree and others, eds., *Papers of Benjamin Franklin*, XI, 380-84.

friends responded by labeling an opposition pamphleteer "a Reptile" who "like a Toad, by the pestilential Fumes of his virulent Slabber" attempted "to blast the fame of a PATRIOT" and describing William Smith, leader of the opposition, as a "consumate Sycophant," an "indefatigable" liar, and an impudent knave with a heart "bloated with *infernal Malice*" and a head full of *"flatulent Preachments."*[87] As for the Presbyterians, they were redesignated "Piss-Brute-arians (a bigoted, cruel and revengeful sect)" by a Franklin party pamphleteer who later reached the apogee of scatalogical polemics when he suggested that now was the time for Smith, president of the college and a director of the hospital, to consumate his alliance with the pamphleteer David Dove, who "will not only furnish you with that most agreeable of all Foods to your Taste, but after it has found a Passage through your Body . . . will greedily devour it, and, as soon as it is well digested, he will void it up for a Repast to the Proprietary Faction: they will as eagerly swallow it as the other had done before, and, when it has gone through their several Concoctions, they will discharge it in your Presence, that you may once more regale on it, thus refined."[88] One shocked outsider wrote to a friend in Philadelphia: "In the name of goodness stop your Pamphleteer's Mouths & shut up your presses. Such a torrent of low scurrility sure never came from any country as lately from Pennsylvan[i]a."[89]

Religious leaders were also drawn into the election campaign. A rural clergyman related that the proprietary leaders had convinced Presbyterian and Anglican ministers in Philadelphia to distribute petitions requesting the preservation of proprietary government. "The Presbyterian ministers, with some others," he lamented, "held Synods about the election, turned their pulpits into Ecclesiastical drums for politics and told their people to vote according as they directed them at the peril of their damnation. . . ."[90] Church leaders such as Tennent, Francis Alison, and Muhlenberg wrote political pamphlets or sent circular letters on the election to every congregation in the province. St. Peters and Christ Church were the scene of preelection rallies as denominational groups assumed an unprecedented role in

164

[87] Quoted in *ibid.,* XI, 384; Gleason, "A Scurrilous Colonial Election and Franklin's Reputation," 82.

[88] [Isaac Hunt], *A Letter From a Gentleman in Transilvania To his Friend in* America *giving some Account of the late disturbances that happen'd in that Government, with some Remarks upon the political revolutions in the Magistracy, and the Debates that happened about the Change* (Philadelphia, 1764); [Isaac Hunt], *A Humble Attempt at Scurrility* (Philadelphia, 1765), 36-37.

[89] Quoted in Gleason, "A Scurrilous Colonial Election and Franklin's Reputation," 82n.

[90] Quoted in Guy Soulliard Klett, *Presbyterians in Colonial Pennsylvania* (Philadelphia, 1937), 256.

politics.[91] A "Gentlemen from Transylvania" charged that Philadelphia's Anglican leaders had "prostituted their Temples . . . as an Amphitheatre for the Rabble to combat in. . . ."[92]

Inflammatory rhetoric, a large polemical literature, the participation of the churches in politics, mobilization of social layers previously unsolicited and unwelcome in political affairs, all combined to produce an election in which almost everybody's integrity was questioned, every public figure's use of power was attacked, and both sides paraded themselves as true representatives of "the people." The effects were dramatic: a record number of Philadelphians turned out for the election. The polls opened at 9 a.m. and remained open through the night as party workers on both sides shepherded in the voters, including the infirm and aged who were carried to the courthouse in litters and chairs. By the next morning, party leaders were still seeking a few additional votes. Not until 3 p.m. on the second day were the polls closed.[93] When the returns were counted, both Franklin and Galloway had lost their seats to men on the proprietary ticket.[94] Franklin did not doubt that he had been defeated by defecting Germans and propertyless laborers "brought to swear themselves intituled to a Vote" by the proprietary leaders.[95] A bit of post-election doggerel caught the spirit of the contest: "A Pleasant sight tis to Behold/ The beggars hal'd from Hedges/ The Deaf, the Blind, the Young the Old:/ T' Secure their priveledges/ They're bundled up Steps, each sort Goes/ A Very Pretty Farce Sir:/ Some without Stockings, some no Shoes/Nor Breeches to their A—e Sir."[96]

165

[91] Thayer, *Pennsylvania Politics*, 97; Klett, *Presbyterians in Pennsylvania*, 256-57; Rothermund, *Layman's Progress*, 126-30; Thomas Stewardson, contributor, "Extracts from the Letter-Book of Benjamin Marshall 1763-1766," *Pennsylvania Magazine of History and Biography*, XX (No. 2, 1896), 207-08.

[92] [Hunt], *A Letter from a Gentleman in Transilvania*, 10.

[93] Tappert and Doberstein, eds., *Journals of Henry Melchoir Muhlenberg*, II, 122-23; William B. Reed, *Life and Correspondence of Joseph Reed* (2 vols., Philadelphia, 1847), I, 36-37; William Logan to John Smith, Oct. 4, 1764, John Smith Papers (Historical Society of Pennsylvania, Philadelphia); Labaree and others, eds., *Papers of Benjamin Franklin*, XI, 390-91. Benjamin Newcomb has studied the election and concluded from it that the Stamp Act roiled Pennsylvania politics and consequently brought about a dramatic increase in electoral participation. See Benjamin H. Newcomb, "Effects of the Stamp Act on Colonial Pennsylvania Politics," *William and Mary Quarterly*, XXIII (April 1966), 257-72. The Stamp Act, however, was hardly mentioned in the outpouring of pamphlets accompanying the election of 1764, which revolved around the move for royal government.

[94] Tappert and Doberstein, eds., *Journals of Henry Melchoir Muhlenberg*, II, 123; Reed, ed., *Life and Correspondence of Joseph Reed*, I, 36-37. For the results of the city elections, see Isaac Norris, "Journal, 1764" (Rosenbach Foundation, Philadelphia).

[95] Labaree and others, eds., *Papers of Benjamin Franklin*, XI, 434. The charge that "the riotous Presbyterians" had deprived Franklin of his seat in the assembly by "Illicit Arts and contrivances" was also communicated to the English ministry. Peter Collinson to Lord Hyde, Oct. 11, 1764, Peter Collinson-Bartram Papers (American Philosophical Society, Philadelphia).

[96] *The Election Medley* (Philadelphia, 1764).

Although the election represents an extreme case and was affected by factors unique to the politics of proprietary Pennsylvania, it reflected a trend in the political life of other cities as well. Political innovations, involving a new set of organizational and propagandistic techniques, a vocabulary of vituperation, resort to violence, attacks on authority and social position, and the politicization of layers and groups in society that had earlier been beyond the political pale, had transformed the political culture of each of these cities in the half-century before 1765.

The extent of these changes can be measured, though imperfectly, by charting electoral participation.[97] In Boston, where the population remained nearly static at about 15,000 from 1735 to 1765, and the number of eligible voters declined markedly between 1735 and 1750 before beginning a slow upward climb, the number of voters participating in General Court elections showed a significant rise.[98] Although voter turnouts fluctuated widely from year to year, a series of peaks in 1732, 1748, 1757, 1760, and 1763 brought the number of voters from 650 in 1732 to 1,089 in 1763 —a 66 percent increase during a period of population stagnation. It is also significant to note that from 1764 to 1775 the General Court elections in Boston never drew as many voters as in the years 1760 and 1763, or, for that matter, as in 1758.[99] These data throw doubt on traditional interpretations of the "democratization" of politics accompanying the Revolutionary

166

[97] Despite the extensive literature on the subject, the extent of the franchise, particularly in the cities, is by no means certain. Robert E. Brown estimates that 56 percent of the adult males were eligible for the vote in Boston but later revises this upward to 75 percent or higher on the basis of literary evidence and inference. Robert E. Brown, *Middle-Class Democracy and the Revolution in Massachusetts, 1691-1780* (Ithaca, 1955), 50, 58, 96. For Philadelphia the estimate is 75 percent. Chilton Williamson, *American Suffrage from Property to Democracy, 1760-1860* (Princeton, 1960), 33-34. For New York, Milton Klein argues that "virtually all the white adult males" *could* obtain the franchise. Klein, "Democracy and Politics in New York," 235. Roger Champagne and Beverly McAnear show that about 65-70 percent of the adult white males *were* qualified to vote. Champagne, "Liberty Boys and Mechanics of New York City," 125-29; and Beverly McAnear, "The Place of the Freeman in Old New York," *New York History*, XXI (Oct. 1940), 418-30. The number of eligible voters in the cities probably never exceeded 75 percent of the taxables, and this percentage seems to have been declining in the eighteenth century as urban poverty and propertylessness increased. Williamson indicates that in Philadelphia in 1774 only 1,423 of 3,124 adult males (about 45 percent) were taxed for real or personal property. Williamson, *American Suffrage*, 33. Of course it is possible that many who were ineligible still voted, as was almost certainly the case in Philadelphia.

[98] Precise population graphs for Boston cannot be devised, but the stagnant population level and the decrease in the number of taxables after 1735 seems firmly established by the scattered census materials and the references to the number of taxables for a number of years in the Selectmen's Records. See Warden, *Boston*, 127-29; Bridenbaugh, *Cities in the Wilderness*, 303n; Carl Bridenbaugh, *Cities in Revolt: Urban Life in America, 1743-1776* (New York, 1955), 5, 216; and *Boston Town Records*, XIV, 13, 100, 280.

[99] *Reports of the Record Commissioners of Boston*, VIII, XII, XVI, XVIII. Scattered vote counts are available for the pre-1717 period for selectmen elections and town meetings.

movement, if we mean by that term the involvement of more people in the electoral process or the extension of the franchise.

In the city and county of Philadelphia a similar rise in political participation can be traced. Four years in which knowledgeable observers remarked on vigorous campaigning and heavy voter turnouts were 1728, 1742, 1754, and 1764.[100] The table below indicates the uneven but generally upward drift of political participation as the eighteenth century progressed.

Year	Taxables	Voters	Percent of Taxables Voting
1728	2963	971	32.8
1742	5240	1793	34.2
1754	6908	2173	31.4
1764	8476	3874	45.7

Extant voting statistics for the city of Philadelphia, exclusive of the surrounding areas of Philadelphia County, are obtainable for only a few scattered years, but a comparison of 1751 and 1764, both years of extensive political activity, shows a rise in voting participation from 40.9 to 54.5 percent of the taxable inhabitants.[101] In 1765, when the proprietary and anti-proprietary parties waged another fierce struggle around the issues raised in the campaign of 1764, the percentage of taxable inhabitants voting in the county and city of Philadelphia increased to 51.2 and 65.1 percent. Never again in the pre-Revolutionary decade would involvement in the electoral process be so widespread, not even in the hotly contested special assembly elections for the city of Philadelphia in April 1776.[102] These figures suggest that the barometric pressure of political culture was on the rise during the half-century preceding the Stamp Act crisis and may, in fact, have reached its pinnacle, prior to the emergence of national political parties, in the early 1760s.[103]

[100] Voters in Philadelphia participated in two assembly elections each October, one for the eight representatives for Philadelphia County and one for two "burgesses" from the city. Thus they were doubly represented in the assembly. These elections were usually held on successive days. Voting statistics are from newspapers, private correspondence, and Isaac Norris, "Journals." The number of taxables for the four years has been extrapolated from the known number of taxables for the years 1720, 1734, 1740, 1741, 1760, and 1767.

[101] Isaac Norris, "Journals, 1764." For another set of totals for Philadelphia County, which vary slightly, see Benjamin Franklin Papers, LXIX, 97 (American Philosophical Society, Philadelphia). The 1765 figures are from *ibid.*, 98, and are reprinted in Labaree and others, eds., *Papers of Benjamin Franklin*, XII, 290-91n.

[102] See David Hawke, *In the Midst of a Revolution* (Philadelphia, 1961), 13-31.

[103] Voting statistics for New York City, where assembly elections were far less frequent, have been found for only two years in the period before 1765. But when combined with statistics for the elections of 1768 and 1769, it appears that in New York the peak of political participation before the Revolution may also have been reached in the early 1760s. See Klein, "Democracy and Politics in Colonial New York," 237.

That an increasing percentage of qualified voters was participating in electoral politics not only by casting their votes but also by taking part in street demonstrations, rallies, and caucuses was emblematic of the changing political culture of the cities. Upper-class leaders, contending for political advantage, had mobilized the electorate and introduced new techniques and strategies for obtaining electoral majorities. Most of these leaders had little taste for the effects of this new kind of politics and perhaps none of them wished to bring political life to the kind of clamorous, unrestrained exercise in vitriol and slander that prevailed in Philadelphia in 1764 and 1765. But piecemeal they had contributed to a transformed political culture which by the 1760s they could only precariously control.

The transformation of politics was not restricted to the cities.[104] But it proceeded most rapidly in the urban centers of colonial life because it was in cities that men in power could influence large numbers of people; that printing presses were located and political literature was most widely distributed; that population density made possible the organization of clubs, mass meetings, and vociferous electioneering tactics; that numerous taverns provided natural nerve centers of feverish political activity; that disparities of wealth were growing most rapidly; and that new attitudes and behavioral patterns first found ideological expression. The countryside was far from immune to the new style of politics and a new political culture, but distances and population dispersion created organizational and communication problems which were far harder to solve than in urban places.

But change occurred everywhere, rendering an older mode of politics obsolete. Internal, local, and intraclass as well as interclass struggles in colonial society had transfigured politics, creating almost by inadvertance a political culture which by 1765 already contained many of the changes in political style and behavior usually associated with the Revolutionary period.[105]

[104] For example, see Kenneth A. Lockridge, *A New England Town, The First Hundred Years: Dedham, Massachusetts, 1636-1736* (New York, 1970), 93-164; and Edward M. Cook, Jr., "Social Behavior and Changing Values in Dedham, Massachusetts, 1700 to 1775," *William and Mary Quarterly*, XXVII (Oct. 1970), 546-80.

[105] For the view that the radicalization process should be associated with the post-1763 period, see Merrill Jensen, "The American People and the American Revolution," *Journal of American History*, LVII (June 1970), 5-35.

The Development of American Citizenship in the Revolutionary Era: The Idea of Volitional Allegiance

by JAMES H. KETTNER*

The concept of American citizenship that developed during the Revolutionary War and achieved full legal form and force in the mid-nineteenth century grew from English roots. It was the end product of a development that stretched over three hundred years, a development in which quasi-medieval ideas of seventeenth-century English jurists were reshaped by the circumstances of life in the New World. The process of change was a gradual one, and at no point did those who participated in it fully perceive its pattern or direction. Americans inherited a complex set of ideas relating to membership, community, and allegiance along with their status as English subjects, and they would adjust, affirm, or repudiate elements of the intellectual whole at different times and in response to varying practical and theoretical concerns. From piecemeal changes and partial modifications, however, a clear line of development emerged as Americans first experienced, then sought to articulate the meaning of their transformation from subjects to citizens.

I. *The English and Colonial Background*

By the late sixteenth century, there had emerged in English law a broad distinction between subjects and aliens, reflecting a clear sense that members of the community ought to enjoy a status different than that accorded to outsiders. While this basic dichotomy already had legal and constitutional reality, there was no explicit theoretical explanation of the source, character, and effects of membership. The intellectual framework within which problems of status were dealt with was flexible and ambiguous, capable of sustaining diverse interpretations and understandings of the relationship between the individual and the community.

The first phase of the conceptual development examined here involved the full articulation of a theory of allegiance and "subjectship." Responding to the controversies and confusion that surrounded the accession of James I to the English throne, Sir Edward

169

*Assistant Professor, University of California, Berkeley, California.

Coke in 1608 in *Calvin's Case* propounded an explicit set of principles and formulations respecting the nature of membership and community that would dominate English law for the next several centuries.[1] His central conclusion was that subjectship involved a personal relationship with the king, a relationship rooted in the laws of nature and hence perpetual and immutable. The conceptual analogue of the subject-king relationship was the natural bond between parent and child. While the law envisioned various types or categories of subjectship, ranging from the fundamental natural status of the native-born subject to the legally-acquired status of the naturalized alien, all varieties of membership mirrored permanent hierarchical principles of the natural order. Once a man became a subject—by birth or otherwise—he remained a subject forever, owing a lasting obedience to his natural superior, the king.

170

The intellectual premises from which Coke derived his conclusions were .those of a man standing midway between the eras historians categorize as "medieval" and "modern," and those premises were destined to fade before the century was out. New conceptions emerged that saw society and government as the product of individual consent and compact, and Coke's quasi-medieval ideas that social and governmental organization grew out of natural principles of hierarchy and subordination became increasingly anachronistic. Yet Coke's conclusions regarding the character of allegiance—his maxims and definitions to the effect that the subject-king relationship was personal, natural, perpetual, and immutable—remained deeply embedded in the law, where they would exercise a profound and lasting influence on the theoretical developments of the future.

Coke pre-empted the discussion and interpretation of subjectship. His analysis preceded the emergence of the new conceptions of the "social compact" and "government by consent" that were articulated in the course of the constitutional crises of the seventeenth century.[2] Coke's authoritative interpretation of allegiance in *Calvin's Case* continued to guide his successors with respect to the legal position of the individual subject, even though his view of society and government was in fundamental conflict with theirs. Seventeenth- and eighteenth-century English jurists never recast the law of allegiance to conform with the new ideas of government by consent. Rather, in dealing with questions of status—in analyzing and giving a theoretical explanation of the long-familiar practice of naturalization, or in deciding cases

---

1. Calvin's Case, 7 Co. Rep. 1a; 77 E.R. 377 (Ex. Ch. 1608).
2. See generally Margaret Atwood Judson, *The Crisis of the Constitution* (New York, 1949).

involving treason, the betrayal of allegiance—they continued to apply the maxims and dicta enunciated by Coke in 1608. By the mid-eighteenth century, then, English concepts of subjectship and community encompassed a central ambiguity: on the one hand, society and government theoretically rested on individual consent and compact; on the other hand, the legal status and obligations of the individual remained natural, perpetual, and immutable.

Across the Atlantic, circumstances almost immediately led men to attenuate and modify the concept of natural allegiance that was part of their legal and intellectual heritage. The changing notions were most apparent in the naturalization policies and practices that quickly became a common feature of the colonial governments. The concerns involved in the incorporation of aliens into the wilderness societies were pre-eminently practical. Little attention was paid to doctrinal consistency, and there was as yet no attempt to rethink the traditional theory of membership from initial premise to ultimate conclusion. Yet while they continued to value their status as subjects and to affirm their allegiance to the king, Americans moved toward a new understanding of the ties that bound individuals into the community.[3]

Naturalization was a legal process involving a form of contract between the individual who chose a new allegiance and a community that consented to adopt him as a member. In English law, the allegiance acquired by the naturalized alien was held to be the "same" as that of a native subject; that is, it was natural, personal, and perpetual. In the colonies, however, men slowly came to see the allegiance of the naturalized subject as reflecting the attributes of the process by which it was acquired; that is, it was volitional and contractual. Moreover, the need to attract settlers by offering special rights and benefits led Americans to soften distinctions between the various ranks and categories of subjects that still could be found in English law. Despite some resistance from the imperial government in England, the colonists gradually came to hold that *all* subjects had a right to share the same benefits and privileges of membership without distinction or discrimination. And if the *condition* of naturalized and native subjects ought to be the same, then their allegiance ought to be the same as well. That allegiance originated in a definable legal act in which the community conferred benefits in return for the subject's obedience and his contribution to the common good. That allegiance was the result of a contract resting on consent.

171

3. See generally James H. Kettner, *The Development of American Citizenship 1608-1870* (unpublished Ph.D. dissertation, Harvard, 1973), ch. 4 [hereafter Kettner, *Am. Citizenship*].

The crisis of the American Revolution impelled the colonists to articulate in theoretical form this new concept of volitional allegiance. As they defended the rights of the colonies against the encroaching power of imperial authorities in London, colonial spokesmen in the years before Independence moved steadily away from the traditional ideas of allegiance that permeated British legal and constitutional thought.[4] By 1776, American theorists had rejected the concept that the colonists were perpetually bound by their subjectship. They denied that their allegiance was natural and indelible. Philosophy, law, and common sense had convinced them that subjects owed obedience to governments only in return for the protection of their fundamental rights. Allegiance was contractual, and contracts could be annulled.

172

The dynamics of the imperial debate, however, allowed Americans to consider the problem of allegiance and subjectship as it pertained to whole communities within the empire and to evade questions concerning the relationship between *individuals* and the society of which they were a part. While the rhetoric of discussion frequently and perhaps necessarily used an "individualistic" vocabulary—men spoke of the relationship between the subject and his sovereign—the whole point of the debate was to delineate and defend the prerogatives of the American *colonies* as though they were homogeneous entities. Massachusetts, New York, and Virginia were subjects writ large. It was *their* relationship with England that American theorists had in mind when they considered the character and the limits of allegiance.

This intellectual perspective was no longer adequate once the colonies broke with the mother country. As thirteen sovereign and independent states were created to supplant the old colonial dependencies, revolutionary leaders found themselves confronted with deeply divided societies. The loyalists—countrymen and quondam fellow subjects—refused to renounce their old allegiance, rejected the claim that the old contract had been abrogated, and resisted the imposition of a new citizenship.

The problem of the loyalists could not be wished away, nor could it be ignored. Yet the principles articulated in the pre-Revolutionary polemics offered no clear guidelines for action. On the one hand, toleration of open disaffection and active opposition to the Revolution threatened the very survival of the cause. On the other hand, the coercion of the unwilling to join the new republics seemed to violate the fundamental principle that legitimate government required the consent of the governed. Lockean contract theory assured Americans that once a society was

---

4. See generally Kettner, *Am. Citizenship*, ch. 6.

formed, the majority could command the obedience of minorities. But what was to be done with those individuals—those *neighbors* —who refused from the beginning to accept the new contract?

The immediate practical problem of what to do with dissidents was more easily solved than the theoretical problems raised by their repudiation of the new republican regimes. Congress and the states enacted a variety of measures to counter and control the threat of subversion from within, and theoretical niceties were frequently forgotten in the heated atmosphere of what was in many respects a civil war. But the fundamental issues involved in the competing claims for individual loyalty could not entirely be evaded. Treason prosecutions during the war necessarily involved questions of allegiance. Post-war diplomatic confrontations between Great Britain and the United States respecting treaty provisions for the recovery of pre-war debts and the compensation for wartime confiscations often hinged upon the party's status as British subject or American citizen.

173

The fragmentation of the community of British allegiance thus posed problems of loyalty, status, and political obligation that had to be confronted and resolved. In the process of facing these issues, Americans developed the idea of volitional allegiance.

The notion that individuals had the right to choose their own loyalty was perhaps embedded in the concept of contractual allegiance from the beginning; yet the transformation of the idea from a mythical construct to a human reality was undeniably the result of the situation created by the Revolution. It would take well into the nineteenth century for Americans to come to terms with this revolutionary legacy, to discover the ramifications and the limitations of the individual's right of election. Jurists, legislators, and theorists would often move slowly, with many a backward glance toward the old, traditional doctrines of subjectship. But once the right was conceded, it could not be revoked. When subjects became citizens, they gained the right to choose their allegiance.

II. *Prosecutions of Loyalists for Treason*

Americans repudiated the authority of Great Britain not as individuals but as organized societies.

Throughout the entire proceeding, it was assumed that the revolutionary assemblies, committees, and conventions that chose the delegates to Philadelphia—as well as the Congressional delegates themselves—truly represented and acted for the whole people. At no time were dissidents considered in any other light than as a minority within legitimate and functioning societies, bound to obey the majority of their fellow members.

Even before the formal break with England, the Continental Congress sanctioned the suppression of anti-Revolutionary activities. Congress was least hesitant to discipline its own Continental Army. The Articles of War, adopted June 30, 1775, provided for the punishment of soldiers who engaged in activities that, for civilians, fell under one of the traditional categories of treason. Courts-martial were empowered to impose penalties short of execution on military men found guilty of mutiny and sedition (the equivalent of "levying war" against constituted authorities) or of supplying, harboring, or corresponding with the enemy (the equivalent of "adhering" or "giving aid and comfort" to the enemy). The discovery that Benjamin Church—a member of the First Continental Congress, and Surgeon-General of the Army—had engaged in "traitorous correspondence" with General Gage impelled Washington to seek a stiffening of the Articles, and on November 7, 1775, Congress empowered courts-martial to impose the death penalty on soldiers convicted of aiding the enemy.[5]

Congress moved more slowly against disaffection among the civilian population. Not until January 11, 1776, did the delegates resolve that any person "so lost to all virtue and regard for his country" as to refuse to receive congressional bills of credit or otherwise discourage their circulation should, on conviction by public committees or other authorities, be "deemed, published, and treated as an enemy of his country, and precluded from all trade or intercourse with the inhabitants of these colonies."[6] This public ostracism was to result from the actions of local bodies, not Congress. Although General Charles Lee of the Continental Army had already brought the power of the military to bear on civilians in Rhode Island and New York by requiring test oaths of suspected persons, a due regard for the distinctions between soldiers and civilians and between Congress and the state authorities led Congress to prohibit any further actions of this nature by its military officers on March 9.[7]

By mid-March, the internal threat seemed drastic enough to justify measures beyond formal, public ostracism.[8] On the 14th

(margin)

5. Bradley Chapin, *The American Law of Treason* (Seattle, 1964), 29-32.

6. *Journals of the Continental Congress, 1774-1789* (Washington, 1904-1937), IV (1776), 49 [hereafter cited, *Jnls. Cont. Cong.*] .

7. *Id.* at 195; B. Chapin, *Am. Law of Treason*, 33-34.

8. A large body of loyalists had already been defeated in armed battle

of that month, Congress recommended that "the several assemblies, conventions, and councils or committees of safety of the United Colonies," immediately disarm all persons "who are notoriously disaffected to the cause of America, or who have not associated, and who shall refuse to associate, to defend, by arms, these United Colonies. . . ."⁹ The suppression of the disaffected was to be carried out by public, not private action. Congress reaffirmed its position on this point on June 18, when it resolved that "no man in these colonies, charged with being a tory, or unfriendly to the cause of American liberty, be injured in his person or property, or in any manner whatsoever disturbed," unless the proceedings were authorized by Congress or by the local authorities.¹⁰

175

Revolutionary leaders found it difficult to take really stern measures against dissidents as long as the colonies technically remained in allegiance to the king. Social pressure and mob action might effectively control the timid and the uncertain, but more drastic powers were needed if the committed opponents of the American cause were to be dealt with. The threat of anarchy was never far below the surface in the troubled months after Lexington, and American leaders had to be concerned lest popular opposition to the "tories" get out of hand and destroy any semblance or order and legitimacy still held by the public authorities. Yet officials hesitated to act in the absence of a clear justification for demanding obedience and loyalty from persons who remained both Americans and British subjects.

The problem came to a head with the discovery of an espionage and counterfeiting ring in New York in early June. The conspirators allegedly received bogus congressional bills from the royal governor, William Tryon—who by now was safely aboard a British warship—using the counterfeit money to depreciate the continental currency and to expedite the recruitment of pro-British forces in the province. The "tory plot" involved both soldiers and civilians, including Thomas Hickey, a member of Washington's personal guard, and David Matthews, mayor of New York City. On June 26, Hickey was found guilty by a court-martial which, under the authority of the Articles of War, ordered

---

at Moore's Creek Bridge in late February, 1776. For the participation of loyalists in early military operations, see Paul H. Smith, *Loyalists and Redcoats: A Study in British Revolutionary Policy* (New York, 1964), 10-31.

9. *Jnls. Cont. Cong.*, IV (1776), 205.

10. *Id.*, V (1776), 464. This resolution was not to prevent the *seizure* for examination and trial of persons suspected of unfriendly acts.

his execution. Two days later, Thomas Hickey became the first American to be hanged in the name of the Revolution.[11]

While the army took care of its own, the public authorities of New York hesitated to move against the civilian conspirators. The provincial congress resolved on June 17 that the colony's courts could not deal with the plot, "being yet held by authority derived from the Crown of Great Britain. . . ."[12] The military had no power to punish civilians; the local government feared to act on its own. The situation demanded decisive measures, and it was left to the Continental Congress to take the initiative.

176   On June 24, 1776, Congress moved to clarify the anomolous legal situation, taking the step that turned disaffection to treason. Recognizing the need to provide a clear legal basis for the suppression of the internal threat, the delegates resolved:

> That all persons residing within any of the United Colonies, and deriving protection from the laws of the same, owe allegiance to the said laws, and are members of such colony; and that all persons passing through, visiting, or make [sic] a temporary stay in any of the said colonies, being entitled to the protection of the laws during the time of such passage, visitation, or temporary stay, owe, during the same time, allegiance thereto:
> That all persons, members of, or owing allegiance to any of the United Colonies, as before described, who shall levy war against any of the said colonies within the same, or be adherents to the king of Great Britain, or other enemies of the said colonies, or any of them, within the same, giving to him or them aid and comfort, are guilty of treason against such colony:

Two additional resolves recommended that the legislatures of the individual colonies pass specific laws punishing counterfeiting and treason.[13]

The resolutions defining allegiance and treason, followed quickly by the Declaration of Independence, provided the individual states with authority to crush internal dissent. The ensuing torrent of legislation that flowed from the state legislatures would not cease until the end of the war. Every state established oaths and declarations to test the loyalty of its inhabitants. Non-jurors

---

11. Curtis P. Nettels, "A Link in the Chain of Events Leading to American Independence," *William and Mary Quarterly*, 3d. ser., (Jan., 1946), 39-40; B. Chapin, *Am. Law of Treason*, 35.

12. C. Nettels, "A Link in the Chain . . . ." 43.

13. *Jnls. Cont. Cong.*, V (1776), 475-76. See also, C. Nettels, "A Link in the Chain . . . ." 38; and B. Chapin, *Am. Law of Treason*, 35-37.

were subjected to penalties ranging from punitive fines, disfranchisement, and deprivation of legal rights to confiscation of their property and banishment. Those loyalists who actively opposed the Revolution, waging war against the American forces or overtly aiding the British, were liable to public execution under most state treason laws.[14]

Once a treason prosecution was begun, the question of the allegiance of the accused became unavoidable, for the essential quality of the crime lay not merely in the specific nature of the act performed but in the intent and status of the performer. A British soldier who "levied war" on the colonies obviously was no traitor. Nor did intent alone suffice to constitute the crime: Joseph Malin of Pennsylvania was acquitted of treason though he confessed to joining a corps of American soldiers, thinking they were British.[15] It was necessary to prove that the person accused had intentionally performed acts that conflicted with obligations he owed as a member of the community. Proof of act, intent, and status were all required before the law judged a man guilty of treason.

177

Treason indictments necessarily included a statement that the accused in fact owed allegiance to the state. Before specifying the acts that one Pennsylvania prisoner had committed "against the Duty of his Allegiance," the state formally charged:

> That John Elwood, late of the County of Bucks, . . . being an inhabitant of and belonging to and residing within the State of Pennsylvania, and under the protection of its Laws, and owing Allegiance to the same State, as a false Traitor against the same, . . . the Fidelity which to the same State he owed, wholly with[drew], and with all his Might intend[ed] the Peace and Tranquillity of this Commonwealth of Pennsylvania, to disturb, and War and Rebellion against the same to raise and to move, and the Government and Independency thereof as by Law established, to subvert, and to raise again, and restore the Government and Tyranny of the King of Great Britain within the same Commonwealth. . . .[16]

---

14. Claude H. Van Tyne, *The Loyalists in the American Revolution* (New York, 1902), chs. IX, X, XII, discusses the punitive laws; Appendices B and C of his work conveniently summarize the major antiloyalist acts. For a particular analysis of the state treason statutes, see B. Chapin, *Am. Law of Treason*, 38-41. J. W. Hurst discusses both statutory and constitutional provisions relating to this crime in his "Treason in the United States," *Harvard Law Review*, LVIII (1944-45), 248-49 n. 35, 256 n. 49.

15. *Respublica v. Malin*, 1 Dall. 33 (Pa. O. & T. 1778).

16. Samuel Hazard *et al.*, eds., *Pennsylvania Archives* (Philadelphia,

Elwood owed allegiance to Pennsylvania because he resided in the state and received the protection of its laws. When he acted against that obligation he was liable to charges of treason.

Hundreds of persons were indicted for treason during the war, but executions for that crime were in fact fairly rare. "Drastic purges and violent assizes were not a part of the Revolution. There was no reign of terror."[17] Most of the injustices committed occurred at the accusation stage, before individuals were brought to trial. It is clear that many more persons were accused of treason and forced to undergo the personal mortification of public obloquy or temporary detention than were ever tried, much less convicted, for that crime. If the cases for which detailed reports are readily accessible are at all representative, the courts took great pains to observe procedural safeguards once the formal machinery of justice was called into play.[18]

It appears to have been a rare case indeed where a person tried, convicted, and sentenced to death for treason did *not* escape the gallows. Governors and legislatures were liberal in granting pardons or in commuting sentences.[19] Convicted men were often given the "option" of accepting their sentence or of enlisting in the state or continental forces—a policy that showed a greater concern for the individual, perhaps, than for the morale and discipline of the army.[20] There was only one known execution for treason in

178

1852-1949), 1st ser., VII, 59-60. Elwood was found guilty and sentenced to hang, but he was later reprieved. *Id.* at 61. He finally received a full pardon. *Colonial Records of Pennsylvania* (Philadelphia, 1852-53), XII, 48. This appears to have been the common form of a treason indictment in Pennsylvania. See, *e.g., Respublica v. Carlisle*, 1 Dall. 34 (Pa. O. & T. 1778).

17. B. Chapin, *Am. Law of Treason,* 71.
18. *Id.* at 63-80.
19. *E.g.,* the General Court at Richmond, Virginia, sentenced at least ten men to hang for treason between April and October, 1782, but all were pardoned. William P. Palmer, ed., *Calendar of Virginia State Papers and Other Manuscripts* (Richmond, 1875-81), III, 120, 194, 361. New York tried a number of persons recruited for loyalist service by Jacob Rosa in 1777. Thirty men were sentenced to hang, and eight were acquitted. All except Rosa and his chief lieutenant, Jacob Middagh, were subsequently pardoned. B. Chapin, *Am. Law of Treason,* 52-53.
20. See, *e.g., Pennsylvania v. Cassedy alias Thompson* (1779), Col. Recs. Pa., XII, 222, 309; *New Jersey v. Bogart, Minutes of the Council of Safety of the State of New Jersey* (Jersey City, 1872), 64, 170. Of seven men tried for treason in connection with a "tory plot" in Maryland, only the leader, Johan C. Frietschie, was hanged. At least one and perhaps as many as four of the others were given the option of enlisting. Dorothy M. Quynn, " The Loyalist Plot in Frederick," *Maryland Historical Magazine,* XL (Sept., 1945), 201-210.

New England during the war, and only four civilians met that fate in Pennsylvania.[21] There were no official executions for treason in Virginia, and apparently many of those sentenced to hang elsewhere in the middle and southern colonies actually suffered lesser punishments.[22] The death penalty seems to have been carried out only where there was clear evidence of active disloyalty, and even then the purpose was as much to warn other potential traitors as to satisfy a patriotic bloodlust.[23]

Nonetheless the distinction between British subject and disloyal citizen emerged out of the treason proceedings. In American eyes, the Revolution fragmented the old community of allegiance, dividing onetime fellow subjects into three separate categories. On the one side were the "real British subjects," including all those whose continued loyalty to the king was uncontested. They had never become citizens of the new republics, and their status during the hostilities was that of alien enemies. On the other side, persons who resided in the states, supported the Revolution, and received the protection of the laws were deemed faithful citizens, entitled to the full privileges of membership. In the middle were the loyalists. They professed a continued allegiance to the British monarch, but in the eyes of "patriot" authorities, the circumstances of their birth, residence, or behavior made them citizens of the new states. Their adherence to Great Britain meant that they were not loyal subjects, but disloyal citizens.

179

---

21. Moses Dunbar was hanged at Hartford, Conn., in March 1777. Epaphroditus Peck, *The Loyalists of Connecticut* (New Haven, 1934), 22-27. The four Pennsylvanians were David Dawson, Abraham Carlisle, John Roberts, and Ralph Morden. I have found nothing relating to Dawson's case. For the others, see generally, Henry J. Young, "Treason and its Punishment in Revolutionary Pennsylvania," *Pennsylvania Magazine of History and Biography*, XC, #3 (1966), *passim* [hereafter, H. Young, "Treason . . . in . . . Pa."], *Respublica v. Carlisle, supra* n. 16; *Respublica v. Roberts*, 1 Dall. 39 (Pa. O. & T. 1778); and John M. Coleman, "The Treason of Ralph Morden and Robert Land," *Pa. Mag. of Hist. & Biog.*, LXXIX (Oct., 1955), 439-451. Samuel Ford and Samuel Lyons were hanged for deserting the provincial navy in 1778, and others may have met a traitor's fate under military authority. *Pa. Archives*, 1st ser., VI, 697-99; *Col. Recs. Pa.*, XI, 565-66, 579, 625.

22. Isaac S. Harrell, *Loyalism in Virginia* (Durham, N.C., 1926), 59; Robert O. Demond, *The Loyalists in North Carolina during the Revolution* (Durham, N.C., 1940), 20. For New York, New Jersey, and Maryland, see B. Chapin, *Am. Law of Treason*, 48-54, 59-60, 77-78.

23. See the Pennsylvania cases *supra*, n.21, and the observation of the judges in the Hardy case, *Col. Recs. Pa.*, xi, 753-4, 761, 764; *Pa. Archives*, 1st Ser., VII, 326-27.

The initial assumption on the American side was that the break with England was the action of a majority, binding the minority of dissenters. The Declaration of Independence, affirmed by the provisional local authorities, had justified the dissolution of the old allegiance on the grounds that George III had defaulted on his obligation to protect his subjects. The congressional resolves of June 24 and the state treason statutes that followed asserted that allegiance was now owed to the new republics. Citizenship supplanted subjectship as the source of protection shifted from George III to the independent states. Revolutionary leaders presumed that the will of the majority was authority enough for the extension of jurisdiction over those who renounced independence and protested their continued loyalty to the king.

III. *The Emergence of the Idea of Volitional Allegiance*

It was inevitable that this presumption would be challenged. Thoughtful loyalists and patriots alike questioned the legitimacy of demanding allegiance and coercing loyalty from individuals who were unwilling participants in the struggle for independence.

Few, perhaps, considered the question as carefully as did Peter Van Schaack, who retired to his New York farm in the winter of 1775-76 to reread Locke, Vattel, Montesquieu, Grotius, Beccaria, and Pufendorf before taking his stand on Independence. Van Schaack had supported the American cause when its main goal had been the redress of grievances within the old imperial system. Yet he was not convinced that the obnoxious British policies were signs of a conspiracy to establish tyranny and to reduce America to slavery.[24] He refused to impute illegitimate motives to the King. When Congress resolved to break the bonds with the mother country, Van Schaack insisted on his right to disagree.

While Van Schaack accepted the ultimate right of revolution, he considered that in the absence of tyranny, "society could not be dissolved, a state of nature did not exist, and a man could not take up arms against the government."[25] The decision whether or not such tyranny existed had to be an *individual* matter:

> Every man must exercise his own reason, and judge for himself; "for he that appeals to Heaven, must be sure that he has

24. After considering the problem, Van Schaack concluded "that taking the whole of the acts complained of together, they do not, I think manifest a system of slavery, but may be fairly imputed to human frailty, and the difficulty of the subject." Henry C. Van Schaack, *The Life of Peter Van Schaack* (New York, 1842), 56. [Hereafter, Van Schaack, *Life*.]

25. William H. Nelson, *The American Tory* (Boston, 1961), 122.

180

right on his side," according to Mr. Locke. It is a question of morality and religion, in which a man cannot conscientiously take an active part, without being convinced in his own mind of the justice of the cause; for obedience while government exists being clear on the one hand, the dissolution of government must be equally so, to justify an appeal to arms. . . .[26]

No majority had the right to impose its opinions on individuals in questions such as this, according to Van Schaack. Even after New York had affirmed the Declaration of Independence and actually assumed the authority and prerogatives of a sovereign state, Van Schaack argued that it was "premature, to tender an oath of allegiance before the government to which it imposes subjection, the time it is to take the place of the present exceptionable one, and who are to be the rulers, as well as the mode of their appointment in future, are known. . . ."[27] Cutting to the very heart of the matter, Van Schaack declared that allegiance to and membership in a political community was ultimately a matter of individual choice:

181

> [A]dmitting that a man is never so clear about the dissolution of the old government, I hold it that *every individual* has still a right to choose the State of which he will become a member; for before he surrenders any part of his natural liberty, he has a right to know what security he will have for the enjoyment of the residue, and "men being by nature free, equal and independent," the subjection of any one to the political power of a State, can arise only from "his own consent." I speak of the formation of a society and of a man's initiating himself therein, so as to make himself a member of it; for I admit, that when once the society *is* formed, the majority of its members undoubtedly conclude the rest.[28]

Van Schaack made the point well. As colonists, the Americans had argued that all legitimate government rested on consent. As

---

26. Van Schaack, *Life*, 57-58.
27. P. Van Schaack to the N.Y. Provincial Convention, Jan. 25, 1777. The letter explained the grounds of Van Schaack's refusal to take the test oath, for which obstinacy he was banished from the state. *Id.*, 72.
28. *Id.*, 73. Van Schaack was consistent in his principles. Once he was convinced that the principles of the British Constitution had been lost and that England was sunk in luxury and vice, he considered himself free to renounce his allegiance and to become a "citizen of the world" until readmitted to the state of New York. He returned to America at the war's end, thus ultimately choosing an American allegiance. *Id.*, 260-63.

founders of new republican states it now seemed inconsistent to insist that individuals could be forced against their will to subject themselves to regimes of which they did not approve. Yet to hold that allegiance was volitional as well as contractual raised questions that were difficult to answer and had implications that were not altogether clear. Indeed, the notion that individual men had the right to choose their own allegiance even after they had enjoyed the protection of the laws in an established society would not be fully accepted until long after the Revolution. It was during the conflict with Great Britain, however, when governments fought over their competing claims to the obedience of the American people, that the first real concessions were made to the right of the individual to decide his own loyalty.

Political theorists had founded political obligation on individual consent long before the American Revolution, of course. But the political ramifications of the idea had never been very deeply explored with respect to the character of allegiance and the relationship between the individual and the community of which he was a member. In Locke's world, men lost the right of autonomous choice as soon as they left the state of nature and submitted to the rule of the majority. Thereafter they were bound by contracts—by the social compact and the contract of government—over which they had no control *as individuals*.[29] Even the original act of volition—the individual's choice to join others to form a community —was more of a theoretical construct than a human reality. Locke did not seriously consider that men in a "state of nature" might have alternative societies to choose among, nor did he explore in depth the validity of the concept of primal consent with respect to those born into already existing societies. His theoretical scheme was thus ill-equipped to deal with the difficult problems of choice raised by the American Revolution.

The colonies' separation from Great Britain did not in fact create a state of nature in which free, autonomous individuals could consider the advantages and disadvantages of submitting to society and government. Britain, of course, continued to insist that the old contracts remained unimpaired, that royal authority over the colonists was still legitimate despite its renunciation by individual rebels or their pretended governments. In the colonies, *ad hoc* provisional governments gradually replaced royal authorities before July, 1776, and they in turn were legitimized or superseded as new state constitutions were drafted and ratified. But there was no general, perceptible break in the actual continuity of government. The Continental Congress defined (and thereby imposed) member-

29. See Kettner, *Am. Citizenship*, 207-9.

ship in the new states even before formalizing independence. And state governments easily and automatically claimed jurisdiction over the same inhabitants and territories that had constituted the colonial dependencies they succeeded.[30]

There were several ways in which this assumption and presumption of jurisdiction could be defended in terms of traditional legal and constitutional theory. One way was to argue that while the contract of government with George III had been broken, the social compact had remained intact. Proceeding from the idea propounded in the pre-Revolutionary debates, that the old colonies had always been separate and complete communities merely sharing a common king, American lawyers could contend that the individual members of the colonial societies were still bound to follow the decisions made by the majority of their fellows. When the majority chose to declare the old government dissolved and a new one erected, minority dissenters were bound to submit. Just as William III had inherited the allegiance of English subjects once "the people" judged that James II had abdicated his throne, so did the new states fall heir to the obedience of all those who had once owed loyalty to George III as the king of their particular colony.[31]

Chief Justice Theophilus Parsons of the Massachusetts Supreme Judicial Court found this argument persuasive as late as 1812. Considering the question whether an infant born in Massachusetts in 1774, who left before Independence and never returned thereafter, was a citizen or an alien, Parsons declared that the Revolution had worked just such an automatic transfer of allegiance:

This people, in union with the people of the other colonies,

183

---

30. See generally, Thad W. Tate, "The Social Contract in America, 1774-1787. Revolutionary Theory as a Conservative Instrument," *W.M.Q.*, 3d. ser., XXII (July, 1965), 375-91. Tate notes that the theory of a broken contract with England was not generally extended to the point of arguing that local or state government was dissolved, except, perhaps, by the Berkshire Constitutionalists in western Massachusetts and the "schismatics" of Vermont and New Hampshire. *Id.*, 388-390. Even where the doctrine *was* successfully applied—as in the "secession" of Vermont—the separation did not occur as the act of autonomous individuals, but as the act of a majority of a whole community that bound all members. The Vermont constitution of July 8, 1777, abjured the king in the usual way, and it explicitly affirmed the right of emigration from one state to another and the right to establish new states in vacant territories: preamble and Art. XVII of the Bill of Rights. Francis N. Thorpe ed., *The Federal and State Constitutions, Colonial Charters, and Other Organic Laws* (Washington, 1909), VI, 3737, 3741.

31. See, *e.g.*, *McIlvaine v. Coxe*, 2 Cranch 280, 317 (U.S. 1805) (argument for defendant).

considered the several aggressions of their sovereign on their essential rights as amounting to an abdication of his sovereignty. The throne was then vacant; but the people, in their political character, did not look after another family to reign; nor did they establish a new dynasty; but assumed to themselves, as a nation, the sovereign power, with all its rights, privileges, and prerogatives. Thus the government became a republic, possessing all the rights vested in the former sovereign; among which was the right to the allegiance of persons born within the territory of the province of Massachusetts Bay.[32]

184

The Court ruled that the infant in question had remained a member of the community of (Massachusetts) allegiance, with all the rights and duties of a citizen.

Parsons personally thought that the bonds of allegiance *could* be broken when the sovereign defaulted on his obligations or when both parties consented to the dissolution of the contract.[33] The Massachusetts courts had already determined that individuals caught up in the Revolution could legitimately change their allegiance with the consent of the government,[34] and they would later hold that persons born within the province could have "been expatriated voluntarily, or by compulsion," during the conflict.[35] Yet, on the whole, the state's claim to obedience took precedence over the individual's right to determine his own loyalty. Massachusetts might *consent* to honor the individual's choice, but within the framework of the contract theory it had no *obligation* to do so.

32. *Ainslie v. Martin*, 9 Mass. 453, 457-58 (1812).

33. *Id.* at 461. John Quincy Adams noted in his diary, Oct. 1, 1787, that Parsons believed that "by the laws of nature every man had a right to put off his natural allegiance, for good cause." Massachusetts Historical Society, *Proceedings*, 2 ser., XVI (1902), 328. Justice Thompson's later claim that Parsons adopted the doctrine of perpetual allegiance to its fullest extent is thus not strictly accurate. See *Inglis v. Trustees of Sailor's Snug Harbor*, 3 Pet. 99, 122-23 (U.S. 1830). Parsons held that a man could sever his allegiance with the default or the consent of the government.

34. *Palmer v. Downer*, 2 Mass. 179n. (1801); *Martin v. Commonwealth*, 1 Mass. 347, 385 (1805); *Gardner v. Ward*, 2 Mass. 244n. (1805); *Kilham v. Ward*, 2 Mass. 236, 239, 268 (1806).

35. *Cummington v. Springfield*, 2 Pickering 394, 395 (Mass. 1824). The phrase quoted is from an opinion given by the Court to the State Senate in the case of George Phipps, June, 1823. The case in question was deemed to fall under the principles established in the Phipps case, and the report cited here consists largely of the opinion given to the Senate in 1823.

An alternative way of justifying the states' assumption of authority over its inhabitants lay in combining the theory of the social contract with the traditional doctrine of conquest. The former readily explained the status of those who voluntarily accepted the new governments. The latter could be used to justify the demands for obedience placed on those who dissented from the Revolution. Coke had claimed in *Calvin's Case*, for example, that the conqueror, holding the power of life and death over the conquered, was entitled to their allegiance.[36] By equating the "disaffected" with the "conquered," Coke's dictum could be applied to legitimize the authority states exercised over the loyalists.

185

The conquest doctrine had the additional advantage from the American point of view of allowing courts to make a distinction between British subjects and American citizens who had been born into a common allegiance. Justice Spencer Roane used the theory that Virginia was a conquering sovereign in order to explain why *antenati* British subjects (those born before Independence) could not claim the rights they would have enjoyed had the state remained a colony:

> They do not become subjects of the conquering power and are not to be considered in that light; because they have not submitted to the conqueror, nor by any compact entitled themselves to the privileges of subjects; and yet they were once inheritable in the territory conquered, and can say as much as the present plaintiffs can say in respect of the territory of Virginia, viz. that, at the time of their birth, they were legitimated here. . . . If, then, the territory of Virginia, had been conquered from Great Britain in the ordinary way, by an existing sovereign, there is no doubt but that, upon the foregoing principles of the common law, the residuary subjects of the British empire, not residing here, nor contracting an allegiance to the conquering power, would have remained aliens, as to the sovereignty established here by such conquest. . . . I see no difference in this respect between a change of the sovereignty of Virginia effected by an existing sovereign, and by a sovereign merely coeval with the change.[37]

For Justice Roane, the Revolution did not therefore involve a mere transfer of allegiance, with the states "inheriting" or succeeding to the loyalty once owed to the king:

> The people themselves who are conquered are legitimated [in the new states] by virtue of the implied compact only,

---

36. See Calvin's Case, 7 Co. Rep. 1a, 17b.
37. *Read v. Read*, 5 Call 160, 199 (Va. Ct. App. 1804).

and cannot claim such legitimation by the paramount title of having been, at the time of their birth inheritable in that territory under another sovereign.[38]

While the Virginia Justice, like his Massachusetts colleague, acknowledged the "natural right" to withdraw allegiance from a tyrant, honoring "the memorable assertion of that right by the American people, who, sword in hand, expatriated themselves from the government which tyrannized over them," he insisted as well that the unwilling could be conquered into a new obedience.[39]

186   Although traditional theory thus offered several ways of justifying the demands for loyalty placed on the former colonists by the new governments, neither the idea of orderly succession nor of conquest seemed to conform adequately to the ideological spirit of the Revolution. Both concepts smacked too much of coercive power and seemed to contradict too blatantly the sense that the war was fought to protect and increase liberty. The need for internal security was clear, of course, and Congress and the states could not ignore the dangers of widespread disaffection. Yet the revolutionary leaders were concerned to keep their cause legitimate and to avoid measures that resembled too closely the arbitrary actions of their former sovereign.

Americans responded to the problem of conflicting loyalties by developing the doctrine of the right of election. The states by no means moved in unison, but all would eventually agree with one lawyer's conclusion that, "In revolutions, every man had a right to take his part. He is excusable, if not bound in duty to take that which in his conscience he approved."[40] The personal choice of allegiance had to be made within a "reasonable" period of time, and once the decision was made it could be considered binding. But the initial concession was clear. Citizenship in the new republics was to begin with individual consent.

The general principle of election seemed clear and fully consonant with the ideals of the Revolution, but its actual application in practice sometimes proved harsh or disingenuous. Most states began with a fairly restrictive policy respecting the

---

38. *Id.* at 199.
39. *Id.* at 201-02.
40. William Tilghman, for plaintiff—in *McIlvaine v. Coxe*, 2 Cranch 280, 281 (U.S. 1805). The principle was perhaps more easily affirmed in cases where Americans were not directly involved. In *Caignet v. Pettit*, 2 Dall. 234, 235 (Pa. S.Ct. 1795), the Court held that a Frenchman "had an undoubted right to dissent from the [French] revolution; and, as a member of the minority, to refuse allegiance to the new government, and withdraw from the territory of *France*."

evidence for election and the time allowed for the exercise of the right. A few states initially assumed that they could claim the allegiance of all their inhabitants at the moment of Independence. If such persons chose to withdraw thereafter, or if they suffered "compulsory expatriation" on conviction or attainder for dis loyalty, they could still be considered to have once been citizens. The disabilities of alienage incurred by this "election" thus could not be removed by later treaty provisions respecting "real British subjects."[41]

Other states were slightly more lenient. Their general policy rested on the concept that citizenship was a contractual relationship in which allegiance was given in return for protection, combined with the idea that Independence had ushered in a brief period of governmental weakness and disorganization that amounted to a virtual state of nature. Election occurred when individuals explicitly acknowledged the legitimacy of the new states or, implicitly, when they accepted the protection of the new constitutions and laws. The time limit for election thus depended upon when legitimate, protective laws came into being in the respective states.

The fact that no treason prosecutions were instituted against civilians until after the states passed treason laws—despite the fact that Congress had already defined the crime—suggests that individuals were generally allowed to choose sides before that time.[42] The assumptions behind this policy were articulated

187

41. See, *e.g., Murray v. Marean* (U.S.C.C., Mass. 1791) cited in John Bassett Moore, ed., *International Adjudications*, mod. ser., III (New York, 1931), 106, (hereafter, Moore, *Int. Adjud.*); *Moore v. Patch* (Mass. 1792) cited in Moore, *Int. Adjud.*, III, 106, 173; *Ainslie v. Martin*, 9 Mass. 453 (1812); and the Connecticut case, *Apthorp v. Backus*, Kirby 407; 1 Am. Dec. 26 (Conn Super. Ct. 1788), where a British subject who acquired lands in the state before the Revolution was held to have once been a citizen. Rhode Island, Connecticut, Virginia, and North Carolina all passed confiscatory acts for disloyalty even before the Declaration of Independence. See Van Tyne, *Loyalists in the Am. Rev.*, App. C. Alexander Hamilton thought that whoever did *not* withdraw from the state became a citizen, though he did not specify the time for withdrawal. He opposed treating all who espoused the British cause as aliens, on the grounds that this admitted the principle that "subjects may at pleasure renounce their allegiance . . ., a principle contrary to law and subversive of government." [A. Hamilton] , "A Letter from Phocion to the Considerate Citizens of New York" and "A Second Letter from Phocion to the Considerate Citizens of New York," in Harold C. Syrett and Jacob E. Cooke, eds., *The Papers of Alexander Hamilton* (New York, 1961), III, 483-97, 530-58. (Hereafter, *Papers*). The quotation is from the first letter, p. 488.

42. B. Chapin, *Am. Law of Treason*, 72, 139 n.39.

in the Pennsylvania case of *Respublica v. Chapman* (1781), a case worth examining in some detail both because of its illustration of contemporary approaches to the problem of conflicting loyalties and because of its later relevance as a precedent in such matters.[43]

Samuel Chapman had resided in Pennsylvania until December 26, 1776, when he departed and joined the British Legion. By a proclamation of the Supreme Executive Council, June 15, 1778, Chapman was required to surrender himself to the state authorities before August 1, and when he ignored the order, he was attainted of treason. Chapman was later captured at sea, taken to Massachusetts (where he was treated as a prisoner-of-war), then extradited to Pennsylvania. Though already convicted of treason by virtue of the attainder, the prisoner was brought before the Supreme Court to give reasons why the judgment should not be executed.

188

The essential point of Chapman's argument was that since there was no legitimate government established in Pennsylvania at the time of his departure from the state, he could receive no protection, owed no allegiance, and was thus not liable to the penalties of treason. The old doctrine of perpetual allegiance, he claimed, "applies only to established and settled governments; not to the case of withdrawing from an old government, and erecting a new one." When such an event took place, every member of the old community "has a right of election." He had signified *his* choice by withdrawing from the state nearly a month before the first legislative act had been passed under the new constitution and nearly three months before all the branches of government were organized and put into operation. A statute of January 28, 1777, revived all the old laws but admitted that they had been in abeyance since May 14, 1776. The state's treason law of February 11, 1777, was not and, under the constitution, could not be retroactive. His attainder, therefore, was illegitimate, unfounded, and utterly void.[44]

The state's Attorney-General countered this argument by contending that even before the new constitution was confirmed, Pennsylvania had been governed by temporary yet legitimate bodies under the authority of the people. He noted that the constitution—"that social compact under which the people of this State are now united"—had been approved on September 8, 1776,

43. *Respublica v. Chapman*, 1 Dall. 53 (Pa. S.Ct. 1781). For additional details of the case, see H. Young, "Treason . . . in . . . Pa.," 301-02. For the use of a case as a precedent, see below, nn. 59, 66.

44. *Respublica v. Chapman*, 1 Dall. 53, 54 (Pa. S.Ct. 1781).

before Chapman withdrew, and that a quorum of the new legislature had met as early as November. Chapman's continued residence in Pennsylvania until December signified his initial acceptance of the new regime, regardless of his later actions.[45]

Chief Justice Thomas McKean saw some validity in both arguments, but his charge to the jury favored Chapman. Treason, claimed McKean, was "nothing more than a criminal attempt to destroy the existence of government," and it might certainly have been committed from the convening of the new legislature (November 18, 1776), before the different qualities of the crime were defined and its punishment declared by positive law. Yet extenuating circumstances tended to absolve the prisoner of this particular crime. From the words of the statute reviving the old laws it could be inferred "that those who framed it, thought the separation from *Great Britain* worked a dissolution of all government, and that the force, not only of the Acts of Assembly, but of the common and statute law of *England*, was actually extinguished by that event."[46] Without the protection of the laws, there evidently could be no allegiance.

All difficulty vanished from the case when one examined the treason act of February 11, 1777. With an evident intent to discriminate between those who owed allegiance and those who did not, the legislature claimed as citizens only those persons *then* or *hereafter* inhabiting the state. Though the policy was not explicitly stated, "we think the desire and intention of the legislature . . . to have been, to allow a choice of his party to every man, until the 11th of February, 1777; and that no act savouring of treason, done before that period, should incur the penalties of the law." Samuel Chapman had made his choice, and within a "reasonable" period of time after Independence. The jury found him not guilty of treason.[47]

Pennsylvania's definition of the time period in which individuals could choose or reject citizenship was perhaps the clearest of all the states', but its stress on the new constitution and the treason statute were representative of a widespread policy. The New York state courts, for example, held that, "Every member of the old government must have the right to decide for himself,

189

---

45. *Id.* at 54-55.
46. *Id.* at 55-58.
47. *Id.* at 58-60. McKean's charge here merely recapitulated and elaborated a position he had already stated in an advisory opinion to President Reed in July, 1779. Reed had asked McKean's opinion concerning the status of persons captured on loyalist privateers—whether they were traitors, pirates, or prisoners-of-war. See H. Young, "Treason . . . in . . . Pa.," 299-300.

whether he will continue with a society which had so funda-
mentally changed its condition." Since the revolutionary government had been "imperfect and inchoate" before April 20, 1777—
the date of the new constitution—it was a "very grave question"
whether treason could have been committed earlier. Whatever
precise time limits were established, it was clear that there had to
be "some personal act, indicative of an assent to become a member
of the new government, and without it, the rights of citizenship
are not acquired."[48]

190

North Carolina permitted election even after its new constitution was established in December, 1776. One case of 1787 implied
that the right to choose was inherent in the fact that the Revolution had created a "state of nature," throwing the inhabitants of
the former colony "into a similar situation with a set of people
ship-wrecked and cast on a maroon'd island—without laws,
without magistrates, without government, or any legal authority.
. . ."[49] Another judge thought that while the state *could* have
claimed the allegiance of all persons resident at the moment of
independence, "whatever were their sentiments or inclinations,"
it nevertheless had granted "the option of taking an oath of
allegiance, or of departing the State," by an act of April, 1777.[50]
The new constitution implied that persons outside the state were
aliens, but statutes allowed absentees to return and be recognized
as citizens as late as October, 1778.[51] British subjects who
never lived in North Carolina and inhabitants who left rather
than swear allegiance within the time allotted by the act of April,
1777, were deemed to have chosen the disabilities of alienage, but
they were not liable to the penalties of disloyalty.[52]

Once a person made his choice of citizenship by swearing
allegiance or by accepting the protection of the laws, and once the
state had acknowledged his membership, he could not change his
mind without risking punishment. This general rule admitted of

---

48. *Jackson v. White*, 20 Johns. Rep. 313, 322, 323, 324 (N.Y. S.Ct.
1822).

49. Judge Ashe, on preliminary motion to dismiss, in *Bayard v.
Singleton*, 1 Martin 48, 1 N.C. 5, 6 (N.C. Super. Ct. 1787).

50. *Hamiltons v. Eaton*, 2 Martin 1, 76, 1 N.C. 641, 688 (U.S.C.C.,
N.C. 1796). The opinion was delivered by Chief Justice Oliver Ellsworth.

51. *Stringer v. Phillips*, 2 Hayward 158, 159, 3 N.C. 204, 205 (N.C.
Super Ct. 1802). See also, R. O. DeMond, *Loyalists in North Carolina*.

52. *Bayard v. Singleton*, 1 Martin 48 1 N.C. 5, 9 (N.C. Super. Ct.
1787), ruled that confiscation was as legally valid as an inquest of office
for taking by escheat the property of an alien. Ellsworth noted that
special considerations might be warranted in cases of forced rather than
voluntary exile or banishment.

some special exceptions, however. Infants might go into exile with their parents without losing the right to claim citizenship at a later date, for they could not be considered capable of making an independent choice during infancy. A child would usually be considered to adopt his father's choice, subject to the "right of disaffirmation, in a reasonable time after the termination of his minority. . . ."[53]

The dependent status of a *feme covert* (married woman) could also temper the *prima facie* evidence of election that residence or exile provided:

> In the relation of husband and wife, the law makes, in her behalf, such an allowance for the authority of her husband, and her duty of obedience [to him], that guilt is not imputed to her for actions performed jointly by them, unless of the most heinous and aggravated nature. . . . A *wife* who left the country in the company of her husband did not *withdraw* herself; but was, if I may so express it, withdrawn by him. She did not deprive the government of the benefit of her personal services; she had none to render; none were exacted of her.[54]

191

Women could commit treason, of course: Esther Marsh was accused of that crime, for example, for helping to supply the British on Staten Island.[55] And women could make individual choices that made them incapable of rights in the new country: the widow of an Irish immigrant who refused to join her husband in New York became an alien after July 4, 1776, and she could take her dower only of lands he had acquired before, not after, Independence.[56] But a woman's status as citizen or alien often depended upon the will of another. Here, as elsewhere, her freedom was limited.

Although states hesitated to demand allegiance from women whose first loyalty was to their husbands or to impose citizenship upon infants incapable of making a choice, they stoutly defended

---

53. Justice Thompson for the majority in *Inglis v. Trustees* of Sailor's *Snug Harbor*, 3 Pet. 99, 126 (U.S. 1830), but see Justice Story's dissenting opinion at 164. The issue of infant election was discussed (but finally evaded) in *Hollingsworth v. Duane*, 12 Fed. Cas. 356 (#6615) (U.S.C.C. Pa. 1801).

54. *Martin v. Commonwealth*, 1 Mass. 347, 391, 392 (1805).

55. *New Jersey v. Marsh* (1778), entries of Jan. 10 and Jan. 14, 1778, *Minutes of N.J. Council of Safety*, 186, 189.

56. *Kelly v. Harrison*, 2 Johns. Cas. 29, 35 (N.Y. S.Ct. 1800). See the similar case in Connecticut, *Sistare v. Sistare*, 2 Root 468 (Conn. Super. Ct. 1796).

their right to define the criteria of membership and to punish persons whose election of citizenship they deemed clear. Public officials and the courts insisted on the legitimacy of penalties imposed for the crime of disloyalty, and they accepted wartime acts specifically claiming the allegiance of named individuals as authoritative evidence of their status.[57] In the long run, such a policy was not necessarily disadvantageous to such persons or their descendants. The peace treaty provision barring "future loss or damage" on account of wartime activities reduced or removed the threat of further punishments for disloyalty, leaving the convicted or attainted loyalist the right to claim the advantages of citizenship. Persons whose sympathies lay with the British and who in fact (if not in law) had chosen to remain subjects might use a wartime attainder to their own advantage after the war, citing it as evidence of their citizenship in the eyes of the law and demanding the rights of the status they had done their best to reject.

192

The case of *McIlvaine v. Coxe*, argued before the United States Supreme Court in 1805, illustrated the possibilities inherent in the situation. Daniel Coxe—a native of New Jersey, onetime member of the colony's Council, and a colonel in the provincial militia—had clearly chosen to side with the British during the Revolution. In 1777, he had fled to British-occupied Philadelphia, where he held office under the king's authority. He followed the British troops to New York in 1779, and he eventually left for England when the royal army evacuated the city. Coxe never swore allegiance to any American state, nor did he ever abjure George III. Indeed, he repeatedly represented himself as a British subject, traded in that capacity, and received a royal pension in compensation for his losses as a loyalist.[58]

McIlvaine's counsel argued that Coxe's actions clearly showed his choice of British subjectship. They cited the Chapman precedent of 1781 to prove the right of election in revolutionary situations.[59] Even if Coxe had owed allegiance to New Jersey by continuing to reside there after the establishment of the new constitution (July 2, 1776) and the state's treason statute (October 4, 1776), his withdrawal, emigration to England, and self-identi-

---

57. In *Camp v. Lockwood*, 1 Dall. 393 (Pa. C.P. 1788), a Pennsylvania court acknowledged the binding force of a Connecticut attainder, deciding that the act barred suit for recovery in all states. *Cooper v. Telfair*, 4 Dall. 14 (U.S. 1800), upheld the validity of a Georgia attainder and denied that it was repugnant to the state's constitution.

58. *McIlvaine v. Coxe*, 2 Cranch 280, 281-83 (U.S. 1808).

59. *Id.* at 284, 322 (argument of counsel).

fication as a British subject proved his expatriation.. The right to choose a new allegiance was inherent in the Revolution, and its validity had been shown by the whole course of American development. "Of all people," argued counsel, "the Americans are the last who ought to call in question the right of *expatriation*. They have derived infinite advantage from its exercise by *others* who have left Europe and settled here."[60]

The old notion of perpetual allegiance founded on *Calvin's Case* had been formulated "when the ideas of the royal prerogative were extravagant and absurd."[61] The New Jersey constitution was based on ideas of contract and consent that repelled the notion that allegiance was immutable, and the ideology of the Revolution implied and included both the right of election and of expatriation. The new states, rightly established, operated by the rule of the majority, of course; but to *institute* that rule, "*individual assent* is necessary, or it deserves the name of usurpation, and ought to be execrated as tyranny."[62] Coxe never gave his consent to the new government. If he owed temporary allegiance between the time of the state's treason act and his withdrawal, his obligation ceased when he departed. If he had become a citizen by coercion, he had the right to shake off that compulsory allegiance which he never recognized.[63] In any event, he must be now considered an alien, not qualified for the rights of citizenship:

> If expatriation be a right when legally exercised, it must induce alienage, and the revolution is a case in point to show that a man is not obliged to continue the subject of that prince under whose dominion he was born; otherwise . . . we must admit that America was not independent until the King of Great Britain acknowledged her independence; and that it was the consequence of, and not antecedent to, the treaty of peace.[64]

The opposing lawyers denied that Coxe had become an alien either during or after the Revolution. The New Jersey constitution of July 2, 1776, had considered every inhabitant a member of the new society, and the decision for independence was an act of the majority binding the minority. Coxe was an inhabitant, thus he

---

60. *Id.* at 284, 325 (argument of counsel).
61. *Id.* at 289. According to Tilghman, the authority of Calvin's Case "is much shaken by the many absurdities it contains. Some of its principles are ridiculous, some contrary to the present law of *England*, and some contrary to our own constitutions."
62. *Id.* at 322 (argument of counsel).
63. *Id.* at 285, 292 (argument of counsel).
64. *Id.* at 329 (argument of counsel).

became a citizen. Even allowing a period of election did not change the case. Coxe had continued in the state after the act of October 4, 1776, by which New Jersey explicitly and unequivocally declared that all persons abiding in its territory and deriving protection from its laws were members owing allegiance. Coxe's attainder in 1778 and the confiscation that followed punished his disaffection but did not alter his citizenship.[65]

194

Coxe's circumstance was not like that of Samuel Chapman of Pennsylvania, for he had remained in the state *after* legitimate government and effective protection began. Coxe rightly suffered the penalties "resulting from his civil relation to the commonwealth"—and he should now be "entitled by natural and equal justice to the benefits of that relation."[66] The doctrine of perpetual allegiance could not decide this case, of course, for the revolutionary situation tore apart the community established by birth under a common sovereign and enabled men to form new contracts of society and government. The place and circumstances of birth did not determine Coxe's allegiance, thus other criteria had to be applied:

> Now, the natural, the only practicable substitute, is this, *that those residing at the time of the revolution in the territory separating itself from the parent country, are subject to the new government, and become members of the new community, on the ground either of tacit consent evidenced by their abiding in such territory; or on the principle that every individual is bound by the act of the majority.*[67]

By continuing to reside in New Jersey, Coxe accepted the contractual relation of allegiance and protection that made him a citizen. He could not thereafter change his citizenship unilaterally. Even if the common law and the constitution of the state admitted the right of expatriation, there was no proof that Coxe had correctly exercised that right, for the contract could only be broken—in the absence of default by the government—by mutual consent.[68] "This public consent," insisted Coxe's counsel, "can be expressed only in one way, *by law;* hence it follows that if the right, strictly speaking, exists, it must be dormant until put in motion by law." The State of New Jersey had never officially recognized or regulated the right; certainly it had done nothing to treat Coxe as anything other than a citizen, albeit a disloyal one. But Coxe had been punished for his disloyalty, and the

---

65. *Id.* at 292-299 (argument of counsel).
66. *Id.* at 300.
67. *Id.* at 312 (argument of counsel).
68. *Id.* at 318.

treaties of 1783 and 1794 prevented any further retribution. He remained a citizen, not an alien. The law must now enforce his rights.[69]

Justice William Cushing handed down the Court's opinion in the case on February 13, 1808.[70] The difficult problems of determining whether the right of expatriation existed in the absence of statutory recognition and of deciding when Coxe lost the right of election were evaded, for there was "no doubt that after the 4th of October 1776, he became a member of the new society, entitled to the protection of its government, and bound to that government by the ties of allegiance." The statute of that date was "conclusive upon the point, . . . [for] the legislature of that state by the most unequivocal declarations, asserted its right to the allegiance of such of its citizens as had not left the state, and had not attempted to return to their former allegiance." The peace treaty did nothing to change Coxe's citizenship, for that agreement merely *recognized* the separate categories of subject and citizen without purporting to *define* their membership. The decision "was left necessarily to depend upon the laws of the respective states, who, in their sovereign capacities, had acted authoritatively upon the subject." New Jersey had declared Coxe a citizen, and he must now be treated as such.[71]

The arguments in *McIlvaine v. Coxe* illustrate clearly the impact of the Revolution on American concepts of allegiance and citizenship. The notion that a person was perpetually bound to the sovereign under whose protection he was born could not survive the actual "dismemberment" of the old empire. The legitimacy of the new governments that emerged from the wreckage of the old community of British allegiance was to derive from individual consent. While lawyers debated the evidence for this consent and the precise time after which it could be presumed to have been given, they agreed that citizenship began with an act of individual will. The opposing lawyers and the Court joined in sustaining the right to elect as an inherent and necessary consequence of the Revolution.

Courts generally pursued a conservative policy with respect to the timing of election into the nineteenth century. As in *McIlvaine v. Coxe*, they insisted that a choice of loyalty had to be made within a short time after the Declaration of Independence, and they allowed no subsequent election of British allegiance *flagrante*

---

69. *Id.* at 320.

70. *McIlvaine v. Coxe*, 4 Cranch 209 (U.S. 1808). Chancellor James Kent considered the principles enunciated in this opinion to be authoritative as late as 1827. James Kent, *Commentaries on American Law*, II (New York, 1827), 33-35. But see below, at n. 82 ff.

71. *McIlvaine v. Coxe*, 4 Cranch 209, 212, 215.

bello.[72] The reasons for this conservatism can be inferred from the arguments and opinions in many of the reported cases. It took time to dissipate the bitterness felt toward natives or long-time residents who took up arms against their neighbors or who otherwise aided the enemy, despite the willingness of many to forgive and forget past hostilities. Punishments meted out to the disloyal on the grounds that they had implicitly chosen citizenship would have been called into question had the courts rejected the states' wartime restrictions on the time limits of election. Moreover, to defer the question of national status until the war's end and to accept as legitimate multiple shifts of loyalty before 1783 seemed to belie the real independence of the states after 1776 and to sanction the British contention that they remained rebellious colonies until the King and Parliament chose to acknowledge their freedom.

196

Eventually the initial insistence on the necessity of an early election would fade. If, during the war, the needs of security demanded that the states be able to identify those over whom they could exercise sovereign power, the concern for individual freedom later helped temper the harshness of this policy. From a post-war vantage point, it often seemed reasonable to accept as decisive a person's choice of allegiance as it appeared at the time of the peace treaty. Even in Massachusetts, where the courts long assumed that all members of the society owed a debt of allegiance to the state at the moment of Independence, judges could later conclude that:

> . . . those who, from timidity, or doubt, or principles of duty and conscience, adhered to their former allegiance, were guilty of no crime for which a punishment could be justly inflicted; and if, from such opinions and impressions, they withdrew from the country, all the evils to which they could justly be subjected would be a complete dissolution of their connection with the country from which they voluntarily withdrew, and the national consequences thereof. They could not be punished for treason, for they had never been united with the new independent society. They had created no new allegiance, for it would be inconsistent with that to which they had a right to adhere. They had an election, and this was to be determined by their own opinions of interest and duty.[73]

72. The policy did not necessarily work both ways, for the courts proved willing to accept British deserters to the American side as citizens if they still adhered to the revolutionary cause in 1783. See *Cummington v. Springfield*, 2 Pickering 394 (Mass. 1824), and *Hebron v. Colchester*, 5 Day 169 (Conn. Super. Ct. 1811).

73. Judge Sedgwick, in *Martin v. Commonwealth*, 1 Mass. 347, 384-85 (1805). New York acknowledged the validity of an election made in 1782, in *Orser v. Hoag*, 3 Hill 79 (N.Y. S.Ct. 1842), a case that arose

Whatever the timing of the individual's election, a choice of British allegiance involved consequences in law that the American courts had to determine. It took time to bring about the spirit of conciliation that the framers of the peace treaty had hoped would characterize the relations between the now separate parts of what had once been a single community. For at least a decade after 1783, many state courts and legislatures refused to concede to British subjects even those rights that the treaty had expressly guaranteed.[74] Not until the Supreme Court's determination of *Ware v. Hylton* (1796), for example, was it made clear that the nation was pledged to enforce the pre-war debts provision, regardless of state legislation designed to obstruct recovery.[75]

197

The task of working out the effect of the Revolution on other rights once held as a consequence of common subjectship continued well into the nineteenth century. American courts rejected the contention that all those born before Independence remained, in some sense, fellow subjects—an argument based on Coke's dictum that a separation of crowns once united left the *antenati* in allegiance to both the old and the new sovereigns, "*ad fidem utriusque regis.*"[76] Yet they hesitated to conclude that all British

---

after the U.S. Supreme Court fixed the principle of relying on the date of the treaty in such questions. See below at n. 82 ff.

74. See *Camp v. Lockwood*, 1 Dall. 393 (Pa. C.P. 1788); *Murray v. Marean*, Moore, Int. Adjud., III, 106, 173; and *Douglass v. Stirk*, Moore, Int. Adjud., III, 106, 174. Maryland's General Court (1790, 1793) initially upheld the right of British creditors to recover though the debtors had paid their debts into the state's treasury and had been released; but the Court of Appeals reversed these decisions: *Dulany v. Wells*, 3 Harris & McHenry 20 (Md. Ct. App. 1795); *Court v. Van Bibber*, 3 Harris & McHenry 140 (Md. Ct. App. 1795). *Ware v. Hylton*, 3 Dall. 199 (U.S. 1796), in turn, reversed the appellate decision. For various legislative strategems to prevent recovery, see Charles R. Ritcheson, *Aftermath of Revolution* (New York, 1969), 63-64.

75. *Ware v. Hylton*, 3 Dall. 199 (U.S. 1796). Some states had moved in this direction already. In New York, the famous case of *Rutgers v. Waddington* (N.Y. Mayor's Ct. 1784) implied that the state's statutes were controlled by the peace treaty: see the documents and account of the case in J. Goebel, Jr., ed., *Law Practice of Alexander Hamilton* (New York, 1964) I, 289-315. For examples of other decisions allowing recovery despite state legislation to prevent it, see: *Hamiltons v. Eaton*, 2 Martin 1 1 N.C. 641 (U.S.C.C. N.C. 1792); *Page v. Pendleton*, Wythe 211 (Va. Ch., 1793); and *Georgia v. Brailsford*, 2 Dall. 402 (U.S. 1793), 3 Dall. 1 (U.S. 1794).

76. Calvin's Case, 7 Co. Rep. 1a, 27b (Ex. Ch. 1608). Coke's doctrines were exhaustively analyzed in a number of cases, as lawyers debated the applicability of his opinion of 1608 to the situation of the *antenati* of the American Revolution. The courts generally concluded that the

subjects immediately incurred all the disabilities of alienage in the new states. The peace treaty had barred "future loss or damage" on account of wartime activities, and although the provision did not necessarily halt non-penal actions that, for example, confiscated property on the grounds of alienage, Jay's Treaty (1794) did guarantee all lands *then* held, providing that neither British subjects, "their Heirs or assigns shall, so far as may respect the said Lands, and the legal remedies incident thereto, be regarded as Aliens."[77]

A long series of judicial decisions worked out the implications of these guarantees and clarified the rights of persons made aliens by the Revolution. The Supreme Court held that the dissolution of the royal government did not automatically create "a dissolution of civil rights, or an abolition of the common law under which the inheritances of every man in the state were held."[78] In order for the states to claim lands held by British subjects, then, they had

---

common allegiance shared before Independence did not persist, and that British subjects who never owed obedience to or received protection from the newly sovereign states became aliens. It was recognized, however, that American citizens might fare better in British courts, where they could claim—as Englishmen in America could not— that they had been born within the king's allegiance and could thus still demand the rights of subjects. See the following cases particularly: *Read v. Read*, 5 Call. 160 (Va. Ct. App. 1804); *Lambert v. Paine*, 3 Cranch 97 (U.S. 1805); *Dawson v. Godfrey*, 4 Cranch 321 (U.S. 1808). *Contee v. Godfrey*, 6 Fed. Cas. 361 (#3140) (U.S.C.C. D.C. 1808), denied that the British-born daughter of an American *antenatus* who had chosen the British side could claim citizenship under the statute 7 Anne c. 5 (discussed in Kettner, *Am. Citizenship*, 20) which in English law had extended subjectship to the foreign-born children of subjects. In this case, the parent's choice of alienage (before the daughter's birth) clearly affected the descendant. On the other hand, *Palmer v. Downer*, 2 Mass. 179n. (1801), suggested that a citizen plaintiff could inherit from a distant ancestor, regardless of any alienage incurred by the parent because of the Revolution, under the statute 11 & 12 Will. III, c. 6 (see Kettner, *Am. Citizenship*, 517, n. 10). *Barzizas v. Hopkins*, 2 Randolph 278 (Va. Ct. App. 1824), held that the foreign-born grandchildren of a native Virginian were aliens and could not inherit, thus denying the applicability of the statute 4 Geo. II, c. 21 (*Kettner, Am. Citizenship* 520).

77. Article 9, Jay's Treaty. Samuel F. Bemis, *Jay's Treaty: A Study in Commerce and Diplomacy* (New Haven, 1923; rev. ed., 1962), App. VIB, 466.

78. *Terrett v. Taylor*, 9 Cranch 43 (U.S. 1815). State courts had moved in this direction earlier, though the principle had not been uniformly acknowledged. See, *e.g.*, *Apthorp v. Backus*, Kirby 407; 1 Am. Dec. 26 (Conn. Super. Ct. 1788) and *Kelly v. Harrison*, 2 Johns. Cas. 29 (N.Y. S.Ct. 1800).

to complete official escheat proceedings; that is, they had to prose-
cute individual cases and could not rely upon a general claim that
the Revolution had divested all such persons of titles to land in
America.[79] The two treaties protected titles that accrued to
British subjects before or during the war, though the agreements
did not protect descents cast or titles acquired after 1783.[80] Thus
British claimants had to prove that they in fact had held some form
of title at the date of the treaty whose guarantees they invoked.[81]

The particular decisions concerning the property of British
subjects drew a clear dividing line between rights acquired before
the peace treaty and those which *might* have accrued thereafter.
Insofar as those whose continued allegiance to the king was clear
were concerned, the treaty thus provided a fixed demarcation line
beyond which such subjects became aliens in the eyes of the law.
By 1830, the Supreme Court was willing to adopt the treaty as a
reference point not only for the rights of "real British subjects" but
for general questions concerning loyalists as well.

199

Justice Joseph Story delivered two opinions that justified
taking 1783 as the cut-off date for the period of election that the
circumstances of the Revolution had made mandatory.[82] In his

---

79. *Fairfax v. Hunter*, 7 Cranch 603 (U.S. 1813), held that an enemy
alien could take lands in Virginia by devise and hold them until formally divested by office found. The state could not grant the lands to
another until its possession was perfected. The treaty of 1794 made such
alien titles indefeasible; that is, it protected them against escheat proceedings on the grounds of alienage by the state. *Terrett v. Taylor*, 9
Cranch 43 (U.S. 1815), and *Jackson v. Clarke*, 3 Wheat. 1 (U.S. 1818),
considered the policy fixed. It was subsequently followed in *Craig v.
Radford*, 3 Wheat. 594 (U.S. 1818); *Orr v. Hodgson*, 4 Wheat. 453 (U.S.
1819); and *Society for the Propagation of the Gospel v. New Haven*,
8 Wheat. 464 (U.S. 1823).

80. *Craig v. Radford* involved a title vested during the war, while
Orr v. Hodgson concerned a title proved to have been held by the alien at
the time of Jay's Treaty. *Dawson v. Godfrey*, 4 Cranch 321 (U.S. 1808),
held that an *antenatus* British subject could not claim the protection of
the peace treaty for a title descending in 1793. *Blight v. Rochester*, 7
Wheat. 535 (U.S. 1822), declared that the treaties protected only those
titles vested in 1783 and 1794, and did not permit aliens to acquire *new*
titles.

81. The Court refused to decide the issue of the validity of a title
where it was not proved that the same was in fact vested at the time of
Jay's Treaty, in *Harden v. Fisher*, 1 Wheat. 300 (U.S. 1816). The Court
held in *Hughes v. Edwards*, 9 Wheat. 489, 501 (U.S. 1824) that the alien
need not show *actual* seisin or possession, declaring that the treaty applied merely to the title "whatever that may be."

82. The two cases were *Inglis v. Trustees of Sailor's Snug Harbor*,
3 Pet. 99 (U.S. 1830); and *Shanks v. Dupont*, 3 Pet. 242 (U.S. 1830). In

view, the common law easily explained a transfer of allegiance from one sovereign to another in cases involving a cession or conquest of territory or when a prince abdicated his government. But the case of a community divided by civil war was more intricate:

> [W]here the old government, notwithstanding the division, remains in operation, there is more difficulty in saying, upon the doctrine of the common law, that their native allegiance to such government is gone, by the mere fact, that they adhere to the separated territory of their birth, unless there be some act of the old government, virtually admitting the rightful existence of the new.[83]

Where two rival claimants demanded an individual's loyalty, *neither* could legitimately "make him responsible, criminally, to its jurisdiction. It may give him the privileges of a subject, but it does not follow, that it can compulsorily oblige him to renounce his former allegiance." The Declaration of Independence was the act of one party only: "It did not bind the British government, which was still at liberty to insist, and did insist, upon the absolute nullity of the act, and claimed the allegiance of all the colonists, as perpetual and obligatory." States on one side of the conflict had no right, by fiat, to force individuals caught up in the situation to become members of the new communities:

> In order, therefore, to make such persons members of the state, there must be some *overt* act or consent on their part, to assume such a character; and then, and then only, could they be deemed, in respect to such colony, to determine their right of election.[84]

the former, Story wrote a dissenting opinion on the major point, which involved the technicalities of a will. However, he agreed with the majority on the question of plaintiff's alienage, though his reasoning varied with that of Justice Thompson, who delivered the majority opinion. In the second case, Story spoke for the majority. In the Inglis case, Justice Johnson applied the now anachronistic claim that the states succeeded to the loyalty of their inhabitants at the moment of Independence. In the Shanks case, he denied the unilateral right of election that he had once considered plausible: "But more mature reflection has satisfied me, that I then gave too much weight to natural law and the suggestions of reason and justice; in a case which ought to be disposed of upon the principles of political and positive law, and the law of nations." Though Johnson thought states should be liberal in allowing a choice of allegiance, he denied that South Carolina had extended a choice to Mrs. Shanks, and he concluded that her "contract" of citizenship thus remained binding. *Inglis v. Trustees of Sailor's Snug Harbor*, at 136; *Shanks v. Dupont*, at 258, 259. Johnson was not supported in this position by any of the other Justices.

83. *Inglis v. Trustees of Sailor's Snug Harbor*, at 157.

84. *Id.* at 157, 159.

The principle that the Americans generally adopted, Story rightly observed, was to consider all persons free to choose sides within a reasonable period of time, "and the fact of abiding within the state, after it assumed independence, or after some other specific period, was declared to be an election to become a citizen." However, such an implicit election:

> . . . could be binding only between him and the state, and could have no legal effect upon the rights of the British crown. The king might still claim to hold him to his former allegiance, and until an actual renunciation on his part, according to the common law, he remained a subject. He was, or might be held to be, bound *ad utriusque fidem regis.*

201

Such a person would be deemed a citizen by the American courts, a subject by the British courts, and either by neutral courts, depending upon the circumstances.[85]

Historically it was true that some persons changed sides during the conflict, and their position remained ambiguous as long as both sides claimed their loyalty. But the treaty ended the anomoly. It "acted, by necessary implication, upon the existing state of things, and fixed the final allegiance of the parties on each side, as it was then *de facto.*" *After* the treaty, then, American courts had no more right to "deem *all* persons citizens who at *any* time before the treaty were citizens" than Great Britain had "to claim as subjects all who previously were subjects." Rather, the agreement that brought peace "ought to be so construed, as that each government should be finally deemed entitled to the allegiance of those who were at that time adhering to it."[86]

Story found this principle simple, rational, and just. It allowed the courts to escape the inconvenience of concluding that the Revolution left many in the position of owing a double allegiance.[87] It had the advantage of giving due weight to the opinions both of the governments and the individuals concerned. Moreover, it could solve difficult questions relating to the evidence for and the timing of election in cases where the individual's choice or capacity to choose was in some doubt.

The utility of this principle was illustrated in *Shanks v. Dupont* (1830), where the Supreme Court considered the status of a woman who had been born in South Carolina and resident there during the war, but who had married a British officer and departed with him for Great Britain in 1782. The case might have involved a whole complex of considerations including the relative weights of place of birth, duration of residence after Independence, marriage

---

85. *Id.* at 160, 161.
86. *Id.* at 162, 163, 164.
87. *Shanks v. Dupont,* 3 Pet. 242, 247 (U.S. 1830).

to an alien enemy, and capacity of a woman *"sub potestate viri"* to choose her own allegiance. Instead, the case became a simple matter of determining *de facto* adherence at the time of the treaty, in which the opinions both of the governments and the individual could be duly considered:

> The governments, and not herself, finally settled her national character. They did not treat her as capable by herself of changing or absolving her allegiance; but they virtually allowed her the benefit of her choice, by fixing her allegiance finally on the side of that party to whom she then adhered.[88]

202

After 1783, concluded Justice Story, Americans had no interest in discriminating against those who had become loyalists or in treating them any differently than as British subjects. Article VI of the peace treaty, he recalled, had barred future confiscations and the further impairment of rights:

> This part of the stipulation, then, being for the benefit of British subjects who became aliens by the events of the war; there is no reason why all persons should not be embraced in it, who sustained the character of British subjects, although one might also have treated them as American citizens.

By international principles, Americans and the British had *equal* rights to claim the allegiance of those who had confronted the Revolution. They could recognize or deny the other's claim. Reason and justice could only conclude that the treaty of 1783 involved a mutual recognition by the governments of the choices that individuals had made at the war's end.[89]

The status of "American citizen" was the creation of the Revolution. The imperial crisis of the pre-war years and the separation from the mother country formalized in 1776 stimulated the articulation of at least some of the major principles that were to shape and define the new status. Despite some initial confusion, Americans came to see that citizenship must begin with an act of individual choice. Every man had to have the right to decide whether to be a citizen or an alien. His power to make this choice was clearly acknowledged to be a matter of right, not of grace, for the American republics were to be legitimate governments firmly grounded on consent, not authoritarian states that ruled by force and fiat over involuntary and unwilling subjects.

Although the right to choose one's loyalty could be regulated, it could not be denied. Individual liberty and the security of the community as a whole could both be served—must both be served

---

88. *Id.* at 248.
89. *Id.* at 249-50.

—by republican citizenship. Americans acknowledged the right of the state to dictate the timing of election, to establish the rules governing its exercise, and to determine its consequences. But the individual alone was responsible for making the choice between subjectship and citizenship.

It was not yet clear how far this right of election could be extended, for the notion that membership in a political community, once formed, was contractual still characterized most discussions of the nature of the relationship between a person who had made his choice, explicitly or implicitly, and the community that accepted him as a member. Some Americans pursued the logic of volitional allegiance to its limits, arguing that the right to join a community logically implied the right to leave it as well. Others were more hesitant, contending that in the absence of default, *both* parties — the citizen and the community—must consent to expatriation. While they acknowledged that allegiance *began* with an act of individual volition, they doubted that the right to *terminate* an obligation once accepted could safely be entrusted to autonomous individuals. The balance between the volitional and contractual aspects of citizenship thus remained an open question even after the immediate effect of the Revolution on the status of its participants had been determined.

Even more perplexing than this was the question whether the Revolution had created one community of allegiance or many. The issue remained at the periphery of the problems of loyalty that Americans dealt with directly in these years, for the particular questions discussed here—the validity of treason prosecutions and of wartime confiscations, and the post-war rights of British subjects in the new states—rarely required a close examination of the possible distinctions between a general American citizenship and membership in a particular state. It was enough to decide that one was a subject or a citizen; to consider whether the latter meant membership in a state or in a nation of states seemed unnecessary.

The question would become a critical one in the years after the Revolution. It would appear in many different contexts and in many different guises: in the development of policies concerning naturalization and expatriation, in debates over the jursidiction of courts and the status of inhabitants of the American territories, in conflicts between nationalists and the advocates of states' rights, and ultimately in the soul-searing crisis of slavery.

By the beginning of the nineteenth century, then, Americans had only begun to discover the complexity of the question, "Who are the People?'" They had committed themselves to certain principles about the acquisition of citizenship, but they had yet to fully develop the meaning of that status.

203

Evangelical Revolt: The Nature of the Baptists' Challenge to the Traditional Order in Virginia, 1765 to 1775

Rhys Isaac*

AN intense struggle for allegiance had developed in the Virginia countryside during the decade before the Revolution. Two eye-witness accounts may open to us the nature of the conflict.

First, a scene vividly remembered and described by the Reverend James Ireland etches in sharp profile the postures of the forces in contest. As a young man Ireland, who was a propertyless schoolmaster of genteel origin, had cut a considerable figure in Frederick County society. His success had arisen largely from his prowess at dancing and his gay facility as a satiric wit. Then, like many other young men at this time (ca. 1768), he came deeply "under conviction of sin" and withdrew from the convivialities of gentry society. When an older friend and patron of Ireland heard that his young protégé could not be expected at a forthcoming assembly, this gentleman, a leader in county society, sensed the challenge to his way of life that was implicit in Ireland's withdrawal. He swore instantly that "there could not be a dance in the settlement without [Ireland] being there, and if they would leave it to him, he would convert [him], and that to the dance, on Monday; and they would see [Ireland] lead the ball that day." Frederick County, for all its geographical spread, was a close community. Young James learned that his patron would call, and dreaded the coming test of strength:

When I viewed him riding up, I never beheld such a display of pride arising from his deportment, attitude and jesture; he rode a lofty elegant

* Mr. Isaac is a member of the Department of History, La Trobe University, Australia. He would like to thank all those who helped this study with encouragement and critical advice, particularly Stephen G. Kurtz, Thad W. Tate, Allan Martin, John Salmond, Inga Clendinnen, and Greg and Donna Dening. A deep debt of gratitude is owed to the Virginia Baptist Historical Society and the Virginia State Library for their cooperation in making available microfilm of the Baptist church books.

horse, . . . his countenance appeared to me as bold and daring as satan himself, and with a commanding authority [he] called upon me, if I were there to come out, which I accordingly did, with a fearful and timorous heart. But O! how quickly can God level pride. . . . For no sooner did he behold my disconsolate looks, emaciated countenance and solemn aspect, than he . . . was riveted to the beast he rode on. . . . As soon as he could articulate a little his eyes fixed upon me, and his first address was this; "In the name of the Lord, what is the matter with you?"[1]

The evident overdramatization in this account is its most revealing feature for it is eloquent concerning the tormented convert's heightened awareness of the contrast between the social world he was leaving and the one he was entering.

205

The struggle for allegiance between these social worlds had begun with the Great Awakening in the 1740s, but entered into its most fierce and bitter phase with the incursions of the "New Light" Separate Baptists into the older parts of Virginia in the years after 1765.[2] The social conflict was not over the distribution of political power or of economic wealth, but over the ways of men and the ways of God. By the figures in the encounter described we may begin to know the sides drawn: on the one hand, a mounted gentleman of the world with "commanding authority" responding to challenge; on the other, a guilt-humbled, God-possessed youth with "disconsolate looks . . . and solemn aspect."

A second scene—this time in the Tidewater—reveals through actions some characteristic responses of the forces arrayed. From a diary entry of 1771 we have a description of the disruption of a Baptist meeting by some gentlemen and their followers, intent on upholding the cause of the established Church:

---

[1] James Ireland, *The Life of the Reverend James Ireland* . . . (Winchester, Va., 1819), 83, 84-85.

[2] For a valuable account of the triumph of evangelicalism in Virginia, 1740 to 1790, see Wesley M. Gewehr, *The Great Awakening in Virginia, 1740-1790* (Durham, N. C., 1930). The rate at which the Separate Baptists were spreading may be seen by the following summary: 1769—7 churches, 3 north of the James River; May 1771—14 churches (1,335 members); May-Oct. 1774—54 churches (4,004 members); 24 north of the James River. *Ibid.*, 117. In the manuscript notes of Morgan Edwards references to *at least* 31 disruptions of meetings, by riot and/or arrest, occurring before 1772 can be identified; 13 of these appear to have been plebeian affairs, 8 gentry-led, and 10 unspecified. Morgan Edwards, Materials toward a History of the Baptists in the Province of Virginia, 1772 *passim,* MS, Furman University Library, Greenville, S. C. (microfilm kindly supplied by the Historical Commission, Southern Baptist Convention, Nashville, Tenn.).

Brother Waller informed us . . . [that] about two weeks ago on the Sabbath Day down in Caroline County he introduced the worship of God by singing. . . . The Parson of the Parish [who had ridden up with his clerk, the sheriff, and some others] would keep running the end of his horsewhip in [Waller's] mouth, laying his whip across the hymn book, etc. When done singing [Waller] proceeded to prayer. In it he was violently jerked off the stage; they caught him by the back part of his neck, beat his head against the ground, sometimes up, sometimes down, they carried him through a gate that stood some considerable distance, where a gentleman [the sheriff] gave him . . . twenty lashes with his horsewhip. . . . Then Bro. Waller was released, went back singing praise to God, mounted the stage and preached with a great deal of liberty.[3]

206

Violence of this kind had become a recurrent feature of social-religious life in Tidewater and Piedmont. We must ask: What kind of conflict was this? What was it that aroused such antagonism? What manner of man, what manner of movement, was it that found liberty in endurance under the lash?

The continuation of the account gives fuller understanding of the meaning of this "liberty" and of the true character of this encounter. Asked "if his nature did not interfere in the time of violent persecution, when whipped, etc.," Waller "answered that the Lord stood by him . . . and poured his love into his soul without measure, and the brethren and sisters about him singing praises . . . so that he could scarcely feel the stripes . . . rejoicing . . . that he was worthy to suffer for his dear Lord and Master."[4]

Again we see contrasted postures: on the one hand, a forceful, indeed brutal, response to the implicit challenge of religious dissidence; on the other, an acceptance of suffering sustained by shared emotions that gave release—"liberty." Both sides were, of course, engaged in combat, yet their modes of conducting themselves were diametrically opposite. If we are to understand the struggle that had developed, we must look as deeply as possible into the divergent styles of life, at the conflicting visions of what life should be like, that are reflected in this episode.

[3] John Williams's Journal, May 10, 1771, in Lewis Peyton Little, *Imprisoned Preachers and Religious Liberty in Virginia* (Lynchburg, Va., 1938), 230-231. A similar account by Morgan Edwards indicates that the men were mounted and mentions who the principals were. Materials, 75-76.

[4] Williams, Journal, in Little, *Imprisoned Preachers,* 231.

Opposites are intimately linked not only by the societal context in which they occur but also by the very antagonism that orients them to each other. The strength of the fascination that existed in this case is evident from the recurrent accounts of men drawn to Baptist meetings to make violent opposition, who, at the time or later, came "under conviction" and experienced conversion.[5] The study of a polarity such as we find in the Virginia pre-Revolutionary religious scene should illuminate not only the conflict but also some of the fundamental structures of the society in which it occurred. A profile of the style of the gentry, and of those for whom they were a pattern, must be attempted. Their values, and the system by which these values were maintained, must be sketched. A somewhat fuller contrasting picture of the less familiar Virginia Baptist culture must then be offered, so that its character as a radical social movement is indicated.

The gentry style, of which we have seen glimpses in the confrontation with Baptists, is best understood in relation to the concept of honor—the proving of prowess.[6] A formality of manners barely concealed adversary relationships; the essence of social exchange was overt self-assertion.

Display and bearing were important aspects of this system. We can best get a sense of the self-images that underlay it from the symbolic importance of horses. The figure of the gentleman who came to call Ireland back to society was etched on his memory as mounted on a "lofty . . . elegant horse." It was noted repeatedly in the eighteenth century that Virginians would "go five miles to catch a horse, to ride only one mile upon afterwards."[7] This apparent absurdity had its logic in the necessity of being mounted when making an entrance on the social scene. The role of the steed as a valuable part of proud self-presentation is suggested by the intimate identification of the gentry with their horses that was constantly manifested through their conversation. Philip Fithian, the New Jersey tutor, sometimes felt that he heard nothing but "Loud disputes

[5] For examples see Edwards, Materials, 34, 54, 55, 73.

[6] For the sake of clarity a single "gentry style" is here characterized. Attention is focused on the forms that appear to have been most pervasive, perhaps because most adapted to the circumstances of common life. It is not, however, intended to obscure the fact that there were divergent and more refined gentry ways of life. The development within the genteel elite of styles formed in negation of the predominant mores will be the subject of a full separate analysis. I am indebted to Jack P. Greene for advice on this point.

[7] J. F. D. Smyth, quoted in Jane Carson, *Colonial Virginians at Play* (Williamsburg, Va., 1965), 103-104. See also the comments of Hugh Jones and Edward Kimber, *ibid.*, 103.

concerning the Excellence of each others Colts . . . their Fathers, Mothers (for so they call the Dams) Brothers, Sisters, Uncles, Aunts, Nephews, Nieces, and Cousins to the fourth Degree!"[8]

Where did the essential display and self-assertion take place? There were few towns in Virginia; the outstanding characteristic of settlement was its diffuseness. Population was rather thinly scattered in very small groupings throughout a forested, river-dissected landscape. If there is to be larger community in such circumstances, there must be centers of action and communication. Insofar as cohesion is important in such an agrarian society, considerable significance must attach to the occasions when, coming together for certain purposes, the community realizes itself. The principal public centers in traditional Virginia were the parish churches and the county courthouses, with lesser foci established in a scatter of inns or "ordinaries." The principal general gatherings apart from these centers were for gala events such as horse race meetings and cockfights. Although lacking a specifically community character, the great estate house was also undoubtedly a very significant locus of action. By the operation of mimetic process and by the reinforcement of expectations concerning conduct and relationships, such centers and occasions were integral parts of the system of social control.[9]

The most frequently held public gatherings at generally distributed centers were those for Sunday worship in the Anglican churches and chapels. An ideal identification of parish and community had been expressed in the law making persistent absence from church punishable. The continuance of this ideal is indicated by the fact that prosecutions under the law occurred right up to the time of the Revolution.[10]

---

[8] Hunter Dickinson Farish, ed., *Journal & Letters of Philip Vickers Fithian 1773-1774: A Plantation Tutor of the Old Dominion* (Williamsburg, Va., 1957), 177-178.

[9] I am unable to find a serviceable alternative for this much abused term. The concept has tended to be directed toward the operations of rules and sanctions, the restraint of the pursuit of self-interest, and the correction of deviant motivation. See *International Encyclopedia of the Social Sciences*, XIV (New York, 1968), 381-396. A different emphasis is adopted in this article, drawing attention to more fundamental aspects, namely, those processes by which cultural criteria of "proper" motivation and "true" self-interest are established and reinforced in a particular society. Closely related are the mechanisms whereby individuals' perceptions and valuations of their own and others' identities are shaped and maintained. My conceptualization derives from the ideas of "reality-maintenance" (almost of continuous socialization) which are fully developed in Peter L. Berger and Thomas Luckmann, *The Social Construction of Reality: A Treatise in the Sociology of Knowledge* (Garden City, N. Y., 1966), 72-73, 84, 166-175, and *passim*.

[10] Little, *Imprisoned Preachers*, 265-266, 291.

Philip Fithian has left us a number of vivid sketches of the typical Sunday scene at a parish church, sketches that illuminate the social nature and function of this institution. It was an important center of communication, especially among the elite, for it was "a general custom on Sundays here, with Gentlemen to invite one another home to dine, after Church; and to consult about, determine their common business, either before or after Service," when they would engage in discussing "the price of Tobacco, Grain etc. and settling either the lineage, Age, or qualities of favourite Horses." The occasion also served to demonstrate to the community, by visual representation, the rank structure of society. Fithian's further description evokes a dramatic image of haughty squires trampling past seated hoi polloi to their pews in the front. He noted that it was "not the Custom for Gentlemen to go into Church til Service is beginning, when they enter in a Body, in the same manner as they come out."[11]

Similarly, vestry records show that fifty miles to the south of Fithian's Westmoreland County the front pews of a King and Queen County church were allocated to the gentry, but the pressure for place and precedence was such that only the greatest dignitaries (like the Corbins) could be accommodated together with their families; lesser gentlemen represented the honor of their houses in single places while their wives were seated farther back.[12]

The size and composition of the ordinary congregations in the midst of which these representations of social style and status took place is as yet uncertain, but Fithian's description of a high festival is very suggestive on two counts: "This being Easter-Sunday, all the Parish seem'd to meet together High, Low, black, White all come out."[13] We learn both that such general attendance was unusual, and that at least once a year full expression of ritual community was achieved. The whole society was then led to see itself in order.

The county courthouse was a most important center of social action. Monthly court days were attended by great numbers, for these were also the times for markets and fairs. The facts of social dominance were there visibly represented by the bearing of the "gentlemen justices" and the respect they commanded. On court days economic exchange was openly merged with social exchange (both plentifully sealed by the taking of

[11] Farish, ed., *Journal of Fithian*, 29, 167.
[12] C. G. Chamberlayne, ed., *The Vestry Book of Stratton Major Parish, King and Queen County, Virginia, 1729-1783* (Richmond, Va., 1931), 167.
[13] Farish, ed., *Journal of Fithian*, 89. See also 137.

liquor) and also expressed in conventional forms of aggression—in banter, swearing, and fighting.[14]

The ruling gentry, who set the tone in this society, lived scattered across broad counties in the midst of concentrations of slaves that often amounted to black villages. Clearly the great houses that they erected in these settings were important statements: they expressed a style, they asserted a claim to dominance. The lavish entertainments, often lasting days, which were held in these houses performed equally important social functions in maintaining this claim, and in establishing communication and control within the elite itself. Here the convivial contests that were so essential to traditional Virginia social culture would issue in their most elaborate and stylish performances.[15]

The importance of sporting occasions such as horse racing meets and cockfights for the maintenance of the values of self-assertion, in challenge and response, is strongly suggested by the comments of the marquis de Chastellux concerning cockfighting. His observations, dating from 1782, were that "when the principal promoters of this diversion [who were certainly gentry] propose to [match] their champions, they take great care to announce it to the public; and although there are neither posts, nor regular conveyances, this important news spreads with such facility, that the planters for thirty or forty miles round, attend, some with cocks, but all with money for betting, which is sometimes very considerable."[16] An intensely shared interest of this kind, crossing but not leveling social distinctions, has powerful effects in transmitting style and reinforcing the leadership of the elite that controls proceedings and excels in the display.

Discussion so far has focused on the gentry, for *there* was established in dominant form the way of life the Baptists appeared to challenge. Yet this way was diffused throughout the society. All the forms of communication and exchange noted already had their popular acceptances with varia-

[14] Charles S. Sydnor, *American Revolutionaries in the Making: Political Practices in Washington's Virginia* (New York, 1965 [orig. publ. Chapel Hill, N. C., 1952]), 74-85. This is the incomparable authority for the nature and function of county court days, and for the rank, etc., of the justices. Chap. 4 makes clear the importance of liquor in social intercourse. That the custom of gentlemen establishing their "liberality" by "treating" their inferiors was not confined to the time of elections is suggested by Col. Wager's report "that he usually treated the members of his militia company with punch after the exercises were over." *Ibid.*, 58.

[15] Farish, ed., *Journal of Fithian, passim;* Carson, *Colonial Virginians at Play, passim.*

[16] Quoted in Carson, *Colonial Virginians at Play,* 160 and *passim.* For evidence of genteel patronage of the sport see *ibid.*, 156-157.

tions appropriate to the context, as can be seen in the recollections of the young Devereux Jarratt. The son of a middling farmer-artisan, Jarratt grew up totally intimidated by the proximity of gentlemen, yet his marked preference for engagement "in keeping and exercising race-horses for the turf . . . in taking care of and preparing game-cocks for a match and main" served to bind him nonetheless into the gentry social world, and would, had he persisted, have brought him into contact—gratifying contact—with gentlemen. The remembered images of his upbringing among the small farmers of Tidewater New Kent County are strongly evocative of the cultural continuum between his humble social world and that of the gentry. In addition to the absorbing contest pastimes mentioned, there were the card play, the gathering at farmhouses for drinking (cider not wine), violin playing, and dancing.[17]

211

The importance of pastime as a channel of communication, and even as a bond, between the ranks of a society such as this can hardly be too much stressed. People were drawn together by occasions such as horse races, cockfights, and dancing as by no other, because here men would become "known" to each other—"known" in the ways which the culture defined as "real." Skill and daring in that violent duel, the "quarter race"; coolness in the "deep play" of the betting that necessarily went with racing, cockfighting, and cards—these were means whereby Virginia males could prove themselves.[18] Conviviality was an essential part of the social exchange, but through its soft coating pressed a harder structure of contest, or "emulation" as the contemporary phrase had it. Even in dancing this was so. Observers noted not only the passion for dancing—"*Virginians* are of genuine Blood—They will dance or die!"—but also the marked preference for the jig—in effect solo performances by partners of each sex, which were closely watched and were evidently competitive.[19] In such activities, in social contexts high or low, enhanced eligibility for marriage was established by young persons who emerged as virtuosos of the dominant style. Situations where so much could happen presented powerful images of the "good life" to traditional Virginians, especially young

[17] Devereux Jarratt, *The Life of the Reverend Devereux Jarratt* . . . (Baltimore, 1806), 14, 19, 20, 23, 31, 42-44. It is interesting to note that although religious observance played a minimal part in Jarratt's early life, the Bible was the book from which he (and other small farmers' sons presumably) learned to read. A base was thereby prepared for evangelical culture. *Ibid.*, 20-21.

[18] Carson, *Colonial Virginians at Play, passim.* For an intensely illuminating discussion of the social significance of "deep play" in gambling see Clifford Geertz, "Deep Play: Notes on the Balinese Cockfight," *Daedalus*, CI (Winter, 1972), 1-37.

[19] Farish, ed., *Journal of Fithian*, 177; Carson, *Colonial Virginians at Play*, 21-35.

ones. It was probably true, as alleged, that religious piety was generally considered appropriate only for the aged.[20]

When one turns to the social world of the Baptists, the picture that emerges is so striking a negative of the one that has just been sketched that it must be considered to have been structured to an important extent by processes of reaction to the dominant culture.

Contemporaries were struck by the contrast between the challenging gaiety of traditional Virginia formal exchange and the solemn fellowship of the Baptists, who addressed each other as "Brother" and "Sister" and were perceived as "the most melancholy people in the world"—people who "cannot meet a man upon the road, but they must ram a text of Scripture down his throat."[21] The finery of a gentleman who might ride forth in a gold-laced hat, sporting a gleaming Masonic medal, must be contrasted with the strict dress of the Separate Baptist, his hair "cut off" and such "superfluous forms and Modes of Dressing . . . as cock't hatts" explicitly renounced.[22]

Their appearance was austere, to be sure, but we shall not understand the deep appeal of the evangelical movement, or the nature and full extent of its challenging contrast to the style and vision of the gentry-oriented social world, unless we look into the rich offerings beneath this somber exterior. The converts were proffered some escape from the harsh realities of disease, debt, overindulgence and deprivation, violence and sudden death, which were the common lot of small farmers. They could seek refuge in a close, supportive, orderly community, "a congregation of faithful persons, called out of the world by divine grace, who mutually agree to live together, and execute gospel discipline among them."[23]

[20] Jarratt wrote of "Church people, that, generally speaking, none went to the table [for communion] except a few of the more aged," Life, 102; and Ireland, "I . . . determined to pursue the pleasures . . . until I arrived to such an advance in years, that my nature would . . . enjoy no further relish. . . . A merciful God . . . would accept of a few days or weeks of my sincere repenting," Life, 59. Likewise it may be noted that religiosity only enters markedly into the old-man phase of Landon Carter's diary. Jack P. Greene, ed., The Diary of Colonel Landon Carter of Sabine Hall, 1752-1778, 2 vols. (Charlottesville, Va., 1965), passim.

[21] David Thomas, The Virginian Baptist . . . (Baltimore, 1774), 59; Robert B. Semple, A History of the Rise and Progress of the Baptists in Virginia, ed. G. W. Beale (Richmond, Va., 1894), 30.

[22] Farish, ed., Journal of Fithian, 69; Upper King and Queen Baptist Church, King and Queen County, Records, 1774-1816, Sept. 16, 1780. (Microfilm of this and subsequently cited Baptist church books kindly provided by the Virginia Baptist Historical Society, Richmond.)

[23] John Leland, The Virginia Chronicle (Fredericksburg, Va., 1790), 27. See also Thomas, The Virginian Baptist, 24-25.

Entrance into this community was attained by the relation of a personal experience of profound importance to the candidates, who would certainly be heard with respect, however humble their station. There was a community resonance for deep feelings, since, despite their sober face to the outside world, the Baptists encouraged in their religious practice a sharing of emotion to an extent far beyond that which would elicit crushing ridicule in gentry-oriented society.[24] Personal testimonies of the experiences of simple folk have not come down to us from that time, but the central importance of the ritual of admission and its role in renewing the common experience of ecstatic conversion is powerfully evoked by such recurrent phrases in the church books as "and a dore was opened to experience." This search for deep fellow-feeling must be set in contrast to the formal distance and rivalry in the social exchanges of the traditional system.[25]

213

The warm supportive relationship that fellowship in faith and experience could engender appears to have played an important part in the spread of the movement. For example, about the year 1760 Peter Cornwell of Fauquier County sought out in the backcountry one Hays of pious repute, and settled him on his own land for the sake of godly companionship. "Interviews between these two families were frequent . . . their conversation religious . . . in so much that it began to be talked of abroad as a very strange thing. Many came to see them, to whom they related what God did for their souls . . . to the spreading of seriousness through the whole neighbourhood."[26]

A concomitant of fellowship in deep emotions was comparative equality. Democracy is an ideal, and there are no indications that the pre-Revolutionary Baptists espoused it as such, yet there can be no doubt that these men, calling each other brothers, who believed that the only authority in their church was the meeting of those in fellowship together, conducted their affairs on a footing of equality in sharp contrast to the explicit preoccupation with rank and precedence that characterized the world from which they had been called. Important Baptist church elections gen-

[24] The Baptists, it was sneered, were "always sighing, groaning, weeping." To which Thomas replied, "It is true lively Christians are apt to weep much, but that is often with joy instead of sorrow." *The Virginian Baptist*, 59.
[25] Chestnut Grove Baptist Church, or Albemarle-Buck Mountain Baptist Church, Records, 1773-1779, 1792-1811, *passim*. Ireland tells how, when he had given the company of travelers to the Sandy Creek Association of 1769 an account of "what the Lord had done for my soul. . . . They were very much affected . . . so much so that one of the ministers embraced me in his arms." *Life*, 141.
[26] Edwards, *Materials*, 25-26.

erally required unanimity and might be held up by the doubts of a few. The number of preachers who were raised from obscurity to play an epic role in the Virginia of their day is a clear indication of the opportunities for fulfillment that the movement opened up to men who would have found no other avenue for public achievement. There is no reason to doubt the contemporary reputation of the early Virginia Baptist movement as one of the poor and unlearned. Only isolated converts were made among the gentry, but many among the slaves.[27]

214

The tight cohesive brotherhood of the Baptists must be understood as an explicit rejection of the formalism of traditional community organization. The antithesis is apparent in the contrast between Fithian's account of a parish congregation that dispersed without any act of worship when a storm prevented the attendence of both parson and clerk, and the report of the Baptist David Thomas that "when no minister . . . is expected, our people meet notwithstanding; and spend . . . time in praying, singing, reading, and in religious conversation."[28]

The popular style and appeal of the Baptist Church found its most powerful and visible expression in the richness of its rituals, again a total contrast to the "prayrs read over in haste" of the colonial Church of England, where even congregational singing appears to have been a rarity.[29] The most prominent and moving rite practiced by the sect was adult baptism, in which the candidates were publicly sealed into fellowship. A scrap of Daniel Fristoe's journal for June 15-16, 1771, survives as a unique contemporary description by a participant:

(Being sunday) about 2000 people came together; after preaching [I] heard others that proposed to be baptized. . . . Then went to the water where I preached and baptized 29 persons. . . . When I had finished we went to a field and making a circle in the center, there laid hands on the persons baptized. The multitude stood round weeping, but when we sang *Come we that love the lord* and they were so affected that they lifted up

---

[27] Thomas, *The Virginian Baptist*, 54. See also Semple, *History of the Baptists in Virginia*, 29, 270, and Leland, *Virginia Chronicle*, 23. I have not as yet been able to attempt wealth-status correlations for ministers, elders, deacons, and ordinary members of the churches. It must be noted that the role which the small group of gentry converts played (as one might expect from the history of other radical movements) assumed an importance out of all proportion to their numbers. See Morattico Baptist Church, Lancaster County, Records (1764), 1778-1814, *passim*, and Chesterfield Baptist Church, Lancaster County, Records, 1773-1788, for the role of the "rich" Eleazer Clay.

[28] Farish, ed., *Journal of Fithian*, 157; Thomas, *The Virginian Baptist*, 34.

[29] Farish, ed., *Journal of Fithian*, 167, 195.

their hands and faces towards heaven and discovered such chearful countenances in the midst of flowing tears as I had never seen before.[30]

The warm emotional appeal at a popular level can even now be felt in
that account, but it must be noted that the scene was also a vivid enactment of *a* community within and apart from *the* community. We must
try to see that closed circle for the laying on of hands through the eyes
of those who had been raised in Tidewater or Piedmont Virginia with the
expectation that they would always have a monistic parish community
encompassing all the inhabitants within its measured liturgical celebrations. The antagonism and violence that the Baptists aroused then also
become intelligible.

215

The celebration of the Lord's Supper frequently followed baptism, in
which circumstances it was a further open enactment of closed community. We have some idea of the importance attached to this public display from David Thomas's justification:

... should we forbid even the worst of men, from viewing the solemn representation of his [the LORD JESUS CHRIST's] dying agonies? May not
the sight of this mournful tragedy, have a tendency to alarm stupid creatures ... when GOD himself is held forth ... trembling, falling, bleeding,
yea, expiring under the intollerable pressure of that wrath due to [sin].
... And therefore, this ordinance should not be put under a bushel, but
on a candlestick, that all may enjoy the illumination.[31]

We may see the potency attributed to the ordinances starkly through the
eyes of the abashed young John Taylor who, hanging back from baptism,
heard the professions of seven candidates surreptitiously, judged them not
saved, and then watched them go "into the water, and from thence, as
I thought, seal their own damnation at the Lord's table. I left the meeting
with awful horror of mind."[32]

More intimate, yet evidently important for the close community, were
the rites of fellowship. The forms are elusive, but an abundance of ritual

[30] Morgan Edwards, Notes, in Little, *Imprisoned Preachers*, 243. See also Leland,
Virginia Chronicle, 36: "At times appointed for baptism the people generally go
singing to the water in grand procession: I have heard many souls declare they
first were convicted or first found pardon going to, at, or coming from the water."

[31] Thomas, *The Virginian Baptist*, 35-36; Albemarle Baptist Church Book,
June 18, 1774.

[32] John Taylor, *A History of Ten Baptist Churches* . . . (Frankfort, Ky.,
1823), 296.

is suggested by the simple entry of Morgan Edwards concerning Falls Creek: "In this church are admitted, Evangelists, Ruling Elders, deaconesses, laying on of hands, feasts of charity, anointing the sick, kiss of charity, washing feet, right hand of fellowship, and devoting children." Far from being mere formal observances, these and other rites, such as the ordaining of "apostles" to "pervade" the churches, were keenly experimented with to determine their efficacy.[33]

Aspects of preaching also ought to be understood as ritual rather than as formal instruction. It was common for persons to come under conviction or to obtain ecstatic release "under preaching," and this established a special relationship between the neophyte and his or her "father in the gospel." Nowhere was the ritual character of the preaching more apparent than in the great meetings of the Virginia Separate Baptist Association. The messengers would preach to the people along the way to the meeting place and back; thousands would gather for the Sunday specially set aside for worship and preaching. There the close independent congregational communities found themselves merged in a great and swelling collective.[34] The varieties of physical manifestations such as crying out and falling down, which were frequently brought on by the ritualized emotionalism of such preaching, are too well known to require description.

Virginia Baptist sermons from the 1770s have not survived, perhaps another indication that their purely verbal content was not considered of the first importance. Ireland's account of his early ministry (he was ordained in 1769) reveals the ritual recurrence of the dominant themes expected to lead into repentance those who were not hardened: "I began first to preach . . . our awful apostacy by the fall; the necessity of repentance unto life, and of faith in the Lord Jesus Christ . . . our helpless incapacity to extricate ourselves therefrom I stated and urged."[35]

As "seriousness" spread, with fear of hell-fire and concern for salva-

216

[33] Edwards, Materials, 56; Albemarle Baptist Church Book, Aug. 1776; Semple, History of the Baptists in Virginia, 81.

[34] Ireland, Life, 191; Taylor, History of Ten Baptist Churches, 7, 16; Semple, History of the Baptists in Virginia, 63; Garnett Ryland, The Baptists of Virginia, 1699-1926 (Richmond, Va., 1955), 53-54.

[35] Ireland, Life, 185. Laboring day and night, "preaching three times a day very often, as well as once at night," he must have kept himself in an exalté, near trance-like condition. His instruction to those who came to him impressed with "their helpless condition" is also illuminating. "I would immediately direct them where their help was to be had, and that it was their duty to be as much engaged . . . as if they thought they could be saved by their own works, but not to rest upon such engagedness." Ibid., 186.

tion, it was small wonder that a gentleman of Loudoun County should find to his alarm "that the *Anabaptists* . . . growing very numerous . . . seem to be increasing in afluence [influence?]; and . . . quite destroying pleasure in the Country; for they encourage ardent Pray'r; strong and constant faith, and an intire Banishment of *Gaming, Dancing,* and Sabbath-Day Diversions."[36] That the Baptists were drawing away increasing numbers from the dominant to the insurgent culture was radical enough, but the implications of solemnity, austerity, and stern sobriety were more radical still, for they called into question the validity—indeed the propriety—of the occasions and modes of display and association so important in maintaining the bonds of Virginia's geographically diffuse society. Against the system in which proud men were joined in rivalry and convivial excess was set a reproachful model of an order in which God-humbled men would seek a deep sharing of emotion while repudiating indulgence of the flesh. Yet the Baptist movement, although it must be understood as a revolt against the traditional system, was not primarily negative. Behind it can be discerned an impulse toward a tighter, more effective system of values and of exemplary conduct to be established and maintained within the ranks of the common folk.

In this aspect evangelicalism must be seen as a popular response to mounting social disorder. It would be difficult—perhaps even impossible—to establish an objective scale for measuring disorder in Virginia. What can be established is that during the 1760s and 1770s disorder was perceived by many as increasing. This has been argued for the gentry by Jack P. Greene and Gordon S. Wood, and need not be elaborated here. What does need to be reemphasized is that the gentry's growing perception of disorder was focused on those forms of activity which the Baptists denounced and which provided the main arenas for the challenge and response essential to the traditional "good life." It was coming to be felt that horse racing, cockfighting, and card play, with their concomitants of gambling and drinking, rather than serving to maintain the gentry's prowess, were destructive of it and of social order generally. Display might now be negatively perceived as "luxury."[37]

Given the absence of the restraints imposed by tight village commun-

---

[36] Farish, ed., *Journal of Fithian*, 72.

[37] Greene, ed., *Landon Carter Diary*, I, 14, 17-19, 21, 25, 33, 39, 44, 47, 52-53; Gordon S. Wood, "Rhetoric and Reality in the American Revolution," *William and Mary Quarterly*, 3d Ser., XXIII (1966), 27-31; Jack P. Greene, "Search for Identity: An Interpretation of the Meaning of Selected Patterns of Social Response in Eighteenth-Century America," *Journal of Social History*, III (1969-1970), 196-205.

ity in traditional Virginia, disorder was probably an even more acute problem in the lower than in the upper echelons of society—more acute because it was compounded by the harshness and brutality of everyday life, and most acute in proportion to the social proximity of the lowest stratum, the enslaved. The last named sector of society, lacking sanctioned marriage and legitimated familial authority, was certainly disorderly by English Protestant standards, and must therefore have had a disturbing effect on the consciousness of the whole community.[38]

218

As the conversion experience was at the heart of the popular evangelical movement, so a sense of a great burden of guilt was at the heart of the conversion experience. An explanation in terms of social process must be sought for the sudden widespread intensification and vocal expression of such feelings, especially when this is found in areas of the Virginia Piedmont and Tidewater where no cultural tradition existed as preconditioning for the communal confession, remorse, and expiation that characterized the spread of the Baptist movement. The hypothesis here advanced is that the social process was one in which popular perceptions of disorder in society—and hence by individuals in themselves—came to be expressed in the metaphor of "sin." It is clear that the movement was largely spread by revolt from within, not by "agitators" from without. Commonly the first visit of itinerant preachers to a neighborhood was made by invitation of a group of penitents already formed and actively meeting together. Thus the "spread of seriousness" and alarm at the sinful disorder of the traditional world tended to precede the creation of an emotional mass movement "under preaching."[39] A further indication of the importance of order-disorder preoccupations for the spread of the new vision with its contrasted life style was the insistence on "works." Conversion could ultimately be validated among church members only by a radical reform of conduct. The Baptist church books reveal the close concern for the disciplinary supervision of such changes.[40]

[38] Gerald W. Mullin, *Flight and Rebellion: Slave Resistance in Eighteenth-Century Virginia* (New York, 1972), *passim*. This article owes an incalcuable debt to Mullin's powerful and creative analysis of the dominant Virginia culture.

[39] Edwards, Materials, 25, 69, 89, 90; Semple, *History of the Baptists in Virginia*, 19-20, 25, 26, 32, 33, 227, 431.

[40] I have closely read the following Baptist church records for the period up to 1790: Broad Run Baptist Church, Fauquier County, Records, 1762-1837; Chesterfield Baptist Church, Recs.; Chestnut Grove/Albemarle Church, Recs.; Hartwood-Potomac Baptist Church Book, Stafford County, 1771-1859; Mill Creek Baptist Church, Berkeley County, Records (1757), 1805-1928; Mill Swamp Baptist Church, Isle of Wight County, Records (1774), 1777-1790; Morattico Baptist Church, Recs.; Smith's Creek Baptist Church, Shenandoah and Rockingham counties, Records, 1779-1809 (1805); Upper King and Queen Baptist Church, Recs.

Drunkenness was a persistent problem in Virginia society. There were frequent cases in the Baptist records where censure, ritual excommunication, and moving penitence were unable to effect a lasting cure. Quarreling, slandering, and disputes over property were other endemic disorders that the churches sought patiently and endlessly to control within their own communities.[41] With its base in slavery, this was a society in which contest readily turned into disorderly violence. Accounts of the occasion, manner, and frequency of wrestling furnish a horrifying testimony to the effects of combining a code of honor with the coarseness of life in the lower echelons of society. Hearing that "by appointment is to be fought this Day . . . two fist Battles between four young Fellows," Fithian noted the common causes of such conflicts, listing numbers of trivial affronts such as that one "has in a merry hour call'd [another] a *Lubber*, . . . or a *Buckskin*, or a *Scotchman*, . . . or offered him a dram without wiping the mouth of the Bottle." He noted also the savagery of the fighting, including "Kicking, Scratching, Biting, . . . Throtling, Gouging [the eyes], Dismembring [the private parts]. . . . This spectacle . . . generally is attended with a crowd of People!" Such practices prevailed throughout the province.[42] An episode in the life of one of the great Baptist preachers, John, formerly "swearing Jack," Waller, illustrates both prevailing violence and something of the relationship between classes. Waller and some gentry companions were riding on the road when a drunken butcher addressed them in a manner they considered insolent. One of the gentlemen had a horse trained to rear and "paw what was before him," which he then had it do to frighten the butcher. The man was struck by the hooves and died soon after. Tried for manslaughter, the company of gentlemen were acquitted on a doubt as to whether the injury had indeed caused the butcher's death.[43] The episode may have helped prepare Waller for conversion into a radically opposed social world.

Nowhere does the radicalism of the evangelical reaction to the dominant values of self-assertion, challenge, and response of the gentry-oriented society reveal itself so clearly as in the treatment of physical aggression. In the Baptist community a man might come forward by way of confession with an accusation against himself for "Geting angry Tho in Just

219

[41] Upper King and Queen Baptist Church, Recs., Jan. 20, 1781; Morattico Baptist Church, Recs., May 30, 1781, *et seq.*; Mill Swamp Baptist Church, Recs., Sept. 17, 1779; Broad Run Baptist Church, Recs., July 27, 1778.
[42] Farish, ed., *Journal of Fithian*, 183; Carson, *Colonial Virginians at Play*, 164-168.
[43] Edwards, Materials, 72.

Defence of himself in Despute." The meeting of another church was informed that its clerk, Rawley Hazard, had been approached on his own land and addressed in "Very scurrilous language" and then assaulted, and that he then "did defend himself against this sd Violence, that both the Assailant and Defendent was much hurt." The members voted that the minister "do Admonish Brother Rawley . . . in the presents of the Church . . . saying that his defence was Irregular."[44]

A further mark of their radicalism, and without doubt the most significant aspect of the quest for a system of social control centered in the people, was the inclusion of slaves as "brothers" and "sisters" in their close community. When the Baptists sealed the slaves unto eternal life, leading them in white robes into the water and then back to receive the bread and wine, they were also laying upon them responsibility for godly conduct, demanding an internalization of strict Protestant Christian values and norms. They were seeking to create an orderly moral community where hitherto there had seemed to be none.

220

The slaves were members and therefore subject to church discipline. The incidence of excommunication of slaves, especially for the sin of adultery, points to the desire of the Baptists to introduce their own standards of conduct, including stable marital relationships, among slaves.[45] A revealing indication of the perception of the problem in this area is found in the recurrent phrase that was sometimes given as the sole reason for excommunication: "walking disorderly." Discipline was also clearly directed toward inculcating a sense of duty in the slaves, who could be excommunicated for "disobedience and Aggrevation to [a] master."[46]

[44] Chestnut Grove/Albemarle Baptist Church, Recs., Dec. 1776; Morattico Baptist Church, Recs., Feb. 17, 1783.
[45] Mill Swamp Baptist Church, Recs., Mar. 13, 1773.
[46] Morattico Baptist Church, Recs., Oct. 8, 1780. The role of the slaves in the 18th-century Baptist movement remains obscure. They always carried with them their slave identity, being designated "Gresham's Bob" or the like, or even "the property of." Yet it is reported that the slaves of William Byrd's great estates in Mecklenburg County were among the first proselytes to the Separate Baptists in Virginia. "Many of these poor slaves became bright and shining Christians. The breaking up of Byrd's quarters scattered these blacks into various parts. It did not rob them of their religion. It is said that through their labors in the different neighborhoods . . . many persons were brought to the knowledge of the truth, and some of them persons of distinction." Semple, *History of the Baptists in Virginia*, 291-292. The valuable researches of W. Harrison Daniel show that hearing of experience, baptism, and disciplining of whites and blacks took place in common. Black preachers were not uncommon and swayed mixed congregations. "In the 1780's one predominantly white congregation in Gloucester County chose William Lemon, a Negro, as its pastor." Segregation of the congregation does not begin to

The recurrent use of the words "order," "orderly," "disorderly" in the Baptist records reveals a preoccupation that lends further support to the hypothesis that concern for the establishment of a securer system of social control was a powerful impulse for the movement. "Is it orderly?" is the usual introduction to the queries concerning right conduct that were frequently brought forward for resolution at monthly meetings.[47]

With alarm at perceived disorder must also be associated the deep concern for Sabbath-day observance that is so strongly manifested in autobiographies, apologetics, and church books. It appears that the Virginia method of keeping the Sabbath "with sport, merriment, and dissipation" readily served to symbolize the disorder perceived in society. It was his observation of this that gave Ireland his first recorded shock. Conversely, cosmic order was affirmed and held up as a model for society in the setting aside on the Lord's Day of worldly pursuits, while men expressed their reverence for their Maker and Redeemer.[48]

When the Baptist movement is understood as a rejection of the style of life for which the gentry set the pattern and as a search for more powerful popular models of proper conduct, it can be seen why the ground on which the battle was mainly fought was not the estate or the great house, but the neighborhood, the farmstead, and the slave quarter. This was a contemporary perception, for it was generally charged that the Baptists were "continual fomenters of discord" who "not only divided good neighbours, but slaves and their masters; children and their parents . . . wives and their husbands." The only reported complaint against the first preachers to be imprisoned was of "their running into private houses and making dissensions."[49] The struggle for allegiance in the homesteads between a style of life modeled on that of the leisured gentry and that embodied in evangelicalism was intense. In humbler, more straitened circumstances a popular culture based on the code of honor and almost hedonist values was necessarily less securely established than among the more affluent gentry. Hence the anxious aggressiveness of popular anti-New Light feeling and action.[50]

---

appear in the records until 1811. Daniel, "Virginia Baptists and the Negro in the Early Republic," *Virginia Magazine of History and Biography,* LXXX (1972), 62, 60-69.

[47] Mill Swamp Baptist Church, Recs., Mar. 13, June 9, 1778; Hartwood-Potomac Baptist Church, Recs., 1776, 9-10.

[48] Ireland, *Life,* 44; Thomas, *The Virginian Baptist,* 34-35.

[49] Thomas, *The Virginian Baptist,* 57: John Blair to the King's Attorney in Spotsylvania County, July 16, 1768, in Little, *Imprisoned Preachers,* 100-101.

[50] Jarratt, *Life,* 23, 31, 38; Farish, ed., *Journal of Fithian,* 73; Semple, *History of the Baptists in Virginia, passim.*

The Baptists did not make a bid for control of the political system—still less did they seek a leveling or redistribution of worldly wealth. It was clearly a mark of the strength of gentry hegemony and of the rigidities of a social hierarchy with slavery at its base that the evangelical revolt should have been so closely restricted in scope. Yet the Baptists' salvationism and sabbatarianism effectively redefined morality and human relationships; their church leaders and organization established new and more popular foci of authority, and sought to impose a radically different and more inclusive model for the maintenance of order in society. Within the context of the traditional monistic, face-to-face, deferential society such a regrouping necessarily constituted a powerful challenge.

222

The beginnings of a cultural disjunction between gentry and sections of the lower orders, where hitherto there had been a continuum, posed a serious threat to the traditional leaders of the community; their response was characteristic. The popular emotional style, the encouragement given to men of little learning to "exercise their gifts" in preaching, and the preponderance of humble folk in the movement gave to the proud gentry their readiest defense—contempt and ridicule. The stereotype of the Baptists as "an ignorant . . . set . . . of . . . the contemptible class of the people," a "poor and illiterate sect" which "none of the rich or learned ever join," became generally established. References in the *Virginia Gazette* to "ignorant enthusiasts" were common, and there could appear in its columns without challenge a heartless satire detailing "A Receipt to make an Anabaptist Preacher": "Take the Herbes of Hypocrisy and Ambition, . . . of the Seed of Dissention and Discord one Ounce, . . . one Pint of the Spirit of Self-Conceitedness."[51]

An encounter with some gentlemen at an inn in Goochland County is recorded by Morgan Edwards, a college-educated Pennsylvania Baptist minister. He noted the moderation of the gentry in this area, yet their arrogant scorn for dissenters in general, and for Baptists in particular, is unmistakable from the dialogue reported. Since Edwards had just come from Georgia, they began with ribald jests about "mr Whitefield's children . . . by the squaw" and continued as follows:

Esq[uire] U: Pray are you not a clergyman? . . .
Capt. L: Of the church of England I presume?

---

[51] Little, *Imprisoned Preachers*, 36; Thomas, *The Virginian Baptist*, 54. See also Semple, *History of the Baptists in Virginia*, 29; Leland, *Virginia Chronicle*, 23; *Virginia Gazette* (Purdie and Dixon), Oct. 31, 1771.

N[orthern] M[inister]: No, Sir; I am a clergyman of a
better church than that; for she is a persecutor.
Omnes: Ha! Ha! Ha! . . .
Esq. U: Then you are one of the fleabitten clergy?
N. M.: Are there fleas in this bed, Sir?
Esq. U: I ask, if you are a clergyman of the itchy true
blue kirk of Scotland? . . .
Capt. L. (whispers): He is ashamed to own her for fear you
should scratch him 'Squire.' . . .
[When they have discovered that this educated man, who shows
such address in fencing with words, is a Baptist minister,
they discuss the subject bibulously among themselves.]
Esq. U: He is no baptist . . . I take him to be one of the
Georgia law[ye]rs.
Mr. G: For my part I believe him to be a baptist minister.
There are some clever fellows among them. . . .
Major W: I confess they have often confounded me with their
arguments and texts of Scripture; and if any other people but
the baptists professed their religion I would make it my
religion before tomorrow.[52]

223

The class of folk who filled the Baptist churches were a great obstacle
to gentry participation. Behind the ridicule and contempt, of course, lay
incomprehension, and behind that, fear of this menacing, unintelligible
movement. The only firsthand account we have of a meeting broken up
by the arrest of the preachers tells how they "were carried before the
magistrate," who had them taken "one by one into a room and examined
our pockets and wallets for firearms." He accused them of "carrying
on a mutiny against the authority of the land." This sort of dark suspicion
impelled David Thomas, in his printed defense of the Baptists, to reiterate
several times that "We concern not ourselves with the government . . .
we form no intrigues . . . nor make any attempts to alter the constitution
of the kingdom to which as men we belong."[53]

Fear breeds fantasy. So it was that alarmed observers put a very crude
interpretation on the emotional and even physical intimacy of this in-
trusive new society. Its members were associated with German Anabap-

[52] Edwards, Materials, 86-88.
[53] John Waller to an unknown fellow Baptist, Aug. 12, 1771, in Little, *Imprisoned
Preachers*, 276; Thomas, *The Virginia Baptist*, 33, 36.

tists, and a "historical" account of the erotic indulgences of that sect was published on the front page of the *Virginia Gazette*.[54]

Driven by uneasiness, although toughened by their instinctive contempt, some members of the establishment made direct moves to assert proper social authority and to outface the upstarts. Denunciations from parish pulpits were frequent. Debates were not uncommon, being sought on both sides. Ireland recalled vividly an encounter that reveals the pride and presumption of the gentlemen who came forward in defense of the Church of England. Captain M'Clanagan's place was thronged with people, some of whom had come forty miles to hear John Pickett, a Baptist preacher of Fauquier County. The rector of a neighboring parish attended with some leading parishioners "who were as much prejudiced . . . as he was." "The parson had a chair brought for himself, which he placed three or four yards in front of Mr. Pickett . . . taking out his pen, ink and paper, to take down notes of what he conceived to be false doctrine." When Pickett had finished, "the Parson called him a schismatick, a broacher of false doctrines . . . [who] held up damnable errors that day." Pickett answered adequately (it appeared to Ireland), but "when contradicted it would in a measure confuse him." So Ireland, who had been raised a gentleman, took it on himself to sustain the Baptist cause. The parson immediately "wheeled about on his chair . . . and let out a broadside of his eloquence, with an expectation, no doubt, that he would confound me with the first fire." However, Ireland "gently laid hold of a chair, and placed . . . it close by him, determined to argue." The contest was long, and "both gentlemen and ladies," who had evidently seated themselves near the parson, "would repeatedly help him to scripture, in order to support his arguments." When the debate ended (as the narrator recalled) in the refutation of the clergyman, Ireland "addressed one of the gentlemen who had been so officious in helping his teacher; he was a magistrate . . . 'Sir, as the dispute between the Parson and myself is ended, if you are disposed to argue the subject over again, I am willing to enter upon it with you.' He stretched out his arm straight before him, at that instant, and declared that I should not come nigher than that

224

---

[54] *Va. Gaz.* (Purdie and Dixon), Oct. 4, 1770. Thomas states that there is no evil which "has not been reported of us." *The Virginian Baptist*, 6. There is in a letter of James Madison a reference to the "Religion . . . of some enthusiasts, . . . of such a nature as to fan the amorous fire." Madison to William Bradford, Apr. 1, 1774, in William T. Hutchinson and William M. E. Rachal, eds., *The Papers of James Madison*, I (Chicago, 1962), 112. See also Richard J. Hooker, ed., *The Carolina Backcountry on the Eve of the Revolution* (Chapel Hill, N. C., 1953), 98, 100-104, 113-117, for more unrestrained fantasies concerning the emergent Southern Baptists.

length." Ireland "concluded what the consequence would be, therefore made a peaceable retreat."[55] Such scenes of action are the stuff of social structure, as of social conflict, and require no further comment.

Great popular movements are not quelled, however, by outfacing, nor are they stemmed by the ridicule, scorn, or scurrility of incomprehension. Moreover, they draw into themselves members of all sections of society. Although the social worlds most open to proselytizing by the Baptists were the neighborhoods and the slave quarters, there were converts from the great houses too. Some of the defectors, such as Samuel Harris, played a leading role in the movement.[56] The squirearchy was disturbed by the realization that the contemptible sect was reaching among themselves. The exchanges between Morgan Edwards and the gentlemen in the Goochland inn were confused by the breakdown of the stereotype of ignorance and poverty. Edwards's cultured facility reminded the squires that "there are some clever fellows among [the Baptists]. I heard one Jery Walker support a petition of theirs at the assembly in such a manner as surprised us all, and [made] our witts draw in their horns."[57] The pride and assurance of the gentry could be engaged by awareness that their own members might withdraw from their ranks and choose the other way. The vigorous response of Ireland's patron to the challenge implicit in his defection provides a striking example.

225

The intensity of the conflict for allegiance among the people and, increasingly, among the gentry, makes intelligible the growing frequency of violent clashes of the kind illustrated at the beginning of this article. The violence was, however, one-sided and self-defeating. The episode of April 1771 in which the parson brutally interfered with the devotions of the preacher, who was then horsewhipped by the sheriff, must have produced a shock of revulsion in many quarters. Those who engaged in such actions were not typical of either the Anglican clergy or the country gentlemen. The extreme responses of some, however, show the anxieties to which all were subject, and the excesses in question could only heighten the tension.

Disquiet was further exacerbated by the fact that the law governing dissent, under which the repressive county benches were intent on acting,

[55] Ireland, Life, 129-134.
[56] Although Samuel Harris, renouncing the world, gave up his newly built country seat to be a meetinghouse for his church, the role of patron died hard. He would kill cattle for love feasts that were held there. Edwards, Materials, 57.
[57] Ibid., 88. The scene was concluded by the genteel Baptist being offered and accepting hospitality. He finally left the neighborhood with an assurance from his host "that he would never talk any more against the Baptists." Ibid., 89.

was of doubtful validity, and became the subject of public controversy in the fall of 1771.[58] This controversy, combined with the appalling scenes of disorder and the growing numbers of Separate Baptists, led the House of Burgesses to attempt action in its spring 1772 session. The Separates had shown renewed tendencies to intransigence as recently as May 1771, when a move was strongly supported to deny fellowship to all ministers who submitted to the secular authority by applying for permission to preach. The fact that eight months later the House of Burgesses received a petition for easier licensing conditions was a sign that a compromise was at last being sought. Nevertheless, prejudices were so strong that the bill that the Burgesses approved was considerably more restrictive than the English act that had hitherto been deemed law in the colony.[59]

226

The crisis of self-confidence which the evangelical challenges and the failure of forceful responses were inducing in the Virginia gentry was subtly revealed in March 1772 by the unprecedented decision of the House, ordinarily assertive of its authority, not to send the engrossed bill to the Council, but to have it printed and referred to the public for discussion. Nearly two years later, in January 1774, the young James Madison, exultant about the progress of the American cause in the aftermath of the Boston Tea Party, despaired of Virginia on account of religious intolerance. He wrote that he had "nothing to brag of as to the State and Liberty" of his "Country," where "Poverty and Luxury prevail among all sorts" and "that diabolical Hell conceived principle of persecution rages." In April of the same year he still had little hope that a bill would pass to ease the situation of dissenters. In the previous session "such incredible and extravagant stories" had been "told in the House of the monstrous effects of the Enthusiasm prevalent among the Sectaries and so greedily swallowed by their Enemies that . . . they lost footing by it." Burgesses "who pretend too much contempt to examine into their principles . . . and are too much devoted to the ecclesiastical establishment to hear of the Toleration of Dissentients" were likely to prevail once again.[60] Madison's foreboding was correct inasmuch as the old regime in Virginia never accomplished a legal resolution of the toleration problem.

The Revolution ultimately enshrined religious pluralism as a funda-

[58] *Va. Gaz.* (Purdie and Dixon), Aug. 15, 22, 1771; *Va. Gaz.* (Rind), Aug. 8, 1771.
[59] *Va. Gaz.* (Rind), Mar. 26, 1772. Especially severe were provisions designed to curb activities among the slaves.
[60] Madison to Bradford, Jan. 24, Apr. 1, 1774, in Hutchinson and Rachal, eds., *Madison Papers*, I, 106, 112.

mental principle in Virginia. It rendered illegitimate the assumptions concerning the nature of community religious corporateness that underlay aggressive defense against the Baptists. It legitimated new forms of conflict, so that by the end of the century the popular evangelists were able to counterattack and symbolize social revolution in many localities by having the Episcopal Church's lands and even communion plate sold at auction. But to seek the conclusion to this study in such political-constitutional developments would be a deflection, for it has focused on a brief period of intense, yet deadlocked conflict in order to search out the social-cultural configurations of the forces that confronted each other. The diametrical opposition of the swelling Baptist movement to traditional mores shows it to have been indeed a radical social revolt, indicative of real strains within society.

227

Challenging questions remain. Can some of the appeal of the Revolution's republican ideology be understood in terms of its capacity to command the allegiance of both self-humbled evangelicals and honor-upholding gentry? What different meanings did the republican ideology assume within the mutually opposed systems of values and belief? And, looking forward to the post-Revolutionary period, what was the configuration—what the balance between antagonistic cultural elements—when confrontation within a monistic framework had given way to accommodation in a more pluralist republican society? These questions are closely related to the subject that this study has endeavored to illuminate—the forms and sources of popular culture in Virginia, and the relationship of popular culture to that of the gentry elite.

Journal of Interdisciplinary History VI:4 (Spring 1976), 545–584.

Gary B. Nash

Urban Wealth and Poverty
in Pre-Revolutionary America

"I thought often of the happiness of new England," wrote Benjamin Franklin in 1772, "where every man is a freeholder, has a vote in public affairs, lives in a tidy, warm house, has plenty of good food and fewel, with whole cloaths from head to foot, the manufacture perhaps of his own family . . ."[1] But less than two decades earlier, already caught in a trough of unemployment and economic depression that would plague the town through the rest of the colonial period, the Boston Overseers of the Poor reported that "the Poor supported either wholly or in part by the Town in the Alms-house and out of it will amount to the Number of about 1000 . . ." Poor relief in Boston, claimed the town officials, was double that of any town of similar size "upon the face of the whole Earth."[2]

228

Writing from Philadelphia in 1756, Mittelberger exclaimed: "Even in the humblest or poorest houses, no meals are served without a meat course." Yet just a few years before, Quaker John Smith wrote in his diary, "It is remarkable what an Increase of the number of Beggars there is about this town this winter." "This is the best poor man's country in the world," pronounced several visitors to Philadelphia in the two decades before the Revolution. But the managers of the Philadelphia almshouse were obliged to report in the spring of 1776 that of the 147 men, 178 women, and 85 children admitted to the Almshouse, only a few blocks from where the Second Continental Congress was debating the final break with England, "most of them [are] naked, helpless, and emaciated with Poverty and Disease to such a Degree, that some have died in a few Days after their Admission."[3]

Gary B. Nash is Professor of History at the University of California, Los Angeles. He is author of *Quakers and Politics: Pennsylvania 1681–1726* (Princeton, 1968) and *Red, White and Black: The Peoples of Early America* (Englewood Cliffs, N.J., 1974).

The author would like to thank Laura Margolin, Billy G. Smith, and John W. Shaffer for research assistance, and James A. Henretta, Jacob M. Price, Stephan Thernstrom, and G. B. Warden for critical comments.

1   Albert Henry Smyth (ed.), *The Writings of Benjamin Franklin*, (New York, 1907), V, 362–363.
2   William H. Whitmore *et al.* (eds.), *Reports of the Record Commissioners of Boston* (Boston, 1885), XIV, 240, 302 (hereafter, *BRC*).
3   Gottlieb Mittelberger (Oscar Handlin and John Clive [eds.]), *Journey to Pennsylvania* (Cambridge, Mass., 1960), 49. Albert C. Myers (ed.), *Hannah Logan's Courtship* (Philadelphia, 1904), 152; Report of the Contributors to the Relief and Employment of the Poor, in *Pennsylvania Gazette*, May 29, 1776.

These comments and reports illustrate how widely contemporary opinion varied concerning the degree of equalitarianism, the extent of poverty, and the chances for humble colonists to succeed in pre-revolutionary society. This is one reason why social historians are setting aside literary sources in order to examine previously unused data that will give a more precise and verifiable picture of how the structure of wealth and opportunity was changing in colonial America, and how alterations in the social profile were causally linked to the advent of the revolutionary movement.

Thus far, their efforts, especially as they pertain to the urban centers of colonial life, have achieved only modest success. They have not gone much beyond Bridenbaugh's impressionistic description of the cities, written two decades ago, and Henretta's more recent analysis of Boston.[4] And even these enticing contributions are shrouded in uncertainties. Bridenbaugh presented only scattered data indicating that the colonial cities faced a growing problem in alleviating the distress of the poor in the half-century after 1725. Henretta, analyzing two tax lists separated by almost a century, attempted to show that significant changes had occurred in the social structure and distribution of wealth in Boston. His data, however, did not allow him to pinpoint when and for what reasons these changes occurred. At present, then, there is reason to believe that the cities of pre-revolutionary British America became more stratified as they grew larger and more commercialized; that they contained a growing proportion of property-less persons; and that they developed genuinely wealthy and genuinely impoverished classes.[5] Although some social historians have been finding that colonial society was assuming structural features commonly associated with European communities, economic historians have been examining statistics on shipbuilding, trade, and wealthholding, and concluding that the American economy was expanding and vibrant throughout the late colonial period. They argue that although the colonists did not benefit equally from this prolonged growth, nearly

229

4 Carl Bridenbaugh, *Cities in the Wilderness: Urban Life in America, 1625–1742* (New York, 1938); Bridenbaugh, *Cities in Revolt: Urban Life in America, 1743–1776* (New York, 1955); James A. Henretta, "Economic Development and Social Structure in Colonial Boston," *William and Mary Quarterly*, XXII (1965), 75–92.

5 For a general formulation of changing social structure see Jackson Turner Main, *The Social Structure of Revolutionary America* (Princeton, 1965). Main makes no detailed analysis of any particular community over time and is therefore unable to delineate the dynamics and extent of change. There are a growing number of studies of land- and wealth-holding in New England towns and Chesapeake counties, but the seaboard cities have thus far escaped analysis.

everybody's standard of living rose. "Even if there were distinct levels
of economic attainment in colonial society," writes McCusker, "and
even if we find that the secular trend in the concentration of wealth
created an increasing gulf between the rich and the poor over the years
separating 1607 and 1775, the fact remains that not only were the rich
getting richer but the poor were also, albeit at a slower rate."[6]

In order to understand the internal sources of revolutionary sentiment in the 1760s and 1770s, we must resolve this apparent confusion
as to how population growth and economic development affected
provincial society. Especially for the northern cities, which became the
focal point of revolutionary agitation, we need to determine the degree
and timing of changes in pre-revolutionary social structure and wealth-
holding; whether the poor were growing proportionately or dis-
proportionately to population increase; whether the level of care for
the impoverished was improving, deteriorating, or remaining steady;
whether the lot of the lower and middle classes was sinking or rising,
both in relative and absolute terms; whether increases in social stratification affected social mobility and, if so, at which levels of society;
and, finally, how these changes were linked, if at all, to the transformation of urban politics and the onset of the Revolution. This essay
cannot provide final answers to any of these questions. That will require the labor of many historians over a period of years. Instead, I
wish to present new data that challenge some of the generally accepted
notions regarding urban social and economic development. They are
suggestive of the unexplored connections between social change and
revolutionary politics in the colonial cities.

We can begin with simple questions: How was the wealth of
northern urban communities divided in eighteenth-century America
and how was this changing? Secular trends in the distribution of wealth
can be measured in two ways: by comparing tax lists over time, and
by analyzing the inventories of estate that were made for thousands
of deceased adults in the colonial cities. Tax records must be used
with caution because what was taxed in one city was not necessarily
taxed in another; because large numbers of free adult males were not

230

6 John J. McCusker, "Sources of Investment Capital in the Colonial Philadelphia
Shipping Industry," *Journal of Economic History*, XXXII (1972), 146–157; James F.
Shepherd and Gary M. Walton, "Trade, Distribution and Economic Growth in Colonial
America," *ibid.*, 128–145; Alice Hanson Jones, "Wealth Estimates for the American
Middle Colonies, 1774," *Economic Development and Cultural Change*, XVIII (1970), esp.
127–140; *idem,* "Wealth Estimates for the New England Colonies about 1700," *Journal of
Economic History*, XXXII (1972), 98–127, esp. 105–107.

included in the tax lists, especially in the last few decades of the colonial period; and because tax lists, based on a regressive taxing system, grossly underestimated the wealth of many individuals, particularly those in the top quarter of the wealth structure. But tax lists did generally include a vast majority of wealth-owners in the urban population, and if allowances are made for the distortions in them, they can be used to ascertain long-range trends.[7]

Inventories of estate, conversely, allow for more refined insights into secular changes in the colonial economy, for they alone offer a continuous data series for urban populations. They also suffer potentially from one major defect—their representativeness in respect to both age and social class. Inventories exist for less than 50 percent of deceased heads of household in Boston and a somewhat smaller proportion of Philadelphians. Moreover, it has been widely suspected that the estates of the wealthier colonists were inventoried more frequently than those of their poorer neighbors. It must also be remembered that the inventories reveal the wealth of persons at the ends of their lives and are thus age-biased.[8] But if the age and class biases are taken into account the inventories are an extraordinarily valuable source for studying social change. Unlike tax lists they are available for every year, and thus allow us to determine how changes in the economy were affecting not only the relative wealth, but also, more importantly, the absolute wealth held at each level of society.

231

The data in Table 1 show a general correspondence in the changing patterns of taxable wealth distribution in the three cities. Although

7 Some of the difficulties in using tax lists are discussed in James T. Lemon and Gary B. Nash, "The Distribution of Wealth in Eighteenth-Century America: A Century of Change in Chester County, Pennsylvania, 1693–1802," *Journal of Social History*, II (1968), 2–7. The primary distortions in the tax lists are that a) certain important forms of urban wealth, including mortgages, bonds, book debts, and ships, were usually not taxed; b) large numbers of persons, too poor to pay a tax, were omitted from the lists, especially in the late colonial period; c) tax assessments tended to represent a smaller percentage of actual wealth as they moved from the bottom to the top of the social scale; d) urban tax lists did not include land held outside the city, usually by the wealthy. All of these biases tend in the same direction—toward minimizing the actual concentration of wealth. As the wealth of the urban elite increased in the eighteenth century, the distortion grew larger; thus the changes indicated in the following analysis of tax data should be regarded as minimally stated.

8 For a discussion of these biases and their correction see Gloria L. Main, "Probate Records as a Source for Early American History, "*William and Mary Quarterly*, XXXII (1975), 89–99; *idem*, "The Correction of Biases in Colonial American Probate Records," *Historical Methods Newsletter*, VIII (1974), 10–28; Daniel Scott Smith, "Underregistration and Bias in Probate Records: An Analysis of Data from Eighteenth-Century Hingham, Massachusetts," *William and Mary Quarterly*, XXXII (1975), 100–110.

Table 1 Wealth Distribution in Three Northern Cities, 1687–1774

	BOSTON 1687	PHILA. 1693	N.Y. 1695	N.Y. 1730	PHILA. 1767	BOSTON 1771	PHILA. 1774
0–30	2.6	2.2	3.6	6.2	1.8	0.1	1.1
31–60	11.3	15.2	12.3	13.9	5.5	9.1	4.0
61–90	39.8	36.6	38.9	36.5	27.0	27.4	22.6
91–100	46.3	46.0	45.2	43.7	65.7	63.4	72.3
91–95	16.1	13.2	13.2	14.2	16.2	14.7	16.8
96–100	30.2	32.8	32.0	25.4	49.5	48.7	55.5
Schutz Coeffic.	.49	.43	.46	.44	.61	.58	.66

SOURCES: The Boston tax list, 1687, *BRC*, I, 91–133; the 1771 valuation list, Massachusetts Archives, CXXXII, 92–147, State House, Boston. (These include 169 persons in 1687 and 631 in 1771 who were listed with no assessable wealth.) The New York tax list, 1695, *Collections of the New-York Historical Society* (New York, 1911–1912), XLIII–XLIV; 1730, New York City Archives Center, Queens College, Flushing, N.Y. (Harlem has not been included since the occupations of its inhabitants were not then urban in character.) For Philadelphia, 1693, *Pennsylvania Magazine of History and Biography*, VIII (1884), 85–105; 1767, Van Pelt Library, University of Pennsylvania, Philadelphia; 1774, Pennsylvania State Archives, Harrisburg, Pennsylvania. (1767 and 1774 include Southwark, an adjacent district, the residents of which by mid-eighteenth century were primary mariners, merchants, and artisans associated with ship-building.)

232

different in their religious, ethnic, and institutional development, Boston, New York, and Philadelphia seemed to follow roughly parallel paths insofar as their wealth structures were affected by growth and participation in the English mercantile world. The wealth profile of the three cities varied only slightly in the late seventeenth century, even though Boston and New York were founded a half-century before Philadelphia, and even though Boston was half as large again as the other cities. Similarly, the configurations of wealth in New York in 1730 and Philadelphia in 1756 are not very different, with the Schutz coefficient of inequality[9] corresponding almost exactly (Tables 1 and

9 The Schutz coefficient, which measures relative mean deviation, is a widely used single-number indicator of inequality (0 = perfect equality; 1.0 = perfect inequality). It is more sensitive than the Gini coefficient to transfers of wealth from the bottom strata to the top but is insensitive to transfers of wealth among people on the same side of mean wealth for the entire society. No method has yet been devised to incorporate into a single coefficient changes in income or property at all levels of society. See Robert R. Schutz, "On the Measurement of Income Inequality," *American Economic Review*, XLI (1951), 107–122; Anthony B. Atkinson, "On the Measurement of Inequality," *Journal of Economic Theory*, II (1970), 244–263.

2). On the eve of the Revolution, taxable assets were divided among Bostonians and Philadelphians in much the same manner, even though Boston's population had stagnated after 1730 while Philadelphia continued to grow rapidly until the Revolution.[10]

These tax lists confirm what some historians surmised even before the advent of quantitative history—that the long-range trend in the cities was toward greater concentration of wealth.[11] At every level of society, from the poorest taxpayer to those who stood in the ninth decile, city dwellers, by the end of the colonial period, had given up a share of their economic leverage to those in the top tenth. Moreover, a close examination of this uppermost layer reveals that even those in the 91 to 95 percentile were not important beneficiaries of this process. In Boston their share of the wealth was actually less in 1771 than in 1687. In Philadelphia their position in 1774 was only slightly better than it had been in 1693. The only impressive gains were made by those in the top 5 percent of society. Into the hands of these men fell all of the relative economic power yielded from below over a century's time. By the eve of the Revolution their share of the taxable wealth in Boston had grown from 30 to 49 percent and in Philadelphia from 33 to 55 percent. Those in the lower half of society were left with only

233

10   The Boston list of 1771 is actually an evaluation of various forms of property and thus differs from the Philadelphia tax assessors lists of 1767 and 1772 in three important respects. First, the Boston list includes important forms of wealth not included on the Philadelphia list, such as ships, stock in trade, the value of commissions in merchandise, and money at interest. Since all these forms of wealth were concentrated in the upper class, the Boston distribution is more accurate than the Philadelphia distribution, which does not take account of these categories. Secondly, on the Boston list, houses and land (valued at one year's rent) are assigned to "such persons as shall appear to have been the actual tenants thereof upon the first day of September last." Thus Boston's renters, who made up about 60% of the taxable inhabitants, were valued with the property of their landlords, distorting the distribution toward greater equality than actually existed. Thirdly, the Boston list exludes nearly 1,000 potentially taxable adults who were omitted because of "age, infirmity, or extreme poverty." This represents about 25-30% of the taxable population in Boston, whereas in Philadelphia about 7% of the taxable population was exempted in 1767 and about 10% in 1774. In both cities but especially Boston, these omissions skew the distribution toward greater equality than actually existed. Although there is no way to weigh these biases mathematically, it can be presumed that the second and third factors tend to cancel out the first in the Boston list of 1771; and that in all tax lists for the colonial period the degree of wealth inequality is understated. The quotations above are from the Massachusetts tax law of 1771 in Ellis Ames and Abner C. Goodell (eds.), *The Acts and Resolves, Public and Private, of the Province of Massachusetts Bay* . . . (Boston, 1886), V, 104, 156–159.

11   See esp., James Truslow Adams, *Provincial Society, 1690–1763* (New York, 1927); Virginia D. Harrington, *The New York Merchant on the Eve of the Revolution* (New York, 1935); Bridenbaugh, *Cities in Revolt.*

Table 2 Philadelphia Wealth Distribution in 1756

	AS ASSESSED ON TAX LIST	MINIMUM WEALTH ADJUSTED	MINIMUM WEALTH ADJUSTED AND SINGLE MEN INCLUDED
0–30	11.4	1.7	1.6
31–60	16.4	15.7	14.0
61–90	32.6	37.3	37.8
91–100	39.6	45.3	46.6
91–95	14.2	12.2	12.6
96–100	25.4	33.1	34.0
Schutz Coeffic.	.35	.44	.45

SOURCE: *Pennsylvania Genealogical Magazine,* XX (1961), 10–41.

234

5.1 percent of the taxable wealth in Boston and 3.3 percent of the wealth in Philadelphia.[12]

Because only a few tax lists from the first half of the eighteenth century have survived, it is still not possible to speak with authority concerning the precise timing of this redistribution of wealth. The data in Table 1 show that New York's wealth was more evenly distributed in 1730 than in 1695, suggesting that if the New York pattern prevailed in the other ports, then the major redistribution came late in the colonial period. But the more equal division of resources in New York in 1730 is partly accounted for by the fact that the largest assessment in that year was for an estate of £670, whereas in 1695 several estates were assessed at more than £2000, thus bending the distribution curve considerably in the direction of inequality. A tax list for Philadelphia in 1756, which on first glance appears to indicate a long-range trend toward equalization of wealth, confirms the point that these lists must be used with caution in order to avoid confusing real changes with changes in the manner of assessment. As shown in Table 2, the distribution of wealth on the Philadelphia tax list of 1756 is far more even than in 1693 or in 1767, apparently indicating a long-range growth toward equality in the first half of the eighteenth

12 Because the Boston lists of 1687 and 1771 are not strictly comparable, these figures must not be regarded as measurements of actual wealth structures, but simply as indicators of the direction and approximate degree of change.

century, and then a dramatic reversal in the next ten years. Two crucial characteristics of the 1756 list nullify this conclusion, however. First, the list omits all single persons, who ordinarily would have been assessed a head tax and counted in the lowest wealth bracket. Secondly, the minimum assessment was levied at £8, whereas, on the 1767 and 1774 assessment lists for the provincial tax, the minimum assessments were £2 and £1 respectively.[13] Both of these artificialities create a wealth distribution curve that reflects far greater equality than actually existed. Table 2 shows the division of wealth after taxpayers in the lowest assessment category (£8) have been revalued so as to correspond to the 1767 pattern, and after the number of taxables has been increased by 11 percent and these single men have been counted in the lowest assessment bracket.[14] These adjustments, which make the various Philadelphia lists more comparable, place the wealth configurations of 1693 and 1756 in close correspondence, and thus suggest that the major change in wealth distribution came during and after the Seven Years' War. But we simply lack sufficient data on the tax-inscribed urban populations of the first half of the eighteenth century to make conclusive statements on the timing involved.

235

Probate records, which, unlike tax lists, are available for every year, generally confirm this long-range picture of change, but yield a more precise picture of the timing.[15] The distribution of wealth in Philadelphia and Boston, as recorded in nearly 4,400 inventories of estate, fluctuated widely in the eighteenth century; but the overall trend was strongly toward a less even division of resources (Table 3 and Charts 1–3).[16] In the lower 60 percent of society, the grasp of ordinary people on the community's wealth, which was never large,

13 In Pennsylvania, when the rate of taxation was 3 or 4 pennies per £ of assessable estate, as in the case of the poor tax, county tax, lamp and watch tax, or paving tax, the assessors set the minimum valuation at from £8 to £12. For the far heavier provincial tax, levied after 1754 at a rate of 18 pence per £ of assessable estate, the minimum assessments were lowered to £1 or £2. This, in itself, suggests the difficulty that laboring-class Philadelphians were having in coping with the heavy provincial taxes after 1754.
14 In five tax lists drawn between 1767 and 1775, and in a tax list for three wards in 1754, the percentage of Philadelphians assessed a head tax varied between 10.0 and 13.3% of the total taxable population.
15 See Appendix A.
16 Boston real estate has been excluded from the data on wealth distribution in order to obtain comparability with the Philadelphia data where inventories only occasionally included real estate. The distribution of real wealth in Boston closely approximated that of personal wealth. The inclusion of real wealth altered the distribution only slightly in

Table 3 Distribution of Inventoried Personal Wealth in Boston and Philadelphia, 1685–1775: Percentage of Inventoried Estates.

	1684–99	1700–15	1716–25	1726–35	1736–45	1746–55	1756–65	1766–75
				Boston				
Low								
0–30	3.3	2.8	2.0	1.9	1.8	1.8	1.4	2.0
31–60	13.9	9.8	7.7	7.4	8.4	8.3	6.0	7.6
61–90	41.6	32.9	28.6	25.1	30.2	34.7	25.1	29.3
91–100	41.2	54.5	61.7	65.6	58.6	55.2	67.5	61.1
High								
91–95	15.3	14.6	13.2	11.4	12.2	15.9	15.5	14.7
96–100	25.9	39.9	48.5	54.2	46.4	39.3	52.0	46.4
Number of Inventories	304	352	314	358	318	532	390	390
				Philadelphia				
Low								
0–30	4.5	4.9	3.9	3.7	2.6	1.5	1.1	1.0
31–60	16.5	16.9	11.1	11.9	9.3	5.5	6.0	4.7
61–90	42.6	37.0	38.1	30.6	36.8	22.9	32.4	24.4
91–100	36.4	41.3	46.8	53.6	51.3	70.1	60.3	69.9
High								
91–95	14.7	16.3	15.7	13.0	20.7	13.8	16.5	14.1
96–100	21.7	25.0	31.1	40.2	30.6	56.3	43.8	55.8
Number of Inventories	87	138	113	154	144	201	279	318

deteriorated substantially, while those in the top tenth, comprising the elite, significantly consolidated their favored position.

It would be unwise to extract too much meaning from these data as to the exact timing of economic changes, for the inventories reflect wealth at the end of colonists' lives rather than the economic outlook in any particular year. But the inventories corroborate the thesis suggested by the tax data, that a major aggrandizement of wealth occurred

---

the 0–30 and 31–60 percentiles, but raised the proportion of wealth owned by those in the 61–90 and 91–95 strata at the expense of those in the top 5% of wealthholders.

Change in Distribution of Inventoried Wealth when Real Estate is Included

0–30	−0.1 to −0.7%
31–60	−1.1 to +0.7%
61–90	+1.1 to +7.9%
91–95	−3.3 to +4.4%
96–100	−0.1 to −11.2%

at the top of society, especially within the uppermost 5 percent.[17] This seems to have occurred somewhat earlier in Boston than in Philadelphia (insofar as the distance between mean and median wealth is a measurement of inequality), as one might expect given the earlier development of the New England port. By 1735, when Boston had nearly reached the limit of population growth in the colonial period, the major changes in the wealth structure had already taken place. Thereafter a ragged pattern emerges from the data. In Philadelphia, the population of which surpassed Boston's in the early 1760s and continued to grow for the rest of the colonial period, the degree of inequality increased steadily, from the settlement of the city in 1682 through the 1740s, and then fluctuated, as in Boston, in the three decades before the Revolution.

237

In spite of the difficulties in interpreting the timing of change, it is clear that by the end of the colonial period the top 5 percent of the inventoried decedents had more than doubled their proportion of the assets left at death in Philadelphia (from 21.7 to 55.8 percent) and almost doubled it in Boston (from 25.9 to 46.4 percent). Almost every other part of the population left smaller shares of the collective wealth, with those in the bottom half absorbing the greatest proportionate losses.

The data on wealth distribution can lead only so far toward an understanding of eighteenth-century social change. First, it is apparent that the growth of the port cities, and their participation in a series of international wars, provided important new opportunities for the accumulation of wealth on a scale not possible in the seventeenth century. The creation of colonial fortunes by as few as 2–3 percent of the city-dwellers was sufficient to alter the indices of inequality by significant amounts.[18] In this sense, tax and probate data only confirm what architectural and social historians have traced in studying the erection of urban mansions and country seats befitting a genuinely

---

17 It would be preferable to chart the Schutz coefficient of inequality annually to determine the timing of change, but the number of inventories is not large enough to allow this. The distance between the annual mean and median wealth of all decedents, which is a rough measurement of the degree of inequality, is displayed in Charts 1A, 2A, and 3A. For a discussion of these problems, see Russell R. Menard, P. M. G. Harris, and Lois Green Carr, "Opportunity and Inequality: The Distribution of Wealth on the Lower Western Shore of Maryland, 1638–1705," *Maryland Historical Magazine*, LXIX (1974), 168–184.

18 A comparison of the graphs of mean wealth for the top 10% and all decedents (Charts 1A, 1B, 1C) demonstrates the power of the uppermost stratum to define the trendline for the society at large.

wealthy class.[19] Secondly, the tax and probate records provide striking evidence that the process of growth and commercialization was creating cities where those in the lower layers of society possessed few taxable assets and virtually no hold on the community's resources. The fact that fully half of Boston's inventoried decedents after 1715 left less than £40 personal wealth and £75 total wealth, while the bottom quarter left only about half this amount, should temper the enthusiasm of those who have argued that colonial communities enjoyed a state of changeless prosperity down to the eve of the Revolution.[20]

238   To get beyond the limitations of these sources we must turn to records of poor relief for a fuller understanding of how and when the social anatomy of the pre-revolutionary cities changed. As in the case of tax and probate records, these materials yield reluctantly to analysis. A casual reading of the Boston town records, for example, tempts one to conclude that the period of greatest distress for the lower class of that city began in the late 1730s and peaked in the early 1750s. A report of the selectmen in early 1736 reported that "the maintenance of the Poor of the Town is a very great and growing charge" and noted that whereas in 1729 £944 had been spent on poor relief, the outlays in 1734 had more than doubled, reaching £2,069. Three years later, the Overseers reported that "our Town-charges to the Poor this Year amounts to about £4,000."[21] What purported to be a fourfold increase in expenditures in eight years, however, turns out on closer examination to be about a threefold increase. Massachusetts was caught in a spiralling inflation during this period and the Overseers, in appealing to the legislature for tax relief, did a bit of inflating of their own. The actual expenditures, converted to English sterling, were £245 in 1729 and £760 in 1737.[22]

19 See, for example, Nicholas B. Wainwright, *Colonial Grandeur in Philadelphia: The House and Furniture of General John Cadwalader* (Philadelphia, 1964); Malcolm Freiberg, *Thomas Hutchinson of Milton* (Milton, Mass., 1971); Bridenbaugh, *Cities in Revolt*, Ch. 6 on "Urban Elegance."
20 See, for example, Jones, "Wealth Estimates for the American Middle Colonies," 119–40; Bernard Bailyn, *The Ordeal of Thomas Hutchinson* (Cambridge, Mass., 1974), 97.
21 Jan. 1, 1735/36, BRC, XII, 121–22; 178; XIV, 13.
22 All values, which in the inventories are given in Massachusetts and Pennsylvania currency, have been converted to sterling. I have used the conversion figures given in *Historical Statistics of the United States, Colonial Times to 1957* (Washington, D.C., 1960), 773, and filled in the missing years from the price per ounce of silver cited in the inventories for these years. For Philadelphia, the yearly sterling equivalents for Pennsylvania currency are taken from Anne Bezanson, Robert D. Gray, and Marian Hussey, *Prices in Colonial Pennsylvania* (Philadelphia, 1935), 431.

Sixteen years later, in 1753, the town petitioned the legislature that poor relief had risen alarmingly to "over £10,000 a year . . . beside private Charity."[23] Because they were reporting their expenditures in "old tenor"—the severely depreciated Massachusetts paper money that had been called in two years before and disallowed after 1751—this figure must be converted to actual expenditures of about £900 sterling. Although this was a substantial increase over a fifteen-year period during which population grew about 25 percent, it was not nearly so great as that which occurred in the next two decades. Poor relief costs rose rapidly between 1751 and 1765, and thereafter, when the city's population remained static at about 15,500, drifted still higher.[24] From annual sterling expenditures of £23–31 per thousand population in the period from 1720 to 1740, poor relief rose to £50 per thousand in the 1740s, £77 in the 1750s, and then skyrocketed to £158 in the early 1770s (Table 4). In New York and Philadelphia poor relief expenditures also began a rapid ascent in the late colonial period, although impoverishment on a large scale began a half-generation later than in Boston. In both cities expenditures of less than £50 sterling per thousand population (which may be taken as a rough measure of public funds needed to support the aged, infirm, orphaned, and incurably ill in the cities during times of economic stability) were required in the period prior to the Seven Years' War.[25]

239

23 BRC, XIV, 240.

24 Several sources can be collated to determine the annual expenditures on the Boston poor from public tax monies. Beginning in 1754 the town records give an annual report of the treasurer on disbursements to the Overseers of the Poor. These reports continue, with a few interruptions, to 1775. The Overseers of the Poor Account Book, 1738–1769, Massachusetts Historical Society, Boston, includes monthly expenditures for the poor and sporadic records, mostly for the 1750s, on disbursements for the workhouse. The expenditures for 1727, 1729, 1734, 1735, and 1737 are given in BRC, XII, 108, 121–122, 178. For the period from 1700 to 1720 I have estimated poor relief costs at one-third the town expenses (given yearly in Boston Town Records), the ratio that prevailed in the five years between 1727 and 1737 when poor relief expense figures are given.

25 The figures for New York have been reconstructed from the Minutes and Accounts of the Church Warden and Vestrymen of the City of New York, 1696–1715, New-York Historical Society; and Minutes of the Meetings of the Justices, Church Wardens, and Vestrymen of the City of New York, 1694–1747, New York Public Library. The salary of the clergymen for the Society for the Propagation of the Gospel, which was included in these expenditures, has been subtracted from the yearly totals. The New York records after 1747 have apparently not survived, but the level of expenditures on the eve of the Revolution was reported by the vestrymen and churchwardens in a petition to the Continental Congress in May 1776. Peter Force, American Archives, 4th Ser., VI (Washington, D.C., 1846), 627. Also see Raymond A. Mohl, "Poverty in Early America, A Reappraisal: The Case of Eighteenth-Century New York City," New York History, L

240

Table 4 Poor Relief in Three Northern Seaports

	BOSTON			PHILADELPHIA			NEW YORK		
	Population	Av. Ann. Expend. (Sterl.) £	Expend. per 1,000 Popul. £	Population	Av. Ann. Expend. (Sterl.) £	Expend. per 1,000 Popul. £	Population	Av. Ann. Expend. (Sterl.) £	Expend. per 1,000 Popul. £
1700–10	7,500	173	23	2,450	119	48	4,500		
1711–20	9,830	181	18	3,800			5,900	249	32
1721–30	11,840	273	23	6,600			7,600	276	25
1731–40	15,850	498	31	8,800	471	49	10,100	351	21
1741–50	16,240	806	50	12,000			12,900	389	21
1751–60	15,660	1204	77	15,700	1083	67	13,200	667	39
1761–70	15,520	1909	123	22,100	2842	129	18,100	1667	92
1771–75	15,500	2478	158	27,900	3785	136	22,600	2778	123

But New York and Philadelphia followed the path of Boston in the third quarter of the century. By the twilight of the colonial period both cities were spending about three times per capita the amount needed to support the poor in the 1740s.

Statistics on rapidly rising expenditures for the relief of the poor cannot by themselves demonstrate that poverty was enshrouding the lives of a rapidly growing part of the urban communities. These data might reveal that public authorities were not supporting a rapidly growing class of poor but were simply becoming more generous in their support of occasional indigency or, alternatively, that the responsibility for poor relief was shifting from private charities to public relief. Neither of these explanations is supportable. Charitable organizations, including ethnic and occupational friendly societies, proliferated after 1750, taking up some of the burden of poor relief. There are also indications that the churches substantially increased their aid to the indigent in the late colonial years.[26] As for the actual numbers of the poor, the records of the overseers of the poor in the three cities, including statistics on admissions to almshouses and workhouses, demonstrate that public officials were coping with greatly swollen poor rolls. In attempting to support more and more penniless, jobless city-dwellers, their major concern was to devise measures for reducing the cost of caring for the destitute under their charge rather than to upgrade the quality of relief. The erection of large almshouses and workhouses, accompanied by the phasing out of the more expensive out-relief system, was the general response to this problem.[27]

New York and Philadelphia reported inconsequential numbers of persons admitted to their almshouses before the middle of the century. In New York, where an almshouse was not built until 1736, the

241

(1969), 5–27. The sources for the Philadelphia data, which are extremely scattered, are given in Nash, "Poverty and Poor Relief in Pre-revolutionary Philadelphia," *William and Mary Quarterly*, XXXIII (1976), 3–30.

26   Bridenbaugh, *Cities in Revolt*, 126–128, 321–325; Nash, "Poverty and Poor Relief," 23–24. To take one example, the charitable expenditures of the Philadelphia Society of Friends, during an era when their membership was not growing, rose from an annual average of £38 in the 1740s and 1750s to £95 annually in the fifteen years before the Revolution. Monthly charity disbursements are given in the Minutes of the Monthly Meeting of Women, Friends of Philadelphia, Vol. F2, Friends Record Center, Philadelphia.

27   David J. Rothman, *The Discovery of the Asylum: Social Order and Disorder in the New Republic* (Boston, 1971). Ch. 1 analyzes this change but associates it primarily with the early nineteenth century.

churchwardens and vestrymen distributed relief to only forty persons or so each year between 1720 and 1735. Most of these were the crippled, sick, aged, or orphaned. By building an almshouse in 1736, which admitted only nineteen inmates in its first year, New York was able to reduce the cost of caring for the poor and to keep annual expenditures under £400 sterling until almost mid-century.[28] The Philadelphia Overseers of the Poor reported that before the 1760s the inmates of the small almshouse, built in 1732, rarely exceeded forty in number, with about the same number of outpensioners. Expenditures on the eve of the Seven Years' War were about £600 sterling per year with another £350 sterling expended by the Pennsylvania Hospital for the Sick Poor.[29] By the most liberal estimates, the number of townspeople receiving out-relief or cared for in almshouses did not exceed nine per thousand population in New York and Philadelphia before the Seven Years' War.[30]

242

In Boston, where the population before mid-century outstripped that of the other two cities by a ratio of about five to three, the shadow of poverty appeared somewhat earlier. As early as 1734 the almshouse held 88 persons and by 1742 the number had risen to 110. In 1756 a room-by-room census listed 148 persons cramped into thirty-three rooms.[31] The number of those supported on out-relief grew even faster, according to a petition in 1757, which estimated that about one thousand Bostonians were receiving poor relief, either as inmates of

28 Churchwardens and Vestrymen's Accounts, New-York Historical Society; Mohl, "Poverty in Colonial New York," 8–13.

29 Report of the Board of Managers, Nov. 3, 1775, Records of the Contributors to the Relief and Employment of the Poor, Almshouse Managers Minutes, 1766–1778, City Archives, Philadelphia. For expenditures, see Nash, "Poverty and Poor Relief," 3–9.

30 Population figures from New York have been calculated from a series of censuses in the eighteenth century. Evarts B. Greene and Virginia D. Harrington, *American Population before the Federal Census of 1790* (New York, 1932), 95–102. The Philadelphia data are constructed from a series of house censuses and lists of taxable inhabitants given in John F. Watson, *Annals of Philadelphia, and Pennsylvania . . .* (Philadelphia, 1857), III, 235–236. See also John K. Alexander, "The Philadelphia Numbers Game: An Analysis of Philadelphia's Eighteenth-Century Population," *Pennsylvania Magazine of History and Biography*, XCVIII (1974), 314–324; Nash and Billy G. Smith, "The Population of Eighteenth-Century Philadelphia," *ibid.*, XCIX (1975), 362–368. The Boston population figures are taken from John B. Blake, *Public Health in the Town of Boston, 1630–1822* (Cambridge, Mass., 1959), 247–249.

31 BRC, XII, 121–122; Lemuel Shattuck, *Report to the Committee of the City Council Appointed to Obtain a Census of Boston for the Year 1845* (Boston, 1846), 4; "A List of Persons, Beds, &c in the Alms House, Aug. 1756," in City of Boston, Indentures, 1734–1751, City Clerk's Office, Boston, vol. 1.

the almshouse or as outpensioners.[32] If this report is accurate, the rate of those receiving public relief had reached sixty two per thousand population in Boston before the onset of the Seven Years' War.

In the third quarter of the century poverty struck even harder at Boston's population and then blighted the lives of the New York and Philadelphia lower classes to a degree entirely unparalleled in the first half of the century. In New York, where the population increased by about half in the third quarter of the century, the rate of poverty jumped fourfold or more. Because the records of the vestrymen and churchwardens for this period have been lost, it is not possible to chart this increase with precision. But a report in the New York *Weekly Gazette* leaves little doubt that change had occurred rapidly after the late 1740s, when New York was still spending less than £400 sterling per year for relief. On March 1, 1771, the *Gazette* reported that 360 persons were confined in the New York almshouse, and during the next twelve months 372 persons were admitted, leaving a total of 425 persons jostling for space in the overcrowded building. Another report in early 1773 revealed that during one month out-relief had been distributed to 118 city-dwellers, suggesting that by 1773 a minimum of 600, and perhaps as many as 800, lower-class New Yorkers were too poor to survive without public assistance.[33] Within one generation the rate of poverty had climbed from about nine per thousand to between twenty-seven and thirty-six per thousand.

For Philadelphia it is possible to be much more precise about the timing and extent of change. As late as 1756 Philadelphia rarely supported as many as 100 indigent persons, at an expense of about £600 sterling. But in the winter of 1761–62 the old system of poor relief broke down as cold weather, rising food and firewood prices, the resumption of Irish and German immigration, and a business depression all combined to place nearly 700 persons in distress.[34] For the next five years the overseers of the poor struggled with a poverty problem which in its dimensions was entirely beyond their experience. They raised the poor rates, conducted charity drives, and petitioned

243

32 BRC, XIV, 302. For another discussion of poverty in Boston see Stephen Foster, *Their Solitary Way: The Puritan Ethic in the First Century of Settlement in New England* (New Haven, 1971), 144–152.
33 *New-York Gazette*, Feb. 11, 1771, Mar. 30, 1772; *New-York Gazette and Weekly Mercury*, Mar. 15, 1773.
34 *Pennsylvania Gazette*, Jan. 7, 1762; Minutes and disbursement book, Records of the Committee to Alleviate the Miseries of the Poor (1762), Wharton-Willing Collection, Historical Society of Pennsylvania.

the legislature for aid in building a new almshouse. "Into rooms but ten or eleven feet square," they reported in 1764, "we have been obliged to put five or six beds", while housing an overflow in a nearby church. By 1766 the almshouse population had swelled to 220.[35]

In despair at their attempts to grapple with the growing poverty problem, the city in 1766 turned over its poor relief system to a group of civic leaders, most of them Quaker merchants. By legislative act the privately incorporated Contributors to the Relief and Better Employment of the Poor were authorized to build a new almshouse and workhouse, curtail out-relief, and use poor tax revenues for escorting the itinerant poor out of the city, while setting the able-bodied resident poor to work at weaving, oakum picking, and cobbling in the workhouse.[36] But from 1768 to 1775 the poverty problem only worsened. An average of 360 persons were admitted annually to the new "Bettering House," and by 1775 the Contributors to the Relief of the Poor warned that they had insufficient funds to maintain the city's destitute, even though they had raised the poor rates to the highest in the colony's history.[37] Including those already in the Bettering House at the beginning of each year, an average of 666 Philadelphians lived a part of their lives each year in this public shelter. Two blocks away about 350 poor persons each year were receiving aid in the Pennsylvania Hospital for the Sick Poor, established in 1751 to restore to health those who might otherwise have left impoverished spouses and children to the public charge.[38] In the decade before the Revolution, the rate of poverty in Philadelphia jumped to about fifty per thousand inhabitants—a fivefold increase in one generation.

In Boston, where poverty had become a serious problem earlier than in New York and Philadelphia, the last twenty years of the colonial period were marked by great hardship. While the city's population stagnated, admissions to the almshouse climbed rapidly:

244

35 Nash, "Poverty and Poor Relief," 9–14; Gertrude MacKinney (ed.), *Votes and Proceedings of the House of Representatives of the Province of Pennsylvania, Pennsylvania Archives,* 8th Ser. (Harrisburg, 1935), VII, 5506, 5535–5536.

36 Nash, "Poverty and Poor Relief," 14–16.

37 Almshouse Managers Minutes, 1768–1778, give monthly figures on admissions and discharges from the almshouse and workhouse. For the 1775 warning see Board of Managers report, Nov. 3, 1775, *ibid.*

38 For the early history of the Hospital, see William H. Williams, "The 'Industrious Poor' and the Founding of the Pennsylvania Hospital," *Pennsylvania Magazine of History and Biography,* XCVII (1973), 431–443. Admission and discharge records, from which these figures have been drawn, are in Attending Managers Accounts, 1752–1781, Pennsylvania Hospital Records (microfilm), American Philosophical Society, Philadelphia.

93 per year from 1759 to 1763; 144 per year from 1764 to 1769; and 149 per year from 1770 to 1775. When added to those already in the almshouse at the beginning of each year, these new inmates brought the almshouse population in the winter months to about 275–300.[39] These figures would probably have soared still higher except for the space limitations of the house and the inability of the town to finance the building of a larger structure. Instead, Boston continued to support large numbers of townspeople on out-relief, whereas New York and Philadelphia relied increasingly on the expedient of committing the poor to large almshouses and workhouses. The records of Samuel Whitwell, a Boston overseer of the poor, reveal that in the years 1769 to 1772 about 15 percent of the householders in his wards were on out-relief—a far higher percentage than in New York or Philadelphia.[40] If Whitwell's wards are representative of the city as a whole, then at least 500 to 600 Bostonians were receiving out-relief as the colonial period closed, in addition to 300 in the almshouse.

245

To prevent the rolls of the poor from swelling still further, Boston's Overseers of the Poor systematically warned out of the city hundreds of sick, weary, and hungry souls who tramped the roads into the city in the eighteenth century. To be "warned out" did not mean to be evicted from Boston. Instead it was a device, dating back to King Philip's War in 1675 when refugees from outlying towns had streamed into the city, for relieving the town of any obligation to support these newcomers if they were in need, or should become so in the future. Migrants warned out of Boston could vote, hold office, and pay taxes; but they could not qualify for poor relief from the city coffers which they helped to fill.[41]

The many thousand entries in the Warning Out Book of the Boston Overseers provides confirmation that the third quarter of the eighteenth century was a period of severe economic and social dislocation. From 1721 to 1742 an average of about twenty-five persons per year had been warned out of the city. The Warning Out Book reveals that from 1745 to 1752 the number climbed to sixty-five per

39 Figures compiled from Admission and Discharge Book, 1758–1774, Records of the Boston Overseers of the Poor, Massachusetts Historical Society.
40 "Account of Payments to the Poor, April, 1769–March 1771, Wards 2 and 12," Records of the Boston Overseers of the Poor. In Philadelphia, the account book of Thomas Fisher, Overseer of the Poor for Lower Delaware Ward in 1774, shows aid to only 7.2% of the taxables. Boston made three attempts between 1748 and 1769 to employ the able-bodied poor in a cloth factory, but all of them failed.
41 Josiah Benton, *Warning Out in New England, 1656–1817* (Boston, 1911), 5–52, 114–116.

year, and then from 1753 to 1764 the number tripled again to about 200 persons per year. In the pre-revolutionary decade newcomers denied entitlement to poor relief rose to just over 450 per year.[42]

It is not possible to ascertain the condition of all of these migrants as they reached Boston in rapidly increasing numbers after the outbreak of the Seven Years' War. But many of them appear to have been disabled veterans; others seem to have been part of the rapidly growing population of jobless, propertyless, drifting persons thrown up by the churning sea of economic dislocation in the early 1760s, when the end of wartime military contracting and the departure of free-spending British military personnel brought hard times to all of the cities. Only six of the fifty adult males warned out of Boston can be found on the 1771 tax list, and all of them were among the bottom tenth of the city's taxpayers. Of 234 adult males warned out in 1768 only twenty-one were listed three years later on the tax list, and again all of them fell into the lowest tenth of the wealth structure. It must be assumed that all of the others died, moved on again, or were simply too poor even to be included on the tax list.

246

By looking at the characteristics of those warned out of Boston in different years, one can gain further appreciation of the change overtaking New England society in the third quarter of the century. Before mid-century, when those entering Boston in quest of opportunity averaged about sixty-five per year, most of the migrants were married couples and their children (Table 5). But during the Seven Years' War the character of the migration began to shift. Married men and women continued to seek out Boston; but single men and women also filled the roads into the city whereas before the war their numbers had been insignificant. From 7 percent of the total migrating body in 1747 they became 25 percent in 1759 and 43 percent in 1771.[43]

The wrenching changes that filled the almshouses and workhouses

42 Bridenbaugh, *Cities in the Wilderness*, 392; "Persons Warned Out of Boston, 1745-1792," Records of the Boston Overseers of the Poor.
43 This analysis is based on a study of persons warned out of Boston in 1747, 1759, and 1771. The "Warning Out Book" gives the relationship of each person in the family group. A full study of the entries in the Warning Out Book, including the place of origin of the migrants, would enlarge our understanding of economic and social dislocation during this period. For a suggestive study see Douglas Lamar Jones, "The Strolling Poor: Transiency in Eighteenth-Century Massachusetts," *Journal of Social History*, VIII (1975), 28-54. After the Seven Years' War, Philadelphia relied increasingly on transporting poor migrants out of the city. The names of these deportees are scattered through the minutes of the Overseers of the Poor, 1768-1774., and in the *Minutes of the Common Council of the City of Philadelphia, 1704-1776* (Philadelphia, 1847), passim.

Table 5 Migration into Boston, 1747–1771

	1747	1759	1771
Single men	3.0%	8.5%	23.4%
Single women	4.0	16.8	20.0
Widows and widowers	7.9	8.9	4.4
Married couples	33.6	27.4	27.5
Children	51.5	38.4	24.7
Total Number	101	190	320

to overflowing, drove up poor rates, redistributed wealth, and crowded the roads leading into the seaboard cities with destitute and unemployed persons in the generation before the Revolution also hit hard at the broad stratum of society just above those whose names appear in almshouse, hospital for the poor, out-relief, and warning out lists. These people—shoemakers rather than laborers, ropemakers rather than mariners, shopkeepers rather than peddlers—were adversely affected in great numbers in Boston beginning in the mid-1740s and in Philadelphia and New York a dozen years later. They have been entirely lost from sight, even from the view of historians who have used tax lists to analyze changing social conditions, because their waning fortunes rendered them incapable of paying even the smallest tax when the collector made his rounds. 247

In Boston this crumbling of economic security within the lower middle class can be traced in individual cases through the probate records and in aggregate form in the declining number of city "taxables." (Table 6). In a population that remained nearly static at about

Table 6 Rateable Polls in Boston, 1728–1771

YEAR	POPULATION	POLLS
1728	12,650	c3,000
1733	15,100	c3,500
1735	16,000	3,637
1738	16,700	3,395
1740	16,800	3,043
1741	16,750	2,972
1745	16,250	2,660
1750	15,800	c2,400
1752	15,700	2,789
1756	15,650	c2,500
1771	15,500	2,588

15,500 from 1735 to the Revolution, the number of rateable polls declined from a high of more than 3,600 in 1735, when the city's economy was at its peak, to a low of about 2,500 around mid-century. This loss of more than a thousand taxable adults does not represent a decline in population but the declining fortunes of more than one thousand householders—almost one-third of the city's taxpaying population. The selectmen made clear that this reduction of the town's taxable inhabitants was caused by an increase in the number of people who had fallen to the subsistence level or below. As early as 1753 they reported that about 220 persons on the tax ledgers were "thought not Rateable ... for their Poverty, besides many Hundreds more for the same reason not Entered in those Books at all." By 1757, at a time when the number of taxable inhabitants had decreased by more than a thousand, they pointed again to this thinning of the tax rolls. "Besides a great Number of Poor ... who are either wholly or in part maintained by the Town, & so are exempt from being Taxed, there are many who are Rateable according to Law either for their Polls or their Tenements that they occupy or both, who are yet in such poor Circumstances that Considering how little business there is to be done in Boston they can scarcely procure from day to day daily Bread for themselves & Families." One can only estimate how numerous these persons were, but if the number of Bostonians receiving partial or full support from public relief funds reached as high as a thousand in the pre-revolutionary generation, as previously estimated, then some 400 other taxpayers may have been living close enough to the subsistence line to have had their taxes abated.[44]

Hard times also struck the laboring classes in Philadelphia, although somewhat later than in Boston. City tax collectors reported to the county commissioners the names of each taxable inhabitant from whom they were unable to extract a tax. The survival of the county commissioners' minutes for the period 1718 to 1776 allows for some precision in tracing this decline.[45] Thousands of entries in the journals chronicle the plight of persons labeled "insolvent," "poor," "runaway," "sickly," or simply "no estate." Taken together these journal entries portray the history of economic distress in Philadelphia

44 BRC, XIV, 13, 100, 280; G. B. Warden, Boston, 1689–1776 (Boston, 1970), 128, 325n; Shattuck, Report to the Committee, 5; BRC, XII, 178; XIV, 302.
45 The manuscript volumes of the County Commissioners' Minutes from 1718 to 1766 are in City Archives, Philadelphia. Another volume, for 1771 to 1774, is at Historical Society of Pennsylvania, and the succeeding volume, extending to Aug. 21, 1776, is in Tax and Exoneration Records, Pennsylvania State Archives, Harrisburg.

during the pre-revolutionary generation. As indicated in Table 7, these Philadelphians constituted a growing part of the taxpaying population. Representing less than thirty per thousand taxables in the period before 1740, they increased to about sixty to seventy per thousand in the years from 1740 to 1760 and then to one out of every ten taxpayers in the pre-revolutionary decade.

By returning to the probate records it is possible to obtain a rough measurement of how all of these trends were affecting people at each level of society in the cities. So far as the individual was concerned— the mariner in Philadelphia or the cabinetmaker in Boston, for example—the distribution of wealth may have had little meaning. Most eighteenth-century city-dwellers probably had only an impressionistic understanding of the relative economic power held by each layer of society and the way in which this was changing. The rich were getting richer, some spectacularly so, while the number of poor grew —that much was undoubtedly clear. But for most city people the preeminent concern was not the widening gap between lordly merchants and humble mechanics but how much they could earn, whatever their occupation, and what it would buy. Regardless of his wealth relative to those at the top of society, the cooper, baker, carpenter, and small shopkeeper had a palpable understanding of how far his income would go in putting food on the table, furniture in the house, and clothes on the backs of his children. Moreover, he was in a position to understand how his standard of living compared to his neighbors, others in his occupational group, and those who had stood in his rank in urban society a decade or so before.

It is precisely these factors that the inventories of estate reveal when studied collectively. The data displayed in Table 8 and Chart 1 and 2 show that Bostonians who at death occupied places in the bottom

Table 7 Indigent Taxables in Philadelphia, 1720–1775

YEARS	AVERAGE NUMBER OF TAXABLES	AVERAGE NUMBER PER YEAR RELIEVED OF TAXES	PERCENTAGE
1720–29	1,060	26	2.5
1730–39	1,450	45	3.1
1740–49	1,950	140	7.2
1750–59	2,620	161	6.1
1760–69	3,260	351	10.8
1770–75	3,850	407	10.6

half of inventoried decedents left markedly smaller estates in the eighteenth century.[46] At the end of the colonial period mean inventoried wealth among these city-dwellers was hardly half of what it had been in the late seventeenth century. Since the standard of living was extremely modest even in the best of times for these families, this decline must have proved especially difficult. Although the wealth of those dying between 1745 and 1755 was increasing, laboring-class householders never attained the level that had prevailed in the period from 1685 to 1710. In the pre-revolutionary decade, three out of every ten inventoried personal estates ranged between £1 and £26 sterling and total estates between £1 and £43 sterling—a level of wealth that indicated a lifetime spent accumulating little more than working tools, clothes, and a few household furnishings.[47] At the bottom of this group were men like mariner James Black, nameless in the historical record except for an inventory listing three coats, four jackets, a chest, and a quadrant, with a total worth of £5-2-0 Massachusetts currency. At the top of this group, stood men like tavern-keeper Francis Warden whose estate, worth £30-10 in Massachusetts currency in 1766, consisted mostly of plain house furnishings, embellished by an occasional "luxury" item such as one silver spoon or a "hand clock" worth one pound.[48]

250

Not until one examines Boston inventories in the top 40 percent of decedents can evidence be found that the eighteenth century provided opportunities for leaving more property than was possible for the same stratum of late seventeenth-century society. About six out of ten Bostonians in this group owned a house and their inventories reveal that most of them could afford pewter on the table, books in

46 A graph of mean inventoried wealth for the lowest three deciles would indicate an even more pronounced downward trend than for the bottom five deciles. Because of the small number of inventories in the early years, the Philadelphia data have been clustered at three and two-year intervals from 1684 to 1694. Until 1701 the number of inventories is too small to permit plotting the uppermost 10%.

47 In order to extract the fullest meaning from these data, yearly mean wealth has been displayed for the bottom half and top tenth of decedents (Charts 1–3), while the ranges of wealth in four strata (lower, middle, and upper thirty percentiles, plus the uppermost tenth) have been grouped by decades (Table 8). Means, medians, and ranges can be constructed for any grouping of years, but the timing of change is most readily discernible when short periods of time are used. Data on the range of wealth at various levels of society, however, are too cumbersome to present annually. For a discussion of these problems see Menard et al., "Opportunity and Inequality."

48 Inventory of James Black, Jan. 10, 1770, Suffolk County Probate Records, LXVIII, 464, Suffolk County Courthouse, Boston; Inventory of Francis Warden, Oct. 3, 1766, ibid., LXV, 377.

251

Table 8 Range of Personal Wealth (£ Sterling) in Boston and Philadelphia Inventories

	1685–99	1700–15	1716–25	1726–35	1736–45	1746–55	1756–65	1766–75
0–30								
Boston	2–70	1–33	1–23	1–17	1–23	1–27	1–19	1–26
Boston[a]	2–86	1–55	1–33	1–26	1–34	1–50	1–31	1–43
Phila.	5–79	5–93	5–60	3–63	5–68	1–56	1–65	4–57
31–60								
Boston	72–206	34–102	24–78	17–65	20–78	28–102	20–67	27–77
Boston[a]	87–292	56–215	34–143	27–132	35–173	51–177	32–146	44–212
Phila.	79–246	94–189	64–222	65–180	69–189	56–183	65–252	57–229
61–90								
Boston	207–711	103–454	79–318	66–273	79–301	103–583	68–397	78–409
Boston[a]	307–1,151	217–736	146–653	138–690	174–720	179–984	149–758	215–1,249
Phila.	252–625	189–577	222–744	189–539	231–1,085	184–1,022	252–1,914	229–1,530
91–100								
Boston	728–2,634	460–4,078	356–6,422	275–9,046	305–5,496	592–3,389	405–6,538	422–3,095
Boston[a]	1,155–3,417	742–11,007	660–7,362	714–9,606	769–7,557	1,005–5,609	769–15,614[b]	1,293–5,138
Phila.	666–1,978	585–2,556	752–4,618	589–5,751	1,165–4,510	1,057–16,000	1,945–22,621	1,530–36,624

a Boston inventories including real wealth.
b Excluding Samuel Waldo with inventoried wealth of £53,265.

Chart 1   Mean Inventoried Personal Wealth in Boston

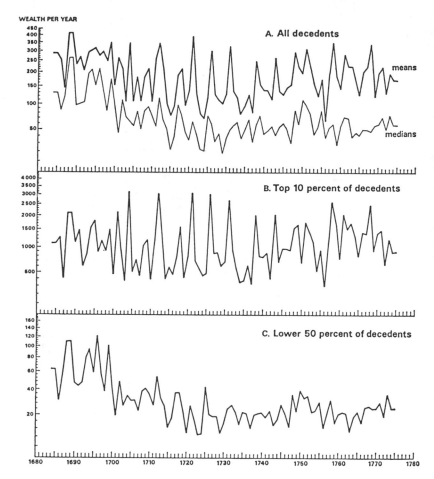

252

the parlor, mahogany furniture, and often the purchase of a slave or indentured servant. Their estates also decreased in value in the early eighteenth century, though not nearly so much as those below them. After about 1740 their fortunes rose appreciably, as shown in the ranges of wealth in Table 8.

It was primarily within the upper tenth of society that Bostonians were able to maintain or better the position of their counterparts from previous years. Even the elite, composed primarily of merchants and large land investors, was not immune to the prolonged period of

Chart 2   Mean Inventoried Real and Personal Wealth in Boston

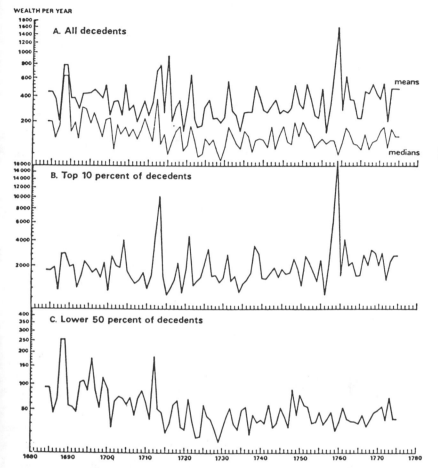

WEALTH PER YEAR

A. All decedents

means

medians

253

B. Top 10 percent of decedents

C. Lower 50 percent of decedents

economic instability, as the jagged lines in Charts 1 and 2 indicate.[49]
Most of the peaks on those charts indicate the fortunes of spectacularly

49 Most of the extreme peaks in Charts 1–3 are explained by the inventories of exceptionally wealthy men. An extreme case, which makes the point clearly, is the peak in
1759 on Charts 2A–B. The estate of Samuel Waldo, a wealthy merchant and land
speculator, was inventoried in this year. Waldo's fortune totaled £1,425 sterling in
personal wealth and £51,840 sterling in real estate. His personal estate was fairly typical
of the top 10% of Boston decedents and therefore caused no sharp upward movement on
Chart 1B. But the extensive land holdings caused a sharp rise in the graph of mean total
wealth among the top 10% of decedents and also among all decedents. I have rejected
the use of "trimmed means" suggested by Gloria L. Main ("The Correction of Biases,"
16–19, 27–28) because in the cities the accumulation of great wealth, though infrequently
on the scale of Waldo's, was an important characteristic of the social structure.

Chart 3[a] Mean Inventoried Personal Wealth in Philadelphia

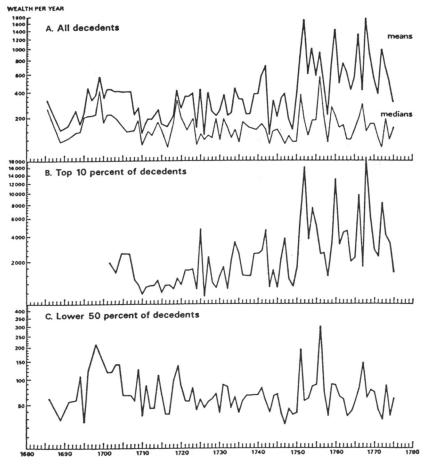

WEALTH PER YEAR

A. All decedents

means

medians

254

B. Top 10 percent of decedents

C. Lower 50 percent of decedents

a The number of inventories for the years before 1701 is insufficient to provide data points for Chart 3 B. In Chart 3 C the data before 1701 have been aggregated at two and three year intervals when necessary to provide a minimum of five inventories for each data point.

successful men such as merchants Peter Faneuil, Charles Apthorp, and Samuel Waldo. It is noticeable that the peaks in personal wealth descend after 1720, which may indicate that the executors of some of Boston's wealthiest men, as was the case with Thomas Hancock, were able to shield their estates from probate. But more likely, these descending peaks reflect Boston's declining position among the American entrepôts in the English mercantile system.[50] Nonetheless, those in the

50 See Main, "The Correction of Biases," 16 for an argument that the rich of Dedham avoided probate in the eighteenth century. Although the estates of some wealthy

top tenth of Boston's inventoried decedents were far better able to maintain their standard of living than the rest of their townsfolk in the first half of the eighteenth century.

In Philadelphia, where population growth continued throughout the colonial period and where only short-lived economic recessions struck before the 1760s, people at every level of society left considerably greater wealth than their counterparts in Boston. There is little doubt that Philadelphia as a whole was more prosperous than Boston after about 1735. Those in the lower half of Philadelphia society, primarily less skilled artisans, merchant seamen, and laborers, left personal estates several times as large as Bostonians of their rank. 255 But in spite of the growth of the city and the rapid development of the Pennsylvania interior in the eighteenth century, these people found themselves struggling to maintain the standard of living of their predecessors, though the decline in their inventoried wealth was minor by comparison to Boston. It must also be noted that the somewhat larger estates left by the lower half after 1750 are deceptive because price inflation raised commodity prices about 50 percent between 1745 and 1775 and thus wiped out most of the gains that are indicated on Chart 3 by the peaks in 1751, 1756, and 1767, and, overall, by the slightly upward trend after 1747.[51]

Among the upper 40 percent of Philadelphians, and especially among the top tenth, sustained urban growth brought greater material rewards as the colonial period drew to a close. This marks a real difference between the two cities. Unlike their Boston counterparts, the merchants, lawyers, land speculators, shopkeepers, and some master artisans in the Quaker city were able to accumulate much larger estates as the eighteenth century progressed. These gains were modest for those from the sixtieth to eightieth percentile. But within the ninth decile the estates of decedents nearly doubled on average between the beginning and end of the colonial period. Among the top tenth, the mean estate more than tripled. Furthermore, those at the pinnacle of Philadelphia society accumulated truly impressive estates in the twilight of the colonial era. In Boston the uppermost wealthholders from 1685 to 1745 consistently outstripped Philadelphia's elite. But after Philadelphia's economy eclipsed Boston's in the 1740s,

Bostonians were not probated, I have found no evidence that the wealthy are underrepresented in the Boston Inventories. On Boston's decline see Jacob M. Price, "Economic Function and the Growth of American Port Towns in the Eighteenth Century," *Perspectives in American History*, VIII (1974), 138–149.
51 For commodity price inflation see Bezanson *et al.*, *Prices in Colonial Pennsylvania*, Ch. 12.

the Quaker city's magnates, capitalizing on the rapid growth of marketable agricultural surpluses from the hinterland and the war-contracting that shifted to the middle colonies in the Seven Years' War, left fortunes that far exceeded the estates of affluent Bostonians. From 1746 to 1775 only three Boston inventories record personal estates of £6,000 sterling or more. Thirty-one Philadelphia inventories exceed £6,000 sterling and many climbed above £15,000.

Several important conclusions can be drawn from this evidence. First, changes in the *share* of wealth held at different levels of society do not necessarily reflect how city-dwellers in a particular stratum were faring in terms of absolute wealth. The mean personal estate of men in the bottom half of Philadelphia's decedents grew somewhat in the last twenty-five years of the colonial period, but this wealth represented a shrinking proportion of the city's inventoried assets because their estates had advanced less rapidly than those above them (Table 2 and Chart 3C). Conversely, Bostonians in the upper tenth controlled a growing proportion of inventoried wealth between 1700 and 1735 even though their estates were shrinking appreciably during this period (Table 2 and Charts 1B and 2B). Secondly, although the long-range trend in the redistribution of wealth was similar in Philadelphia and Boston, the actual experiences of people in the same stratum differed widely between the two cities. Philadelphians had their economic problems, including trade recessions in the mid 1720s and late 1740s. But they suffered neither the extreme fluctuations that characterized Boston's economic environment, nor the half-century of currency depreciation that cut into the material well-being of most Bostonians but seems to have had its most devastating effects on the laboring classes. Philadelphia was a city in which the statistical probability of duplicating the success of Benjamin Franklin was extraordinarily small for those beginning at the bottom. But the deterioration of earning power in Philadelphia did not extend so far up in the social ranks as it did in Boston and did not erode the economic security of those in the bottom two-thirds of society as extensively as in the New England port.[52] The inventoried estates of Bostonians in the bottom 60 percent of society fell by more than half in the first half of

256

---

52 The data presented here bear on the material estates of groups of people and not on opportunity for individuals at different levels of society at different points of time. Although some inferences can be made regarding changes in opportunity, we need life-cycle analyses for each of the cities before firm conclusions can be made regarding social mobility. I have made an initial effort toward this end in "Up From the Bottom in Franklin's Philadelphia," unpub. paper delivered at the Stony Brook Conference on Quantification in the Study of Early American Social History, June, 1975.

the eighteenth century; in Philadelphia the decline was about 25 percent. In Boston only men in the top 20 percent died at the end of the colonial period with larger estates than similarly-placed men of the late seventeenth century. In Philadelphia every one in the top 50 percent of society left more personal wealth after 1756 than had men of this rank a half century before.

Thirdly, contrary to the theory of economic development advanced by most economists of capitalist societies, the concentration of wealth in the hands of the entrepreneurial class did *not* benefit all ranks of society.[53] In fact, the upper-class consolidation of wealth between 1685 and 1775 was accompanied by the erosion of real assets held at death by those in the lower four-fifths of Boston society and the lower 60 percent of Philadelphia society. Though examples of spectacular individual ascent from the bottom could be found in both cities, the chances of success at any level of society below the upper class seem to have been considerably less in the eighteenth century than before. We will need life-cycle analyses for all the port towns before any firm conclusions can be reached concerning changes in opportunity for movement off the bottom, but the probate data and the records of poor relief make a presumptive case that for most city-dwellers, including many shopkeepers and professionals as well as laboring people, the dominating fact of eighteenth-century life, as wealth was becoming more concentrated, was not material success but economic stasis.

Taken together, these data on wealth distribution, inventoried wealth, poor relief, warnings out, and tax forgiveness indicate that life in the seaport cities was changing profoundly in the eighteenth century. These changes were manifested in the growth of poverty after 1740 that was chronic enough to embrace at least one-fifth of the heads of household by the eve of the Revolution. They were evidenced in the general weakening of economic leverage of the artisan and shopkeeper class and the fall from taxable status of large numbers of these people. They were apparent in the augmentation of power in the hands of merchants, lawyers, and land speculators—a consolidation of wealth that took most visible form in the building of lavishly appointed city houses and the increase in four-wheeled carriages, usually attended by liveried slaves, which rolled through the city streets at a time when the poorhouses were bulging with inmates.

53 See, for example, W. W. Rostow, *The Process of Economic Growth* (New York, 1959), 292–296.

This restructuring of colonial society was highly visible to rich and poor alike.[54]

The causes of this transformation can only be tentatively explored in this essay. It will require a mammoth investigation of shifts in the operation of the Atlantic economy and the links between the mercantile cities and the agricultural hinterlands before we will comprehend what was occurring in these seabord centers of colonial life. But two factors seem to hold special explanatory potential in unraveling the economic and social mechanisms at work. First, the pressure of population on land, already explored by a number of historians, seems to have severely restricted opportunity in older agricultural areas. This factor may have set hundreds of people from the small inland towns on the road to the coastal cities after the 1740s and may have held there, especially in Philadelphia and New York, hundreds of new immigrants who otherwise would have sought their fortune on the frontier. Compounding the seriousness of this rural dislocation was the role which stiffening Indian resistance to further land encroachments played in the third quarter of the century. The Cherokee, Delaware, and Shawnee resistance movements of 1758–1761, and Pontiac's pan-Indian movement of 1763–1765, may hold explanations for the bottling up of the new immigrants who flooded into the colonies from northern Ireland and Germany after the Seven Years' War.[55]

Secondly, the cycle of wartime boom and post-war recession, which occurred almost once a generation between the late seventeenth

258

54 For the imitation of English aristocratic life in Philadelphia, see Wainwright, *Colonial Grandeur*; Margaret B. Tinkcom, "Cliveden: The Building of a Colonial Mansion," *Pennsylvania Magazine of History and Biography* LXXXVIII (1964); Carl and Jessica Bridenbaugh, *Rebels and Gentlemen: Philadelphia in the Age of Franklin* (New York, 1942), Ch. 6. The *Wöchenliche Philadelphische Staatsbote* reported in December, 1767 that fifty German city-dwellers were walking the streets with their children crying for bread. Starving Germans, sometimes with naked children, were reported in the city in 1772. See O. Seidensticker, *Geschichte der Deutschen Gesellschaft von Pennsylvanien* (Philadelphia, 1876), 149–152.
55 Philip J. Greven, Jr., *Four Generations: Land and Family in Colonial Andover, Massachusetts* (Ithaca, N.Y., 1970); Charles S. Grant, *Democracy in the Connecticut Frontier Town of Kent* (New York, 1961); Kenneth Lockridge, "Land, Population, and the Evolution of New England Society, 1630–1790," *Past & Present*, 39 (1968), 62–80; Rowland Berthoff and John M. Murrin, "Feudalism, Communalism, and the Yeoman Freeholder: The American Revolution Considered as a Social Accident," in Stephen G. Kurtz and James H. Hutson (eds.), *Essays on the American Revolution* (Chapel Hill, 1973). For information on Indian resistance see David H. Corkran, *The Cherokee Frontier: Conflict and Survival, 1740–1762* (Norman, Okla., 1962); Randolph C. Downes, *Council Fires on the Upper Ohio: A Narrative of Indian Affairs in the Upper Ohio Valley until 1795* (Pittsburgh, 1940); C. A. Weslager, *The Delaware Indians: A History* (New Brunswick, N.J., 1972).

century and the Revolution, seems to have had an unusually dis-
figuring effect on urban societies. International conflict made merchant
princes out of military contractors in all three northern cities. In Boston,
for example, Andrew and Jonathan Belcher profited mightily from
Queen Anne's War. A generation later, another conflict—King George's
War—brought great wealth to Benjamin Colman, Thomas Hancock,
Benjamin Hallowell, and others. The same was true in New York and
Philadelphia where the Seven Years' War enriched merchants such
as Charles Ward Apthorp, William Bayard, Oliver DeLancey, David
Franks, John Baynton, and Joseph Fox. But at the same time, these
wars left in their wake hundreds of broken and impoverished war
veterans from the Canadian expeditions and privateering voyages, and
hundreds of destitute war widows. Equally important, financing the
wars required the imposition of heavy new taxes, which fell with
severity upon the lower and middle classes. Added to this, urban
artisans and laborers found that commodity prices rose rapidly, especially after 1760, while their wages failed to keep pace.[56]

    259

    The case of Boston is especially illuminating. The Cartagena and
Louisburg expeditions of 1743–1745, whatever they may have done
for Yankee self-esteem, imposed heavy taxes on the middle and lower
classes, drained the provincial treasury, and left hundreds of families
in Boston fatherless and husbandless. Eight years later Boston's leaders
were still lamenting the staggering burden which the war had imposed.[57]

    Compounding the postwar problems was the growth of satellite
ports such as Salem, Newburyport, and Marblehead in the second
quarter of the century. Growing rapidly, they chipped away at the
mainstays of Boston's economy—shipbuilding, the carrying trade in
fish, and distilling. As Boston's selectmen explained in a series of
petitions to the General Court for tax relief, the loss of shipbuilding
contracts led to a decline in the trade of coopers, bakers, tanners,
tallowchandlers, victuallers, and many others. Shipbuilding in 1747–48,
they reported, produced 10,140 tons (in several earlier years it had

56 Bridenbaugh, *Cities in Revolt*, 43–97; Virginia D. Harrington, *The New York
Merchant on the Eve of the Revolution* (New York, 1935); William S. Sachs, "The Business
Outlook in the Northern Colonies, 1750–1775," unpub. Ph.D. diss., (Columbia University, 1957), Ch. 2; W. T. Baxter, *The House of Hancock: Business in Boston, 1724–1775*
(Cambridge, 1945), 92–107; Nash, "Up From the Bottom," 15–22.
57 Warden, *Boston*, 127–134. The lingering effects of the war were discussed by an
anonymous writer in the *Boston Independent Advertiser*, Feb. 8, 1748, who claimed that
nearly one-fifth of the province's adult males had been lost in the war, and five years
later by an anonymous writer in *Industry & Frugality Proposed . . .* (Boston, 1753).

exceeded 14,000 tons). But in 1755–56, only 2,162 tons emerged from the Boston shipyards. Distillers reported a 50 percent decline in their volume, skinners declared a drop in skins dressed yearly from about 30,000 to 6,000 between 1746 and 1756; and at one point in the late 1740s twenty-five of the town's thirty butchers took their business elsewhere. "We are in a low impoverished condition," wrote Charles Chauncy in 1752, in attempting to promote a linen manufactory, which, for a brief time, was seen as a way of employing "some hundreds of Women and Children" so that they might do "a great deal towards supplying themselves with Bread, to the easing the Town of its Burthen in providing for the poor."[58] Capping Boston's difficulties was inflation, which had been a problem since about 1715 but reached crisis proportions in the late 1740s. The erosion of purchasing power, in an era when prices rose much faster than laboring men's wages, may have been one of the major factors in the decline of inventoried wealth in the lower two-thirds of society. The runaway inflation was finally halted in 1750 with the calling in of paper money and a drastic devaluation, but laboring Bostonians, rightly or wrongly, felt the cure struck particularly hard at them.[59]

260

The onset of the Seven Years' War brought temporary relief to the city as war contracts, enlistments, and spending by British soldiers sparked a commercial revival. But the return of prosperity was short lived. With the end of the American phase of the war in 1760 came a serious bottoming out of the economy and the beginning of a depression that hit the city hard in the 1760s. The beginning of the postwar depression coincided with natural disaster. In March, 1760, the worst fire in colonial history consumed the houses, stores, and possessions of 377 Bostonians. That 218 of these fire victims were

58 Some of the petitions are in *BRC*, XII, 119, 198; XIV, 12, 220–221, 238–240, 280; and in Massachusetts Archives, CXVII, 55–68, 395–396. For Boston's economic difficulties, also see Price, "American Port Towns," 140–149; James G. Lydon, "North Shore Trade in the Early Eighteenth Century," *American Neptune*, XXVIII (1968), 261–274; Charles Chauncy, *The Idle-Poor Secluded from the Bread of Charity by the Christian Law* (Boston, 1752).

59 For the decline of purchasing power see Andrew McF. Davis, *Currency and Banking in the Province of Massachusetts-Bay* (New York, 1901), 378. In 1739 William Douglas analyzed the effect of currency depreciation on workingmen's budgets, showing that a carpenter whose daily wages had risen from five to twelve shillings from 1712 to 1739 was earning, by the later date, only the equivalent of 3s 4d in buying power at current prices. *A Discourse Concerning the Currencies of the British Plantations* . . . (Boston, 1740), 22–23. Malcolm Freiberg, "Thomas Hutchinson and the Province Currency," *New England Quarterly*, XXX (1957), 190–208.

described as poor is one indication of how widespread poverty had become in the town.[60]

In the aftermath of the Seven Years' War Boston's economic malaise spread to New York and Philadelphia. The Quaker city had been the main port of entry for German and Scottish-Irish immigrants since the 1720s and, in the twenty years before the outbreak of the final Anglo-French conflict in North America, an average of more than a dozen ships per year disgorged passengers. But as late as the mid-1750s the city's almshouse contained no more than sixty inmates, a good indication that those who chose to remain in Philadelphia were easily absorbed into the economy. After the reopening of the oceanic road to the colonies following a wartime hiatus from 1755 to 1760, however, the arriving Rachel Rhumburgs, Daniel O'Neals, and Patrick McGuires found high prices, few jobs, and foreboding talk of deteriorating relations between colonists and native Americans in the areas of new settlement. The wartime boom, which had sent per capita imports of British goods soaring to an all-time high, turned with shocking swiftness into a postwar recession. Merchants who had overextended their credit in building up large inventories of goods found themselves bankrupt; ships lay idle, leaving hundreds of mariners without employment; and money was scarce, particularly after the restrictive Currency Act of 1764. Five years after the bubble of wartime prosperity broke, a Philadelphia doctor, whose work in the poor German and Irish neighborhoods of Mulberry Ward put him in intimate touch with the lower class, wrote of the continuing depression. "Our tradesmen begin to grow clamourous for want of employment [and] our city is full of sailors who cannot procure berths. Who knows," he added prophetically, "what the united resentments of these two numerous people may accomplish."[61]

In New York, the prosperous center of British military activities

261

60 Warden, *Boston*, 149–152; "List of Losses by Fire, 1760," Manuscript Division, Boston Public Library; *BRC*, XXIX, 89–100; Baxter, *House of Hancock*, 150–159.

61 German ship arrivals are given in Ralph Beaver Strassburger and William John Hinke, *Pennsylvania German Pioneers: A Publication of the Original Lists of Arrivals in the Port of Philadelphia from 1727 to 1808*, (Norristown, Pa., 1934), I, xxix. Immigration from Northern Ireland is traced in R. J. Dickson, *Ulster Emigration to Colonial American, 1718–1775* (London, 1966), Appendix E. Arthur L. Jensen, *The Maritime Commerce of Colonial Philadelphia* (Madison, Wis., 1963), 118–122; Harry D. Berg, "The Economic Consequences of the French and Indian War for the Philadelphia Merchants," *Pennsylvania History*, XIII (1946), 185–193; Joseph A. Ernst, *Money and Politics in America, 1755–1775: A Study in the Currency Act of 1764 and the Political Economy of Revolution* (Chapel Hill, 1973), 102–103. Benjamin Rush to Ebenezer Hazard, Nov. 8, 1765, in L. H. Butterfield (ed.), *Letters of Benjamin Rush* (Princeton, 1951), Pt. 1, 18.

and colonial privateering exploits during the Seven Years' War, the postwar recession, combined with price inflation, also struck with severity. "Everything is tumbling down, even the traders themselves," explained John Watts, one of the chief beneficiaries of military contracts.[62] Three years later, "A Tradesman" complained of the "dismal Prospect before us! a long Winter, and no Work; many unprovided with Fire-Wood, or Money to buy it; House-Rent and Taxes high; our Neighbours daily breaking their furniture at Vendue in every Corner." During the remainder of the colonial era, the economy in New York, as in Philadelphia, was buffeted by violent fluctuations. The chief victims, wrote one New Yorker in 1767, were "the poor industrious tradesmen, the needy mechanic, and all men of narrow circumstance." New York, like the other cities, rallied briefly in the early 1770s, but the prosperity of an earlier era was never recovered.[63]

262

Before we can go much farther in our understanding of the dynamics of urban colonial society it will be necessary to explore a number of questions. To what extent did Anglo-American business cycles affect the economy at large and various occupational and social groups in particular? Did the movement toward a wage labor market, where indentured servants and slaves were replaced in the northern cities by free workers who could be hired and fired at the employer's will, create a new class of urban poor? Precisely how did the international wars of the eighteenth century affect the structure of opportunity in the seaboard cities? To what extent did Indian resistance against further land encroachments in the interior lead to an increase of migration into the cities, in a kind of eastward movement, in the late colonial period? Was occupational specialization and the exposure of a growing part of the urban workforce to the increasingly severe fluctuations of a market economy making entry into some crafts more difficult? How was the burden of price inflation, in Boston between about 1715 and 1750 and in New York and Philadelphia

62 To Scott, Pringle, Cheap, and Co., Feb. 5, 1764, quoted in Ernst, *Money and Politics in America*, 90. See also the descriptions of business failures and hard times in "To my Countrymen, the Inhabitants of the Province and City of New-York," *New-York Gazette or Weekly Post-Boy*, Aug. 26, 1762; Harrington, *New York Merchant*, 313–320. For the effect of economic cycles on one merchant see Philip L. White, *The Beekmans of New York in Politics and Commerce, 1647–1870* (New York, 1950), Ch. 12.
63 *New-York Journal*, Dec. 17, 1767. "Probus," in *New-York Journal*, Nov. 19, 1767. See also Ernst, *Money and Politics*, 251–260; Harrington, *New York Merchant*, 316–351.

from 1745 to 1775, distributed among urban dwellers? Finally, was poverty in the city a transitional state, endured for brief periods by newcomers and recently freed indentured servants who then went on to better things; or, alternatively, was it becoming a way of life for an increasing number of city dwellers? From the data presented above come indications rather than clear-cut answers to these questions. But the evidence of considerable economic distress and thwarted aspirations in the late colonial period is compelling.

If it can be assumed that the urban people of the 1760s responded not only to high principles enunciated in revolutionary pamphlets, but also to the conditions of their lives, then this evidence suggests that we need a new assessment of the forces that brought the Revolution into being. Those "mindless mobs," so roundly dismissed at the time for their inability to act except out of passion, may not have been so incapable of determining how their life chances had been affected in the decades before 1776. Accordingly, careful attention must be paid to the printed attacks on the wealthy that appeared with increasing frequency in newspapers and tracts in the late colonial period. "Poverty and discontent appear in every Face (except the Countenances of the Rich)," stormed a pamphleteer in Boston in 1750. The author went on to remark that it was no wonder that a handful of merchants, who had fattened themselves on war contracts and through manipulating the unstable money market, could "build ships, Houses, buy Farms, set up their Coaches, Chariots, live very splendidly, purchase Fame, Posts of Honour" and so forth while the bulk of the population languished. Was it equitable, asked a writer in the *New-York Gazette* in 1765, "that 99, rather 999, should suffer for the Extravagance or Grandeur of one? Especially when it is considered that Men frequently owe their Wealth to the impoverishment of their Neighbours?" Was supporting the poor an act of charity or simple justice, asked another New York writer in 1769, reminding his audience that "it is to the meaner Class of Mankind, the industrious Poor, that so many of us are indebted for those goodly Dwellings we inhabit, for that comfortable Substance we enjoy, while others are languishing under the disagreeable Sensations of Penury and Want."[64]

63

64 Vincent Centinel (pseud.), *Massachusetts in Agony; or, Important Hints to the Inhabitants of the Province: Calling aloud for Justice to be done to the Oppressed* ... (Boston, 1750), 3–5, 8, 12–13. *New-York Gazette*, July 11, 1765, quoted in Bernard Friedman, "The Shaping of the Radical Consciousness in Provincial New York," *Journal of American History*, LVI (1970), 794. *New-York Gazette or Weekly Post-Boy*, Nov. 13, 1769; also *ibid.*, Dec. 24, 31, 1767, Jan. 7, 21, 1768. I have attempted a fuller analysis of the growing

Understanding how life in the cities was changing may also render far more comprehensible political factionalism in the late colonial period and the extraordinary response to the attempts at imperial reform initiated after the Seven Years' War. The rise of radical leaders such as James Otis and Samuel Adams in Boston, for example, cannot be separated from the years of economic difficulty, spreading poverty, and the limited chances of advancement that so many people in the city experienced. Nor can the widespread support of revolutionary radicals in New York and Philadelphia be understood without reference to the new conditions in the cities at the end of the colonial period. In this sense, understanding whether Otis was clinically mad is less important than perceiving that in his venomous attacks on the wealthy, powerful, aristocratic, in-bred Hutchinsonian circle, the members of which had repeatedly demonstrated their insensitivity to lower-class Bostonians, Otis had struck a resonant chord. When a conservative writer attacked Otis and his colleagues in 1763 as "the darling idols of a dirty, very dirty, witless rabble commonly called the little vulgar," he was not unmindful of the prior attacks by Otis on those in Boston who "grind the faces of the poor without remorse, eat the bread of oppression without fear, and wax fat upon the spoils of the people."[65] When the Stamp Act riots came, it was entirely appropriate from the lower-class point of view that the initial targets should be the luxuriously appointed homes of Andrew Oliver, Benjamin Hallowell, and Thomas Hutchinson, the last detested by the lower class since the late 1740s as the architect of a merciless deflationary policy that in the long run may have benefitted the mechanic and shopkeeping class but was seen at the time as primarily beneficial to the rich. Rich men began burying their treasures and sending valuable possessions to the homes of poorer friends, indicating that Governor Francis Bernard was close to the mark in concluding that the Boston crowd was engaged not only in a political response to new imperial regulations but also in "a war of plunder, of general levelling, and taking away the distinction of rich and poor."[66]

Much more work must be done before firm pronouncements can be made about linkages between the changing dynamics of urban

264

---

attack on the wealthy in my essay "Social Change and the Growth of Pre-revolutionary Urban Radicalism," in Alfred Young (ed.), *The American Revolution: Explorations in the History of American Radicalism* (forthcoming).

65 *Boston Evening Post*, Mar. 14, 1763; *Boston Gazette*, Jan. 11, 1762, Supplement.

66 Bernard to the Board of Trade, Aug. 31, 1765, in William Cobbett (ed.), *The Parliamentary History of England* (London, 1813), XVI, 129–131.

societies and the onset of the revolutionary movement. The challenge at hand is not to make simplistic connections between the decline of mean inventoried wealth and the advent of revolutionary sentiment or between the rise of urban poverty and the beginnings of the imperial crisis. It is far from certain that rapid social change brings social unrest, or even that those who suffer the most are the first to rise against the causes of their suffering. What is needed, rather, is a deeper understanding of how changing social and economic circumstances, beginning in the early eighteenth century and accelerating in the last generation of the colonial period, eroded the allegiance of many urban dwellers to the British mercantilistic system and also to their own internal social systems. The collapse of the Atlantic economy at the end of the Seven Years' War, coming near the end of a long period of urban change, seems to have shaped the way these people thought about the future far more profoundly than has been recognized. Nobody before the 1760s thought to associate economic dislocation in Boston, or the rise of poverty in New York, with a mercantile system that provided a handsome flow of credit and cheap manufactured goods, as well as military protection. But the economic shocks beginning at the end of the Seven Years' War began to focus thought in an entirely new way—both in reference to participation in the British mercantile world and in regard to the internal structuring of urban society, where elements of the elite were increasingly being viewed as conscience-less aggrandizers of wealth and power. It is the large body of evidence, indicating how the conditions of life and the promise for the future were changing in the cities, that makes far more comprehensible than a purely ideological interpretation can do, both the creation and reception of revolutionary sentiment.

265

Appendix A

The analysis that follows is based on data derived from 2,957 inventories of wealth for Boston, located at Office of the Recorder of Wills, Suffolk County Court House, Boston; and 1,434 inventories for Philadelphia, located in Office of Register of Wills, City Hall Annex. Inventories in both Massachusetts and Pennsylvania meticulously recorded all forms of personal property, including slaves, servants, household possessions, currency, bonds, mortgages, book debts, silver plate, stock in trade, ships, livestock, and other forms of moveable property. Boston inventories also recorded real estate, usually including real property outside Suffolk County, but Philadelphia inventories only occasionally listed real property. For more detailed information on the process of inventorying see the articles by Alice Hanson Jones, cited in note 6.

Three tests have been made to check the inclusiveness and cross-sectionality of the inventories. First, the number of inventories was compared to the estimated number of burials to determine the percentage of decedents whose estates were inventoried. By aggregating burials and inventories for 5-year periods, it was determined that the estates of between 35–55% of Boston's males were inventoried. Although the variation in 5-year periods is considerable, there was no trend toward greater or less inventory coverage. In Philadelphia, where burial statistics began in 1729 and were not regularly available until 1747, the percentage of male decedents with inventories ranged from about 14 to 23%. The much lower incidence of inventories in Philadelphia may be because the city was the major port of arrival in America for German, Scottish-Irish, and English immigrants and therefore the burials included a large number of transients and persons only recently arrived in the city. The number of Boston burials is taken from John B. Blake, *Public Health in the Town of Boston, 1630–1822* (Cambridge, Mass., 1959), 250. For the number of burials in Philadelphia and the sources from which they are derived, see Nash, "Slaves and Slaveholders in Colonial Philadelphia," *William and Mary Quarterly*, XXX (1973), 227, 231. Secondly, the Philadelphia inventories were checked against the tax lists for three dates (using only the names of persons dying within 4 years of the tax lists), to ascertain whether the wealth bias inherent in all probate records changed appreciably, with the following results:

Position of Inventoried Philadelphia Decedents on Previous Tax List

Wealth Quintile		1709	1756	1722
Low	1	2 (5.4%)	8 (7.8%)	2 (3.3%)
	2	5 (13.5%)	11 (10.8%)	4 (6.6%)
	3	7 (18.9%)	16 (15.7%)	9·(14.8%)
	4	8 (21.6%)	29 (28.4%)	15 (24.6%)
High	5	15 (40.5%)	38 (37.3%)	31 (50.8%)

266

Thirdly, the occupations of the decedents were checked for three periods to determine how representative the inventories were in this regard and whether the degree of occupational bias changed. The following table, representing the occupations of about half of the decedents, shows the occupational representativeness of the probate data. The percentage of taxpayers in the various occupations is from Price, "American Port Towns," 177–183.

Occupations of Boston and Philadelphia Decedents with Inventories

	Percentage of Inventories			% of
	1684–1725	1726–1750	1751–1775	Taxpayers
Building crafts				
Boston	4.1	3.9	4.3	10.1 (1790)
Philadelphia	8.6	7.9	5.9	11.3 (1774)
Professionals				
Boston	1.2	2.0	2.7	4.1
Philadelphia	2.1	2.2	3.5	3.4
Shipbuilding crafts				
Boston	2.7	4.3	4.4	8.6
Philadelphia	1.0	0.8	2.6	4.9
Mariners				
Boston	21.8	22.7	21.1	9.3
Philadelphia	8.0	8.6	10.1	8.7
Merchants and Shopkeepers				
Boston	15.5	13.1	14.6	13.5
Philadelphia	24.3	26.2	21.1	10.0

All three tests of the reliability of the inventories reveal, as expected, that biases are inherent in this kind of data. But there is a remarkable degree of consistency in both the wealth and occupational bias, warranting the conclusion that the inventories reveal real changes in the structure of eighteenth-century society rather than random changes in the pattern of will-leaving or inventory-taking. No attempt has been made to correct for age or wealth in calculating the distribution of inventoried wealth. Since I am not calculating the wealth distribution for the living population, as in the case of the tax lists, it is necessary only to insure that the distortions in the sample remain reasonably constant in order to establish change over time. The overrepresentation of mariners in the Boston inventories and of merchants in the Philadelphia inventories serves as a warning that comparisons are better made for one city at different points in time than for two cities.

Families and Farms:
Mentalité in Pre-Industrial America

James A. Henretta

T

HE history of the agricultural population of pre-industrial America

268 remains to be written. As a result of quantitative investigations of wealth distribution and social mobility; of rates of birth, marriage, and death; and of patterns of inheritance, officeholding, and church membership, there is an ever-growing mass of data that delineates the *structures* of social existence in the small rural communities that constituted the core of American agricultural society in the North before 1830. But what of the *consciousness* of the inhabitants, the mental or emotional or ideological aspects of their lives? And what of the relationship between the two? Can a careful statistical analysis of people's lives—a precise description of their patterns of social action—substantiate at least limited statements as to their motivations, values, and goals?

A number of historians have attempted to establish a connection between the subsistence activities of the agricultural population and its institutional, ideological, and cultural existence. Consider, for example, the entrepreneurial interpretation implicit in James T. Lemon's highly regarded quantitative analysis of the eighteenth-century agricultural society of Southeastern Pennsylvania:

> A basic stress in these essays is on the "liberal" middle-class orientation of many of the settlers. . . . "Liberal" I use in the classic sense, meaning placing individual freedom and material gain over that of public interest. Put another way, the people planned for themselves much more than they did for their communities. . . . This is not to say that

Mr. Henretta is a member of the Department of History at the University of California, Los Angeles. Earlier versions of this paper were presented at the University of Rochester, the Charles Warren Center at Harvard, and the Shelby Cullom Davis Center at Princeton. Mr. Henretta wishes to express special gratitude for the written criticisms and suggestions offered by Patricia Wilson, Jonathan Wiener, Fred Matthews, Jeffrey Nelson, Richard Dunn, Gary Nash, Peter Kolchin, Daniel Scott Smith, and Sam Bass Warner, and for the oral commentaries of Lawrence Stone, R. Jackson Wilson, and Bernard Bailyn.

the settlers were "economic men," single-minded maximizing material-
ists. Few could be, or even wanted to be. Nevertheless, they defended
their liberal propensities in a tenacious manner. . . . Undoubtedly their
view was fostered by a sense that the environment was "open." As
individualists, they were ready in spirit to conquer the limitless continent, to subdue the land.[1]

However overburdened with reservations and qualifications, the general
thrust of this depiction of values and aspirations is clear enough. Lemon's
settlers were individualists, enterprising men and women intent upon the
pursuit of material advantage at the expense of communal and non-economic
goals.

269

Can the "consciousness" with which Lemon has endowed these early
Pennsylvanians be verified by historical evidence? The question is important,
for many of the statistical data presented by Lemon do not support this
description of the inhabitants' "orientation," "spirit," or "propensities."
Take the pattern of residence. It is true that the predominance of isolated
farmsteads—rather than nucleated villages—suggests that these men and
women were planning "for themselves much more than . . . for their
communities." But what of the presence of clusters of ethnic and religious
groups? Such voluntary concentrations of like-minded settlers indicate the
importance of *communal* values, of people who preferred to share a religious
or ethnic identity. Here the author's evidence contradicts his conclusion.
"Most of the people who came during this period," Lemon writes of the
years between 1700 and 1730, "settled together in areas and communities
defined by nationality or denomination. . . . Language and creed thus exerted
considerable influence on the whereabouts of people. Yet groups were mixed
in several areas, for example on the Lancaster Plain."[2]

This exception only confirms the rule. Nearly every historian who has
studied ethnic settlement patterns in the colonial period has stressed the
existence of communal concentrations. In the Middle Colonies, for example,
patterns of spatial segregation appeared among the Dutch in Newark, New
Jersey, and to some extent among Quakers and Seventh Day Baptists in the
same area. Most of the German immigrants who arrived in Lancaster,
Pennsylvania, in 1744 settled on the lots laid out by Dr. Adam Simon Kuhn,
the leading German resident, rather than on land offered by the English
proprietor, Alexander Hamilton. These linguistic and religious ties extended
beyond settlement patterns to encompass economic relationships. Every one
of the one hundred names inscribed in the account book of Henry King—

[1] *The Best Poor Man's Country: A Geographical Study of Early Southeastern
Pennsylvania* (Baltimore, 1972), xv.
[2] *Ibid.*, 221.

shoemaker, butcher, and currier of Second River, New Jersey, in 1775—was of Dutch origin; and the main business connections of the merchants of Lancaster, whether they were Jewish or Quaker or German, were with their co-religionists in Philadelphia.[3]

Is an individualist spirit fully compatible with these communal settlement patterns and this religiously determined economic activity? It is possible, of course, that these ethnic or linguistic preferences facilitiated the pursuit of individual economic gain, and that the patronage of the shop of a fellow church member brought preferred treatment and lower prices. But the weight of the evidence indicates that these decisions were not made for narrowly economic or strictly utilitarian reasons: the felt need to maintain a linguistic or religious identity was as important a consideration as the fertility of the soil or the price of the land in determining where a family would settle. The "calculus of advantage" for these men and women was not mere pecuniary gain, but encompassed a much wider range of social and cultural goals.[4]

270

These ethnic, linguistic, or religious ties did not reflect a coherent ideological system, a planned *communitarian* culture similar to the highly organized Moravian settlement at Bethlehem, Pennsylvania.[5] These bonds among families, neighbors, and fellow church members were informal; nonetheless, they circumscribed the range of individual action among the inhabitants of Pennsylvania and laid the foundations for a rich and diverse cultural existence. These community-oriented patterns of social interaction emerge clearly from Lemon's quantitative data, yet they do not figure prominently in his conclusion. He has not explained the complexity of the settlers' existence but has forced their lives into the mold of a timeless, placeless concept of "liberal individualism."

A similar discrepancy between data and interpretation appears in Lemon's analysis of the economic goals and achievements of the inhabitants of eighteenth-century Pennsylvania. What becomes of the open environment and the conquering spirit when "tenant farming was much more frequent than we might expect[.] . . . [I]n 1760 and 1782 about 30 per cent of

[3] Dennis P. Ryan, "Six Towns: Continuity and Change in Revolutionary New Jersey, 1770-1792" (Ph.D. diss., New York University, 1974), 57-71; Jerome H. Wood, Jr., "Conestoga Crossroads: The Rise of Lancaster, Pennsylvania, 1730-1789" (Ph.D. diss., Brown University, 1969), 53, 114-115, 129-131.
[4] Nor, in E. A. Wrigley's definition, was their society modern—one in which "the unit is the individual or, at the widest, the nuclear family" and "the utilities to be maximized are concentrated in a narrower band and are pursued with a new urgency" ("The Process of Modernization and the Industrial Revolution in England," *Journal of Interdisciplinary History*, III [1972], 233, 229).
[5] Gillian Lindt Gollin, *Moravians in Two Worlds: A Study of Changing Communities* (New York, 1967).

Lancaster's and Chester's married taxpayers were landless" and an additional 15 percent of the total number of taxpayers in Chester County were single freemen—mostly young men without landed property. With nearly 45 percent of the members of the adult white male population without land of their own, the gap between evidence and conclusion is so obvious that it must be confronted; and what better way than by evoking the spirit of Frederick Jackson Turner? "As long as the frontier was open . . . ," Lemon writes, "many people were able to move, and as a result frustrations were dampened and the liberal values of the original inhabitants of the colony were upheld."[6]

This is an appealing interpretation, especially since it admits the necessary connection between the structure of opportunity offered by a given environment and the consciousness of the inhabitants, but it is not completely satisfactory. It assumes that the migrants came with "liberal" values, with an expectation that most adult males would own a freehold estate and that anything less than this would generate anger and frustration. Neither the basic proposition nor its corollary is acceptable, for both fail to convey the settlers' conception of social reality, their understanding of the structural components of age and wealth.

To be "young" in this agricultural society (as in most) was either to be landless or without sufficient land to support a family. As Philip J. Greven, Daniel Scott Smith, and Robert A. Gross have shown, male parents normally retained legal control of a sizable portion of the family estate until death, in order to ensure their financial well-being in old age, and the economic security of their widows was carefully protected by dower rights.[7] Nor were

271

[6] Lemon, *Best Poor Man's Country*, 94, 97; James T. Lemon and Gary B. Nash, "The Distribution of Wealth in Eighteenth-Century America: A Century of Change in Chester County, Pennsylvania, 1693-1802," *Journal of Social History*, II (1968), Table I. Since indentured and hired servants are not included in the categories of married freeholder or single freeman, the proportion of landless males may be greater than 45%.

[7] Philip J. Greven, Jr., "Family Structure in Seventeenth-Century Andover, Massachusetts," *William and Mary Quarterly*, 3d Ser., XXIII (1966), 234-256, and *Four Generations: Population, Land, and Family in Colonial Andover, Massachusetts* (Ithaca, N.Y., 1970); Daniel Scott Smith, "Parental Power and Marriage Patterns: An Analysis of Historical Trends in Massachusetts," *Journal of Marriage and the Family*, XXXV (1973), 419-428; Robert A. Gross, *The Minutemen and Their World* (New York, 1976), 210, n. 22. These authors interpret this use of economic power as an attempt by parents to control the marriage age and the subsequent family life of their children. This may have been the *effect* of delayed transmission; the prime *cause*, however, was probably the parents' concern with financial security during their old age. The exercise of parental authority (with the resulting generational conflict) was not an end in itself but simply the by-product of the prudent fiscal management of productive property. Some of the difficulties in interpreting these data are explored by Maris Vinovskis, "American Historical

these cultural restraints on the transmission of improved property the only, or even the main, obstacle to the economic prospects of the next generation. For the high rate of natural increase constantly threatened to overwhelm the accumulated capital resources of many of these northern farm families. There was never sufficient cleared and improved property, or livestock, or farm equipment, or adequate housing to permit most young men and women to own a farm. In five small agricultural towns in New Jersey in the 1770s, for example, one half of all white males aged eighteen to twenty-five were without land, while another 29 percent of this age group owned fifty acres or less. And in Concord, Massachusetts, the percentage of landless males (many of whom were young) remained at 30 percent from 1750 to 1800. This correlation between age and wealth persisted throughout the life-cycle; all of the males in the lowest quintile of the taxable population in East Guilford, Connecticut, in 1740 were below the age of forty, while every person in the highest quintile was that age or above.[8]

The accumulation of financial resources by aging men brought them higher status and political power. In Concord, between 1745 and 1774, the median age of selectmen at the time of their first election to office was forty-five, a pattern that obtained in Dedham and Watertown as well.[9] Indeed, the correlation among age, wealth, status, and power in these agricultural communities indicates the profound importance of age as a basic principle of social differentiation. And so it appeared to the Reverend William Bentley of Salem on a visit to Andover in 1793; the country people, he noted, assembled to dance "in classes due to their ages, not with any regard to their condition, as in the Seaport Towns."[10] In such an age-stratified society economic "success" was not usual (and not expected) until the age of thirty-five, forty, or even forty-five. Propertied status was the product of one or two decades of work as a laborer or tenant, or of the long-delayed inheritance of the parental

---

Demography Review Essay," *Historical Methods Newsletter*, IV (Sept. 1971), 141-148.
   [8] Ryan, "Six Towns," 273 (Table 61); Robert A. Gross, "The Problem of Agricultural Crisis in Eighteenth-Century New England: Concord, Massachusetts as a Test Case" (unpub. paper, 1975), 7; John J. Waters, "A Yankee Village's Last Hundred Years: Guilford, Connecticut in the Eighteenth Century" (unpubl. paper, 1975), Table 1. The Wisconsin tax lists for 1860 indicate that a man one year older than another had, on the average, 7.8% more wealth than his younger counterpart. Lee Soltow, *Patterns of Wealthholding in Wisconsin Since 1850* (Madison, Wis., 1971), 8. Soltow finds a "pattern of wealth increase from age 20 to 50 or 55, with a tapering after this age" in rural areas; and that age and nativity account for roughly 60% of the inequality in the distribution of wealth (*ibid.*, 46, 42).
   [9] Gross, *Minutemen*, 196; Kenneth A. Lockridge and Alan Kreider, "The Evolution of Massachusetts Town Government, 1640 to 1740," *WMQ*, 3d Ser., XXIII (1966), 566.
   [10] *The Diary of William Bentley, D.D.* . . . , II (Salem, Mass., 1907), 17.

farm. The ownership of a freehold estate was the *goal* of young male farmers and their wives; it was not—even in the best of circumstances—a universal condition among adult males at any one point in time. Age stratification thus constituted an important aspect of what Michael Zuckerman has neatly conceptualized as the "social context" of political activity in these small and ethnically homogeneous agricultural settlements.[11] The economic dependence and powerlessness of young adults was a fact of life, the proper definition of social reality.

If cultural norms legitimated an age-stratified society in the minds of most northern farmers, then the character of social and economic life accustomed them to systematic inequalities in the distribution of wealth. Consider the evidence. In southeastern Pennsylvania in 1760 and again in 1782, the top 40 percent of the taxable population owned 70 percent of the assessed wealth, while the top 10 percent controlled 33 percent. On the 1784 tax list of Newtown, Long Island, the proportions were nearly identical, with the top 40 percent owning 73 percent of the wealth, and the richest 10 percent holding 37 percent. In both places, inequality increased steadily from the end of the seventeenth century even as the rate of natural population growth declined—a clear indication of advancing social differentiation (and not simply age stratification). And in Newtown, at least, the bulk of the poor population in 1784 was composed not of "younger sons or older men" but of workers in the prime of their productive lives.[12]

273

The westward migration of this excess farm population was of crucial importance, although not for the precise reasons suggested by Turner and Lemon. Young men and women without a landed inheritance moved to newly settled communities not as yeomen but as aspirants to that status; they hoped to make the difficult climb up the agricultural "ladder" from laborer to tenant to freeholder. This geographical movement, in turn, helped to maintain social stability in long-settled agricultural towns. One-third of all

[11] "The Social Context of Democracy in Massachusetts," *WMQ*, 3d Ser., XXV (1968), 523-544. Zuckerman's analysis is not sufficiently critical of Robert E. Brown's work, even as it provides a better conceptual framework for evaluating the importance of a widespread suffrage. Age stratification is ignored, as are economic inequality and the increasing appearance of religious conflict. For a more detailed analysis of Zuckerman's work (and that of Greven, John Demos, and Kenneth Lockridge) see James A. Henretta, "The Morphology of New England Society in the Colonial Period," *Jour. Interdisciplinary Hist.*, II (1971), 379-398.
[12] Lemon, *Best Poor Man's Country*, 11 (Table 1); Jessica Kross Ehrlich, "A Town Study in Colonial New York: Newtown, Queens County (1642-1790)" (Ph.D. diss., University of Michigan, 1974), 178, 164 (Table 13). The data for Concord indicate that in 1770-1771 the top 20% of the population owned 48% of the land and 56% of the town's wealth but paid only 42.7% of the total tax (Gross, *Minutemen*, 212, 220, 231).

adult males in Goshen, Connecticut, in 1750 were without land; but two decades later a majority of these men had left the town and 70 percent of those who remained had obtained property through marriage, inheritance, or the savings from their labor. A new landless group of unmarried sons, wage laborers, and tenant farmers had appeared in Goshen by 1771, again encompassing one-third of the adult males. A similar process of out-migration and property accumulation would characterize many of the lives of this landless group, but throughout the northern region there was a steady increase in the number of permanent tenant farmers as the century progressed.[13]

274   The renewed expropriation of aboriginal lands during the early nineteenth century brought a partial reversal of this trend. Massive westward migration enabled a rapidly growing Euro-American population to *preserve* an agricultural society composed primarily of yeoman freeholding families in many eastern areas, and to *extend* these age- and wealth-stratified communities into western regions.[14] This movement did not, however, produce less stratified communities in the Northwest states, nor did it assure the universal ownership of land. Within a few decades of settlement the wealth structure of the frontier states was nearly indistinguishable from that in the agricultural areas of the more densely settled east. In Trempealeau County, Wisconsin, in 1870 the poorest 10 percent of the propertied population owned less than 1 percent of all assessed wealth, while the most affluent 10 percent controlled 39 percent. This distribution was almost precisely the same as that in those regions of Vermont from which many of the inhabitants of this farming county had recently migrated.[15] "On no frontier," Neil McNall concludes from an intensive study of the settlement of the rich Genesee

[13] Jackson Turner Main, *The Social Structure of Revolutionary America* (Princeton, N.J., 1965), 176. For a carefully documented analysis of the agricultural ladder see Clarence H. Danhof, *Change in Agriculture: The Northern United States, 1820-1870* (Cambridge, Mass., 1969), 78-115.

[14] The alternative was a class-stratified society, composed of a few owners of large properties and a mass of wage laborers—an agricultural proletariat. See, for example, J. Harvey Smith, "Work Routine and Social Structure in a French Village: Cruzy in the Nineteenth Century," *Jour. Interdisciplinary Hist.,* V (1975), 362.

[15] Merle Curti et al., *The Making of an American Community: A Case Study of Democracy in a Frontier County* (Stanford, Calif., 1959), chap. 4. Inequality in the Old Northwest was less acute than in Frederick and Berkeley counties in the Shenandoah Valley of Virginia in 1788, where the top 10% of the landowners held nearly 50% of the land, or in the "cotton South," where the top decile controlled between 50% and 55% of the total wealth in 1850 and 1860. See Robert D. Mitchell, "Agricultural Change and the American Revolution: A Virginia Case Study," *Agricultural History,* XLVII (Apr. 1973), 131, and Gavin Wright, "'Economic Democracy' and the Concentration of Agricultural Wealth in the Cotton South, 1850-1860," *Agricultural Hist.,* XLIV (1970), 63-85.

Valley in upstate New York between 1790 and 1860, "was there an easy avenue to land ownership for the farmer of limited means."[16]

Evidence from a variety of geographic locations indicates, therefore, that Lemon has presented an overly optimistic description of the agricultural economy of early America and has falsely ascribed a "liberal" consciousness to the inhabitants of eighteenth-century Pennsylvania. His analysis is not unique. A number of historians of colonial New England have offered similar interpretations of an entrepreneurial mentality among the majority of the agricultural population. Sometimes the ascription is implicit and perhaps inadvertent, as in the case of Philip Greven's path-breaking analysis of Andover, which focuses attention on the single economic variable of land transmission. Was the preservation of a landed inheritance the concern of *most* Andover families or only that of the very select group of substantially endowed first settlers and their descendants whom Greven has studied? The pattern of family life, geographic mobility, and economic values may have been very different among later arrivals to Andover—those who had less land to pass on to the next generation—yet this group constituted a majority of the town's population by the eighteenth century. Or what of the pervasive entrepreneurial outlook among Connecticut farmers which is posited by Richard L. Bushman in his stimulating examination of the transition *From Puritan To Yankee?*[17] Bushman's interpretation of the Great Awakening is predicated upon the emergence of an accumulation-oriented pattern of behavior, and yet little—if any—evidence is presented to demonstrate its existence among the mass of the population.

Indeed, the only work which attempts explicitly to demonstrate the predominance of entrepreneurial values among the farming population of New England is the small but influential study by Charles S. Grant, *Democracy in the Connecticut Frontier Town of Kent.* According to Grant, the one-hundred-odd male settlers who arrived in Kent during the late 1730s and the 1740s were "remarkably uniform . . . prosperous enough to buy proprietary shares and to accumulate large amounts of land." They were "versatile and ambitious," and the economic opportunity available in Kent—"fertile (but stony) farming land, . . . deposits of iron ore, and abundant water power for . . . mills"—induced in these settlers "not placid contentment, but an almost

275

[16] Neil Adams McNall, *An Agricultural History of the Genesee Valley, 1790-1860* (Philadelphia, 1952), 240-241. For the rapid and extensive emergence of farm tenancy in Illinois and Iowa see Paul W. Gates, "Frontier Estate Builders and Farm Laborers," in Richard Hofstadter and Seymour Martin Lipset, eds., *Turner and the Sociology of the Frontier* (New York, 1968), 105, 115-116.

[17] Subtitled: *Character and the Social Order in Connecticut, 1690-1765* (Cambridge, Mass., 1967). The possible bias in Greven's work is suggested in Vinovskis, "American Historical Demography Review Essay," *Historical Methods Newsletter,* IV (Sept. 1971), 142-145.

frenzied determination to try a hand at everything."[18] Thus "virtually every family settled on a farm which . . . usually produced a salable surplus"; "virtually every family had some member involved as operator or part owner of an ironworks"; and "virtually every early settler was an avid land speculator." By the time of the American Revolution this activity had produced "a population raised on an economic tradition of land speculation and individualistic venturing" which refused to make "economic sacrifices" for the sake of Independence.[19] While Grant indicates that there may have been "humble subsistence farmers" and "obscure yeomen" in the town, he "is impressed not so much with the contented subsistence way of life as with the drive for profits." Indeed, he devotes a chapter to "The Drive For Profits," and concludes it by stressing the acquisitiveness of the economic elite, the "aggressive opportunists" whose ethical standards were "part and parcel of the spirit of Kent." "One sees in certain of the Kent settlers not so much the contended yeoman, certainly not the 'slave' toiling for his master, but perhaps the embryo John D. Rockefeller."[20]

276

Even when stated in more historically realistic language, Grant's argument is not sustained by his evidence. He begins by distorting much of the allegedly opportunistic and profit-seeking economic activity in Kent by calling it "nonagricultural." In actuality, most of the nonfarm enterprises were sawmills, gristmills, fulling mills, and tanneries. These were profit-seeking businesses, but they were also social necessities in a rural community; all were intimately connected to agricultural production. With the exception of the iron industry (the development of which lends some support to Grant's thesis), these enterprises produced primarily for a local market and were so crucial to the welfare of the inhabitants that they were supported by communal action. Following the long New England tradition of material inducements to skilled artisans, the proprietors of the town voted an extra lot in the first division to Ebenezer Barnum "on condition he build a sawmill by the last of December next and also a gristmill in two years."[21] Thus the mere existence of most of these "non-agricultural" enterprises will not substantiate Grant's interpretation. They were traditional, not new, enterprises, practical necessities rather than dramatic innovations, and the product of communal legislation as much as of an adventurous individualism.

A second distortion appears when Grant argues that "the most signifi-

[18] (New York, 1961), 99, 29, 169-170.
[19] Ibid., 170, 42, 53, 171.
[20] Ibid., 78, 29, 54, 53.
[21] This vote (as well as the fact that there was a common field system in Kent in the early 1740s) is mentioned in Grant's "A History of Kent, 1738-1796: Democracy on Connecticut's Frontier" (Ph.D. diss., Columbia University, 1957), 43, 57-58, although not in the published version.

cant aspect of this enterprise . . . would seem to be the magnitude of profit-seeking activity." "Altogether," he indicates, "209 men were investors in nonagricultural enterprise at Kent between 1739 and 1800."[22] But what is the significance of this number? Neither in his monogragh nor in his dissertation does Grant indicate the aggregate number of adult males who lived in Kent during this sixty-year period; yet this total is crucial, for it represents the number of *potential* investors. The statistical material that is available suggests that at least one thousand (and probably one thousand five hundred) adult males worked and resided in Kent during this period; thus the 209 resident "profit-seekers" constituted only 15-20 percent of the potential investing population.[23] What Grant has depicted as the activity and the ethos of most of the inhabitants of Kent becomes, at most, the enterprise and outlook of a well-to-do upper class.

277

In an attempt to demonstrate the pervasiveness of this entrepreneurial outlook in Kent, Grant adduces another type of evidence. His position—based more on assumption than on argument—is that the sale of "surplus" agricultural products on the market constitutes prima facie evidence of a profit-oriented attitude. Considered abstractly, this is a weak line of reasoning, if only because of the word "surplus" itself. This term, as it was widely used in America until the middle of the nineteenth century, clearly indicated that market sales were a secondary rather than a primary consideration: the "surplus" was what was left over after the yearly subsistence requirements of the farm household had been met.[24]

Even if this faulty reasoning is ignored, the factual evidence will not sustain Grant's argument that a majority of these farmsteads produced a surplus which could be sold or exchanged. Grant himself states that 40 of the 103 farms in Kent in 1796 could provide only enough foodstuffs for the sustenance of their occupants. And this estimate is undoubtedly too low, since his computations assume a grain harvest of twenty-five bushels per acre for both corn and wheat. Such yields might be attained on the best land (and then only for the first harvests), but reliable data from areas as far apart as Massachusetts, Pennsylvania, Virginia, and North Carolina indicate average yields of fifteen bushels per acre for corn and eight to twelve bushels for wheat.[25] If these yields are assumed, the proportion of Kent farmsteads that

[22] Grant, *Democracy in Kent*, 44.
[23] Grant notes that 474 adult males lived in Kent between 1738 and 1760 and that 525 adult males lived in or moved through Kent in the four years 1774-1777. Since some of these 999 men were undoubtedly "double-counted," the total number was somewhat less; but because this calculation pertains only to 26 years out of a total of 62, the total number of resident adult males during this period must have been at least 1,000.
[24] Danhof, *Change in Agriculture*, 17-18.
[25] Grant, *Democracy in Kent*, 34, n. 3. The computations appear only in the

produced even a small salable surplus drops from two-thirds to one-third;
only the most productive farms—15-20 percent of the total—could have
produced enough to engage in extensive market transactions.

Why was this the case? Was the soil too poor? The climate too
forbidding? Or were the aspirations of the settlers too limited? What was the
economic and cultural consciousness of the mass of the agricultural population? These questions raise fundamental issues pertaining to the nature of
social reality and the sources of human motivation; and their resolution must
begin with an investigation of the epistemological premises of the entrepreneurial school of agricultural historians. Once again, Charles Grant offers an
278 ideal entrée, this time as he explicitly acknowledges the source of his
interpretation: "Hofstadter suggests," Grant explains in a footnote, "that
where the yeoman practiced only subsistence farming, he did so out of
necessity (lack of transportation and markets) and not because he was
enamored of this way of life. The yeoman farmer wanted profits."[26] At issue
here is not the validity of the argument but the assumptions on which it is
based. Following Hofstadter, Grant effects a radical disjunction between the
constraints imposed by the material and social environment and the yeoman's
consciousness. The "drive for profits" simply exists, even given the "lack of
transportation and markets." The subsistence way of life does not seem to
affect or alter the sensibility of the farmer; consciousness is divorced from
condition.

Contemporary observers who spoke to this issue assumed a rather different relationship between environmental opportunities and human goals. "We
know," wrote one migrant to the Genesee Valley in 1810, "that people who
live far from markets and cannot sell their produce, naturally become
indolent and vicious." "There can be no industry without motive," another
migrant warned the readers of *The Plough Boy* in 1820, "and it appears to
me [that without markets] there is great danger that our people will soon

dissertation, pp. 67-68, 78-79, where heavy reliance is placed on the yields reported in
American Husbandry. This anonymous work, published in 1775, is criticized for its
inflated estimates of farm yields in Harry Roy Merrens, *Colonial North Carolina in
the Eighteenth Century: A Study in Historical Geography* (Chapel Hill, N.C., 1964),
chap. 6, n. 11. Merrens also provides more reliable estimates (pp. 110.ff.), as does
Lemon, "Household Consumption in Eighteenth-Century America and Its Relationship to Production and Trade: The Situation Among Farmers in Southeastern
Pennsylvania," *Agricultural Hist.*, XLI (1967), 59-70, and *Best Poor Man's Country*, 152-153 (Table 27). In Concord, average grain yields—corn and wheat combined—increased from 12.2 to 15 bushels per acre between 1771 and 1801 (Gross,
Minutemen, 231), while Mitchell reports wheat yields of 10 bushels per acre in the
newly settled Shenandoah Valley ("Agricultural Change," *Agricultural Hist.*,
XLVII [1973], 129).
[26] Grant, *Democracy in Kent*, 191. The reference is to Richard Hofstadter, "The
Myth of the Happy Yeoman," *American Heritage*, VII (Apr. 1956), 43-53.

limit their exertions to the raising of food for their families."[27] A somewhat similar point had been made in the mid-eighteenth century by William Byrd II when he came upon a fertile allotment that "would be a valuable tract of land in any country but North Carolina, where, for want of navigation and commerce, the best estate affords little more than a coarse subsistence." All were agreed that "convenience and a ready market is the life of a settler—not cheap lands."[28]

Such astute contemporary perceptions constituted the empirical foundations for the argument propounded in 1916 by Percy Bidwell, the leading modern historian of early American agriculture. Why should the farmer specialize, "why should he exert himself to produce a surplus," Bidwell asked in his classic analysis of the rural economy of New England, when there was no market in which to sell it, when "the only return he could expect would be a sort of psychological income . . . ?"[29] Bidwell's logic is still compelling, for it is based on epistemological principles that command assent. It recognized, if only implicitly, that there was a considerable diversity of motivation and of economic values among the farm population. In this respect, it echoed the observation of another contemporary. "Farming may be so conducted as to be made profitable, or merely to afford a living[,] or to run out the farm," a Massachusetts writer noted in 1849. "Taking the land as it averages in the state, this depends more on the farmer than on the soil." At the same time, Bidwell insisted that everyone was affected by the structural possibilities and limitations of the society, whatever their cultural propensities or economic aspirations. There was a direct relationship between the material environment, on the one hand, and the consciousness and activity of the population on the other. This understanding informs Bidwell's account and renders it far superior to that of the entrepreneurial school of agricultural historians. "Potatoes are very much used and increased attempts are making to raise them for market," Bidwell quotes the Reverend Samuel Goodrich of Ridgefield, Connecticut (c. 1800), "but the distance from the market is so great that it is not expected the practice will be general."[30] Acquisitive hopes had yielded to geographic realities.

A convincing interpretation of northern agriculture must begin, therefore, not with an ascribed consciousness but rather with an understanding of

[27] Quoted in McNall, *Agricultural History of the Genesee Valley*, 104.

[28] Louis B. Wright, ed., *The Prose Works of William Byrd of Westover: Narratives of a Colonial Virginian* (Cambridge, Mass., 1966), 184; McNall, *Agricultural History of the Genesee Valley*, 96.

[29] Percy W. Bidwell, "Rural Economy in New England at the Beginning of the Nineteenth Century," Connecticut Academy of Arts and Sciences, *Transactions*, XX (1916), 330.

[30] *Ibid.*, 317n; The Massachusetts quotation is from Danhof, *Change in Agriculture*, 134.

the dimensions of economic existence. These varied significantly from one region to another, primarily as a result of differential access to an urban or an international market. Yet in every area similar cultural constraints circumscribed the extent of involvement in the market economy. Indeed, the tension between the demands of the market and the expectations stemming from traditional social relationships was a fact of crucial significance in the lives of this pre-industrial population.

Given the absence of an external market, there was no alternative to subsistence or semi-subsistence production.[31] Following the settlement of an inland region, for example, there would be a flurry of barter transactions, as 280 established settlers exchanged surplus foodstuffs, seeds, and livestock for the scarce currency and manufactured items brought by newly arrived migrants. Subsequently, the diversification of the local economy created a small demand for farm produce among artisans and traders. Yet neither of these consuming groups was large. Migrants quickly planted their own crops, and most rural artisans cultivated extensive gardens and kept a few head of livestock. The economy had stabilized at a low level of specialization.

This system of local exchange, moreover, did not constitute a market economy in the full sense of the term. Many of these transactions were direct ones—between producers of different types of goods and services—without the involvement of a merchant, broker, or other middlemen. Farm men and women exchanged wheat for tools, meat for furniture, or vegetables for cloth, because their families had a specific personal use for the bartered product. They would attempt to drive a hard bargain or to make a good deal in their negotiations with the blacksmith, cabinetmaker, or seamstress—to insist, for example, on a carefully crafted, high-quality product. Yet their goal was not profit but the acquisition of a needed item for use. "Robt Griffins wife got 10 cocks of hay from me which she is to pay in butter," Matthew Patten of Bedford, New Hampshire, noted in his diary in the 1770s; "I asked her 2£ for a cock." Even when an artisan or merchant would "sell" goods to a farmer and record the obligation in monetary terms, it was assumed that the debt would continue (usually without interest) until it was balanced in a subsequent barter transaction of "Country Produce at Market Price."[32]

---

[31] By these terms I mean limited participation in a commercial market economy. As the preceding quotations suggest, most farm families had enough land, equipment, and labor to raise as much food as they could consume. Thus their living standards (in terms of calories and protein) could rise even if they did not engage in extensive market transactions. The pressure of population on resources inhibited such advances, but there were no near-famines or subsistence crises in the northern colonies, as there were, for instance, in France in the 1690s.

[32] Max George Schumacher, *The Northern Farmer and His Markets during the Late Colonial Period*, Dissertations in American Economic History (New York,

A market existed, therefore, and it regulated the overall terms of trade among farmers, artisans, and merchants. But this price system was not sovereign; it was often subordinated, in the conduct of daily existence, to barter transactions based on exchange value—what an item was worth to a specific individual. Some goods could not be purchased at any price because they were spoken for by friends, neighbors, or kinfolk. "I went to joseph Farmers and [to] Alexanders to buy some corn," Patten noted in 1770, "but Farmers was all promised and Alexander wood [would] not take 2 pistereens a bushel and I got none."[33] The maximizing of profit was less important to these producers than the meeting of household needs and the maintaining of established social relationships within the community. And it was this "subsistence farm society" which Jackson T. Main correctly specifies as "the most common type throughout New England and perhaps in the entire North" until the end of the eighteenth century.[34] As Bidwell argued, "the revolution in agriculture, as well as the breaking down of the self-sufficient village life, awaited the growth of a [large, urban] non-agricultural population."[35]

A commercially oriented agriculture began to develop after 1750, in response to lucrative urban and European markets for American grain. Yet the size of these new trading networks should not be overestimated. The meat exports of the entire state of Connecticut between 1768 and 1773 would have been absorbed by an additional urban population of twenty-two thousand—a city the size of New York; and the shipments of grain from

281

1975), 88, 83. For further detail see *The Diary of Matthew Patten of Bedford, N.H. from Seventeen Fifty-Four to Seventeen Eighty-Eight* (Concord, 1903).

[33] Schumacher, *Northern Farmer*, 20. My argument in these two paragraphs is based on Michael Merrill's "Self-Sufficiency and Exchange in the Rural Economy of the United States," *Radical History Review*, VII (1977).

[34] Main, *Social Structure*, 18. Another important characteristic of many of these communities was an extensive debt structure. Grant notes a "vast tangle of debts" in Kent, with each adult male having an average of 20 creditors in the 1770s. There was no concentration of debts in the hands of a moneylending class; most of the obligations were small, often ran for years, and frequently cancelled each other out. When Elizur Price died in 1777, he had 20 creditors but was himself owed money by 17 men. In more commercial settlements there was a distinct financial elite. When Elisha Hurlbut, a merchant of Windham, Conn., died in 1771, he was owed a total of £590 by no fewer than 77 debtors, and during the preceding 12 years had initiated 212 debt actions (13% of the total) in Windham County Court. See William F. Willingham, "Windham, Connecticut: Profile of a Revolutionary Community, 1775-1818" (Ph.D. diss., Northwestern University, 1972), 77-91, 240-261. The debt structure in Newtown, N.Y., remained extensive as late as 1790, while that in Lancaster, Pa., conformed to the Windham pattern. Ehrlich, "Town Study in Colonial New York," 151-154; Wood, "Conestoga Crossroads," 167-168.

[35] Bidwell, "Rural Economy," Conn. Academy of Arts and Sci., *Trans.*, XX (1916), 353.

Connecticut ports were even smaller. Exports of wheat and flour from the Middle Colonies during these years were far more substantial, with the annual average equivalent to 2.1 million bushels of wheat. Still, the amount of wheat consumed by the residents of these colonies was nearly twice as large (3.8 million bushels per year). And wheat was normally cultivated on only one-third of the acreage devoted to the production of grain, most of which was corn that was consumed by livestock. The "surplus" wheat exported to foreign markets thus remained a relatively small part of total production (15-20 percent), even for commercially minded family farmers.[36] As late as 1820, "the portion of farm products not consumed within the northern rural community" and sold on all outside markets, both foreign and domestic, amounted to only 25 percent of the total.[37]

Given the existence of a growing European market—a demand for wheat that brought a price rise of 100 percent during the second half of the eighteenth century—the slow and limited commercialization of northern agriculture is significant. Far more dramatic changes were occurring in the South, on slave plantations rather than on family farms. During the years from 1768 to 1773 wheat and flour exports from Virginia and Maryland amounted to 25 percent of the total from the "bread-basket" colonies of New York and Pennsylvania. This "striking expansion of the wheat belt" to the southern colonies after 1750 clearly indicated, as Max Schumacher has argued, "that production on the individual [northern] farms was not elastic enough to cope with the rising wheat market."[38]

The high cost of inland transport was one factor that inhibited the expansion of northern wheat production. A bushel of wheat could be shipped 164 miles on the Hudson River from Albany to New York City in 1769 for fourpence, or 5 percent of its wholesale value, but the proportion rose to 18 percent for a journey of the same distance on the shallow and more difficult waters of the upper Delaware River in Pennsylvania. And the cost of land transportation was much higher. Even in 1816, when the price of grain was high in Philadelphia, the cost of transporting wheat from 50 miles outside the city amounted to one-fourth of the selling price.[39]

Technological restraints and cultural preferences placed even greater limitations on the expansion of wheat production on the family farms of the

---

[36] Schumacher, *Northern Farmer*, 33, 42 and 42n for the macro-estimates; Lemon, *Best Man's Poor Country*, Tables 27 and 28, and 180-181 indicates that 8 of 26 cultivated acres on a typical farm of 125 acres would be planted in wheat and that 50 bushels of grain (out of a total of 295) would be available for sale or exchange.

[37] Danhof, *Change in Agriculture*, 11, 2.

[38] Schumacher, *Northern Farmer*, 142. See also pp. 110, 154, 167.

[39] *Ibid.*, 57-59; George Rogers Taylor, *The Transportation Revolution, 1815-1860* (*Economic History of the United States*, IV [New York, 1951]), 133.

north. Thomas Jefferson isolated the crucial variable when he noted, in 1793, that planters "allow that every laborer will manage ten acres of wheat, except at harvest." The inefficiency of the sickle, which limited the amount a worker could reap to one-half or three-quarters of an acre per day, placed a severe constraint upon the cultivation of wheat. Large-scale production— with annual yields of 1,000 bushels from 100 acres—was attempted only by those northern producers who were prepared to bid for scarce wage labor during the short harvest season or who controlled a captive labor supply of indentured servants or black slaves. In Somerset County, New Jersey, one farmer relied on the assistance of six blacks to harvest his 80 acres of wheat, while a Trenton proprietor had three blacks to reap 20 acres.[40] Such entrepreneurial farmers were exceptions. They entered the market not only to buy necessities and to sell their surplus but also to buy labor—slaves, servants, wage workers—in order to make a profit. Their farms were "capitalistic" enterprises in the full sense of the term: privately owned productive properties which were operated for profit through a series of market-oriented contractual relationships.

Even in the most market-oriented areas of the Middle Colonies, many farmers participated in the commercial capitalist economy in a much more limited way and with rather different goals. Lacking slaves or indentured servants and unwilling to bid for wage labor, they planted only 8 to 10 acres of wheat each year, a crop that could conveniently be harvested by the farmer, one or two growing sons, and (in some cases) his wife. Of the normal yield of 80 to 100 bushels, 60 would be consumed by the family or saved for seed; the surplus of 20 to 40 bushels would be sold on the Philadelphia market, bringing a cash income in the early 1770s of £5 to £10 sterling. The ordinary male farmer, Lemon concludes, was content to produce "enough for his family and . . . to sell a surplus in the market to buy what he deemed necessities."[41] There was little innovative, risk-taking behavior; there was no

[40] Jefferson to President Washington, June 28, 1793, in Andrew A. Lipscomb and Albert E. Bergh, eds., *The Writings of Thomas Jefferson*, IX (Washington, D.C., 1903), 142.

[41] Lemon, *Best Poor Man's Country*, 180; see also Tables 27 and 28 and pp. 179-183. Was there a "motivationally subsistent agricultural class" in the North similar to that found among the poor white population in the South? "A common practice of [southern white cotton] farmers in plantation areas," Julius Rubin has argued, "was to raise the minimal amount of cash crop needed to buy a narrow and rigid range of necessities: tobacco, lead, powder and sugar." For these men, mere participation in the international economy was neither an indication of nor conducive to the development of an entrepreneurial mentality. See Julius Rubin, "Urban Growth and Regional Development," in David T. Gilchrist, ed., *The Growth of the Seaport Cities, 1790-1825: Proceedings of a Conference Sponsored by the Eleutherian Mills-Hagley Foundation March 17-19, 1966* (Charlottesville, Va., 1967), 15. Two other

determined pursuit of profit. Indeed, the account books of these farm families indicate that they invariably chose the security of diversified production rather than hire labor to produce more wheat or to specialize in milk production. Economic gain was important to these men and women, yet it was not their dominant value. It was subordinate to (or encompassed by) two other goals: the yearly subsistence and the long-run financial security of the family unit.

Thus, the predominance of subsistence or semi-subsistence productive units among the yeoman farming families of the northern colonies was not only the result of geographic or economic factors—the ready access to a reliable, expanding market. These men and women were enmeshed also in a web of social relationships and cultural expectations that inhibited the free play of market forces. Much of the output of their farms was consumed by the residents, most of whom were biologically or legally related and who were not paid wages for their labor. A secondary group of consumers consisted of the inhabitants of the local area, members of a community often based on ties of kinship, language, religion, or ethnicity. An impersonal price system figured prominently in these transactions, but goods were often bartered for their exchange value or for what was considered a "just price." Finally, a small (but growing) proportion of the total production of these farms was "sold" on an external market through a series of formal commercial transactions.

If freehold ownership and participation in these urban and international markets meant that northern agriculture did not have many of the characteristics of a closed peasant or a pre-capitalist economy,[42] they do not imply that

---

works that begin to examine the values, behavior, and life style of the poor white agricultural population of the South are Rhys Isaac, "Evangelical Revolt: The Nature of the Baptists' Challenge to the Traditional Order . . . ," *WMQ*, 3d Ser., XXXI (1974), 345-368, and Aubrey C. Land, "Economic Base and Social Structure: The Northern Chesapeake in the Eighteenth Century," *Journal of Economic History*, XXV (1965), 639-654.

[42] There are a number of other reasons for not describing this as a "peasant society," as Kenneth A. Lockridge has done in *A New England Town, The First Hundred Years: Dedham, Massachusetts, 1636-1736* (New York, 1970). Dedham was simply not analogous to the subjugated aboriginal settlements which Eric Wolf depicted as "closed corporate peasant communities" ("Closed Corporate Peasant Communities in Mesoamerica and Central Java," *Southwestern Journal of Anthropology*, X [1957], 1-18). A more realistic comparison is with the peasant societies of early modern Western Europe; and the differences are sufficiently great as to render use of the term unwise in the American context. There were few landlords and no nobility in the northern colonies; the settlement pattern was diffuse rather than nucleated by the 18th century; the central government was weak; the role of the church was limited and the established Congregational churches of New England were non-hierarchical in structure; and the system of property relationships was

this system of production and exchange was modern or that its members were motivated primarily by liberal, entrepreneurial, individualist, or capitalist values. Nor is it sufficient to describe these farming communities as "transitional" between the ideal-types of traditional and modern or pre-capitalist and capitalist. To adopt such an idealist approach is to substitute typology for analysis, to suggest a teleological model of historical development, and to ignore the specific features of this social and economic system. Rather, one must point to its central features: the community was distinguished by age- and wealth-stratification and (usually) by ethnic or religious homogeneity, while on the family level there was freehold property ownership, a household mode of production, limited economic possibilities and aspirations, and a safety-first subsistence agriculture within a commercial capitalist market structure. And then one must seek an understanding of the "coping strategies" used by individuals, groups, and governments to reconcile the competing demands, the inherent tensions, and the immanent contradictions posed by this particular configuration of historical institutions and cultural values.

285

It would be premature, at this point, to attempt a complete analysis of the *mentalité* of the pre-industrial yeoman population. Yet a preliminary examination may suggest both a conceptual framework for future research and the character of certain widely accepted values, goals, and behavioral norms. An important, and perhaps controversial, premise should be made explicit at the beginning. It is assumed that the behavior of the farm population constitutes a crucial (although not a foolproof) indicator of its values and aspirations. This epistemological assumption has an interpretive implication, for it focuses attention on those activities that dominated the daily lives of the population—in the case of this particular society, on the productive tasks that provided food, clothing, and shelter.

---

contractual and malleable. Finally, these American farming communities constituted the central core of the society; they were not "part-societies" and "part-cultures" (in the definition of peasant society advanced by Robert Redfield), dependent upon and exploited by a metropolitan elite.

If a historical analogy is required, then the "post-reform" peasant societies of 19th-century Western Europe are the most appropriate, not those of the ancien régime. See, for example, Walter Goldschmidt and Evelyn Jacobson Kunkel, "The Structure of the Peasant Family," *American Anthropologist*, N.S., LXXIII (1971), 1058-1076. Then, too, the pattern of *family* behavior and values may be similar among small freeholding farmers, whether they live in a yeoman or in a peasant *society*: compare, for example, Greven's Andover families with those analyzed in Lutz K. Berkner, "The Stem Family and the Development Cycle of the Peasant Household: An Eighteenth-Century Austrian Example," *American Historical Review*, LXXVII (1972), 398-418.

This process of production and capital formation derived much of its emotive and intellectual meaning from the cultural matrix—from the institutional character of the society. Work was arranged along familial lines rather than controlled communally or through a wage system. This apparently simple organizational fact was a crucial determinant of the historical consciousness of this farming population. For even as the family gave symbolic meaning and emotional significance to subsistence activities, its own essence was shaped by the character of the productive system. There was a complex relationship between the agricultural labor and property system of early America and its rural culture; and it is that matrix of productive activities, organizational structures, and social values which the following analysis attempts (in a very preliminary fashion) to reconstruct.[43]

286

Because the primary economic unit—the family—was also the main social institution, production activities had an immense impact on the entire character of agrarian life. Family relationships could not be divorced from economic considerations; indeed, the basic question of power and authority within the family hinged primarily on legal control over the land and—indirectly—over the labor needed to work it. The parents (principally the husband) enjoyed legal possession of the property—either as freeholders, tenants, or sharecroppers—but they were dependent on their children for economic support in their old age. Their aim, as Greven has pointed out, was to control the terms and the timing of the transfer of economic resources to the succeeding generation.[44]

The intimate relationship between agricultural production and parental values, between economic history and family history, is best approached through a series of case studies. The first of these small family dramas began in 1739 with the arrival in Kent, Connecticut, of Joseph Fuller. At one time or another Fuller was an investor in an iron works, a "typical speculative proprietor," and a "rich squatter" who tried to deceive the Connecticut authorities into granting him (and his partner Joshua Lassell) 4,820 acres of provincial land. Fuller's energy, ambition, and activities mark him as an

[43] The exciting work of E. P. Thompson on the agricultural society of 18th-century England, "The Moral Economy of the English Crowd in the Eighteenth Century," *Past and Present*, L (Feb. 1971), 76-136, and "Patrician Society, Plebian Culture," *Jour. Soc. Hist.*, VII (1974), 382-405, focuses on conflicts engendered by consumption shortages and by asymmetrical authority relationships. It assumes, but does not investigate in detail, class- or wealth-related production differences. A similar concentration on authority, especially in its religious aspects, characterizes the excellent work of Rhys Isaac (see n. 41 above). Ultimately, it will be necessary to specify the relationships among productive activity, religious inclination, and the system of authority.
[44] Greven, "Family Structure," *WMQ*, 3d Ser., XXIII (1966), 234-256, and *Four Generations*.

entrepreneur, even a "capitalist." Yet his behavior must be seen in the widest possible context, and the motivation assessed accordingly. When this restless man arrived in Kent at the age of forty (with his second wife), he was the father of seven sons, aged two to sixteen; thirteen years later, when his final petition for a land grant was rejected, he had nine sons, aged eleven to twenty-nine years, and five daughters. With fourteen children to provide with land, dowries, or currency, Fuller *had* to embark on an active career if he wished to keep his children (and himself and his wife in their old age) from a life of landless poverty.

In the event, fecundity overwhelmed the Fullers' financial ingenuity. None of the children of Joseph Fuller ever attained a rating on the tax list equal to the highest recorded for their father, and a similar pattern prevailed among the sons of the third generation. The total resources of the Fuller "clan" (for such it had become) grew constantly over time—with nine second- and twelve third-generation males appearing on the tax lists of Kent—but their per capita wealth declined steadily.[45] The gains of one generation, the slow accumulation of capital resources through savings and invested labor, had been dispersed among many heirs.

287

Such divisions of limited resources inevitably roused resentment and engendered bitter battles within farm families. Ultimately, the delicate reciprocal economic relationship between parents and children might break down completely. Insufficiency of land meant that most children would have to be exiled—apprenticed to wealthier members of the community or sent out on their own as landless laborers—and that parents would have to endure a harsh old age, sharing their small plot with the remaining heir. High fertility and low mortality threatened each generation of children with the loss of class status; the unencumbered inheritance of a freehold estate was the exception, not the rule.

Even in these circumstances—as a second example will suggest—the ideal for many dispossessed children remained property ownership and eventual control of the transfer process with regard to their own offspring. "My parents were poor," an "Honest Farmer" wrote to the *Pennsylvania Packet* in 1786,

and they put me at twelve years of age to a farmer, with whom I lived till I was twenty one. . . . I married me a wife—and a very working young woman she was—and we took a farm of forty acres on rent. . . . In ten years I was able to buy me a farm of sixty acres on which I became my own tenant. I then, in a manner, grew rich and soon added another sixty acres, with which I am content. My estate increased

[45] Grant, *Democracy in Kent*, 101, "Diminishing Property: Three Generations of Fullers," Table 13. See also pp. 17, 47-50, 67, 71.

beyond all account. I bought several lots of out-land for my children, which amounted to seven when I was forty-five years old.

About this time I married my oldest daughter to a clever lad, to whom I gave one hundred acres of my out-land.[46]

Was this "success story" typical? Did the "Honest Farmer" minimize the difficulties of his own ascent and exaggerate the prospects of his seven children, each of whom would have to be provided with land, livestock, or equipment? It is clear, at any rate, that this Pennsylvanian enjoyed a crucial advantage over Joseph Fuller; he could accumulate capital through the regular sale of his surplus production on the market, and offer economic assistance to his children. His grandchildren, moreover, would grow up in the more fully developed commercial economy of the early nineteenth century. Ten years of work as a farm laborer—and an intense commitment to save— would now yield a capital stock of five hundred dollars. With this sum invested in equipment, livestock, and supplies, it would then be feasible to rent a farm, "with the prospect of accumulating money at a rate perhaps double that possible by wage work."[47] To begin with less than five hundred dollars was to increase dependence on the landlord—to accept a half-and-half division of the produce rather than a two-thirds share. In either case, there was a high financial and psychological price to be paid. For many years these young adults would be "dependent," would work as wage laborers without security, as sharecroppers without land, or as mortgagors without full independence; their labor would enrich freeholders, landlords, and bankers even as it moved them closer to real economic freedom.

This process is readily apparent in a third case study, an archetypical example of the slow but successful accumulation of productive agricultural property in the mid-nineteenth century. In 1843 a young farmer in Massachusetts bought an old farm of 85 acres for $4,337; "in order to pay for it, I mortgaged it for $4,100, paying only $237, all that I had, after buying my stock." Nine years later it was clear that some progress had been made, for he had "paid up about $600 on the mortgage, and laid out nearly $2,000 in permanent improvements on my buildings and farm." This hard-working farmer was "a little nearer the harbor than I was when I commenced the voyage," but he was still $3,500 in debt and had interest payments of $250 to make each year.[48] These obligations might be met in ten or fifteen years, but

---

[46] Quoted in Stevenson W. Fletcher, *Pennsylvania Agriculture and Country Life, 1640-1840* (Harrisburg, 1950), 315.

[47] Danhof, *Change in Agriculture*, 91 and 78-115.

[48] *Ibid.*, 112; quotations are from Amasa Walker, ed., *Transactions of the Agricultural Societies in the State of Massachusetts, for 1852 . . .* (Boston, 1853), 93-94.

by then new debts would have to be incurred in order to provide working capital for his children. This farmer would die a property owner, but at least some of his offspring would face a similarly time-consuming and difficult climb up the agricultural ladder.

Two features of the long-term process of capital formation through agricultural production revealed by these case studies stand out as particularly important, one static and the other dynamic. The recurrent factor was the continual pressure of population on the existing capital stock; the rate of natural increase constantly threatened to outstrip the creation of new productive resources: cleared land, machinery, housing, and livestock. This danger is demonstrable in the case of the Fuller clan, and its specter lurks in the prose of the "Honest Farmer" and his younger accumulation-oriented counterpart in Massachusetts. Economic prosperity was the result of unremitting labor by each generation. Only as farm parents began consciously to limit their fertility were they able to pass on sizable estates to their children—and this occurred primarily after 1830.[49]

What changed—from the seventeenth to the early nineteenth century—was the increased rate of capital formation stemming from the expansion of the market economy; the growing importance of "unearned" profits because of the rise in the value of land and of other scarce commodities; and the extent to which middlemen dominated the processes of agricultural production and of westward migration. These three developments were interrelated. All were aspects of an increasingly important system of commercial agriculture that generated antagonistic social relationships and incipient class divisions. These alterations brought greater prosperity to those farmers whose geographic locations and cultural values were conducive to market activity. The new structural possibilities undoubtedly induced other producers (who might otherwise have been content with their subsistence existence) to raise their output, perhaps even to alter their mode of production by hiring labor or purchasing farm machinery. Certainly, the boom in land values enabled those settlers with substantial estates to reap windfall profits. They had not always purchased their land with speculative resale in mind, but they benefited nonetheless from social and economic forces beyond their control: the surge in population and in agricultural prices both in the American colonies and in Western Europe. Finally, there were individuals and groups who sought to manage the new system of production and exchange. By the mid-eighteenth century, merchants and land speculators had appeared as

289

[49] Robert Wells, "Family Size and Fertility Control in Eighteenth-Century America: A Study of Quaker Families," *Population Studies*, XXV (1971), 73-82, traces the beginning of this process, while the sequel is explored by Richard A. Easterlin, "Population Change and Farm Settlement in the Northern United States," *Jour. of Econ. Hist.*, XXXVI (1976), 45-75.

crucial factors in the westward movement of population, and within another fifty years bankers and mortgage companies were also extracting a share of agricultural production. At some times and places the monetary liens imposed by middlemen and substantial landowners were justified; they represented fair returns for services rendered. More often, the farm population—especially those of its members who were young or landless—paid a disproportionate price for access to the productive system because bankers, speculators, and merchants were able to use their political and economic power to set the terms of exchange in order to gain a greater share of the growing wealth of the society than was warranted by their entrepreneurial contribution.[50]

290

Even as this process of economic specialization and structural change was taking place, the family persisted as the basic unit of agricultural production, capital formation, and property transmission. This is a point of some importance, for it suggests that alterations in the macro-structure of a society or an economic system do not inevitably or immediately induce significant changes in its micro-units. Social or cultural change is not always systemic in nature, and it proceeds in fits and starts. Old cultural forms persist (and sometimes flourish) within new economic structures; there are "lags" as changes in one sphere of life are gradually reconciled with established values and patterns of behavior.

And so it was in the case of the pre-industrial yeoman family. Changes in societal structure did not alter the basic character of the farm family (although the proportion of such families in the population steadily decreased). As the case studies suggest, the agricultural family remained an extended lineal one; each generation lived in a separate household, but the character of production and inheritance linked these conjugal units through a myriad of legal, moral, and customary bonds. Rights and responsibilities stretched across generations. The financial welfare of both parents and children was rooted in the land and in the equipment and labor needed to farm it. Parents therefore influenced their children's choice of marriage partners. Their welfare, or that of their other children, might otherwise be compromised by the premature division of assets which an early marriage

---

[50] On this controversial topic see McNall, *Genesee Valley*, 14, 48, 63-64, 240-241, and chap. 4. A favorable view of the tenancy system is offered by Sung Bok Kim, "A New Look at the Great Landlords of Eighteenth-Century New York," *WMQ*, 3d Ser., XXVII (1970), 581-614. Kim succeeds only in demonstrating that their own financial interests often prompted landlords to offer reasonable terms to their tenants; he does not demonstrate the inherent superiority of the tenancy system or that it was not more exploitative than, for instance, the grants of the New England governments during the 17th century or of the U.S. government under the Homestead Acts.

entailed.[51] The line was more important than the individual; the patrimony was to be conserved for lineal purposes.

The historical significance of these lineal values was immense. The emphasis on the line or upon the welfare of the entire family, for example, inhibited the emergence of individualism. When the members of this agricultural society traced the contours of their cultural landscape, they began with the assumption—as John Demos has amply demonstrated—that the basic unit was a family, "a little commonwealth," not a man (and still less a woman) "for himself," in their disparaging phrase.[52] This stress on family identity also shaped the character—and often confined the scope—of entrepreneurial activity and capitalist enterprise. Lemon's analysis indicates that most male farmers in Pennsylvania preferred family labor (including the assistance of nearby relatives) to that provided by indentured servants, slaves, or wage laborers. Religious membership was also circumscribed by cultural values, especially in the Congregational churches of New England. As Edmund Morgan argued thirty years ago (in an hypothesis recently supported with quantitative evidence by Gerald Moran), Puritanism quickly became a "tribal" cult, with family lineage the prime determinant of elect status.[53]

Nevertheless, lineal values were not always dominant. And they were often affected by the emergent market economy; indeed, the commercial family-capitalism of the early modern period and the small father-son businesses of the nineteenth century represented striking adaptions of the lineal ideal.[54] Equally significant alterations took place in rural areas, in response to the pressure of population on agricultural resources. In the seventeenth century many settlers had attempted to identify the family with a specific piece of land, to ensure its continued existence by rooting it firmly in space. Thus, in 1673, Ebenezer Perry of Barnstable, Massachusetts, entailed his land to his son Ebenezer and to the latter's "eldest son surviving and so on

291

[52] John Demos, *A Little Commonwealth: Family Life in Plymouth Colony* (New York, 1970), 77-78.
[53] Edmund S. Morgan, *The Puritan Family: Religion and Domestic Relations in Seventeenth-Century New England* (Boston, 1944), chap. 6; Gerald Francis Moran, "The Puritan Saint: Religious Experience, Church Membership, and Piety in Connecticut, 1736-1776" (Ph.D. diss., Rutgers Univ., 1974). Moran has analyzed the membership of a number of Congregational churches in Connecticut between the time of their founding (1630s and 1640s) and 1800. He finds that 60 to 70% of all members during that period were either the original founders or their descendants.
[54] See, for example, Bernard Bailyn, "Communications and Trade: The Atlantic in the Seventeenth Century," *Jour. Econ. Hist.*, XIII (1953), 378-387, esp. 380-382.

to the male heirs of his body lawfully begotten forever."[55] Other early inhabitants of Massachusetts preferred to bequeath the family homestead to the youngest son—ultimogeniture—both because this would allow elder siblings to leave the farm at an early age and because the youngest son often came to maturity just as the parents were ready to retire. In either case, the transmission of property was designed to link one generation with the next, and both with "family land."

When the pressure on family resources made it impossible to provide all surviving sons with a portion of the original family estate, the settlers devised alternative strategies of heirship. Some parents uprooted the family and moved to a newly settled area where it would be possible to maintain traditional lineal ties between generations. "The Squire's House stands on the Bank of [the] Susquehannah . . . ," Philip Fithian reported from the frontier region of northeastern Pennsylvania in 1775. "He tells me . . . he will be able to settle all his Sons and his fair Daughter *Betsy* on the Fat of the Earth."[56] Other farmers remained in the old community and sought desperately to settle their children on nearby lands. The premature death of one son brought the Reverend Samuel Chandler of Andover, Massachusetts, to remember that he had "been much distressed for land, for his children," and to regret that "he took so much care . . . [for] one is taken away and needs none."[57] From nearby Concord, Benjamin Barrett petitioned the General Court for a grant of land in New Hampshire, since he and many other residents were "without land for their posterity"; yet when this request was granted, none of the petitioners migrated to the new settlement. When Barrett died in 1728, the income from these western lands helped to settle two sons on his Concord estate and two younger sons on farms in nearby Worcester County.[58]

This imaginative use of western land rights to subsidize the local settlement of offspring may have been fairly widespread. Of the forty-one men who were the original purchasers of proprietary shares in Kent, Connecticut, twenty-five did not become inhabitants of the town but sold their rights to residents, relatives, and neighbors. Still, the limited availability of

292

[55] Quoted in John J. Waters, "The Traditional World of the New England Peasants: A View from Seventeenth-Century Barnstable," *New England Historical and Genealogical Register*, CXXX (1976), 4.
[56] July 26, 1775, Robert Greenhalgh Abion and Leonidas Dodson, eds., *Philip Vickers Fithian: Journal, 1775-1776, Written on the Virginia-Pennsylvania Frontier* . . . (Princeton, N.J., 1934), 71; Jack Goody, "Strategies of Heirship," *Comparative Studies in Society and History*, XV (1973), 3-20.
[57] Samuel Chandler, diary entry for Dec. 23, 1745, quoted in Greven, *Four Generations*, 254.
[58] Gross, *Minutemen*, 80.

arable land in the older communities of New England and the Middle
Colonies ruled out this option for most parents. The best they could do was to
finance the migration of some children while keeping intact the original
farmstead. Both in Newtown, Long Island, and in German areas of Pennsylvania in the eighteenth century, fathers commonly willed the family farm to
the eldest son, requiring him to pay a certain sum of money to his younger
brothers and his sisters. In other cases, the farm was "sold" to one son or son-
in-law, with the "profits" of the transaction being divided among the other
children—daughters usually receiving one-half the amount bestowed on the
sons.[59]

These attempts by individual farmers to preserve a viable family estate
reflected a set of values that was widespread in the community and which
eventually received a formal legal sanction. When the appraisers of intestate
property in Concord, Massachusetts, reported that a property could not be
divided "without Spoiling the Whole," the probate court granted the farm
intact to one heir (usually the eldest son), requiring him to compensate his
brothers and sisters for their shares in the estate.[60] Such rulings confirmed the
societal norm: even as New England parents wrote wills that divided their
lands, they encouraged or directed their children to reconstitute viable
economic units, with regard to both size and access. As Mark Hasket of
Rochester, Massachusetts, wrote in his will: "my sons shall not any of them
debar or hinder one another from having a way over each others Land when
and where there may be ocation for it."[61]

There were other respects in which the central position of the lineal
family (rather than the conjugal unit or the individual) was reflected in the
legal system. On the death of her husband, a wife normally received the
"right" to one-third of the real property of the estate. Yet this control was
strictly limited: it usually lapsed upon remarriage and, even more significant,
did not include the privilege of sale. The widow's "third" had to be
preserved intact, so that upon her death the property could revert to the heirs
of the estate. More important than the economic freedom of the widow—her
rights as an individual—was the protection of the estate and the line of

293

[59] Ehrlich, "Town Study in Colonial New York," 123-127; John C. Gagliardo,
"Germans and Agriculture in Colonial Pennsylvania," *Pennsylvania Magazine of
History and Biography*, LXXXIII (1959), 192-198; Greven, *Four Generations*, 234-
245. Ryan records a typical intergenerational arrangement: "Samuel Day, having
seven sons, could only provide an estate for three sons, leaving them to pay sons
David, Robert, Abraham and Jared £100 apiece" ("Six Towns," 85).

[60] Gross, "Problem of Agricultural Crisis in Eighteenth-Century New England,"
8. Of the landed estates settled in probate in Concord between 1738 and 1775, 60%
were not divided; only 25% were divided among three or more heirs.

[61] Quoted in Waters, "Traditional World of New England Peasants," *NEHGR*,
CXXX (1976), 7; Danhof, *Change in Agriculture*, 80.

succession. These deeply held values were preserved even in the more diverse, money-oriented economy of eastern Massachusetts in the eighteenth century; the law was changed to permit widows to sell family property, but the court carefully regulated such transactions to ensure that the capital of the estate would be used for the support of the child-heirs.[62] Property was "communal" within the family, with the limits of alienation strictly limited by custom or by law. Even as the link to the land was broken the intimate tie between the estate and the lineal family was reaffirmed.

294

These traditional notions of family identity were subjected to considerable strain by the mid-nineteenth century. The psychological dimensions of the economic changes that diminished the importance of the family farm as the basic productive unit are revealed, in an oblique fashion, in the naming patterns practiced by parents in Hingham, Massachusetts. During the colonial period, most parents in this agricultural settlement did not perceive their children as "unique *per se.*" If a child died, his or her existence was perpetuated indirectly, for the same forename was normally given to the next infant of the same sex, especially when the dead child carried the same name as one of the parents. This necronymic pattern, with its obvious emphasis on the line rather than the individual, persisted in Hingham until the 1840s. So also did the tendency of parents to name their first children after themselves—to entail the parental name, as it were, and thus to stress the continuity between generations.[63] As economic change altered the structure and character of Hingham society, these lineal conceptions of identity gradually yielded to more individualistic ones. After 1800 first sons were given the same forenames as their fathers but a distinctive middle name. This was a subtle and complex compromise, for these middle names were often family names as well (the mother's surname, for example)—yet another manifestation of the persistence of traditional forms in a time of transition.

It is significant that this shift toward a distinctive personal identity—toward individualism—has been traced in Hingham, Massachusetts, one of the oldest English settlements in America, and not on the frontier. A similar development may have resulted from (or accompanied) the westward movement, but it is equally likely—Frederick Jackson Turner to the contrary—that lineal family values were *more* important than individualism in the new

---

[62] Alexander Keyssar, "Widowhood in Eighteenth-Century Massachusetts: A Problem in the History of the Family," *Perspectives in American History*, VIII (1974), 100-111.

[63] Daniel Scott Smith, "Child-Naming Patterns and Family Structure Change: Hingham, Massachusetts, 1640-1880" (unpub. paper, 1975), 10. Over 60% of first sons and over 70% of first daughters bore the same forename as their parents in 17th-century Hingham families, and the proportions remained high until the first children of the 1861-1880 marriage cohorts, when "the respective fractions are two-fifths and one-sixth."

farming communities of the old Northwest. For farm families usually trained and encouraged their children "to succeed *them*, rather than to 'succeed' by rising in the social system."[64] The young adults of thriving farm communities were not forced to confront the difficult problems of occupational choice and psychological identity as were those from depressed and overcrowded rural environments or growing cities. The dimensions of existence had expanded in the East, even as the eighteenth-century patterns of farm life, community stratification, and family identity were being recreated, in a modified form, in the new settlements of the West.

In some of these older and crowded communities in New England and the Middle States, lineal family values remained important well into the nineteenth century because they were consistent, at least temporarily, with rural industrialization and an emergent market economy. Fathers and mature sons continued to farm the (now depleted or subdivided) land while mothers, daughters, and younger sons turned their talents and energies to the production of textiles, shoes, and other items. The period between 1775 and 1815 was "the heyday of domestic manufactures" in America.[65]

295

The family factory assumed major economic importance as a result of the commercial dislocations produced by the War for Independence; household production of linen and woolen cloth was increased to compensate for the lack of English imports. Subsequently, this enlarged productive capacity was systematically organized by American entrepreneurs. In some cases, merchants sought out new markets for household manufactures and then capitalized part of the productive process itself, providing necessary materials and credit through the "putting out" system. Tens of thousands of "Negro shoes" were sold to southern slaveholders by Quaker merchants from Lynn, Massachusetts; and this productive network extended far back into the New England countryside. An even more important product of the rural family factory was wearing apparel. In New York State the production of textiles increased steadily until 1825, when the per capita output of household looms amounted to 8.95 yards.[66]

[64] The quotation refers to the socialization process in a "tradition-directed" culture, as described by David Riesman, *The Lonely Crowd: A Study of the Changing American Character* (New Haven, Conn., 1950), 40, 17-18. See also Joseph F. Kett, "Adolescence and Youth in Nineteenth-Century America," *Jour. Interdisciplinary Hist.*, II (1971), 283-299. As Nancy Cott and R. Jackson Wilson have pointed out to me, the agricultural journals of the 1830s are filled with articles and letters expressing parental concern over the urban migration of farm youth; such sentiments suggest the persistence of lineal, farming-oriented values.

[65] Lewis C. Gray, *History of Agriculture in the Southern United States to 1860*, I (Washington, 1933), 455; Rolla Milton Tryon, *Household Manufactures in the United States, 1640-1860* (New York, 1966 [orig. publ. Chicago, 1917]), esp. 243-276.

[66] Paul G. Faler, "Workingmen, Mechanics and Social Change: Lynn, Massa-

This extraordinary household output was made possible not only by the existence of a regional or national market—the product of a mature merchant-directed commercial capitalism—but also by the peculiar evolution of the factory system. By the late eighteenth century certain operations which were difficult in the home—such as fulling, carding, dyeing, and spinning in the case of textile production—had been assumed, with constantly increasing efficiency, by small mills. This process of specialization was as yet incomplete; eventually the weaving of cloth (as well as the preparation of the yarn) would be removed from the home and placed in the factory. For the moment—indeed for more than a generation—this final stage in the "evolution of the simple household industry into the . . . factory system" was held in abeyance by technological constraints, and the family factory reigned supreme.[67] Rural industrialization expanded the productive capacity of the society and systematically integrated female labor into the market economy; but it did so without removing the family from the center of economic life.

One result was to perpetuate, for another generation, the delicate and reciprocally beneficial economic relationship between eastern farm parents and their offspring. The intergenerational exchange of youthful labor for an eventual inheritance had been threatened in the mid-eighteenth century by land scarcity, which diminished the financial security of aging parents and their ability or willingness to assist their children. Some young adults implicitly rebuked their parents by migrating; others stayed and exercised a gentle form of coercion. Nineteen percent of all first births registered in Concord, Massachusetts, in the 1740s were premaritally conceived, and the proportion rose to 40 percent in Concord, Hingham, and many other northern communities by the end of the century. "If they were again in the same circumstances," one observer noted, these young men and women "would do the same again, because otherwise they could not obtain their parents' consent to marry."[68] Once the legal and financial concessions were extracted from reluctant parents, marriage quickly followed. Both parents and children shunned illegitimacy; both accepted the cultural norm of stable family existence.

Whatever their economic weakness and vulnerability to youthful persuasion, parents retained significant power over their offspring. Affective bonds remained strong, and they were augmented by the power of the state.

chusetts, 1800-1860" (Ph.D. diss., University of Wisconsin, 1971), 41-43; Taylor, *Transportation Revolution*, 212-213; Tryon, *Household Manufactures*, 190, 276-279, 370-371, and Tables 12, 16, 18.
[67] Tryon, *Household Manufactures*, 243-259, 272-276; Danhof, *Change in Agriculture*, 20-21.
[68] Quoted in Daniel Scott Smith and Michael S. Hindus, "Premarital Pregnancy in America, 1640-1971: An Overview and Interpretation," *Jour. Interdisciplinary Hist.*, V (Spring 1975), 557; Gross, *Minutemen*, 217, 235.

Young men who wished to work outside the household unit before they attained their legal majority were obliged to buy their economic freedom, undertaking in written contracts to pay their parents a certain sum in return for the privilege. Similarly, the first New England mill girls turned at least a portion of their earnings over to their parents; they were working outside the home but not for themselves as unattached individuals.[69] The lineal family remained predominant, in large part because there were few other institutions in early nineteenth-century America that could assume its social and economic functions—few schools, insurance companies, banks, or industries to provide training and capital for the new generation, and comfort and security for the old. Only a major structural change in the society itself—the widespread appearance of non-familial social, economic, and political organizations—would undermine the institutions of lineage; until this occurred there were simply no "alternatives to the family as a source of provision for a number of crucially important needs."[70]

The lineal family—not the conjugal unit and certainly not the unattached individual—thus stood at the center of economic and social existence in northern agricultural society in pre-industrial America. The interlocking relationship between the biological life cycle and the system of agricultural (and domestic) production continued to tie the generations together even as the wider economic structure was undergoing a massive transformation and as the proportion of farming families in the population was steadily declining. Most men, women and children in this yeoman society continued to view the world through the prism of family values. This cultural outlook—this inbred pattern of behavior—set certain limits on personal autonomy, entrepreneurial activity, religious membership, and even political imagery.[71] Lineal family values did not constitute, by any means, the entire world view—the *mentalité*—of the agricultural population, but they did define a central tendency of that consciousness, an abiding core of symbolic and emotive meaning; and, most important of all, they constituted a significant and reliable guide to behavior amid the uncertainties of the world.

[69] Joseph F. Kett, "Growing Up in Rural New England, 1800-1840," in Tamara K. Hareven, ed., *Anonymous Americans: Explorations in Nineteenth-Century Social History* (Englewood Cliffs, N.J., 1971), 1-16; Joan W. Scott and Louise A. Tilly, "Women's Work and the Family in Nineteenth-Century Europe," *Comparative Studies in Soc. and Hist.*, XV (Jan. 1975), 36-64.
[70] Michael Anderson, *Family Structure in Nineteenth-Century Lancashire* (Cambridge, 1971), 96.
[71] An extended discussion of the importance of family imagery in 18th-century politics, political theory, and the War for Independence is Edwin G. Burrows and Michael Wallace, "The American Revolution: The Ideology and Psychology of National Liberation," *Perspectives in Am. Hist.*, VI (1972), 167-306.

CULTURE AND CAPITALISM IN PRE-REVOLUTIONARY AMERICA

JOSEPH J. ELLIS

Mount Holyoke College

DURING THE MIDDLE DECADES OF THE EIGHTEENTH CENTURY THERE began to appear, for the first time, published prophecies of imminent American cultural greatness. In 1758, for example, an elderly Connecticut woman named Martha Brewster, who described herself as "a humble widow," published a collection of *Poems on Diverse Subjects*. One of them, entitled "A Dream," described her vision of a future in which Americans dominated the world in philosophy, literature, and the arts; her grandsons, she predicted, would come of age in an America bursting with creative genius. There were "Four Ages of Man," she observed, the "budding, blooming, ripening, withering States," and the English colonies in North America were moving rapidly towards their age of bloom.[1] The following year *The New American Magazine* appeared in Woodbridge, New Jersey; its editor, who wrote under the pseudonym "Sylvanus Americanus," described himself as a combination of Virgil and Cicero. He foresaw the emergence of an Augustan Age "this side the Atlantic" now that the French had been defeated and the continent was safely under the aegis of English influence.[2] In Boston that same year Jonathan Mayhew, the leading New England minister of the day, proclaimed that providence had vanquished the French menace and thereby paved the way for "a mighty empire . . . in numbers little inferior perhaps

---

[1] Martha Brewster, *Poems on Divers Subjects* (New London, 1758), 3-4, 34.
[2] *The New American Magazine*, Jan. 1759; see also Samuel Neville, *The History of North America From the First Discovery Thereof* (Woodbridge, New Jersey, 1761) for a reprint of the magazine essays.

to the greatest in Europe, and in felicity to none." Mayhew saw a bucolic empire of "happy fields and villages," but he also conjured up the image of a "spacious kingdom of learning" where poetry and philosophy would coexist with "the purest religion since the time of the apostles."[3]

When news of the total defeat of the French armies in Canada reached the colonies in 1760, it touched off another round of effusive declarations. Ezra Stiles delivered a Thanksgiving sermon to his congregation in Newport, Rhode Island, and focused on the propitious signs that "This Land may be renowned for Science and Arts." Stiles did not specify the time when cultural greatness would arrive, but he did indicate that it was both imminent and inevitable. "Not only science, but the elegant Arts are introducing apace," he noted, "and in a few years we shall have . . . Painting, Sculpture, Statuary, but first of all the greek Architecture in considerable Perfection among us."[4] In Philadelphia a young graduate of the Pennsylvania Academy by the name of Francis Hopkinson put the same vision to verse:

299

> Fair Science softning, with reforming Hand,
> The native Rudeness of a barbarous Land
> . . . .
> It must be so, prophetic Fancy cries,
> See other *Popes*, and other *Shakespeares* rise.[5]

Hopkinson not only wrote poems, he also composed songs, played musical instruments, and painted portraits, as if he was anticipating that several of the muses would pay him a personal visitation. His friend and classmate, Nathaniel Evans, predicted that Philadelphia was the worthy successor to London and Rome as the cultural capital of the world:

> O would the Muses, sweet celestial Maids!
> In this fair Land vouchsafe to fix their Seat,
> . . . .
> Much do we need their Aid, and sacred Lore,
> To virtuous Acts to animate the Soul.[6]

Meanwhile, Philadelphia's most prominent resident wondered why America had not already surpassed England in the arts. "Why should that petty Island," asked Benjamin Franklin, "which compar'd to America is

[3] Jonathan Mayhew, *Two Discourses* (Boston, 1759), 13, 57.
[4] Quoted in Edmund S. Morgan, *The Gentle Puritan: A Life of Ezra Stiles, 1727–1795* (New Haven: Yale Univ. Press, 1962), 214.
[5] Francis Hopkinson, *Science, A Poem* (Philadelphia, 1762), 6, 16.
[6] Nathaniel Evans, *Ode, on the Late Glorious Successes of His Majesty's Arms, and Present Greatness of the English Nation* (Philadelphia, 1762), 12.

but like a stepping Stone in a Brook, scarce enough of it above Water to keep one's Shoes dry; why, I say, should that little Island, enjoy in almost every Neighbourhood, more sensible, virtuous and elegant Minds, than we can collect in ranging 100 Leagues of our vast Forests?" Although Franklin did not answer his own question, he expressed confidence that the passage of time would work to America's advantage: "'tis said," he coyly observed, "the Arts delight to travel Westward."[7]

Franklin was merely reiterating an old and venerable idea which had been given its most eloquent and familiar contemporary expression in 1726 by the Anglican divine, George Berkeley. In his "Verses on the 300 Prospect of Planting Arts and Learning in America," Berkeley had described the New World as the ideal environment for the flowering of the arts and sciences, the worthy heir of the cultural traditions established by the Greeks, continued by the Romans during the reign of Augustus, and most recently nourished in England from the late sixteenth to the early eighteenth centuries. In the grand cyclical pattern of civilization, Berkeley asserted, there was a continual rising and falling of empires and a discernible westward drift to the movement of history. This boded well for the American colonies:

> There shall be sung another golden age,
> The rise of empire and of arts,
> The good and great inspiring epic rage,
> The wisest heads and noblest hearts.
>
> Not such as Europe breeds in her decay;
> Such as she bred when fresh and young,
> When heavenly flame did animate her clay,
> By future poets shall be sung.
>
> Westward the course of empire takes its sway;
> The first four acts already past,
> A fifth shall close the drama with the day;
> Time's noblest offspring is the last.[8]

Berkeley's imagery rested on several key assumptions worthy of notice because they were shared by American commentators like Franklin and

[7] Leonard Labaree et al., eds., *The Papers of Benjamin Franklin* (New Haven: Yale Univ. Press, 1960–   ), 10:232–33.

[8] Alexander C. Fraser, ed., *The Works of George Berkeley, D. D.* (4 vols., Oxford, 1901), 4:364–65 for the poem. For a discussion of Berkeley's vision of America and his influence see R. C. Cochrane, "Bishop Berkeley and the Progress of the Arts and Learning: Notes on a Literary Convention," *Huntington Library Quarterly*, 17 (1954) 229–49, and Kenneth Silverman, *A Cultural History of the American Revolution* (New York: Crowell, 1976), 9–11, 238–39.

Stiles. First, Berkeley presupposed a close connection between what he called "The rise of empire and of arts." Only a society with burgeoning political, economic, and military power could be expected to produce first-rate art and literature in great abundance. Second, he posited a kind of global conservation of cultural energy principle: only one nation could possess the requisite ingredients for artistic greatness at any one moment in history; the muses travelled in a flock; they left one country *en masse* when it began to decline, flew west, then landed in a rising nation-state. Third, Berkeley described the movement of civilization towards America in terms that were at once optimistic and fatalistic. The imminent migration of the arts and learning across the Atlantic was part of a grand historical design outside of human control. Americans were destined to be its beneficiaries whether they liked it or not.

301

Although originally published in 1752, Berkeley's poem did not receive widespread circulation in the colonial press until the late 1750s and early 1760s. Its popularity, in short, was part of the upsurge of interest in America's cultural prospects that surfaced in the years immediately preceding the constitutional crisis with England. Berkeley's verses did not *cause* this upsurge of interest; as the most graceful expression of the belief in American cultural ascendancy, it was simply the best remembered and most frequently cited version of an increasingly popular theme. John Adams recalled that "the observation that arts, sciences, and empire had travelled westward" was a commonplace when he was a young lawyer in Massachusetts, "and in conversation it was always added since I was a child, that the next leap would be over the Atlantic into America."[9]

In the years between the Peace of Paris (1763) and the Declaration of Independence, the assertion that America was predestined to burst forth in a sudden frenzy of artistic and literary creativity appeared in several different guises. Berkeley's poem, often accompanied by editorials endorsing its uplifting message, cropped up sporadically in colonial newspapers and magazines. Traveling actors recited addresses on the theme before the start of plays in makeshift theaters. Ministers committed to a millennial view of history periodically made reference to the prominence of the arts under Christ's thousand-year reign. Whig political pamphlets occasionally included the claim that imperial taxation policies were but another sign of English degeneration and decline that would drive the muses towards America. Even English commentators referred to the inevitable rise of American culture. In 1774 *Lloyd's Evening Post* of London printed an account of two Americans who visited the city in 1974 and

---

[9] Adams to Benjamin Rush, May 21, 1807 in Charles Francis Adams, ed., *The Life and Works of John Adams* (10 vols., Boston, 1856), 9:600.

found it in ruins, much like Rome. "The next Augustan age will dawn on the other side of the Atlantic," wrote Horace Walpole. "There will, perhaps, be a Thucydides at Boston, a Xenophon at New York, and, in time, a Virgil at Mexico." But most published discussions of high culture in America, it should be noted, were quite brief, quick asides made in passing, part of an essay or sermon devoted to another topic.[10]

There were two exceptions. In September of 1770 John Trumbull read *An Essay on the Use and Advantages of the Fine Arts* to the graduating class at Yale. Trumbull's version of cultural history followed the conventional formula: he located the source of the arts in classical Greece; then the muses appeared in Rome with Augustus, Cicero, and Horace; and then the arts blossomed in Elizabethan England with the appearance of Spencer and Shakespeare. There was "a short eclipse [during] the luxurious reign of Charles II," but the emergence of Pope and Addison signalled that English culture had revived and "shone forth with superior brightness in the prosperous days of William and Anne." Trumbull placed a great deal of emphasis on the connection between high culture and what he called "the unconquered spirit of freedom." Under oppressive regimes and arbitrary rulers like Charles II, the arts tended to atrophy. But when governments adopted liberal policies "the fine Arts have been studiously cultivated and hath shined forth with peculiar lustre." He claimed, for example, that the American opposition to the Stamp Act and to English imperial policies "have awakened the spirit of freedom" and thereby demonstrated that America was fertile ground for creative artists. He concluded with a rapturous poetic vision *a la* Berkeley:

> In mighty pomp America shall rise;
> Her glories spreading to the boundless skies;
> Of ev'ry fair, she boasts the assembled charms;
> The Queen of Empires and the Nurse of Arms.
>
> See bolder Genius quit the narrow shore,
> And unknown realms of science dare t'explore;
> Hiding in the brightness of superior day
> The fainting gleam of Britain's setting ray.
>
> This land her Steele and Addison shall view,
> The former glories equal'd by the new;
> Some future Shakespeare charm the rising age,
> And hold in magic chains the [g]listning stage.[11]

[10] F. J. Hinkhouse, *The Preliminaries of the American Revolution as Seen in the English Press, 1763–1775* (New York: Oxford Univ. Press, 1926), 106–07 for the newspaper account; Silverman, *Cultural History*, 288–89 for the Walpole quotation.
[11] John Trumbull, *An Essay on the Use and Advantages of the Fine Arts* (New Haven, 1770), 5–7, 11, 13–15.

The other full-scale exploration of the role of the arts in America was also a commencement address, this one delivered at Princeton in 1771 and published in Philadelphia the following year. Written by two graduating seniors, Hugh Henry Brackenridge and Philip Freneau, *A Poem on the Rising Glory of America* neatly summarized the arguments offered by various champions of American cultural ascendancy during the preceding decade. Brackenridge and Freneau also traced the transit of culture from Athens to Rome to England; they too proclaimed that the inevitable next stop was America:

> we too shall boast   *303*
> Our Alexanders, Pompeys, heroes, kings
> That in the womb of time yet dormant lye
> Waiting the joyful hour for life and light.[12]

The time was rapidly approaching, they assured their listeners, when there would be a new Pope writing classical verse by the Schuylkill River and a new Hampden by the Susquehanna. Moreover, the young prophets were millennialists who claimed that America's reign of cultural supremacy would last exactly one thousand years. And when it ended, human history would also cease; America was "the final stage . . . of high invention and wond'rous art,/Which not the ravages of time shall waste."[13] Like Trumbull, Brackenridge and Freneau exalted the miraculous influence of freedom. The muses could only sing, they claimed, "Where freedom holds the sacred standard high." History was like a westward moving caravan, a wagon train in which political, military, and cultural greatness were linked together and freedom provided the fuel. Brackenridge and Freneau were even more specific: the particular kind of freedom most efficacious was commercial freedom, the freedom to trade. Each and every cultural accomplishment, they wrote, "Derives her grandeur from the pow'r of trade."

> For commerce is the mighty reservoir
> From whence all nations draw the streams of gain.
> 'Tis commerce joins discover'd worlds in one.[14]

---

[12] Hugh Henry Brackenridge and Philip Freneau, *A Poem on the Rising Glory of America* (Philadelphia, 1772), 21.

[13] Ibid., 25.

[14] Ibid., 3, 16–17; see also William Smith, *An Oration . . . before . . . the American Philosophical Society* (Philadelphia, 1773) for the similar claim that thoughtful colonists "anticipate the rising Grandeur of America . . . [and] trace the Progress of the Arts, like that of the Sun, from East to West. . . . THAT *Day* hath even now more than dawned upon us."

It was an unwieldy and implausible combination. Historic inevitability, the millennium, freedom, commerce, culture—all quite large and intractable concepts—were fused together in *Rising Glory* and molded into yet another exuberant forecast of American leadership in the arts. Where, one might reasonably ask, were all these ideas coming from? How and why did such optimism originate in pre-revolutionary America? Given the paucity of the previous colonial contribution to the arts and sciences, how could such extravagant expectations achieve credibility?

One conclusion seems incontrovertible: American cultural expectations were *not* based on a mounting list of past literary and artistic accomplish-
ments. Even the most enthusiastic prophets of the coming cultural apotheothis recognized that colonial America had made few, if any, major contributions to learning and the arts during the first century and a half of settlement. Greatness lay ahead, in the future and not in the past. In fact, the past looked almost completely barren.

In poetry, the verse of Edward Taylor, the most talented poet of colonial America, was buried in trunks awaiting discovery by twentieth-century historians. In painting, the emergence of Benjamin West and John Singleton Copley in the 1750s created considerable excitement that America might at last produce an artist of recognized genius. But first West and then Copley felt obliged to leave America in order to develop their talents. Once they had settled in London, neither artist ever returned, primarily because, as Copley put it, "in comparison with the people [of England] . . . , we Americans are not half-removed from a state of nature." In literature as in painting, Americans looked to England for models, inspiration, and approval. Benjamin Franklin's essays were conscious attempts to duplicate the urbanity of Addison and Steele. And William Byrd's *History of the Dividing Line*, another important American work not published in the eighteenth century and therefore unknown, represented Byrd's effort to show that he was a London gentleman frolicking in the Virginia woods. The one enduring and original philosopher in colonial America, Jonathan Edwards, was a cult hero to a small number of New Light ministers in New England, but Edwards' treatise on free will remained an intellectual weapon in local theological wars between competing sects. Edwards himself was dismissed by his parishioners and spent his latter years ministering to Indians in western Massachusetts, isolated and unappreciated.

Soon after the start of the American Revolution, it is true, Americans would begin to ransack their past for cultural accomplishments in a patriotic effort to provide the new nation with a respectable legacy in the arts and sciences. Then men like Franklin and Edwards would loom large. But in pre-revolutionary America, most especially during the middle decades of the eighteenth century, those colonists who gave any thought to the matter at all actually undervalued native writers, artists, and thinkers and felt obliged to apologize for their crudeness. Colonial Americans were profoundly aware that they lived on the periphery of a civilization whose center was London. Pre-revolutionary America was a provincial society whose leading members aped the manners of the English aristocracy and whose past accomplishments in the arts were derivative gestures, copies rather than originals. This, at least, was the dominant attitude of most aspiring artists and intellectuals by the middle years of the eighteenth century.[15]

All this makes it even more remarkable to see incredibly optimistic assertions of national ascendancy in the arts. Since these predictions pre-dated the debates over Parliament's right to tax the colonies, they cannot be attributed solely to the political crisis and patriotism of the 1760s and 1770s. Nor did the optimistic estimates depend upon proto-nationalistic pride in the cultural achievements of preceding generations. If one takes the rhetoric of these cultural projections seriously, it seems to suggest a sudden, almost explosive, flowering of the arts in an environment that previously produced shrivelled, unimpressive vegetation. The questions posed earlier thus seem even more vexing and perplexing: how could such buoyant and unprecedented expectations develop in provincial America?

*   *   *

Clues pointing toward an answer can be found in the demographic and economic evidence recently generated by historians of early America. Since most eighteenth-century commentators on the arts presumed that high culture was permanently linked to social and economic development, then the direction and pace of that development in pre-revolutionary America becomes highly significant. And the bulk of the evidence suggests not only that mid-eighteenth-century America was experiencing explosive rates of social and economic growth, but also that a good many colonists were aware of these trends. The effusive vision of an American

[15] For a recent analysis of American provincialism and cultural defensiveness, see Jack P. Greene, "Search for Identity: An Interpretation of Selected Patterns of Social Response in Eighteenth-Century America," *Journal of Social History*, 3 (1970), 189–224; John Clive and Bernard Bailyn, "England's Cultural Provinces: Scotland and America," *William and Mary Quarterly*, 3d Ser.,9 (1954), 200–13; Kenneth S. Lynn, *Mark Twain and Southwestern Humor* (Boston: Little, Brown, 1959), 3–22 for scrutiny of William Byrd; Vincent Buranelli, "Colonial Philosophy," *William and Mary Quarterly*, 3d Ser.,16 (1959), 343–62 for Edwards' philosophical legacy.

Athens was in part the result of a straightforward and conscious extrapolation from the visible and much discussed maturation of colonial society. At deeper and less conscious levels, however, the buoyant optimism that surfaced in pre-revolutionary America represented an early manifestation of a new, more liberal way of thinking made possible by the social and economic changes of the era and by the attitudes these changes encouraged.

Certain basic facts are beyond dispute. We now know, for example, that the American population grew at a relatively steady rate of 3 percent a year during the first three-quarters of the eighteenth century. This rate
306 of increase, which exceeded the modern definition of an "exploding population" (i.e., 2.6 percent per year), was primarily the result of a higher annual birth rate (55 births per 1000 inhabitants) than the annual death rate (27 per 1000). Immigration from Europe accounted for only about 20 percent of the overall increase in the white population during the half-century before the Revolution. America's overall growth rate was five to six times greater than England's: in 1700 there were 20 Englishmen to each American colonist; by 1775 the ratio was 3 to 1. The American population was also unusually young; in 1775 between 45 and 50 percent of the whites were under the age of sixteen, a fact which assured that the rapid rate of population growth would continue well into the future.[16]

Modern scholarship on the economic growth of the colonies allows for less precise conclusions, primarily because of important regional differences, the incomplete character of the data available, and disagreements over the meaning of the evidence that does exist. Nevertheless, it is clear that the total output of the American colonies increased dramatically during the eighteenth century, most probably at a rate slightly slower than the rate of population increase. Between 1730 and 1750, for example, the population of Pennsylvania rose by about 130 percent and the amount of bread, wheat, and flour exported from Philadelphia went up approximately 120 percent. The major cause of the rapid growth in total output was the increasing size of the population, although there is also evidence for an increase in per capita production of about .5 percent annually between 1720 and 1775. Despite periodic depressions, an unfavorable balance of trade with England, credit problems, and a persistent shortage

---

[16] Robert V. Wells, *The Population of the British Colonies in America before 1776: A Survey of Census Data* (Princeton: Princeton Univ. Press, 1975), 69–171; Daniel S. Smith, "The Demographic History of Colonial New England," *Journal of Economic History*, 32 (1972), 165–83; D. V. Glass and D. E. C. Eversley, ed., *Population in History* (London, 1965), especially the essay by J. Potter, "The Growth of Population in America, 1700–1860"; James Henretta, *The Evolution of American Society, 1700–1815* (Lexington, Mass.: D. C. Heath, 1973), 5–39.

of currency, the total wealth of the American colonies rose steadily throughout the eighteenth century, so that by the eve of the Revolution the American population as a whole had a higher standard of living than any European country and, according to the most recent and exhaustive analysis, "the highest achieved for the bulk of the population in any country up to that time." This rise in total wealth helped to mask, or at least mute, a parallel development: the widening gap between rich and poor. Several local studies of the distribution of wealth in pre-revolutionary America show that as the colonial economy became more commercial and capitalistic, the resulting wealth was distributed more unevenly. But the dramatic increase in the total wealth meant that even *307* the poorer half of the population enjoyed a higher standard of living than their parents or grandparents.[17]

Eighteenth-century estimates of American social and economic growth may have lacked the precision of modern studies, but the rough outlines of demographic developments were well known. Benjamin Franklin's *Observations on the Increase of Mankind,* written in 1751 and first published in 1755, estimated that the overall population of the colonies was doubling every twenty to twenty-five years. At this rate, he reasoned, the people in America "will, in another Century be more than the people of England, and the greatest Number of Englishmen will be on this Side the water." Throughout the 1750s Ezra Stiles also amassed statistical evidence on New England that confirmed Franklin's estimates. He published his findings in *A Discourse on the Christian Union* (1761), identifying the underlying causes of America's explosive growth rate as "*Free polity, free religion, free property* and *matrimony.* . . ."[18]

With the outbreak of the Anglo-American debate over Parliament's authority in the colonies, a host of American pamphleteers, including Franklin, John Dickinson, John and Sam Adams, and Tom Paine, focused attention on the demographic growth of the colonies and their increasing economic importance to the empire. Paine's *Common Sense,* which fused

---

[17] Marc Engal, "The Economic Development of the Thirteen Colonies," *William and Mary Quarterly,* 3d Ser., 32 (1975), 191–222; Alice Hanson Jones, "Wealth Estimates of the American Middle Colonies, 1774," *Economic Development and Cultural Change,* 18 (1970), part two, 118–19, 130; George R. Taylor, "American Economic Development Before 1840," *Journal of Economic History,* 24 (1964), 427–44; Simon Kuznets, "Notes on the Pattern of United States Economic Growth," Robert Fogel and Stanley Engerman, eds., *The Reinterpretation of American Economic History* (New York: Harper and Row, 1971), 17–24; Henretta, *Evolution of American Society,* 41–81, 103–06.

[18] Labaree, ed., *Franklin Papers,* 4:225–34; Stiles, *Discourse on the Christian Union* (Boston, 1761), 97–113, 123; see also James H. Cassedy, *Demography in Early America: Beginnings of the Statistical Mind, 1600–1800* (Cambridge, Mass.: Harvard Univ. Press, 1969), 111–16.

together Berkeley's vision of American destiny, Franklin's demographic argument, and Paine's own belief in the progressive unfolding of liberal values in the New World, represented the logical culmination of this tradition by insisting that the growth of American power made independence inevitable. "As I have always considered the independency of this continent, as an event which sooner or later must arrive," he wrote, "so from the late progress of the continent to maturity, the event cannot be far off." The major claim of Paine's enormously influential pamphlet, and the meaning of its title, was that the awareness of American demographic and economic growth had become commonplace, a matter of

308 common sense.[19]

The euphoric predictions of American cultural greatness, then, derived at least a measure of their credibility from the increased awareness of long-range social trends that, correctly it turned out, placed America on the upward curve of history. But these same demographic and economic trends also had less visible consequences, consequences which made eighteenth-century Americans particularly receptive to the buoyant way of thinking exhibited by prominent colonists like Franklin and Paine.

Population expansion and economic growth were slowly transforming daily life in the towns and rural villages where the vast majority of colonists lived and died. The community studies produced by a rising generation of colonial historians have focused scholarly attention on the ways in which the stability, harmony, and cohesion of seventeenth-century villages were eroded during the course of the eighteenth century and the bonds which tied communities and families together were gradually unravelled. Doubtless the self-sufficient agrarian communities of seventeenth-century New England were not as placid and free of conflict as some historians would have us believe. And despite population pressures, the declining crop yields of farm land, tensions between propertied fathers and landless sons, increasing social stratification, and the steady commercialization of agriculture, many villages remained traditional agrarian communities committed to harmony and order throughout the eighteenth century. Nevertheless, it now seems clear that colonial communities were at various stages of a major social transformation in the middle decades of the eighteenth century, that the ties which bound individuals together were dissolving, and that due subordination of individual

[19] For an incisive analysis of this literature, see J. M. Bumsted, "'Things in the Womb of Time': Ideas of American Independence, 1633–1763," *William and Mary Quarterly*, 3d Ser., 31 (1974), 533–64; see also Edwin G. Burrows and Michael Wallace, "The American Revolution: The Ideology and Psychology of National Liberation," *Perspectives in American History*, 6 (1972), 167–306. For the Paine quotation, see Philip S. Foner, ed., *The Complete Writings of Thomas Paine* (2 vols., New York: Citadel, 1945).

interests to communal goals could no longer be taken for granted. Even in rural villages which looked much the same in 1750 as they had in 1650, where ministers and magistrates continued to exalt the old virtues of austerity, deference, and self-restraint, new and more liberal attitudes towards authority and personal freedom were crystallizing.[20]

Because the belief in the power and preferability of individual freedom has become an unquestioned article of faith in modern America, it seems sacrilegious to notice that it has a history, meaning that it came into existence at a certain time and under certain conditions, that it is not an eternal verity. But it is crucial to recognize how alluringly new liberal values were in pre-revolutionary America, especially if we are to fathom the utopian expectations harbored by the revolutionary generation. We need to recover a fresh appreciation of the exciting, almost magical, possibilities that presented themselves when eighteenth-century Americans began to think about the unprecedented productivity that would result if the energies of ordinary Americans were released on the world. Logically and chronologically, the belief in an American Athens was linked to the emergence of a liberal mentality that exalted the untapped power that would be generated within individuals and society at large when traditional impediments to thought and action were obliterated. In short, both political independence and cultural greatness appear to have derived a portion of their plausibility and much of their appeal from a new-found respect, even fascination, for the future of freedom in a society already on the road towards capitalism.[21]

309

---

[20] The major community studies are: Philip J. Greven, Jr., *Four Generations: Population, Land, and Family in Colonial Andover, Massachusetts* (Ithaca: Cornell Univ. Press, 1970); Kenneth A. Lockridge, *A New England Town: The First Hundred Years* (New York: Norton, 1970); Michael Zuckerman, *Peaceable Kingdoms: New England Towns in the Eighteenth Century* (New York: Knopf, 1970); Paul Boyer and Stephen Nissenbaum, *Salem Possessed: The Social Origins of Witchcraft* (Cambridge: Harvard Univ. Press, 1974); Robert A. Gross, *The Minutemen and Their World* (New York: Hill and Wang, 1976). The best study of an entire colony is Richard Bushman's *From Puritan to Yankee: Character and the Social Order in Connecticut, 1690–1765* (Cambridge, Mass.: Harvard Univ. Press, 1965). Of the several excellent review essays analyzing this literature, I found John Murrin, "Review Essay," *History and Theory*, 11 (1972), 236–75 and Rhys Isaac, "Order and Growth, Authority and Meaning in Colonial New England," *American Historical Review*, 76 (June, 1971), 728–37 most helpful. Robert Gross also allowed me to read an unpublished paper, "Communities in Colonial New England: An Historiographic Review," which I found quite insightful.

[21] Three recent scholarly articles have addressed the problems posed by the coexistence of "traditional" and "modern" or "liberal" attitudes in revolutionary America: Joyce Appleby, "Liberalism and the American Revolution," *New England Quarterly*, 49 (1976), 3–26; Michael Zuckerman, "The Fabrication of Identity in Early America," *William and Mary Quarterly*, 3d Ser., 34 (1977), 183–212; James Henretta, "Families and Farms: Men-

*   *   *

One rather critical question remains unanswered: granted that many Americans derived considerable encouragement from a crude but accurate assessment of their growth in population and economic productivity; granted also that the social changes sweeping through pre-revolutionary America eroded the communal values that had formerly confined individual behavior and thereby "prepared" colonists for liberal ideals; but why did forecasts of inexorable demographic and economic advances lead to the assurance that the *arts* were also about to flower in America? What was the connection between material growth and the arrival of the muses?

This is not an easy question to answer, in part because the prophets of America's cultural destiny, from Berkeley onward, assumed that the connection was so obvious that it required no explanation. Berkeley, for example, simply asserted that empires and the arts rise together. John Trumbull spoke of the simultaneous flowering of "arts and arms." Brackenridge and Freneau presumed that America's "rising glory" would include cultural as well as economic prominence. The familiar references to Athens, Rome, and Shakespeare's England served as an implicit historical explanation—the arts would accompany American prosperity and power because that was the way it had always happened in the past. But no one spelled out the reasons why economic and cultural development were expected to go hand in hand.

Eighteenth-century Americans felt no need to explain themselves on this issue because they presumed that the artistic, political, and economic life of any society, including their own, was a single thing and not several different things. They had yet to create a language which would allow them to refer conveniently to a separate, self-contained sphere of aesthetics and refined taste.[22] And they had no need for such a language because it was inconceivable to them that the arts could flourish, or even exist at all, independent of favorable social and economic developments. If we are to understand the revolutionary generation on its own terms, we need to jettison certain modern ways of thinking and their related vocabularies. Our presumption that it is possible to think and talk about the arts as distinct from society—or, for that matter, the isolated individual as dis-

310

---

talité in Pre-Industrial America," ibid., 3d Ser., 35 (1978), 3–32. While in this paragraph and throughout this essay I emphasize the influence of emerging liberal values, largely because they help explain the boundless optimism of several commentators on the arts, I realize there is another side to the story; namely, the persistence of older, more traditional attitudes. These attitudes underlay the apprehension towards high culture that found their fullest expression in the 1770s and 80s and I have analyzed them at length in a longer work in progress.

[22] On this point see Raymond Williams, *Culture and Society, 1780–1950* (London: Chatto and Windus, 1958).

tinct from society—is a legacy of the nineteenth century. Eighteenth-century Americans had not learned to make these distinctions. They lacked our modern understanding of the word "culture" as a transcendent realm of sensibility divorced from ordinary events because they retained the traditional assumption that social and aesthetic life was indivisible and interconnected. A flourishing high culture was but one manifestation of social health. Economic prosperity was another manifestation of the same health. Politics, the arts, economic development, and demography were not separate spheres of human activity but interlaced strands comprising the social fabric.

A common refrain, running through the Whig literature on both sides of *311* the Atlantic, linked artistic creativity and economic productivity by making them both natural consequences of liberal political conditions. According to this formulation, a nation's health varied directly with the amount of freedom or liberty the government allowed. In one of his early essays, entitled "Of the Rise and Progress of the Arts and Sciences," David Hume had put it unequivocally: "it is impossible for the arts and sciences to arise, at first, among any people unless that people enjoy the blessings of free government." Hume also insisted that as soon as arbitrary and despotic policies became the norm, "from that moment they [the arts and sciences] naturally, or rather necessarily decline, and seldom or never revive in the nation, where they formerly flourished."[23] In a long series of essays, published in England during the 1720s as *Cato's Letters,* John Trenchard and Thomas Gordon made the preservation of civil liberty the prerequisite for commercial prosperity, legal justice, and everything else worth living for, including the arts. According to "Cato," "*Polite Arts and Learning [are] naturally produced in Free States, and marred by such as are not free.*"[24] The Earl of Shaftesbury had worked out a similar scheme even earlier. In 1710 Shaftesbury argued that the Glorious Revolution of 1688 had established the proper conditions for the flowering of the arts in England. He claimed that it was "easy . . . to apprehend the advantages of our Britain in this particular, and what effect its established liberty will produce in everything which relates to art. . . ." For Shaftesbury, "the high spirit of tragedy can ill subsist where the spirit of liberty is wanting."[25]

[23] T. H. Green and T. H. Grose, eds., *Essays: Moral, Political and Literary by David Hume* (2 vols., London: Longmans, 1898), I.
[24] Quoted in Silverman, *Cultural History,* 219.
[25] John M. Robertson, ed., *Shaftesbury's Characteristics of Men, Manners, Opinions, Times, Etc.* (2 vols., New York: Dutton), I, 141–43.

Literate colonists like Franklin, Stiles, and Trumbull were familiar with these English writings. *Cato's Letters* enjoyed an especially wide circulation in the colonies during the middle decades of the eighteenth century and played an important role in shaping American attitudes towards Parliamentary power in the pre-revolutionary era. But here is another instance when printed words only confirmed attitudes that colonists had begun to acquire from their own experience. When Stiles associated the emergence of an American Athens with "the spirit of freedom," when Trumbull linked the rise of indigenous American poetry and painting with "the absence of constraints," and when Brackenridge and Freneau claimed 312 that greatness in the arts only appeared "Where freedom holds her sacred standard high," they were not just echoing the essays of Shaftesbury and Hume. They were embracing the new and intoxicating liberal idea that was barely beginning to enter the consciousness of American colonists by the middle third of the eighteenth century: namely, that if all the artificial restraints and regulations imposed on human activity were removed, the result would not be chaos but harmony; moreover, that the religious and political health as well as the economic and cultural productivity of such a society would increase dramatically.

Although the long-range social changes that were slowly eroding the communal ethos of local life operated at different levels and speeds from region to region, the benign implications of freedom first became visible throughout the colonies in the aftermath of the Great Awakening. As the religious revivals swept through New England and the middle colonies in the 1740s, they left a trail of ecclesiastical wreckage. The power of the clergy had been eroded; established churches were splintered into several competing sects. The communal cohesion that depended on religious consensus deteriorated even further. The bond between church and state was also weakened, since the proliferation of sects made it difficult for any one religious group to maintain that it alone should enjoy political support. For many ministers the disorder and disarray were ominous symptoms of God's wrath and the collapse of religious uniformity was a source of considerable unease. But for some observers the new arrangement produced unforeseen and extraordinarily positive consequences. As Stiles saw it, for example, the breakdown of the traditional religious order allowed men and ideas to interact in exciting new ways. Stiles did not worry about chaos or religious anarchy because, he insisted, the multiplicity of sects "will unavoidably become a mutual balance upon one another." He compared the interaction of religious groups with a chemical reaction: "Their collisions, like the action of acids," he wrote, "will subside in harmony and union, not by the destruction of either but in the friendly cohabitation of all. . . . Indeed mutual oppression will more and more subside from the mutual balance of one another."[26]

Other Americans were also discovering that freedom was a safe and many splendored thing at this same time. During a controversy over the establishment of King's College in 1752, for example, William Livingston opposed Anglican domination of the college. When his Anglican critics charged that he was challenging their supremacy only because he wanted to give Presbyterians control over the school, Livingston repudiated the notion that any single interest group ought to enjoy favored status. He argued that the ultimate authority over King's College should be lodged with the New York legislature, where the clash of various factions would serve as a check against arbitrary rule by any one sect. Livingston claimed that "the Jealousy of all Parties combating each other would inevitably produce a perfect Freedom for each particular Party." Franklin, who was a genius at making the most novel ideas sound like folksy, self-evident truths, expressed the same faith in free and unhampered debates. "Light often arises from a collision of opinions," he wrote in 1760, "as fire from flint and steel; and if we can obtain the benefit of the *light*, without danger from the *heat* sometimes produc'd by controversy, why should we discourage it?" Similarly, during the public debate over the imposition of an excise tax in Massachusetts in 1754, several merchants opposed the tax on the grounds that it would discourage industriousness and thereby lower productivity. Regulations were unnecessary, they argued, because the competition among merchants created a harmonious network of interest groups which not only policed themselves but also generated wealth that would benefit the public.[27]

These scattered celebrations of the inherent tractableness and latent power of freedom—usually described as a release from the constraints imposed by religious, political, or economic regulations—were the first manifestations of a genuinely new and modern way of thinking about growth and development. One can discover the early glimmerings of this mentality in late seventeenth-century England, where advocates for religious toleration began to question the value of religious uniformity and proponents of a free trade policy began to criticize the mercantile assump-

313

---

[26] Stiles, *The Christian Union*, 51–54; Gilbert Tennent, *A Persuasive to the Right Use of the Passions in Religion* (Philadelphia, 1760), passim; John Brown, *An Address to the Principal Inhabitants of North America* (Philadelphia, 1763), 13–15. See also Richard Bushman, *From Puritan to Yankee*, 267–90; Sidney E. Mead, *The Lively Experiment: The Shaping of Christianity in America* (New York: Harper and Row, 1963), 16–37.

[27] Milton M. Klein, ed., *The Independent Reflector . . . By William Livingston* (Cambridge, Mass.: Harvard Univ. Press, 1963), 195–96; Labaree, ed., *Franklin Papers*, 9:61; James Lovell, *Freedom, the First of Blessings* (Boston, 1754), passim.

tions of the Board of Trade. During the course of the eighteenth century Scottish thinkers, most especially Lord Kames, David Hume, John Millar, and Adam Smith, made this new attitude toward freedom into the centerpiece of a school of thought for which Smith's *An Inquiry into the Wealth of Nations* represented the culminating philosophical statement. By the 1780s James Madison, who was thoroughly familiar with the writings of the Scottish *philosophes*, used their arguments in *Federalist 10* to claim that the constant clash of interest groups in the new nation would provide a source of stability for the allegedly fragile republican government. And by the third decade of the nineteenth century the principle of
314 *laissez-faire* had entrenched itself as an established feature of an unofficial American creed that glorified the hurly-burly of the capitalistic marketplace.[28]

From a long-range perspective, then, it is possible to see the sporadic endorsements of freedom which first began to surface in America during the middle years of the eighteenth century as the earliest symptoms of a mentality which, in its fully-developed form, became the dominant ideology of liberal, capitalist society. It is probably no accident that the initial formulations of what was to become known as the bourgeois or market mentality appeared in the pre-revolutionary era, just when the economy was becoming commercialized and when the majority of colonists, farmers as well as merchants, were discovering that their livelihood depended upon the buying and selling of commodities in the marketplace. For our purposes, however, it is critical to recognize that the emerging commitment to the benign and powerful effect of unregulated conditions was not solely or even primarily a commitment to *economic* development. The crystallizing ideas and attitudes which we now recognize as essential for the triumph of capitalism were originally believed to be all-purpose agents capable of liberating religion, politics, trade, and the arts from past constrictions.

And so another piece of the puzzle falls into place. Excessively optimistic predictions of America's cultural growth became commonplace in the

[28] Joyce Appleby, "Ideology and Theory: The Tension Between Political and Economic Liberalism in Seventeenth-Century England," *American Historical Review*, 81 (1976), 499–515; Duncan Forbes, "'Scientific' Whiggism: Adam Smith and John Millar," *Cambridge Journal*, 7 (1954), 653–70; David M. Potter, *People of Plenty: Economic Abundance and the American Character* (Chicago: Univ. of Chicago Press, 1954), passim. Albert O. Hirschman, *The Passions and the Interests: Political Arguments for Capitalism before its Triumph* (Princeton: Princeton Univ. Press, 1977), provides a compelling explanation for the seductive power of free-market rationales in the seventeenth and eighteenth centuries. For an overview of colonial attitudes towards work, freedom and prosperity that emphasizes the staying power of traditional, pre-capitalistic values, see J. E. Crowley, *This Sheba, Self: The Conceptualization of Economic Life in Eighteenth-Century America* (Baltimore: Johns Hopkins Univ. Press, 1974).

middle years of the eighteenth century, at a time when colonists were first becoming aware of the rapid growth of America's population and economy. Moreover, virtually all the predictions of imminent artistic greatness contained some reference to the important role that freedom would play in generating the cultural apotheosis. This emphasis on freedom, usually defined as the release from traditional sources of authority, accompanied the development of a market mentality, which in turn coincided with the collapse of the traditional social structure and the emergence of a market-oriented economy in colonial America. The affinity that so many commentators presumed to exist between economic and cultural growth in America, or between the rise of empire and the arts, 315 now comes into sharper focus. Commercial and cultural ascendancy were described as synonymous because they were regarded as the mutual beneficiaries of the same liberating process. Artistic creativity and economic productivity, culture and capitalism, were expected to flourish together in the free and stimulating conditions of the American marketplace. Needless to say, the members of the revolutionary generation were in for a huge disappointment.

The Material Lives of Laboring
Philadelphians, 1750 to 1800

Billy G. Smith

JOHN Shenton, a Philadelphia mariner, sailed four times to Antigua on the snow *Mary* between October 1750 and November 1752. He earned between £13 and £15 per voyage, plus 3s. 6d. for each day he may have worked unloading or stowing cargo, for an annual income of approximately £32 during those years. Shenton's personal expenses must have been minimal, for room and board were provided on ship, and the only financial difficulties he may have encountered would have resulted from supporting a wife and children, if he had such. The material conditions that he and his hypothetical family experienced, however, are not clear to us.

Fifteen years later, Joseph Graisbury earned about £180 annually by outfitting some of Philadelphia's wealthiest citizens in the latest fashions from Holland-cloth breeches to silk vests. He bought a house worth £120 in Lower Delaware ward, in which he resided with his wife, at least seven children, all under eight years of age, and a slave. But the standard of living provided by his tailoring, and the ways it varied during the decade before the Revolution, are unknown.

Late in the 1780s, John and Elizabeth Baldwin performed occasional jobs for the Pennsylvania Hospital for the Sick Poor. John whitewashed fences and walls for 5s. 5d. per day, and spread dung on the hospital's garden for 1s. 6d. per day. Elizabeth washed clothes, cleaned rooms, made candles, cooked, and nursed, usually for 2s. 6d. per day. The couple and their two children lived in a "brick tenement" rented from the hospital for £12 annually and may at times have paid 9d. for a meal at the hospital. Again, the material circumstances of their lives and the nature of their struggle to make ends meet cannot be clearly understood from these fragmentary data.[1]

Mr. Smith is a member of the Department of History at Douglass College of Rutgers University. He wishes to thank David E. Dauer, Gary B. Nash, John K. Alexander, Michaele Cohen, P. M. G. Harris, and Carole Srole for their critical comments. An earlier form of this article appears in the *Working Papers*, Regional Economic History Center, Eleutherian Mills–Hagley Foundation, II, No. 4 (Greenville, Del., 1979).

[1] These vignettes are drawn from information in the U.S. Bureau of the Census, *Heads of Families of the First Census of the United States taken in the Year 1790: Pennsylvania* (Washington, D.C., 1908), 245, and in the following manuscript records:

These vignettes provide glimpses into the material world of urban laboring people in America during the second half of the eighteenth century. They are a summons to research the day-to-day lives of ordinary Americans rather than a basis for easy generalizations about their physical existence. Despite limited evidence, historians usually describe the living standards of the urban lower classes as comfortable, perpetuating the hoary myth that labor scarcity in early America inevitably meant high wages for anyone who cared to work. Thus Sam Bass Warner finds Revolutionary Philadelphia a city of "abundance for the common man." "An unskilled laborer without connections," Warner claims, "could find work with board and wages to begin accumulating a little money for tools," and the "earnings of the ordinary artisan . . . could support a wife and children without their having to take outside employment."[2] Carl Bridenbaugh states that the "lower sort" received "very high wages" and that "a hardworking man could support his wife and family and even lay by a little money for the future."[3] Philadelphians, in particular, Bridenbaugh believes, "enjoyed continuing prosperity and a steady rise in the standard of living."[4] In the Quaker City as in the colonies generally, according to John J. McCusker, "not only were the rich getting richer but the poor were also."[5] Jackson Turner Main concurs: "The general standard of living was high." Indeed, conditions in the Pennsylvania capital were so favorable that even the "poor laborer," Main avers, "could normally expect to become a small property owner."[6]

Similarly, paucity of evidence has not restrained historians from using the supposedly favorable economic circumstances of laboring people to

---

Business Papers of Samuel Coates and John Reynell, 1755-1767, Coates and Reynell Papers, Historical Society of Pennsylvania, Philadelphia; ledger of Joseph Graisbury, 1759-1773, Forde and Reed Papers, Hist. Soc. Pa., hereafter cited as ledger of Graisbury; transcripts of the 1767 Tax Assessors' Reports, Van Pelt Library, University of Pennsylvania, Philadelphia; Philadelphia City Constables' Returns for 1775, Philadelphia City Archives, City Hall Annex; and Matron and Steward's Cash Books, Pennsylvania Hospital Records, American Philosophical Society, Philadelphia.

[2] Sam Bass Warner, Jr., *The Private City: Philadelphia in Three Periods of Its Growth* (Philadelphia, 1968), 7. See also David Hawke, *In the Midst of a Revolution* (Philadelphia, 1961), 38, and Stephen E. Lucas, *Portents of Rebellion: Rhetoric and Revolution in Philadelphia, 1765-76* (Philadelphia, 1976), 20.

[3] *Cities in Revolt: Urban Life in America, 1743-1776* (New York, 1955), 148, 284.

[4] Carl and Jessica Bridenbaugh, *Rebels and Gentlemen: Philadelphia in the Age of Franklin* (New York, 1942), 10-11, 13.

[5] "Sources of Investment Capital in the Colonial Philadelphia Shipping Industry," *Journal of Economic History,* XXXII (1972), 146-157. See also James F. Shepherd and Gary M. Walton, "Trade, Distribution, and Economic Growth in Colonial America," *ibid.,* 128-145, and Alice Hanson Jones, "Wealth Estimates for the American Middle Colonies, 1774," *Economic Development and Cultural Change,* XVIII (1970), 127-140.

[6] *The Social Structure of Revolutionary America* (Princeton, N.J., 1965), 279, 194.

interpret their political motivations and behavior. Charles S. Olton argues that "the mechanic class" in Revolutionary Philadelphia was "preponderantly composed of independent entrepreneurs" whose "common interests" help explain their political activity.[7] Other historians, generalizing on the meaning of the Revolution, assert that it did not result from "belly factors" or "rising misery" but "took place in a basically prosperous . . . economy." Americans in general, it is said, did not confront, and were not roused to rebellion by, the "predicament of poverty."[8]

Little has been done to test the comfort of the urban "lesser sort" by measuring their living standards. Reviewing the literature, Philip S. Foner concludes that "we can but guess at the actual wages of eighteenth-century workers"—a fundamental issue—because "we have no reliable statistics on pay scales."[9] Main's work on the social structure of Revolutionary America took a tentative step in this direction, but we have not advanced far since then.[10] Recent studies of the Philadelphia poor by Gary B. Nash and John K. Alexander contradict the prevailing rosy view of the lives of laboring people.[11] Nash discovers growing problems of poverty and unemployment during the late colonial period, which he regards as symptoms of structural weaknesses in the urban economy, and he undertakes to show how changes in the "material conditions of life . . . for city dwellers" generated a "revolutionary commitment within the middle and lower ranks of colonial society."[12]

318

[7] *Artisans for Independence: Philadelphia Mechanics and the American Revolution* (Syracuse, N.Y., 1975), 8-9.

[8] Hannah Arendt, *On Revolution* (New York, 1963), esp. chap. 1. See also Bernard Bailyn, "The Central Themes of the American Revolution: An Interpretation," in Stephen G. Kurtz and James H. Hutson, eds., *Essays on the American Revolution* (Chapel Hill, N.C., 1973), 12.

[9] *Labor and the American Revolution* (Westport, Conn., 1976), 12.

[10] While Main's collection in *Social Structure* of massive amounts of data is admirable, his methodology at times is imprecise and faulty. Examining the economic mobility of taxpayers in two Philadelphia wards, for example, he draws optimistic conclusions about the material circumstances of urban laborers (*ibid.*, 192-194, 195, n.49). However, no laborers lived in either of the two wards in the year he chose. For a darker view of the economic mobility of poor Philadelphians see Gary B. Nash, "Up From the Bottom in Franklin's Philadelphia," *Past and Present*, No. 77 (Nov., 1977), 57-83. For other criticism of Main see Jesse Lemisch, "The American Revolution Seen from the Bottom Up," in Barton J. Bernstein, ed., *Towards a New Past: Dissenting Essays in American History* (New York, 1968), 8, 33.

[11] Nash, "Poverty and Poor Relief in Pre-Revolutionary Philadelphia," *William and Mary Quarterly*, 3d Ser., XXXIII (1976), 3-30, and "Urban Wealth and Poverty in Pre-Revolutionary America," *Journal of Interdisciplinary History*, VI (1976), 545-584. A recent excellent study that focuses more on the responses of wealthier Philadelphians to poverty is John K. Alexander, *Render Them Submissive: Responses to Poverty in Philadelphia, 1760-1800* (Amherst, Mass., 1980).

[12] Gary B. Nash, "Social Change and the Growth of Prerevolutionary Urban Radicalism," in Alfred F. Young, ed., *The American Revolution: Explorations in the*

We still lack a systematic investigation sensitive to changes in the material welfare of the urban laboring classes during the late eighteenth century. Historians have not studied the relation between wages and living costs, the regularity of employment opportunity, or the cyclical factors that affected income, prices, and work availability. Basic questions consequently remain unanswered. How did the supposed high wages translate into purchasing power? How did the seasonality of work affect income? How close to the margin did working people live, and how seriously did fluctuations in the economy affect them? How often did they experience periods of hardship or prosperity? Were the material conditions of their lives generally improving or deteriorating? The evidence available to answer such questions is more limited than that for the study of the wealthy or even of the institutionalized poor for whom government records exist. But it is possible, nonetheless, to find out a good deal about the material lives of laborers and artisans—and this inquiry is essential to a full understanding of the social, political, and economic history of the period.

My purpose in this article is to measure as precisely as the sources permit the household budgets, wages, and material conditions of Philadelphia's lower sort—those people who lived just above the poverty line and generally did not receive public assistance—during the second half of the eighteenth century. A large range of property, wealth, and economic interests existed among urban laborers, and the failure of historians clearly to specify the people being examined has generated some of the current confusion in studies of eighteenth-century labor.[13] To avoid compounding this confusion, this article focuses on two categories of less-skilled artisans—cordwainers (shoemakers) and tailors—and two unskilled groups—laborers and mariners. Several factors determine the selection of these four groups. Of all major occupations, they were the most heavily concentrated near the bottom of the economic order; tax collectors assessed two-

319

History of American Radicalism (DeKalb, Ill., 1976), 7; Nash, *The Urban Crucible: Social Change, Political Consciousness, and the Origins of the American Revolution* (Cambridge, Mass., 1979).

[13] Historians have defined the urban lower sort imprecisely, partly because 18th-century terms were imprecise. Staughton Lynd, for example, used the term "mechanics" as it was employed in the 18th century, as "all groups below merchants and lawyers," including "anyone who worked with his hands" ("Mechanics in New York Politics, 1774-1788," *Labor History*, V [1964], 225-246). Herbert Morais equated "craftsmen" and "lower class" ("Artisan Democracy and the American Revolution," *Science and Society*, VI [1942], 227-241). Eric Foner has described several divisions within Philadelphia's middle and lower orders (*Tom Paine and Revolutionary America* [New York, 1976]). James H. Hutson mistakenly identified a highly skilled artisan group of ship carpenters as part of the "lower sort" in "An Investigation of the Inarticulate: Philadelphia's White Oaks," *WMQ*, 3d Ser., XXVIII (1971), 3-25. See also Jesse Lemisch and John K. Alexander, "The White Oaks, Jack Tar, and the Concept of the 'Inarticulate,'" *ibid.*, XXIX (1972), 109-134; Simeon J. Crowther, "A Note on the Economic Position of Philadelphia's White Oaks," *ibid.*, 134-136; and Hutson, "Rebuttal," *ibid.*, 136-142.

thirds of their members the minimum rate in 1772. The four groups composed not only a substantial portion of the lower sort, accounting for almost half of those in the bottom third of the tax structure in 1772, but also a sizable segment of the city's population—at least one-third and probably one-half of the free male workers.[14] The variety of economic functions performed by members of these groups should make their experiences representative of Philadelphia's laboring people. Mariners and many laborers served in the maritime sector; other laborers depended on the construction and shipbuilding industries as well as on a host of miscellaneous jobs; cordwainers and tailors worked as artisans supplying consumer goods and services.

320   The following pages give an account of the costs of four basic necessities—food, rent, fuel, and clothing—in order to construct a typical household budget. A consideration of actual and real wages (the latter adjusted by the cost of living), of income, and of the material conditions of the four occupational groups will follow.[15]

Food was the most important item in every household budget. The series of eighteenth-century Philadelphia wholesale prices developed by Anne Bezanson and her associates cannot be used to make accurate estimates of expenditures for food because neither the retail mark-up nor the effect of the international market on wholesale prices can be deduced from these data.[16] Fortunately, accounts of daily purchases, specifying the quantity and price of each commodity, by the Pennsylvania Hospital from the mid-1750s until well into the nineteenth century provide a wealth of

[14] These four groups composed about 1/3 of the city's taxables on seven tax lists between 1756 and 1798. This must represent a minimum figure for their proportion of the entire working population, as many of the poor, because of their mobility or poverty, were missed or excused by the assessors and thus did not appear on the rolls. The underrepresentation of mariners on the tax lists is discussed in detail below. The 1756 tax list was published by Hanna Benner Roach, comp., "Taxables in the City of Philadelphia, 1756," *Pennsylvania Genealogical Magazine*, XXII (1961), 3-41. Transcripts of the Tax Assessors' Reports for 1767 are in the Van Pelt Lib. The 1772, 1780, 1789, and 1798 provincial tax lists are in the City Archs. Figures for the 1774 tax list are based on an analysis in Jacob M. Price, "Economic Function and the Growth of American Port Towns in the Eighteenth Century," *Perspectives in American History*, VIII (1974), 123-186.

[15] A word of caution concerning the data in this article should be offered. No historical statistics are completely accurate, and statistics from the colonial period are generally less accurate than those from later eras of American history. The best one can hope for are reliable estimates. In this study the relative values—the indices of change of prices, budgets, and wages—are generally more reliable than the estimates of absolute budgets and wages.

[16] Anne Bezanson, Robert D. Gray, and Miriam Hussey, *Prices in Colonial Pennsylvania* (Philadelphia, 1935), and *Wholesale Prices in Philadelphia, 1784-1861*, 2 vols. (Philadelphia, 1936-1937); Anne Bezanson et al., *Prices and Inflation during the American Revolution: Pennsylvania, 1770-1790* (Philadelphia, 1951).

information about the retail prices of food and the consumption standards of Philadelphia's lower sort.[17]

The hospital's purchases reveal that Philadelphians could select from an impressive variety of food. Flour, bran, oats, barley, and rice products constituted a large part of their diet; they also dined on fresh and salted pork, mutton, veal, beef (including calf's head), chicken, goose, turkey, pigeon, and rabbit, as well as such seafoods as shad, herring, oysters, and clams. Vegetables included white and sweet potatoes, turnips, parsnips, corn, beans, peas, asparagus, and cucumbers, and Philadelphians ate apples, oranges, peaches, lemons, raisins, currants, and cranberries in season. Butter, cheese, and eggs seem to have been plentiful, while salt, pepper, mustard, horseradish, sugar, molasses, syrup, and vinegar were used to flavor food. The Quaker City residents washed all this down with milk, coffee, several types of tea, chocolate, and unfermented cider, and they lifted their spirits with hard cider, rum (both the local and the more expensive West Indian variety), wine, and "small" and "strong" beer.

The cost of items purchased by the hospital provides an annual average retail price of each foodstuff during the second half of the century.[18] To construct an accurate food-budget index that measures the cost of food for an individual or family, a weighting system based on the quantity of each of the foodstuffs consumed is necessary. For the purposes of the present investigation, reliable food consumption patterns of Philadelphia's lower sort can be derived from the records of the Pennsylvania Hospital. Because the hospital was a publicly funded institution established for the poor, and because it experienced continuous financial problems, we may reasonably assume that the types and proportions of foods eaten by laboring Philadelphians resembled the diet of the patients.[19]

To establish a reliable laborer's diet, I have computed the proportion of each of the nineteen most common foodstuffs purchased by the hospital in

[17] Matron and Steward's Cash Books, Pa. Hosp. Recs. Since the hospital purchased in bulk, it probably bought food at a discount. Estimations of the food budget of laboring people based on these retail prices thus probably err on the conservative side.

[18] To account for seasonal variation in the cost of food, prices from Feb., May, Aug., and Nov. of each year have been collected and the mean prices during each of the four months have been weighted equally to compute the average annual price of each commodity. The price relative of each commodity and the evenly weighted index of all items are available in Billy G. Smith, " 'The Best Poor Man's Country': Living Standards of the 'Lower Sort' in Late Eighteenth-Century Philadelphia," *Working Papers*, Regional Econ. Hist. Research Center, II, 50, 64-68.

[19] William H. Williams, "The 'Industrious Poor' and the Founding of the Pennsylvania Hospital," *PMHB*, XCVII (1973), 431-443; Nash, "Poverty and Poor Relief," *WMQ*, 3d Ser., XXXIII (1976), 7-8. Eighteenth-century medical practice discouraged wealthier citizens from entering hospitals, and the diet standards provided there undoubtedly reflected that fact.

1772.[20] The caloric requirements of laboring Philadelphians have been used to determine the amount of each food they consumed. Nutritionists consider that a twentieth-century man of average physical activity needs between 3,000 and 3,200 calories each day; men engaged in heavy labor require approximately 4,550.[21] Men of the colonial period perhaps needed somewhat fewer calories because of their slightly smaller stature, though this may well have been offset by the additional energy required in the absence of modern labor-saving machinery.[22] It seems unlikely that an eighteenth-century laborer could long have been adequately sustained on fewer than 3,000 to 3,200 calories daily. Accordingly, I have constructed a diet of 3,000-3,200 calories in which the nineteen foodstuffs were consumed in the same proportion as they were purchased by the Pennsylvania Hospital (Table I).[23]

Although the method of establishing this diet is not completely satisfactory, comparisons with other real and estimated patterns of food consumption indicate that the Philadelphia laborer's diet was minimal in both quality and cost. Grains constituted the mainstay of the American table generally. Daily rations of the Continental army in 1775 included one pound of bread and a small amount of cornmeal.[24] Prisoners in early nineteenth-century Philadelphia ate 1.25 pounds of bread, supplemented by cornmeal.[25] James T. Lemon finds that the wills of Pennsylvania farmers specified that their widows should receive five hundred pounds annually, or 1.37 pounds daily of grain products.[26] The proposed diet of laboring

322

[20] The amount the Pennsylvania Hospital spent on various foods between May 3, 1772, and May 3, 1773, is in its report to the assembly. See Charles F. Hoban, ed., *Votes of the Assembly* (Samuel Hazard *et al.*, eds., *Pennsylvania Archives*, 8th Ser. [Philadelphia and Harrisburg, Pa., 1852-1949]), VII, 7069, hereafter cited as *Votes of Assembly*.

[21] Mary Davis Rose, *Laboratory Handbook for Dietetics*, ed. Clara Mae Taylor and Grace Macleod, 5th ed. rev. (New York, 1949), 15-36, hereafter cited as Rose, *Laboratory Handbook*.

[22] Eighteenth-century Americans apparently were not as short as is sometimes believed. Sixty-seven inches was the mean height of 130 mariners who applied for certificates of citizenship in Philadelphia between 1795 and the end of the century. Seamen's Protective Certificate Applications to the Collector of Customs for the Port of Philadelphia, Records of the Bureau of Customs, Record Group 36, National Archives.

[23] Caloric estimates are from Rose, *Laboratory Handbook*. Neither fish nor peas are included in the diet because the method of purchasing them does not permit calculating their unit price.

[24] U.S. Bureau of the Census, *Historical Statistics of the United States: Colonial Times to 1970*, II (Washington, D.C., 1975), 1175.

[25] James Mease, *The Picture of Philadelphia* . . . (Philadelphia, 1811), 167.

[26] James T. Lemon, "Household Consumption in Eighteenth-Century America and Its Relationship to Production and Trade: The Situation among Farmers in Southeastern Pennsylvania," *Agricultural History*, XLI (1967), 63-64, 68.

TABLE I
ESTIMATED PHILADELPHIA LABORER'S DIET

Foodstuff	Annual Quantity Consumed	Daily Caloric Intake	1762 Cost per Week in Pence
Wheat flour[a]	365.0 lb.	1600	12.73
Cornmeal	45.0 lb.	199	.71
Rice	15.7 lb.	68	.68
Bran	52.6 lb.	110	.69
Meat		528	11.65
beef	100.2 lb.		
mutton	18.2 lb.		
pork	9.1 lb.		
veal	47.0 lb.		
Potatoes	6.6 lb.	7	.19
Turnips	27.6 lb.	12	.50
Butter	12.8 lb.	117	5.09
Milk	38.1 gal.	281	7.81
Salt	21.9 lb.	b	.37
Pepper	.1 lb.	b	.06
Sugar	16.8 lb.	83	2.16
Molasses	4.9 gal.	174	3.16
Beverages			.92
coffee	.7 lb.	b	
tea	.2 lb.	b	
chocolate	.2 lb.	b	
Total		3179	46.72

[a]Includes both middling and common flour.
[b]Not included in caloric calculations.

Philadelphians, which allows 1.31 pounds of grains daily, closely resembles that of soldiers, prisoners, and widows. Meat furnished a significant proportion of the caloric intake of Americans. The Continental army allotted one pound of beef a day to soldiers; Philadelphia prisoners ate one-half pound; .41 pounds has been estimated as the daily fare of both Pennsylvania widows and American adults generally.[27] The laborer's diet, as

[27] These figures are computed from *Historical Statistics*, II, 1175; Mease, *Picture of Philadelphia*, 167; Lemon, "Household Consumption," *Agric. Hist.*, XLI (1967),

constructed, includes .48 pounds of meat daily, similar to that of prisoners and widows, and to the overall American consumption, but not quite half the rations of soldiers. Contemporary comments indicating that "most labourers and mechanics eat a portion of [meat] at breakfast and supper" suggest that, if anything, the diet estimate cuts the meat allotment to the bone.[28] Milk, sugar, and molasses served as less important energy sources. Most Americans apparently drank milk even though it soured quickly in warm weather. Both Bostonians of the "middling figure" in the early eighteenth century and Continental soldiers during the Revolution consumed a quart daily; Philadelphia laborers are estimated to have drunk .4 quarts per day.[29] Sugar and molasses were important food flavorings, and the latter was also used in making the "small beer" popular among Pennsylvanians.

324

If the laborer's diet included more grains and less meat than other real and estimated patterns of consumption, it was also cheaper to purchase. Retail prices gathered from the hospital records indicate that in 1762 (the base year for all the indices constructed in this article) Philadelphians would have paid 3.88s. per week, or £10.12 per year, for the diet served up in Table I.[30] Estimates by Main and David Klingaman exceed this amount. Main puts the cost of food for a single man at £10-13 annually during this period, and Klingaman calculates the per capita food budget in Philadelphia at £11.88 per year between 1768 and 1772. The Continental army rations, because they included more meat than the diet specified in Table I, cost even more: £14.38 per year at Philadelphia 1762 prices.[31]

63; and David Klingaman, "Food Surpluses and Deficits in the American Colonies, 1768-1772," *Jour. Econ. Hist.*, XXXI (1971), 559-560.

[28] Mease, *Picture of Philadelphia*, 121. The proportional relationship of the foodstuffs composing the diet in Table I closely resembles the proportions of foodstuffs issued occupants of Philadelphia's almshouse during the late 18th century. In 1792 and 1793 the almshouse supplied its inhabitants with .32 pounds of meat for every pound of cereals, while the diet in Table I allots .36 pounds of meat for every pound of cereals. Daily Occurrences Docket, Feb. 5, 1793, Guardians of the Poor, Phila. City Archs., hereafter cited as Daily Occurrences Docket.

[29] *Historical Statistics*, II, 1175; Carl Bridenbaugh, "The High Cost of Living in Boston, 1728," *New England Quarterly*, V (1932), 800-811.

[30] All values in this article are in Pennsylvania currency unless otherwise indicated. Conversion rates to sterling before the Revolution are available in *Historical Statistics*, II, 1198. For the 1790s, values are converted from dollars to Pennsylvania pounds at the rate of 7.5s. per dollar. The superior data on prices and wages available for the year 1762 determined its selection as the base year for all indices in this article. For accuracy and convenience, money values are given in decimal notation: £10.12 is £10. 2s. 5d.

[31] The currency of Main's estimate is unclear. If it is pounds sterling, the equivalent in Pennsylvania currency is between £16.67 AND £21.67 (*Social Structure*, 115). Klingaman's estimate in pounds sterling is converted into Pennsylvania currency at the rate of .6 pounds sterling per each Pennsylvania pound, and then adjusted to

Other miscellaneous records of expenditures for food corroborate the conservative nature of this budget.[32]

Although the diet in Table I is imprecise, for the purposes of this study it need be only a reliable estimate, and it does appear a reasonable, if minimal, diet for Philadelphia's lower sort both in pattern of consumption and in price. In any case, minor alterations in the diet will not significantly affect the overall conclusions of this investigation.

Using this diet and the food-price series developed above, I have constructed a food-budget index that measures the cost of the diet in each year relative to its cost in 1762 (Table II, column 1).[33] For example, in 1762 the diet cost £10.12; in 1770 its cost was 90 percent of that, or £9.11. Food prices climbed more than 20 percent from the war years of   *325*

---

the 1762 food prices found in this article ("Food Surpluses," *Jour. Econ. Hist.*, XXXI [1967], 567). Data on the Continental army rations are in *Historical Statistics*, II, 1175.

[32] During the third quarter of the 18th century, 1s. per day "diet money" was customarily allowed both sea captains and their "boys" (Journal of John and Peter Chevalier, Nov. 29, 1770, July 19, 1773; Clifford Papers, III, 1760-1762; bills and receipts, Coates and Reynell Papers, Boxes 1751-1754 and 1755-1767, all at Hist. Soc. Pa.). In the 1770s, John Fitch's journeymen silversmiths paid 8s. 2d. weekly for board (ledger of John Fitch, Case 33, Hist. Soc. Pa.). Simultaneously, master tailors thought that it cost 1.5s. per day to feed a journeyman; calculated from information in the minutes of the Taylors Company, Hist. Soc. Pa. Ten shillings per week was the cost for board in the Pennsylvania Hospital and the workhouse before the Revolution. After the Revolution, the hospital both paid and charged workmen 9d. per meal, while the lowest price for patients' board fluctuated between 7s. 6d. and 12s. 6d. per week (Matron and Steward's Cash Books, Pa. Hosp. Recs.).

[33] The formula used to construct this index is

$$I = \frac{\sum\left[P_oQ\left(\dfrac{P_1}{P_o}\right)\right]}{\sum P_oQ}$$

where I = food-budget index; P_o = prices of each foodstuff in base year 1762; P_1 = prices of each commodity in a given year; and Q = quantities of each food consumed by families in 1772. This is the most widely used measurement in cost-of-living studies. A slight upward bias is built into this measurement as it is assumed that the pattern of consumption remains constant. Consumption patterns change, however, as consumers tend to purchase more of those items the prices of which rise least or fall most over time. Arithmetic rather than geometric indices are used in this article because the former make more economic sense even though the latter possess superior mathematical qualities. For an explanation of the construction of an index and a discussion of the benefits and liabilities of arithmetic and geometric indices see R. G. D. Allen, *Index Numbers in Theory and Practice* (Chicago, 1975), 1-48, and Irving Fisher, *The Making of Index Numbers: A Study of Their Varieties, Tests, and Reliability*, 3d ed. rev. (New York, 1927).

TABLE II
HOUSEHOLD BUDGET INDICES
(BASE YEAR = 1762)

Year	(1) Food-Budget Index: 19 Items Weighted by Laborer's Diet	(2) Rent Index	(3) Firewood Price Index[b]	(4) Clothing Price Index	(5) Household Budget Index[e]
1754	94		59[c]	92	89[f]
1755	89		60	83	84[f]
1756	99		52		92[g]
1757	98[a]		78[c]		95[g]
1758	80[a]		56[c]		76[g]
1759	89		95[c]		90[g]
1760	95		91		94[g]
1761	86		88		86[g]
1762	100	100	100	100	100
1763	115		91	100	107
1764	101		116[c]	94	102
1765	91		96[c]	82	94
1766	90		58[c]	73	90
1767	94	112	81[c]	88	96
1768	86		71	81	90
1769	81		71	83	88
1770	90		73	88	94
1771	96		71	79	95
1772	99		91	85	99
1773	90		76[d]	76	92
1774	100		61	79	96
1775	89	111	76	80	92
1776	97		82	251	121
1783	154	252	118	188	180
1784	147		160	99	164
1785	123		116	92	143
1786	124		111	110	142
1787	119		105	99	134
1788	99		74	139	123
1789	107	165	76	82	115
1790	134		79	92	131
1791	130		97	92	131
1792	131		106	110	136
1793	143		111	119	144
1794	161		130	137	158
1795	207		197	114	186
1796	227		215	132	201
1797	192		212	150	185
1798	183	184	182	129	176
1799	188		174	105	174
1800	201		177	125	185

[a] Interpolated from the wholesale cost of nine food items in Anne Bezanson, Robert D. Gray, and Miriam Hussey, *Prices in Colonial Pennsylvania* (Philadelphia, 1935), 422–423.
[b] Includes oak and pine wood only. Mean prices for April, May, and June of each year are used to construct the index unless otherwise indicated.
[c] Index based on mean price for entire year.
[d] Interpolated from price in 1772 and 1774.
[e] Budget based on expenditure for food, fuel, clothing, and rent unless otherwise indicated.
[f] Based on food, fuel, and clothing costs.
[g] Based on food, fuel, and rent costs.

the 1750s to 1763 (see Figure I),[34] fell to their pre-war level by the late 1760s, and then rose gradually until the outbreak of the Revolutionary War. The diet's cost was 50 percent higher during the early 1780s but decreased steadily until 1788, when it again began to rise steeply, increasing more than 100 percent by the mid-1790s.

The food-budget index functions as a barometer of a family's food expenditures. Nutritionists consider that, on average, an adult female and a child require 83 and 60 percent, respectively, of the calories needed by an adult male.[35] The median size of families in the four occupational groups in Philadelphia during the mid-1770s was four—two adults and two children—and that composition forms the basis of all computations of household budgets in this article.[36] Consumption at these rates, when applied to the £10.12 cost of the diet in Table I in 1762, produces an estimated family food budget of £30.66 for the base year of the food-budget index.

Even though Philadelphia was located in a grain- and animal-producing region, its people could not buy food as cheaply as might be expected. Because foodstuffs composed the primary exports of the area, overseas demand drove up local prices and caused rapid and wide fluctuations in food costs. The assize of bread, for example, was legally bound to the price of wheat or flour, and as the export prices of those commodities increased, so did the price of loaves in the city's bakeries.[37]

During difficult times, laboring families adopted several strategies to trim food costs. They could produce their own food, although the crowded alleys where most lived made gardening impractical, and the possession of a cow even less feasible.[38] Many undoubtedly kept hogs, notching their ears for identification and allowing them to roam freely through the streets to feed on garbage. Poorer Philadelphians most often reduced their food costs by eating larger quantities of flour, cornmeal, and rice,

[34] Rising food prices during the early 1760s may have been even more dramatic than the food-budget index indicates. In 1761 the assembly passed a law regulating the assize of bread; in changing the measurement of loaves from troy to avoirdupois weight, the law reduced the size of the cheapest loaf by approximately 25%. James T. Mitchell and Henry Flanders, eds., *The Statutes at Large of Pennsylvania from 1682 to 1801* (Philadelphia and Harrisburg, Pa., 1896-1911), II, 61-63, VI, 69-71, hereafter cited as *Pa. Statutes.*

[35] Rose, *Laboratory Handbook,* 15-36.

[36] Household size is calculated by matching people in the four occupational groups on the 1772 tax list with the Constables' Returns of 1775, City Archs., which give the name of the household head and composition of the household.

[37] *Pa. Statutes,* II, 61-63, VI, 69-72, VIII, 130-138, 308-309, 429-435, XIV, 510-511. Philadelphians continually complained that forestalling and engrossing drove up the cost of food. Because of these "different manoevers," one drayman grumbled, "a number of worthy families were sorely distressed, and the common day laborers almost starved" ("A Drayman," *Independent Gazetteer* [Philadelphia], Apr. 9, 1791).

[38] Only 3% of the members of the four occupational groups were taxed for a cow in 1772.

FIGURE I

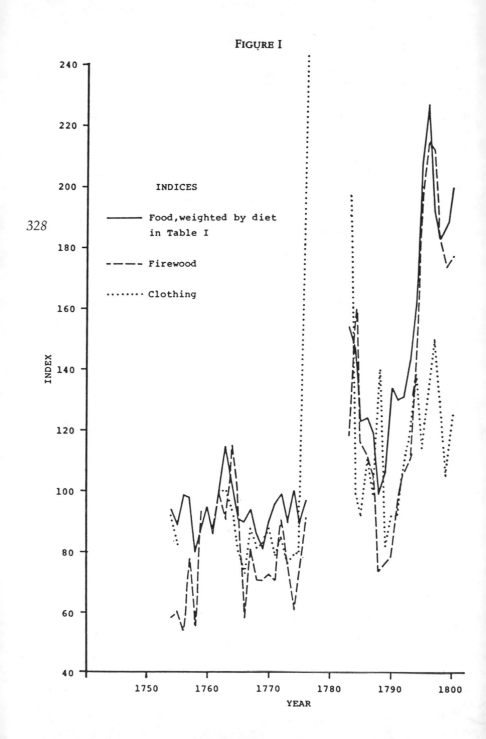

328

foods with the highest caloric yield for the money. Carried to its extreme—the consumption of grains only—a family food budget could be trimmed by as much as 45 percent, though this resulted in a bland, unnutritious diet. Such a strategy would have been debilitating, increasing susceptibility to the diseases that plagued the city.[39] "Most who are used to hard labour without doors begin to fail soon after [age] thirty," one contemporary wrote, "especially if they have been obliged to live on a poor diet that afforded but little nourishment or was unwholesome."[40]

The cost of shelter constituted the second major component of the household budget. Constables' returns and tax assessors' reports for various years provide sufficient data to construct an index of rents (Table II, column 2).[41] Laboring families lived predominantly as tenants and boarders; fewer than one in ten owned their homes.[42] In 1767, laborers, mariners, cordwainers, and tailors paid average annual rents of £10.08, £11.86, £21.98, and £22.81, respectively. During the decade before Independence housing costs remained stable, as cheap dwellings multiplied on the outskirts of the city. Rents of poorer Philadelphians doubled during the Revolutionary War, reflecting the general inflation, declined during the Confederation era, and then climbed slightly during the following decade.

Laboring Philadelphians commonly crowded into small narrow wooden houses. Typically, Philip Mager, a tailor with a wife and four children, leased a two-story wooden tenement twelve feet wide and eighteen feet deep. Mariner Richard Crips and his family rented an eleven-by-fourteen

329

---

[39] On the threat of disease and high mortality in Philadelphia see Billy G. Smith, "Death and Life in a Colonial Immigrant City: A Demographic Analysis of Philadelphia," *Jour. Econ. Hist.*, XXXVII (1977), 863-889.

[40] "Phileleutheros," *Pennsylvania Gazette and Weekly Advertiser* (Phila.), Feb. 2, 1780. Other comments on the inferior quality of food consumed by poorer citizens are "Citizens," *Gazette of the United States* (Phila.), Mar. 23, 1796, and "A Speculator," *Pa. Gaz.*, Mar. 16, 1785.

[41] Rents are calculated from information contained in the Constables' Returns of 1762 and 1775 and the tax lists of 1783, 1789, and 1798, all at City Archs., and from the 1767 Tax Assessors' Reports, Van Pelt Lib. These computations represent the minimal expense for shelter since they do not include the ground rent and taxes that many tenants complained they had to pay. "A Poor Tradesman," *Pennsylvania Packet, and Daily Advertiser* (Phila.), Oct. 20, 1784; "A Tenant," *Pennsylvania Evening Herald, and American Monitor* (Phila.), July 16, 1785. For a complete explanation of the method of determining rents see Billy G. Smith, "The 'Lower Sort' in Revolutionary Philadelphia" (Ph.D. diss., University of California at Los Angeles, in progress), chap. 3.

[42] Only 4% of laborers and mariners, and 14% of cordwainers and tailors, owned their homes, based on the 1767 Tax Assessors' Report, Van Pelt Lib., the tax lists of 1772, 1783, 1789, 1798, and the Constables' Returns of 1775, City Archs. This contradicts Main's assertion that the "great majority of artisans . . . were homeowners" (*Social Structure*, 80). Main believes that over half of cordwainers owned their homes and that "three-fourths of all artisans were homeowners" (*ibid.*, 132).

foot, single-story dwelling in the northern suburbs. In his two-story wooden box, eighteen feet square, in Harmony Alley, tailor William Smith may have found himself in even more cramped quarters. Like many other poor men, he did not have a separate kitchen, so his wife prepared meals in the fireplace not only for their three children but also for two boarders.[43] Many families saved expenses by taking in lodgers or by doubling up with other families. Laborer Martin Summers and his family, for example, lived with cordwainer Henry Birkey, his wife, and three children, and divided the £18 annual rent. With his wife and four young children, Christian Fight, a Knight of St. Crispin, shared his abode and £12 lease with fellow shoemaker Christian Nail and his family.[44] By contrast, wealthier citizens frequently occupied three-story brick houses of comparable width but two or three times as deep, with such outbuildings as kitchens, wash houses, and stables. Many owned two-story brick kitchens of a size equal to or greater than most of the dwellings of the lower sort.[45]

330

Before the Revolutionary War, laboring Philadelphians inhabited back alleys and rooming houses scattered throughout the city, though they tended to congregate on its perimeters. As the rapidly expanding population pressed on available housing, central-city estate values rose and tenements were hurriedly constructed in the suburbs. During the final quarter of the century poorer Philadelphians radiated increasingly to the fringe areas of the city—to Mulberry Ward and the Northern Liberties in the north, and Dock Ward and Southwark in the south. A 1795 ordinance prohibiting the erection of wooden structures in the city both reflected and stimulated residential change. Judged from the ratio of taxpayers to houses, conditions in poorer areas must have deteriorated during the second half of the century. In Mulberry Ward the number of houses rose at an annual rate of 2.5 percent while taxpayers increased by 3.1 percent each year; simultaneously, both houses and taxpayers grew by only .4 percent annually in Walnut Ward in the middle of the city.[46] By the close of the century, expensive two- and three-story brick houses filled the center

[43] These conditions are reconstructed from descriptions of dwellings contained in United States Direct Tax of 1798: South Ward, XXVI, Form A, reel 2, frame 169, East Northern Liberties, XLIII, Form A, reel 3, frames 51, 122, City Archs. Occupational information is from Cornelius William Stafford, *The Philadelphia Directory, for 1797* ... (Philadelphia, 1797), 51, 122, 169. Information on family composition is in U.S. Census Office, *Return of the Whole Number of Persons within the Several Districts of the United States: Second Census* (Washington, D.C., 1800), reel 8, frames 74, 134, and reel 9, frame 90.

[44] Constables' Returns for 1775, North Ward, City Archs.

[45] See, for example, the descriptions of houses in High Street Ward in U.S. Direct Tax of 1798, I, Form A, reel 1, City Archs.

[46] Mulberry Ward contained 488 and 1,343 houses in 1749 and 1790, respectively, and 309 and 1,372 taxpayers in 1741 and 1789. During the same years, houses in Walnut Ward increased from 104 to 125, and taxpayers grew from 98 to 122. The numbers of houses in 1749 and taxables in 1741 are given in John F. Watson, *Annals of Philadelphia, and Pennsylvania, in the Olden Times* ... (Phila-

of the city, while laborers and less-skilled artisans crowded into frame
tenements in the fringe wards and suburbs. Though still blurred, a dis-
tinctly modern pattern of residential segregation by economic strata began
to emerge by 1800.[47]

Philadelphians cooked their meals and heated their homes with firewood, an essential ingredient in their household budgets. Private business
documents and records of the Pennsylvania Hospital permit the construction of an index of firewood prices (Table II, column 3).[48] Only the costs
of oak and pine are tabulated, for these were the cheapest available fuels
and the ones most likely used by the lower sort. The cost of wood spiraled
upward from the war years of the 1750s to a peak in 1764 (see Figure I),
plummeted for the next two years, then fluctuated until Independence.
Like food prices and house rents, firewood prices climbed during the Revolutionary War, declined during the 1780s, and rose again in the subsequent decade.

331

In 1762 Philadelphians spent an average of 22s. 11d. for the cheapest
cord during the spring months. Poorer citizens, frequently buying quantities smaller than a full cord and most often during the winter when prices
were at their peak, may well have paid two or three times that amount.[49]
The quantity of wood burned by a typical household is difficult to determine because of the paucity of evidence and seasonal variations in the use
of fuel. Four journeymen silversmiths employed by John Fitch each
burned an average of 4.88 cords annually from 1772 to 1775.[50] This appears at least a fair indication of use by laboring Philadelphians; much less
would hardly have sufficed for their cooking and heating requirements,

---

delphia, 1884), II, 404-407, III, 236. Taxables in 1789 are from my analysis of the
1789 Provincial Tax List, City Archs. The number of houses in 1790 is from Benjamin Davies, *Some Account of the City of Philadelphia* ... (Philadelphia, 1794), 17.

[47] This analysis of residential patterns is based on information in Smith, "The
'Lower Sort' in Revolutionary Philadelphia," chap. 6.

[48] Matron and Steward's Cash Books, Pa. Hosp. Recs. The following are at Hist.
Soc. Pa.: Samuel Morris's Day Book, 1755-1767; bills, receipts, and accounts of
the Shippen Family, XXVIII-XXX, 1754-1822; Jour. of John and Peter Chevalier; bills and receipts of John Cadwalader, Cadwalader Collection; Business Papers of Levy Hollingsworth, Hollingsworth Collection, Sec. VII: Bills, 1751-1789,
and Sec. III: Invoices, 1764-1789; and Thomas A. Biddle Shipbook.

[49] The price of firewood varied seasonally, often costing twice as much in winter
as in spring. Moreover, in his construction of a working-class Philadelphia family
budget in the early 19th century, Matthew Carey estimated that a cord was nearly
twice as high when bought in small parcels (*An Appeal to the Wealthy of the Land* ...
[Philadelphia, 1833], 10).

[50] Ledger of John Fitch, Case 33, Hist. Soc. Pa. One contemporary estimated
that a "genteel" Philadelphia family burned 25 cords annually during the 1790s;
estimate of Joseph Nourse in Ellis Paxson Oberholtzer, *Philadelphia: A History of
the City and Its People*, I (Philadelphia, n.d.), 400.

particularly in their draughty wooden homes. Thus a poor family spent a substantial sum, an estimated £5.60 in 1762, for fuel.[51]

The great demand for wood by both private and commercial users undoubtedly drove up its cost. Households alone burned more than 20,000 cords in 1772. Bakers, brickmakers, blacksmiths, and iron manufactures likewise needed fuel, while coopers, house carpenters, shipwrights, and lumber exporters must have added to the city's wood requirements. So vital was firewood that local regulations proscribed its purchase for re-sale in the city between September and March.[52] As the forests surrounding the city were depleted, small boats brought wood from New Jersey and the Delaware Valley; as the carrying distance increased, so did the price of fuel. The problem evoked numerous charity drives to supply wood to the city's poor, as well as recurrent demands to regulate the amount charged by carters and boatmen for carrying firewood.[53]

332

Reasonable estimates of clothing costs can be made. The city's workhouse spent at least £3 annually to outfit John Peter Operting, a "labouring lunatic," during the 1760s. Main has calculated £4.17 as an average annual clothing allowance for adult males during this period.[54] In 1770, the most essential and least expensive attire could be purchased in Philadelphia for about £3.74. For that sum a man could buy a pair of coarse laborer's shoes (9s.), a pair of stockings (2s. 6d.), a pair of cloth breeches (15s. 7d.), a cloth coat (29s. 5d.), two shirts (6s. 2d. each), and a felt hat (6s.).[55] This wardrobe would have been minimal, not quite equalling the standard of dress annually issued to the inmates of the city's almshouse during the early nineteenth century, and far inferior to the silk garments fashionable among wealthier citizens.[56] If materials were purchased, and the coat, breeches, and shirts made at home, clothing costs could be cut to £2.5.[57] This figure, 40 percent below Main's estimate, can be used to compute the

---

[51] The £5.60 figure is the product of the 1762 average price per cord, 22.92s., and the estimated 4.88 cords burned per year. An artisan in Charleston, S.C., thought firewood cost him £3 sterling each year or £5 Pennsylvania currency, and winters are much milder in Charleston than in Philadelphia. Main, *Social Structure*, 118.

[52] Mease, *Picture of Philadelphia*, 125-126; Bridenbaugh, *Cities in Revolt*, 27, 235.

[53] Bridenbaugh, *Cities in Revolt*, 27, 235, and *Rebels and Gentlemen*, 235.

[54] Gertrude MacKinney, ed., *Votes and Proceedings of the House of Representatives of the Province of Pennsylvania* (Samuel Hazard et al., eds., Pa. Archs., 8th Ser.), VI, 5451, 6345; *Pa. Gaz.*, July 14, 1763; Main, *Social Structure*, 116.

[55] Ledger of Graisbury; Matron and Steward's Cash Books, Pa. Hosp. Recs.

[56] Clothing Issues Ledger, 1805-1831, Guardians of the Poor, City Archs.

[57] Spinning the yarn and weaving the cloth domestically might save a bit more money, but this would have been difficult for many poorer households because of the considerable time and skill required, as well as the substantial investment. A spinning wheel cost £1, or about four day's wages for a laborer, in 1788 (Matron and Steward's Cash Books, Pa. Hosp. Recs.).

clothing costs for a laboring family. The price of women's dress probably matched that of men's, while cordwainers' and tailors' records indicate that children's shoes, breeches, and coats cost about 70 percent of those of men.[58] Thus in 1770 a laboring family of four would have spent roughly £8.5 for clothing. Prices for basic articles of clothing other than shoes are unavailable for the entire period, but an index constructed from the cost of materials—thread, flax, tow, flannel, and linen—for certain articles of apparel (stockings, breeches, shirts, and coats) can serve as a proxy for the changes in the cost of clothing.[59] This index, combined with the price index of shoes and each index weighted according to its proportion of the 1770 clothing budget estimate given above, provides a clothing-price index (Table II, column 4) graphed in Figure I.

333

The family budget for laborers, mariners, cordwainers, and tailors constructed from calculations of the price of food, rent, fuel, and clothing averaged £60.82 in 1762.[60] The costs of the items in this budget are below other observed costs and estimates made by other historians. Not only is the budget thus minimized, but many necessities for a "decent competency" are excluded. Rum, apparently a vital element of the lives of eighteenth-century Americans,[61] may have cost laboring Philadelphians £3 annually but has not been included in the household budget. Taxes likewise are excluded; they amounted to £2-3 per year for poorer Philadelphians at the end of the colonial period.[62] Although the Pennsylvania Hospital provided low-cost services, medical treatment was expensive. Smallpox variolation cost £3, not including wages lost during the required quarantine period of one or two weeks, and the inoculation had to be renewed every four or five years.[63] Death imposed a financial burden; in the early 1760s interment in private cemeteries could cost as much as £11.[64] Child-bearing also was dear: midwives charged about 15s. before the Revolutionary War.[65] All of these necessities, along with soap, starch,

[58] Ledger of Graisbury. Main estimates that the cost to clothe a child ran about 80% of the expense of outfitting an adult, or about £3.33 (Pa. currency) annually during this period (Social Structure, 116).

[59] Prices of these articles are from the Matron and Steward's Cash Books, Pa. Hosp. Recs. Unfortunately, these records are incomplete and do not contain any data on clothing costs from 1756 through 1761.

[60] In 1762, food, fuel, and clothing cost £30.66, £5.60, and £9.66, respectively. Laborers, mariners, cordwainers, and tailors paid rent of £9, £10.58, £19.63, and £20.37, respectively, or an average of £14.90 for the four groups.

[61] W. J. Rorabaugh, The Alcoholic Republic: An American Tradition (New York, 1979), 7-11.

[62] Nash, "Up From the Bottom," Past and Present, No. 77 (Nov., 1977), 76.

[63] George W. Norris, The Early History of Medicine in Philadelphia (Philadelphia, 1886), 112.

[64] Norris Stanley Barratt, Outline of the History of Old St. Paul's Church, Philadelphia, Pennsylvania (Philadelphia, 1917), 43.

[65] Matron and Steward's Cash Books, Pa. Hosp. Recs.

candles, chamber pots, brooms, cutlery, and furniture, have been excluded from the estimated budget.

The index of the average household budget of the four occupational groups, which measures the relative cost of purchasing the 1762 budget in nearly every year from 1754 to 1800, appears in Table II, column 5, and is graphed in Figure II.[66] The cost of this budget increased sharply toward the end of the French and Indian War, fell precipitously in 1765 to its prewar level, and rose gradually during the following decade. The significant jump in 1776 marked the beginning of the exorbitant inflation during the Revolutionary War. The index plummeted from 1783 to 1789, then climbed rapidly to a peak more than twice as high as in the 1770s.

334

Laborers, mariners, cordwainers, tailors, and their families frequently found it hard to earn enough money to meet their basic expenses. Relatively low wages (compared to the cost of living) and irregular employment made life unpredictable for laboring people and undercut their attempts to achieve more than a minimal degree of physical well-being or economic security. The following section compares the wages and incomes of the four groups with the cost of their household budget and considers the factors responsible for their struggle to maintain their subsistence.

Contradicting Carl Bridenbaugh's contention that "few day laborers . . . were to be found in any [colonial] city," Philadelphia's tax lists reveal that laborers formed the second largest occupational group in the city, their number exceeded only by mariners.[67] Laborers composed between 5 and 14 percent of taxpayers during the second half of the century. Their proportion of the working population undoubtedly was greater than this percentage, however, because many poorer citizens were excused from paying taxes and many taxpayers with undesignated occupations probably were unskilled. Laborers were concentrated at the very bottom of the tax hierarchy: in 1772, assessors appraised nine of every ten laborers at the

[66] Except for the years 1754 through 1761, the annual costs of food, rent, fuel, and clothing are summed for each year and divided by the estimated 1762 budget to compute the index of household budgets. Because of limitations in the data, the household-budget index for 1754 and 1755 is calculated by dividing the total expenditure for food, fuel, and clothing in those years by the total cost of these items in 1762. Similarly, the index for 1756 through 1761 is constructed by dividing the outlay for food, fuel, and rent in those years by the total price of these items in 1762. Rent and clothing accounted respectively for 25 and 14% of the total 1762 household budget. Unless the cost of those two items fluctuated very significantly during the few years for which data are not extant—and there is no reason to believe that they did—the household-budget index for 1754-1761 should accurately reflect variations in the cost of the budget.

[67] Bridenbaugh, *Cities in Revolt*, 148. The proportion of the taxpayers who were laborers is from my analysis of the tax lists cited in n. 14.

FIGURE II

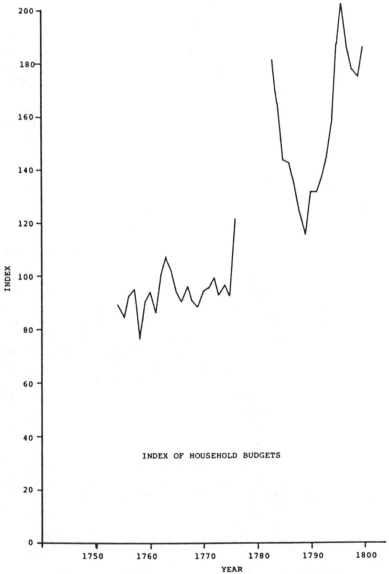

INDEX OF HOUSEHOLD BUDGETS

335

minimum rate. Many worked in construction or shipbuilding, or hauled goods to and from ships, warehouses, and stores; others found jobs in breweries and distilleries or as street pavers, hay mowers, potato diggers, dung spreaders, whitewashers, swamp drainers, sawyers, chimney sweeps, and the like.

Using data on laborers' earnings contained in the ledgers of the Pennsylvania Hospital, government records, and a host of private business accounts, I have constructed an index of laborers' actual wages, and I have used the household budget index as an inflationary scale to produce an index of laborers' real wages (Table III).[68] Real wages peaked during the French and Indian War (see Figure III), plunged during the last two years *336* of that conflict, rose during the mid-1760s, and then declined steadily during the last decade before the Revolutionary War. Although they fluctuated, real wages in the 1780s approximated those of the 1770s and began to rise during the final decade of the century.

If employed for six days each week throughout the year, a laborer would have earned £59.3 in 1762, the base year of the wage indices. Because this hypothetical annual income assumes full employment, however, it must be considered a high figure, rarely if ever attained. The supply of jobs depended on a variety of factors, among them the cycles of nature that affected activity in the city nearly as much as on the farm. Severe winter weather halted maritime commerce, shipbuilding, and housing construction. Ice in the Delaware River, as well as the seasonal shipment of agricultural produce, caused ship arrivals during January and February to average less than a third their usual number for the rest of the year.[69] Jobs for outdoor workers declined correspondingly. Newspaper and broadside commentators characterized winter as a season when the city had "little occasion . . . for the labour of the Poor," and when "for want of Employment, many . . . are reduced to great Straits and rendered burthensome to their neighbors."[70] Thus when laborer James Thompson for "want of work" entered the almshouse in January 1789, he joined many laboring Philadelphians in similar circumstances who annually swelled the ranks of

[68] Only laborers performing unskilled tasks and receiving wages "not found" (not supplied board) are considered. Hardly any short-term laborers were supplied board. The indices of all real wages in this article are calculated by solving the following equation for each year:

$$I_R = I_W/I_H$$

where I_R = index of real wages, I_W = index of actual wages, and I_H = index of household budget.

[69] This is based on ship arrivals in 1756, 1759, and 1762, reported weekly in the *Pa. Gaz.* during these years.

[70] *Pa. Packet*, Dec. 12, 1787; *Whereas the Number of Poor In and around this City . . .* [Philadelphia, 1764], broadside, Evans no. 9870, as quoted in Alexander, *Render Them Submissive*, 14-15.

TABLE III
INDICES OF LABORERS' WAGES
(BASE YEAR = 1762)

Year	Laborers' Actual Wages	Laborers' Real Wages	Number of Observations	Sources
1751	92		6	a
1752	90		11	a
1753	89		15	a
1754	86	97	18	a, i
1755	85	101	28	a, b, c
1756	92	100	11	a
1757	92	97	1	c
1758	90	118	13	b, c
1759	92	102	7	b, d
1760	118	126	34	b, e, m, p, t
1761	116	135	3	r, v
1762	100	100	17	b, c, k, p, w
1763	90	84	18	b, h, p, y
1764	86	84	12	b, c, f, m, x
1765	92	98	3	b, c, k
1766	105	117	6	b, f, k
1767	105	109	10	b, f, k
1768	101	112	11	f, k, m, s
1769	84	95	14	b, c, j, m
1770	89	95	35	b, m, n, q
1771	87	92	12	b, n
1772	82	83	5	b, z
1773	68	74	12	b, n, o, z
1774	79	82	13	b, m
1775	74	80	13	b
1776	93	77	8	b, m
1783	125	69	9	b, x
1784	110	67	22	b, u, x, z[1]
1785	126	88	57	b, l, n, u, x, z[1]
1786	120	84	16	b, u, x
1787	104	78	29	b, u, x, z[1]
1788	117	95	15	b, u
1789	88	77	17	b, m, x, z[1]
1790	86	66	14	b, l, z[1]
1791	97	74	25	b, g, z[1]
1792	119	88	15	b, z[1]
1793	117	81	11	b, n, z[1]
1794	143	90	28	b, z[1]
1795	174	94	12	b, l, z[1]
1796	170	85	12	b, z[1]
1797	178	96	2	b, z[1]
1798	197	112	9	b, z[1]
1799	197	113	11	b, z[1]
1800	162	88	10	b, l, z[1]

NOTES TO TABLE III

The location for all sources below is the Historical Society of Pennsylvania, Philadelphia, unless otherwise noted.

a. Bills and receipts, Coates and Reynell Papers, Boxes 1751-1754 and 1755-1767.

b. Matron and Steward's Cash Books, Pennsylvania Hospital Records, American Philosophical Society, Philadelphia.

c. Minutes of the County Commissioners.

d. Ledger of Isaac Zane, 1748-1759.

e. Clifford Papers, Correspondence, II, 1760-1762.

f. Account Book, Folder: Brigantine *Elizabeth* Accounts, Richard Waln Collection.

g. Dutilh and Wachsmuth Papers, Miscellaneous Box 1704-1800, folder 32.

h. Isaac Norris Cash Book.

i. The accounts of building the addition to the statehouse in the early 1750s are in the Norris Fairhill Papers.

j. Minutes of the Friendship Carpenter's Company, 1768-1776.

k. Minutes of the Commissioners for Paving Streets.

l. U.S. Department of Labor, "Wages and Hours of Labor," *Bulletin of the United States Bureau of Labor Statistics*, CXXVIII (Washington, D.C., 1913), 21.

m. Bill, receipts, and accounts, Shippen Family Papers, XXVIII-XXX.

n. Cadwalader Collection, Incoming Correspondence, bills and receipts, Boxes 1-6, 12-14.

o. Ledgers of Joshua Humphreys, 1766-1777, 1772-1773, 1784-1805, Joshua Humphreys Papers.

p. Ledger of Mifflin and Massey, 1760-1763.

q. Journal of John and Peter Chevalier.

r. Ledger of Joseph Wharton, Wharton Papers.

s. Business Papers of Levy Hollingsworth, Hollingsworth Collection, Sec. VII: bills 1751-1789, Sec. III: invoices, 1764-1789.

t. Samuel Morris Day Book, 1755-1767, and Ledgers, 1755-1772, 1761-1763.

u. Thomas A. Biddle Shipbook.

v. Forde and Reed Papers.

w. Account of Richard Meadow, Ball Papers.

x. Business Records of Stephen Girard, American Philosophical Society, Philadelphia.

y. Philip Benezet's Account with Sloop *Sally*, Dreer Collection.

z. *Minutes of the Supreme Executive Council of Pennsylvania: Colonial Records of Pennsylvania* (Harrisburg, Pa., 1852).

z¹. Donald R. Adams, Jr. "Wage Rates in Philadelphia, 1790-1830" (Ph.D. diss., University of Pennsylvania, 1967).

---

the institutional poor during the winter months.[71] Cyclical variations in the cost of living corresponded to the seasonality of employment. During the winter, firewood prices often doubled or tripled, and the variety of foodstuffs available in the markets narrowed, restricting the options of the lower sort in limiting their food budgets. "Winter is fast approaching," wrote John Edgworth, a laborer, "whose dire effects the very Rich and oppulent will feel, much more [the] poor."[72] Another Philadelphian noted

[71] Daily Occurrences Docket, Jan. 20.

[72] Records of Pennsylvania's Revolutionary Governments, Clemency File, 1775-1790, RG 27, roll 38, frame 642, Pennsylvania State Archives, Harrisburg, hereafter cited as Recs. of Pa.'s Revolutionary Governments.

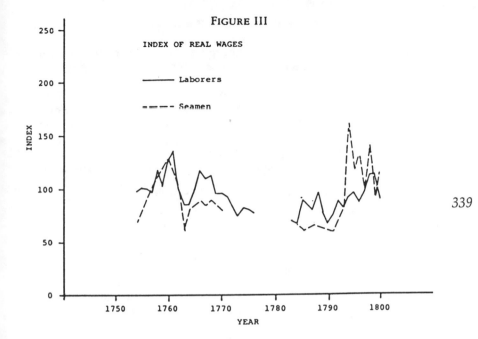

FIGURE III

INDEX OF REAL WAGES

——— Laborers

– – – Seamen

339

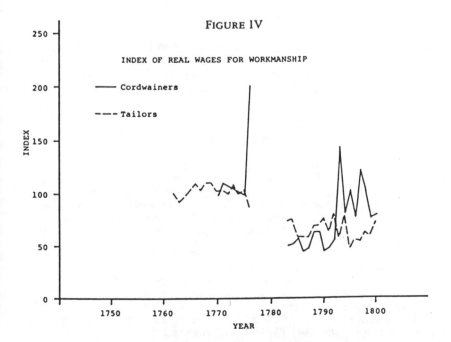

FIGURE IV

INDEX OF REAL WAGES FOR WORKMANSHIP

——— Cordwainers

– – – Tailors

that "collections (time immemorial) have been made every winter, either by means of charity sermons among the different sects, or private subscriptions, for the poor."[73]

Epidemics, illness, and injury also limited the regularity of work. Recurrent smallpox and yellow fever epidemics caused mass evacuations of the city, so that laboring people who, in the words of one observer, "have neither place to remove to, or funds for their support," were left without work for long periods until panic subsided.[74] It is sadly ironic that during the 1790s, just as laborers' wages increased, their earning capacity was badly disrupted by the serious epidemics of that decade. Philadelphians who worked outdoors were peculiarly susceptible to such ailments as rheumatism and frostbite, and to on-the-job injuries. And, as a contributor to the *Pennsylvania Journal* observed, "a labouring man, who has a wife and children, if he falls into sickness . . . falls into distress."[75] Thus laborer Eneos Lyon, injured while sinking a pump and rendered "incapable of labouring for a livelyhood," had little choice but to enter the almshouse. When mariner Thomas Loudon was admitted, the almshouse clerk noted that he suffered from the "casualties, and accidents in his Way of life, and the vicissitudes of fortune to which such men are liable seems now to manifest itself."[76]

Cyclical variations in the city's economy also influenced the amount of work available to unskilled workers. Two examples will suffice. Economic dislocations following the French and Indian War curtailed employment opportunities for many poor citizens. In 1764 city leaders complained about the "want of Employment, which was reducing a large number of residents to great Straits."[77] Two years later, Philadelphia's grand jury admitted that many "labouring People & others in low Circumstances . . . who are Willing to work cannot obtain sufficient Employment."[78] During the 1790s, on the other hand, Philadelphia's rapidly expanding maritime commerce brought a high demand for the services of laborers and mariners.[79]

[73] *Indep. Gaz.*, Dec. 12, 1785, as quoted in Alexander, *Render Them Submissive*, 16.

[74] "A Useful Hint," *Mercury Daily Advertiser* (Phila.), Aug. 19, 1797, as quoted in Alexander, *Render Them Submissive*, 130. During the last half of Oct. 1793, at the peak of a yellow fever epidemic, 1/4 of the families in the city received money, provisions, and firewood distributed at City Hall. Many Philadelphians were reduced to begging their daily bread from bakers. "Money, Provisions, and Firewood," *Federal Gazette and Philadelphia Daily Advertiser*, Nov. 2, 1793, and "Loaf Bread Baker," *ibid.*, Nov. 6, 1793.

[75] *Pennsylvania Journal and Weekly Advertiser* (Phila.), Sept. 27, 1786, as quoted in Alexander, *Render Them Submissive*, 12.

[76] Daily Occurrences Docket, Apr. 29, Nov. 17, 1800.

[77] *Whereas the Number of Poor*, Evans no. 9870.

[78] *Votes of Assembly*, VII, 5830.

[79] For a detailed analysis of Philadelphia's economic cycles see Smith, "The 'Lower Sort' in Revolutionary Philadelphia," chap. 5.

A comparison of incomes and household budgets discloses the nature of the struggle to make ends meet. In 1762, a laborer would have spent about £55 for food, rent, fuel, and clothing for himself and his family. If fully employed, his total annual wages of nearly £60 met these basic expenses. If he were partially employed (a more reasonable assumption) for five out of every six work days, or ten of every twelve months, his income fell £6 shy of these necessities. Other members of his family therefore had to work to secure its subsistence. For example, Rachael, the wife of weaver James Brown, made rifle cartridges and soliders' clothing during the Revolutionary War to earn needed money.[80] After the war, laborer Samuel Cryndal found that in addition to "what little he Earned . . . his wife's Industry" was essential for his family to make "out a living although a very Poor one."[81] Women toiled for the Pennsylvania Hospital as nurses, clothes washers, chimney sweeps, potato diggers, cooks, maids, whitewashers, soap makers, and bakers, and in wealthier homes as servants. The range of money-making activities for children was more limited. They gathered twigs to sell for firewood, tended cattle, and carried dairy produce from the countryside. Children in poorer households undoubtedly were often apprenticed at a young age because of the financial burden they posed.

341

Limited evidence suggests that women received roughly one-half the wages of men, and children somewhat less than that.[82] A working woman in 1762 thus might have contributed an additional £25 to the household. This would have covered the deficit for the four necessities and the extra expenses of taxes, medical bills, candles, soap, and other miscellaneous items, while perhaps even providing a few luxuries such as rum, tobacco, or "sweet meats." This degree of comfort was most likely to have been achieved when the index of real wages was one hundred or greater, as during the French and Indian War, the mid-1760s, and the late 1790s.

Much more prevalent was a situation in which the income of a family barely matched the cost of basic necessities. This condition characterized the postwar depression of 1762-1765 and most of the 1770s, 1780s, and early 1790s, when real wages fluctuated 20-25 percent below their 1762 level and posed severe economic problems for laborers and their families. At the partial level of employment assumed above, a laborer's earnings would have averaged £14 below the cost of essentials. The combined income of husband and wife would barely have covered food, fuel, rent, and

[80] Petitions for Revolutionary War Pensions, W15879, Nat'l Archs.

[81] Recs. of Pa.'s Revolutionary Governments, roll 37, frames 1242-1243.

[82] Women employed by the Pennsylvania Hospital earned about half the wages paid men even when performing the same jobs. This also appears a common wage proportion between the sexes in the 19th century. See Edith Abbot, *Women in Industry: A Study in American Economic History* (New York, 1910), 262-316.

clothing, and the few remaining pounds could not have met additional expenses, much less permit savings or minor luxuries.[83]

Unskilled workers and their families in Philadelphia generally lived on the edge of, or occasionally slightly above, the subsistence level; simply to maintain that level both spouses had to work. Life was hard at the best of times and disastrous at the worst. Consequently, institutional aid to the poor rose to unprecedented levels during the second half of the century.[84] When Hugh Porter's rheumatism became inflamed, Lenoard (*sic*) Croneman broke his thigh, and John Drew suffered frostbitten feet, they joined hundreds of laborers who depended on public or private assistance for fuel, clothing, and food.[85] Others, like laborer Samuel Cryndal, were forced to more drastic measures; his financial problems during the post-Revolutionary depression "obliged him to bind his Eldest child out, tho very young," because Cryndal could not support the boy.[86]

A detailed examination of the causes of variations in real wages and material conditions is beyond the scope of this study, but some tentative explanations can be offered. The supply of unskilled laborers and the demand for their services determined their economic condition. Migration patterns influenced the size of the labor pool, while fluctuations in the city's economy, particularly in maritime commerce, housing construction, and shipbuilding—the areas in which most unskilled workers were employed—defined the demand side of the economic equation. During the quarter century preceding the Revolutionary War, Philadelphia's population, augmented by heavy European immigration, grew faster than these three sectors of its economy. Between 1756 and 1774, laborers increased from 5 to 14 percent of the taxable work-force. Simultaneously, when the volume of the three economic sectors is measured on a per capita basis—the best available indicator of the relative numbers of jobs in these areas—one finds that Philadelphia's maritime commerce remained stagnant, housing construction grew only slightly, and shipbuilding declined. This ac-

342

[83] In 1774, the cost of the four basic necessities was £52.72, while a laborer, employed at 83% of full capacity, and his wife might earn £58.30. The resulting per capita estimated income of £8.74 sterling for a laborer's family of four agrees with the calculations of other historians. David Klingaman computes the per capita income in Philadelphia in about 1770 at between £6.5 and £9 sterling ("Food Surpluses and Deficits," *Jour. Econ. Hist.*, XXXI [1971], 569). Alice Hanson Jones figures a range of £8.4 to £14 sterling per capita income in the American colonies in 1774 ("Wealth Estimates," *Econ. Development and Cultural Change*, XVIII, Pt. II [1970], 128, Table 51).

[84] Nash, "Poverty and Poor Relief," *WMQ*, 3d Ser., XXXIII (1976), 3-30; George W. Geib, "A History of Philadelphia, 1776-1789" (Ph.D. diss., University of Wisconsin, 1969), 203-205.

[85] Daily Occurrences Docket, Mar. 1, June 2, 1800, June 22, 1801.

[86] Recs. of Pa.'s Revolutionary Governments, roll 37, frames 1242-1243.

counts for much of the gradual decrease in laborers' real wages before the Revolutionary War.[87]

After booming briefly at the close of the war, the city's shipbuilding and maritime commerce slumped during the 1780s, and the housing industry remained dormant throughout the decade. The real wages of laborers, who composed a constant 7 percent of the taxable work-force, were correspondingly depressed until the early 1790s. Better times returned with the outbreak of hostilities between France and England in 1793. Philadelphia's neutral carrying and re-export trades flourished, and this commercial expansion underlay much of the vigorous shipbuilding and housing construction during the decade. As laborers declined from 7 percent of the work-force in 1789 to 5 percent in 1798, their real wages and material conditions improved.

343

Mariners composed the largest occupational group in the city during the late eighteenth century, accounting for as much as 20 percent of the free male work-force on the eve of the Revolutionary War. They numbered only about 5 percent of taxpayers, for their mobility and poverty excluded the vast majority of them from the tax rolls.[88] Only 164 seamen appear on the 1772 tax list, for example, but other sources indicate a much greater number of sailors in the city. During the 1770s, about two hundred ship captains belonged to Philadelphia's Society for the Relief of Poor and Distressed Masters of Ships, Their Widows and Children.[89] Since vessels averaged approximately six crew members, the city probably contained roughly 1,200 merchant seamen in the early years of the decade. Between July 1, 1770, and July 1, 1771, custom officials collected a tax of 71,164 pence from Philadelphia sailors at the rate of sixpence for each month they drew wages.[90] This suggests a total of 1,186 seamen in the city, assuming each mariner worked ten months during the year, and a larger number if they worked less than that. Corroborating this estimate is a remark by the customs house officer in 1770 that "there are not less than a thousand Seamen here at this time."[91]

Most sailors were concentrated at the bottom of the economic ladder of freemen; tax collectors assessed 70 percent of them the minimum tax in

[87] This and the following paragraph are based on an analysis of the city's economy in Smith, "The 'Lower Sort' in Revolutionary Philadelphia," chap. 5.

[88] The county commissioners recorded the names of citizens too poor to pay taxes. Three volumes of their minutes, from 1718 to 1766 are in the City Archs. Another volume, from 1771 to 1774, is at Hist. Soc. Pa., and a final volume, from 1774 to 1776, is in the Tax and Exoneration Records, Pa. St. Archs.

[89] Quarterly Payments, 1768-1776, Hist. Soc. Pa.

[90] By an act of Parliament in 1696, this tax, which supported the Greenwich Hospital for disabled seamen, was assessed on every sailor who served on a ship owned by a citizen of the British Empire. The collections from Philadelphia mariners during 1770-1771 are recorded in the Customs House Papers, XI, 1409, Hist. Soc. Pa.

[91] *Ibid.*, X, n.p.

1772. A sizable majority of Philadelphia mariners spent a considerable portion of their lives as common seamen, forming a kind of deep-sea proletariat. Some of the rest came from farms near the city and served only briefly before the mast, while others occasionally signed on for short voyages and worked in less-skilled jobs when ashore. Most mariners were men with few skills, lured to the sea neither by a sense of adventure nor by hopes for advancement, but by the opportunity for employment.[92]

From mariners' wage rates recorded by merchants engaged in the overseas trade, I have constructed indices of the actual wages of seamen, mates, and captains, and, deflating by the household budget, an index of seamen's real wages (Table IV).[93] In 1762, common seamen earned an average of £4.1 per month, and mates £5.4.[94] The maximum annual income of seamen, £49, fell short of the cost of the four basic necessities and also of the maximum earnings of day laborers. Longer periods of continual employment and the food and lodging supplied sailors on board ship somewhat offset this difference. As with laborers, however, periodic unemployment prevented seamen from earning the maximum income. Job opportunities varied seasonally; mariners paid only 12 percent of their taxes during the winter months. More important was the turn-around time of ships in port, on the order of thirty-six days in Philadelphia at mid-century.[95] In foreign ports sailors filled part of that slack period unloading and stowing cargo. In Philadelphia, however, in the words of an Admiralty Court judge, "merchants find it more for their interest . . . to hire other

344

[92] This paragraph is based on an analysis of several hundred seamen in the Ship's Crew Lists and the Seamen's Protective Certificate Applications, Records of the Bureau of Customs, RG 36, Nat'l Archs., and the Maritime Records of the Port of Philadelphia, 1789-1860, Library of Congress. Samuel Eliot Morison mistakenly characterizes most seamen as young, adventure-seeking boys attracted by the romance of the sea and kept there by hopes of promotion or rum (*The Maritime History of Massachusetts, 1783-1860* [Boston, 1921], 106).

[93] Bus. Papers, Boxes 1751-1754, 1765-1767, Coates and Reynell Papers; Clifford Papers, Correspondence, II, 1760-1762; Account Book, Folder: Brigantine *Elizabeth* Accounts, Richard Waln Collection; Ships and Shipping Folder, Etting Papers; Customs House Papers; Dutilh and Wachsmuth Papers, Miscellaneous Boxes 1726-1856 and 1704-1800; Thomas Mason's Journal, 1775, Misc. Letters of Thomas and John Mason, Henry Pleasant's Papers; Jour. of John and Peter Chevalier; Philip Benezet's Account with Sloop *Sally*, Dreer Collection; Claude W. Unger Collection; Boats and Cargoes, Society Misc. Collection; Biddle Shipbook, 1784-1792—all at Hist. Soc. Pa. Business Records of Stephen Girard, Am. Phil. Soc. Donald R. Adams, Jr., "Wage Rates in Philadelphia, 1790-1830" (Ph.D. diss., University of Pennsylvania, 1967), 213.

[94] These figures do not include the privilege of carrying their own freight aboard ship to sell in their home port, but this was more often reserved for captains than for the entire crew.

[95] James F. Shepherd and Gary M. Walton, *Shipping, Maritime Trade, and the Economic Development of Colonial North America* (Cambridge, 1972), 198.

TABLE IV
INDICES OF MARINERS' WAGES
(BASE YEAR = 1762)

Year	Seamen's Actual Wages	Seamen's Real Wages	Mates' Actual Wages	Captains' Actual Wages
1750	73		79	80
1751	72		79	80
1752	69		78	80
1753	65		79	80
1754	61	69	74	80
1755	67	80	74	80
1756	85	92	84	80
1757	98	103		107
1759	109	121		107
1760	121	129	130	
1762	100	100	100	100
1763	67	63	93	107
1764	83	81	91	93
1765	79	84	93	93
1766	79	88	93	93
1767	82	85	93	93
1768	81	90	93	93
1770	76	81	86	93
1772				93
1784	109	66	139	160
1785	82	57	130	133
1786	82	58	112	107
1787	80	60	93	107
1789				100
1790	77	59	93	120
1791	77	59	93	120
1792	95	70	95	113
1793	121	84	125	120
1794	255	161		
1795	218	117	216	
1796	264	131	209	180
1797	182	98	233	250
1798	246	140	223	250
1799	155	89	265	250
1800	209	113	233	250

Coates and Reynell Papers, Boxes 1751-1754; Clifford Papers, Correspondence, II, 1760-1762; Account Bk., Folder: Brigantine *Elizabeth* Accounts, Richard Waln Coll.; Ships and Shipping Folder, Etting Papers; Customs House Papers; Dutilh and Wachsmuth Papers, Misc. Boxes 1726-1856 and 1704-1800; Thomas Mason's Journal, 1775, Misc. Letters of Thomas and John Mason, Henry Pleasant's Papers; Jour. of John and Peter Chevalier; Philip Benezet's Account with Sloop *Sally*, Dreer Coll.; Biddle Shipbook, 1784-1792—all at Hist. Soc. Pa.; Bus. Recs. of Girard, Am. Phil. Soc.; Adams, "Wage Rates in Philadelphia," 213.

than the mariners to lade and unlade vessels" because it was cheaper to employ stevedores by the day than to pay the crew monthly wages and supply them with provisions.[96]

Living on the edge of subsistence, merchant seamen with families faced many of the same economic problems as did laborers. When John Machman was unable to get a berth on a ship during winter, when John Quail suffered from rheumatism and venereal disease, when James Union came down with a fever, they landed in the almshouse, and their families suffered. Mary Lewis and Mary Winger, wives of sailors on the frigate *City of Philadelphia* in 1800, ended up in the almshouse when unable to support themselves, the former because she was pregnant and the latter because she was ill. Even mariners' wives who had jobs struggled to provide for themselves and their children. When a constable picked up eight-year-old William Thomas for begging in the street, the boy explained that while his father "has been gone to sea" his mother "goes out washing of Cloaths for a livelihood ... [and] leaves him at home to take care of his Brother." When his brother cried from hunger, William went soliciting bread.[97]

346

The pay of mariners responded to fluctuations in the city's economy in much the same fashion as did that of laborers. The demand for sailors, and the significant role that war played in shaping that demand, were key factors determining their material comfort. Their wages were abnormally high during the French and Indian War, partly because privateering attracted many men who hoped to strike it rich and left few able seamen in the city.[98] As shipping activity slackened during the early 1760s and again in the 1780s, so did mariners' wages. The boom in the export and re-export trades during the 1790s raised seamen's wages after 1793.

Cordwainers and tailors formed the two largest groups of artisans, each accounting for about 5.6 percent of the taxable work-force during the second half of the century. Although cordwainers were scattered throughout the tax structure except at the very top, most found a place near the bottom of the economic scale. Forty percent were assessed the minimum tax in 1772.

More than 250 bills for shoes contained in the Pennsylvania Hospital records and merchants' papers permit construction of individual price se-

[96] *Admiralty Decisions in the District Court of the United States, for the Pennsylvania District, by the Hon. Richard Peters* ... (Philadelphia, 1807), I, 255, II, 413. The practice of hiring men other than mariners to stow and unload the cargo seems to have been common in pre-Revolutionary Philadelphia as well. See Bus. Papers, Box 1755-1767, Coates and Reynell Papers, Hist. Soc. Pa.

[97] Daily Occurrences Docket, Feb. 6, 1790, Jan. 18, 1793, Mar. 17, Apr. 7, May 22, 1800, Aug. 29, 1801.

[98] Included in the wills recorded in Philadelphia between 1755 and 1760 are those of many lower-class men who were going to sea on privateers (Will Book K [1752-1757], Will Book L [1757-1760], Register of Wills, City Hall Annex, Philadelphia). See also Virginia D. Harrington, *New York Merchants on the Eve of the Revolution* (New York, 1935), 303-307.

ries for a variety of shoes. Price relatives of each of these have been weighted equally to produce a retail price index for shoes (Table V, column 1).[99] This index does not accurately indicate cordwainers' wages since the costs of raw materials and labor are included in the price of shoes. However, this retail price index and a price index of raw materials can be employed to create an index of cordwainers' wages. According to a broadside issued during the Revolutionary War, the cost of raw materials in 1774 averaged 57 percent and labor 43 percent of the retail price of shoes.[100] The Philadelphia wholesale price index of leather, hides, and sole leather developed by Anne Bezanson represents the cost of raw materials for shoes (Table V, column 2).[101] Using the actual price of raw materials in 1774, Bezanson's wholesale price index, and the retail price index of shoes computed above, I have calculated an index of cordwainers' wages for their labor (Table V, column 3) and, adjusting for the cost of the household budget, an index of their real wages (Table V, column 4).[102]

347

Except for a large increase reflecting the rapid inflation of late 1776, cordwainers' actual and real wages remained stable during the years immediately preceding Independence (see Figure IV). Real wages were markedly lower in 1783 than before the war and continued at about the same level until the early 1790s. They more than doubled in 1793 and remained relatively high for much of the rest of the period.

Though evidence is sparse, a few available sources permit rough approximations of the earnings of cordwainers. Their incomes can be estimated from information contained in their 1779 broadside and in the labor conspiracy trial of Philadelphia journeymen shoemakers in 1806. The broadside indicates that in 1774 a master cordwainer received 4s. 9d. for the craftmanship involved in each pair of shoes.[103] Journeymen testified at the

---

[99] Price series for slippers, "channel pumps," "dress shoes," and "ordinary" shoes for adult males, as well as for "Negroes shoes," boys' shoes and cobbling charges for "soaling" and "heel-taping," are constructed from bills, receipts, and accounts, Shippen Fam. Papers, XXVIII-XXX, 1754-1822, and bills and receipts, Coates and Reynell Papers, Hist. Soc. Pa.; Matron and Steward's Cash Books, Pa. Hosp. Recs.

[100] To the Inhabitants of Pennsylvania . . . (Philadelphia, 1779), broadside, Hist. Soc. Pa.

[101] Bezanson et al., Prices and Inflation, 332-342; Bezanson, Gray, and Hussey, Wholesale Prices in Philadelphia, I, 385.

[102] The index of cordwainers' wages was calculated by solving the following equation for each year:

$$I_W = \frac{I_P - (.57) I_M}{.43}$$

where I_W = index of cordwainers' wages, I_P = retail price index of shoes, and I_M = price index of raw materials.

[103] To the Inhabitants, broadside, Hist. Soc. Pa.

TABLE V
INDICES OF SHOE COSTS AND CORDWAINERS' WAGES FOR WORKMANSHIP
(BASE YEAR = 1762)

	(1)	(2)	(3)	(4)
Year	Retail Prices of Shoes	Wholesale Prices of Raw Materials	Cordwainers' Actual Wages for Workmanship	Cordwainers' Real Wages for Workmanship
1762	100	100	100	100
1763	115			
1764	112			
1767	92			
1768	88			
1769	88			
1770	91	90	92	98
1771	96	90	104	109
1772	97	90	106	107
1774	96	96	96	100
1775	94	97	90	98
1776	181	133	243	201
1783	103	113	88	49
1784	100	110	86	52
1785	94	103	82	57
1786	91	113	62	44
1787	87	102	64	48
1788	89	99	77	63
1789	88	101	72	63
1790	89	113	58	44
1791	90	110	63	48
1792	91	107	75	55
1793	150	107	206	143
1794	115	110	122	77
1795	151	121	190	102
1796	117	93	149	74
1797	146	86	225	122
1798	136	103	178	101
1799	113	107	131	75
1800	124	108	144	78

348

Bills, receipts, and accounts, Shippen Fam. Papers, XXVIII-XXX, 1754-1822; bills and receipts, Coates and Reynell Papers, Hist. Soc. Pa.; Matron and Steward's Cash Books, Pa. Hosp. Recs.

trial that they produced about six pairs of common shoes per week.[104] A master thus might have earned 28.5s. weekly, or £74.1 in 1774, if fully employed. Masters collected an additional shilling on every pair made by their journeymen, so each journeyman might have contributed as much as £15.6 to his master's income in 1774.[105]

Master cordwainers enjoyed a relatively comfortable material position during most of the period. Food, rent, fuel, and clothing would have cost £62.9 in 1774. In that year a master, working without assistants, might have earned £74.1 if fully employed. Thus he would need to have been employed 85 percent of his possible working time to meet the cost of those four necessities. If he enjoyed the services of a journeyman or a few apprentices, the profits accrued from their labor would have covered his family's additional miscellaneous expenses. If he worked alone, however, earnings by his wife or children probably would have been required. Assuming that his wife could earn approximately one-half the income of a male laborer, her contribution of £19.4 would have helped to provide the four necessities and some minor luxuries, with perhaps a bit left over for savings. The relatively favorable circumstances of master cordwainers deteriorated after the Revolution. The combined incomes of husband and wife, even if both were employed fulltime, could not quite meet the cost of the four necessities.[106] Master cordwainers who hired journeymen, and the few who owned servants and slaves, were in the best position to survive the economic dislocations of the 1780s, but nearly all were forced to cut their living standards drastically until the early 1790s.

Journeymen cordwainers earned appreciably less than their masters. In 1774 they received 3s. 9d. for a pair of shoes, yielding £58.5 for a year of full employment. But, as they testified at their trial, work was seasonal, and winter was usually a slack period.[107] Although slightly better off than

349

[104] Job Harrison testified that in 1799 he earned about 48.75s. ($6.50) per week making shoes for 9s. each. At this rate, he must have produced 5.4 shoes in a week of work. Those shoes had linings and required slightly more time to make than common shoes, so the latter could probably be made at the rate of six shoes per week. Philadelphia's cordwainers frequently observed the holiday of "Saint Monday" in the alehouse, and thus probably averaged slightly more than one pair of common shoes per day. John R. Commons et al., eds., A Documentary History of American Industrial Society, III: Labor Conspiracy Cases, 1806-1842, Pt. I (Cleveland, Ohio, 1910), 63, 73-74, 83-84, 121-124, hereafter cited as Documentary History; Foner, Tom Paine, 36.

[105] In 1774 masters typically sold shoes for 11s., of which they paid 6s. 3d. in material costs and 3s. 9d. in journeymen's wages, leaving a profit of 1s. To the Inhabitants, broadside, Hist. Soc. Pa.

[106] The hard times of the 1780s are reflected in the "value" of cordwainers' occupations assessed by tax collectors in 1783 and 1789. In 1783, the occupations of 17.5% of cordwainers were assessed at £25 or less. By 1789, 40% of cordwainers were assessed that amount. Tax list 1783 and 1789, City Archs.

[107] Documentary History, III, Pt. I, 114, 123-124. Work also fluctuated annually. The shoe market in 1769, for instance, was said to be "much overdone," and few

common laborers, journeymen shoemakers were hard pressed to meet the £64.3 cost of basic necessities during the early 1770s. The depression of the 1780s severely affected their material condition, not only by driving wages down but by limiting the available work. Hugh Dugan, sent into the almshouse as a pauper in 1789, was one of many cordwainers forced to rely on public assistance.[108] Even during good times, journeymen made little money to spare. At their trial they declared that they earned 45s. per week, or £117 annually during the late 1790s.[109] But their estimated family budget during that period averaged £120 per year, so that their income barely matched the cost of the four necessities. As a result, a number of shoemakers, like John and Esther Dougherty and their three children, spent time in a relief institution.[110]

350

Shoemaking was organized on a small scale during the colonial period, and on the eve of the Revolution as many as half of Philadelphia's taxable cordwainers functioned as masters.[111] Few owned a shop; nearly all toiled at home, mainly on "bespoke work," that is, shoes made to order for local customers. Masters invested in few unfree laborers; 7 percent owned servants and only one possessed a slave in 1772, although some directed as many as three or four apprentices.[112] Through their organization of the Cordwainers Fire Company, which served as a guild, and their political activity, master cordwainers were able to control shoe prices and the wages of their journeymen and to maintain their profits at a fairly constant level before the Revolutionary War.[113] When England dumped shoes on the American market after the war, Philadelphia's cordwainers were hard hit: the profits of masters and wages of journeymen were alike depressed.

---

jobs were then available (Thomas Clifford to Edward and William Gravena, May 23, 1773, Thomas Clifford Letter Book, Clifford Papers, 1767-1773, Hist. Soc. Pa.).

[108] Daily Occurrences Docket, Feb. 18, 1789.

[109] Because many journeymen were forced to do "market work," which paid only half as much as "bespoke work," this probably was near a maximum. *Documentary History*, III, Pt. I, 73-74, 86.

[110] Daily Occurrences Docket, Aug. 23, 1800.

[111] While there are no records that indicate the total number of masters and journeymen during this period, several sources give clues to the proportion of each. By identifying as many masters and journeymen as possible, and then determining their common and distinguishing characteristics, an approximation of their numbers can be obtained. For a complete explanation of the methodology see Smith, "Living Standards of the 'Lower Sort,'" *Working Papers*, Reg. Econ. Research Center, II, 23, n. 103, and Thomas Smith, "Reconstructing Occupational Structures: The Case of Ambiguous Artisans," *Historical Methods Newsletter*, VIII (1975), 136-146.

[112] These figures are calculated from the tax list of 1772 and the Account of Servants and Apprentices Bound before John Gibson, Dec. 5, 1772, to May 21, 1773, Hist. Soc. Pa.

[113] Olton, *Artisans for Independence*, 21-22; minutes of the Cordwainers Fire Company, Hist. Soc. Pa.

Both groups consequently pushed for protective legislation for their products.

The rising demand for Philadelphia-made footwear, in conjunction with several national tariffs on shoes beginning in 1789, stimulated higher prices for shoes during the final decade of the century. Locally, the growth in the city's inhabitants, and thus their demand for shoes, outstripped the increase in the number of shoemakers. Between 1789 and 1798, the proportion of cordwainers in the taxable work-force declined from 7.5 to 5.2 percent. Simultaneously, protective tariffs enlarged the national market, and European wars created a greater international need for American shoes.[114] During the 1790s, the United States shifted from a net importer of eighty thousand pairs of shoes annually to a net exporter of fifty thousand pairs.[115] Masters and journeymen struggled with one another for the greater profits on their product, as each group formed its own organization to further its interests. Their conflict culminated in America's first labor conspiracy trial in 1806.[116]

351

Tailors and breeches-makers were the wealthiest of the four occupational groups considered in this article, but they still clustered near the bottom of the tax hierarchy. Assessors taxed 41 percent of them the minimum rate in 1772. But one-fourth of them, those who catered to the city's wealthy citizens, appeared in the top third of the tax structure. Tailors' bills scattered through merchants' papers and the Pennsylvania Hospital's records can be used to determine their earnings.[117] These bills distinguish the charge for labor from the cost of materials and are sufficiently detailed to permit construction of individual series of wages for making a number of articles of clothing.[118] Wage relatives for labor costs for sewing these articles have been weighted equally to create an index of tailors' wages (Table VI, column 1). When this index is adjusted by the household budget, an index of real wages results (Table VI, column 2).

[114] Olton, *Artisans for Independence*, 102-103; Blanche Evans Hazard, *The Organization of the Boot and Shoe Industry in Massachusetts before 1875* (Cambridge, Mass., 1921), 39-40.
[115] Adam Seybert, *Statistical Annals . . .* (New York, 1969 [orig. publ. 1818]), 94-95, 100-101, 108, 160-161, 162-163.
[116] For changes in shoemaking during this period see Hazard, *Organization of the Boot and Shoe Industry*, 24-45, and *Documentary History*, III, Pt. I, 19-58.
[117] Bills, receipts, and accounts, Shippen Fam. Papers, XXVIII-XXX, 1754-1822; bills and receipts of John Cadwalader, Cadwalader Coll.; bills and receipts, Coates and Reynell Papers; Bus. Papers of Hollingsworth, Hollingsworth Coll., Sec. VII: bills, 1751-1789; Sec. III: invoices, 1764-1789; Samuel Morris Day Book, 1755-1767; ledger of Graisbury—all at Hist. Soc. Pa.; Matron and Steward's Cash Books, Pa. Hosp. Recs.
[118] Individual series of wages for making each of the following articles of clothing have been constructed: cloth and "superfine" suits, cloth and silk breeches, cloth coats, damask and silk vests, Holland "draws," "ordinary" shirts and trousers, and "Negroes" cloth coats and breeches.

TABLE VI
INDICES OF TAILORS' WAGES FOR WORKMANSHIP
(BASE YEAR = 1762)

Year	(1) Tailors' Actual Wages	(2) Tailors' Real Wages
1762	100	100
1763	100	93
1764	99	97
1765	98	104
1766	98	109
1767	99	103
1768	99	110
1769	97	110
1770	97	103
1771	98	103
1772	98	99
1773	99	108
1774	96	100
1775	100	109
1776	104	86
1783	132	73
1784	124	76
1785	84	59
1786	82	58
1787	78	58
1788	84	68
1789	79	69
1790	100	76
1791	82	63
1792	109	80
1793	82	57
1794	123	78
1795	90	48
1796	112	56
1797	100	54
1798	110	62
1799	102	59
1800	134	72

352

Bills, receipts, and accounts, Shippen Fam. Papers, XXVIII-XXX, 1754-1822; bills and receipts of John Cadwalader, Cadwalader Coll.; bills and receipts, Coates and Reynell Papers; Bus. Papers of Hollingsworth, Hollingsworth Coll., Sec. VII: bills, 1751-1789, Sec. III: invoices, 1764-1789; Samuel Morris Day Book, 1755-1767; ledger of Graisbury—all at Hist. Soc. Pa.; Matron and Steward's Cash Books, Pa. Hosp. Recs.

Because the amount of available work fluctuated, the real wages of tailors do not translate exactly into their real incomes. But, as in the case of cordwainers, it is unlikely that wages varied inversely with demand for clothes. Real wages and real income should have been isomorphic, and changes in the former should be indicative of changes in the latter. Real wages varied little before the Revolutionary War (see Figure IV), perhaps reflecting the success of the Taylors Company of Philadelphia, formed in 1771 by masters in an attempt to standardize their pay.[119] This wealthiest of the four occupational groups was hard hit after the war as real wages fell 25-40 percent and remained at a low level during the 1790s.

Tailors' incomes and living standards can be roughly approximated from the few available sources. Naturally, a crucial determinant of a tailor's income was his status as either journeyman or master. Journeymen probably made up 40 or 50 percent of the tailors in the city during the second half of the century.[120] The master tailors of the Taylors Company limited journeymen to a maximum of 4s. per day, which, assuming full employment, would have yielded £62.4 annually during the years immediately preceding the Revolutionary War.[121] Journeymen tailors thus had to work fulltime at maximum wages to earn the £63 cost of essentials, but their work, like that of cordwainers, varied seasonally.[122] During the two decades following the war, their economic condition deteriorated seriously.

An appraisal of the income of master tailors is more difficult. The ledger of Joseph Graisbury records his average income from 1765 to 1769 at £182 per year, but he was one of the wealthiest tailors in the city.[123] His tax rate in 1767 exceeded the median tailor's assessment nearly fourfold, and he was even more exceptional in owning both his home and a slave. The majority of master tailors must have earned considerably less than Graisbury though still more than journeymen, perhaps on the order of £100 annually during the pre-war years. This estimate is congruent with the appraisal of the income of master cordwainers. Masters in both crafts probably enjoyed similar living standards before Independence, but tailors' real wages plummeted during the 1780s and continued at a much lower plateau during the century's final decade.

The findings of this study challenge the customary maxims concerning the elevated wages, comfortable material conditions, and abundant oppor-

353

[119] Members of the society agreed to abide by only two articles: neither to charge a lower price for workmanship than that agreed upon by the society, nor to pay more to journeymen than the society specified. Disciplinary action was taken several times against members who violated these rules (minutes of the Taylors Co., Hist. Soc. Pa.).
[120] These estimates have been arrived at by the method described in n. 111.
[121] Minutes of the Taylors Co., Hist. Soc. Pa.
[122] Winter was invariably a slack season for Joseph Graisbury (ledger of Graisbury, *passim*).
[123] *Ibid.*

tunities for economic advancement enjoyed by laboring people in early American urban society. Its analysis of the incomes and living costs of the lower sort in one city paints a markedly darker portrait of their economic circumstances than that generally limned by historians. A knowledge of the material position of laboring people during the latter half of the eighteenth century in British America is essential if we are to assess such vital issues as the effect of class structure on the turbulent political events of the period, or the eventual impact of industrialization on the lives of Americans.

354 Unskilled workers and journeymen artisans in the "lesser" crafts in Philadelphia often encountered very serious difficulties in meeting their families' basic needs. Many, if not most, lived in poverty or on its edge. The severity of their struggle simply to maintain, or rise slightly above, the subsistence level depended to a great extent on the size and composition of their households. Unmarried, healthy males generally found it easy enough to earn a living wage. But most laboring Philadelphians were married and had at least two children, usually quite young.[124] Because their employment opportunities were circumscribed and their wages low, women and children rarely could earn their keep, but as a supplement to the wages of the household head, their income was essential to the maintenance of the family. Only in the best of times, during the French and Indian War or the late 1790s, could male heads of household in the four occupational groups earn enough money to pay for basic necessities. Those a step higher in the economic hierarchy, like master cordwainers and tailors, who were able to profit from the labor of journeymen, apprentices, and in a few instances servants and slaves, enjoyed a more comfortable existence. However, in periods of depression, such as the early 1760s and the 1780s, they, too, faced serious hardships, and other members of their household had to contribute to the family income.

The number of urban laboring people in colonial America was greater, and their economic plight more precarious, than has been commonly assumed. It has been estimated that about one-third of the residents of eighteenth-century European cities were laboring poor who frequently became destitute at times of crisis.[125] A similar proportion of Philadelphians—perhaps between one-fourth and one-third of the free population—experienced analogous conditions. Their material position was extremely vulnerable, and they were easily driven below the subsistence

[124] It is important to note the significance of life cycle in assessing the situation of the "lower sort." Studying the career patterns of the members of the four occupational groups considered in this article, I found an extremely weak correlation between their life cycle and either their tax assessment or occupational status. Most of the unskilled and the "lesser" artisans remained in the same economic circumstances for the duration of their residence in the city. See Smith, "The 'Lower Sort' in Revolutionary Philadelphia," chap. 4.

[125] Jeffry Kaplow, "The Culture of Poverty in Paris on the Eve of the Revolution," *International Review of Social History*, XII (1967), 278-291.

level by such ordinary occurrences as business cycles, seasonal unemployment, illness, injury, pregnancy or child-care requirements, or epidemics that disrupted the city's economy. As a result, private and public aid to the poor rose to unprecedented levels during the late colonial period and the 1780s, and increasingly not only the aged, infirm, widowed, and orphaned but able-bodied working men and women as well found themselves on the charity rolls.[126]

The late colonial period was not one during which Philadelphia's laboring people enjoyed steadily increasing prosperity. Indeed, they lived so near subsistence before the Revolutionary War that there appears to be no lower level from which they could have risen. The increasing wealth usually thought to have characterized the colonies in general and Philadelphia *355* in particular during this period did not trickle down to the lower sort. If anything, the opposite occurred. Philadelphia's poorer residents experienced relative prosperity during the late 1750s and early 1760s but generally suffered declining living standards from the end of the French and Indian War until Independence. For the city's laboring people, the Confederation era was a period of adversity that ended for many, although not all, only by the mid-1790s.

The material standards of Philadelphia's laboring people were spartan. The budgets constructed in this article are extremely lean ones, generally based on estimates of minimal expenditures for four necessities and omitting many essentials of a decent competency. If the lower sort met the cost of the budget, they still lived very sparely, even by contemporary standards, for they dined like prisoners, dressed in the same fashion as almshouse inmates, and crowded into cramped quarters. Any reduction in income or increase in expenses meant significant sacrifices. Hard-pressed families ate more grains, doubled or tripled up in houses, went without essential clothing, shivered through winters with insufficient fuel, forewent smallpox inoculation but were unable to flee the city in times of epidemic. Some undoubtedly were pushed into an underground economy, stealing their necessary provisions. Others turned to public and private charities, and many landed in relief institutions that often were little more than prisons for the poor. The spectre of poverty and deprivation haunted their lives. In these circumstances, dreams of wealth or home ownership, if such dreams existed, would have been shattered by a reality where even a decent competency was difficult to maintain. If this were the best poor man's country for urban laboring people at the time (and that remains a disputed question), it still was a world requiring constant vigilance and struggle to survive.

[126] Nash, "Poverty and Poor Relief," *WMQ*, 3d Ser., XXXIII (1976), 3-30; Geib, "History of Philadelphia," 203-205.

Ordering the Backcountry:
The South Carolina Regulation

Rachel N. Klein

IN 1769 a group of South Carolina frontiersmen chained John Harvey to a tree and took turns administering five hundred lashes while members of the party beat drums and played a fiddle. Harvey, a "roguish and troublesome" man, was believed to have stolen a horse.[1] He was one of many such "troublesome" persons brought under the lash by men who called themselves "Regulators." Supported by thousands of inland settlers, Regulators acted from 1767 through 1769 as the primary enforcers of order in the backcountry. The leaders were ambitious, commercially oriented slaveowners who struggled to assume control of their own region by suppressing threatening groups. Their actions and their demands open a window onto the values, fears, and early experience of an emerging planter class.

Regulators banded together in response to a wave of crime that swept the backcountry during the mid-1760s. Newspapers abounded with accounts of violent robberies perpetrated by groups of wandering bandits, and settlers feared for their lives and property. Lacking local courts and jails, and frustrated by the leniency of the Charleston criminal justice system, they took the law into their own hands. Regulators punished suspected robbers by whipping or houseburning. Some they drove from the colony, and others they carried to the Charleston jail. Gradually broadening their activities, they whipped "whores" and forced the idle to

Ms. Klein is a member of the Department of History at Pomona College. Earlier versions of this article were presented at the annual meeting of the Organization of American Historians in 1979 and at a colloquium of the Institute of Early American History and Culture in 1980. The author wishes to thank the participants at those sessions for their comments. In addition, she would like to thank Edmund S. Morgan, Steven H. Hahn, David Brion Davis, and George D. Terry for their helpful advice on earlier drafts.

[1] South Carolina Council Journal, Feb. 3, 1772, hereafter cited as Council Jour. All manuscripts cited are in the Department of Archives and History, Columbia, S.C., unless otherwise noted. Regulators were practicing an age-old European ritual by which groups would play music or make loud noise while publicly, and often brutally, punishing blatant offenders of community standards. See E. P. Thompson, " 'Rough Music': Le Charivari anglaise," *Annales*, XXVII (1972), 285-312.

work. Not until 1769, with the passage of South Carolina's Circuit Court Act, did the insurgents finally disperse.[2]

Impelled to action by the spread of banditry, Regulators also enumerated a series of smouldering backcountry grievances which they presented in the form of a lengthy Remonstrance to the assembly. Focusing on robbers and vagrants, they demanded local courts, jails, and other measures for suppressing crime. They complained of absconding debtors and the excessive fees charged by Charleston lawyers. They requested local civil courts, local mechanisms for processing land warrants, and greater representation in the assembly. Regulators revealed their commercial aspirations by calling for premiums on their crops.[3]

In his excellent study of the Regulator uprising published nearly twenty years ago, Richard Maxwell Brown concluded that the most active insurgents were acquisitive men whose primary purpose was "to stamp out crime and chaos so that ambition and enterprise could gain their rewards." Describing the backcountry as a region divided between "two societies," Brown argued that Regulators represented respectable, hard-working settlers who were struggling to suppress the various "low," lawless, and disorderly segments of the inland population. He found that 32 of the 120 known Regulators were or would become justices of the peace, and that 21 were militia or ranger officers before the Revolution. At least 31 acquired slaves, and at least 17 eventually owned ten slaves or more. Almost all known Regulators were landowners, and 19 accumulated one thousand or more acres. In addition, Regulators won support from the wealthiest and most widely respected men of the region. Brown minimized the extent of sectional conflict between coast and frontier. He argued that coastal leaders were far more alarmed by Regulator methods than by their demands, and pointed out that the struggle with England, rather than any fundamental lack of sympathy, delayed response to key Regulator demands.[4]

Without challenging Brown's basic interpretation, this article explores the social conflict in the backcountry and the broader social transformation from which that conflict emerged. Building on Brown's study, it will more fully and precisely analyze just what the Regulators were regulating.

On the eve of the uprising, South Carolina was divided into two geographically, socially, politically, and economically distinct regions. The coastal area, which extended about sixty miles inland, contained rich lands ideally suited to the production of rice and indigo. Over the preceding

---

[2] Richard Maxwell Brown, *The South Carolina Regulators* (Cambridge, Mass., 1963), *passim*.

[3] Richard J. Hooker, ed., *The Carolina Backcountry on the Eve of the Revolution: The Journal and Other Writings of Charles Woodmason, Anglican Itinerant* (Chapel Hill, N.C., 1953), 213-246.

[4] Brown, *S.C. Regulators*, 113-134, 144, and *passim*.; quotation on p. 134.

century, French, English, and Barbadian immigrants had settled the lowcountry area, where they lived amidst an overwhelming slave majority. By the mid-1760s, the coastal region was split into twenty parishes, but social and political life centered in the port city of Charleston.

Farther inland the coastal swamps gave way to a pine belt, sandhill, and red-clay region that rose gradually into a fertile piedmont plateau. Tied to the coast by the Savannah, Santee, and Peedee river systems, South Carolina's extensive backcountry remained unsettled by whites until colonists virtually wiped out the Yamassee Indians in the war of 1715-1717. During the 1730s, Governor Robert Johnson embarked upon a plan to draw white settlers into ten new townships; he hoped that a 358 yeoman frontier would protect the coast in the event of slave insurrection or Indian war. Initially, the project floundered, but by the middle decades of the eighteenth century interior settlements were expanding rapidly as migrants from Pennsylvania, Virginia, and North Carolina joined European immigrants and settlers from the coastal parishes. By the late 1760s, the region contained between thirty thousand and thirty-five thousand inhabitants and about three-fourths of the colony's white population, yet it had only two representatives in the assembly from the one, vaguely defined parish of St. Marks.[5]

Although the backcountry remained predominantly an area of small farms and few slaves, some frontiersmen were beginning to acquire black labor for the production of commercial crops. By the mid-1760s, indigo was already a leading backcountry commodity, particularly in the middle regions of the colony below the fall line. Indigo could be profitably grown by large and small planters alike, and the compactness of the finished dye facilitated transport.[6] Settlers were also producing some tobacco for market. In 1768 a Charleston observer noted that "several large quantities of excellent tobacco, made in the back settlements, have been brought to this market." One year later, petitioners requested the establishment of inland tobacco inspection sites, and in 1770 Lieutenant Governor William

[5] *Ibid.*, 3, 13-18.

[6] Eighteenth-century Americans generally used the word "planter" as a synonym for "farmer" or "yeoman." Not until the 19th century did they narrow the definition to include only substantial holders of land and slaves. The 18th-century backcountry presents a particular problem of definition because the planter class of later years was in process of formation. Families that were prosperous small slaveholders in the 18th century emerged later as owners of substantial numbers of slaves. Included in the Regulator movement were a number of settlers who were producing cash crops. By 1790 some of these men held more than 20 slaves. I use "planter" to describe that rising segment of the population. "Farmer" is used in reference to those who were producing crops primarily for home use; most were nonslaveholders. The division between planters and prosperous farmers was not, of course, absolute. In any case, it is not possible to be more precise because there are no census reports or surviving tax records from which individual slaveholdings could be determined for the pre-Revolutionary period.

Bull informed Lord Hillsborough that "tobacco, tho' a bulkey commodity, is planted from one hundred and fifty to two hundred miles from Charleston, where the Emigrants from Virginia find the weed meliorate as they come south; and they cultivate it now with great advantage not withstanding the distance of carriage to market."[7]

Indigo and tobacco were not the only burgeoning backcountry crops. The introduction, by 1760, of a store and mills in the village of Pine Tree Hill (later Camden) encouraged the expansion of wheat production in an area that would later become a center of Regulator activity. In 1760 the *South Carolina Gazette* reported "fine Carolina flour Just arrived from *Pine-tree-Hill*" available at the Charleston store of Ancrum, Lance, and Loocock. By 1770, William Bull could exult that "flour is a growing article in our exportation; above four thousand barrels are now exported when formerly we imported more." Hemp production was also on the rise, and prosperous planters, particularly those below the fall line at the Wateree River swamps, were producing some rice for export. Although few inventories list herds of more than one hundred head of cattle, many settlers owned more livestock than could have been used simply for home consumption. Frontier farmers apparently contributed various livestock products, as well as certain food crops, to the roster of the colony's exports.[8]

359

[7] *American Husbandry*, I (London, 1775), 431; William Gerard De Brahm, "Philosophico-Historico-Hydrogeography of South Carolina, Georgia, and East Florida . . . ," in Plowden Charles Jennett Weston, ed., *Documents Connected with the History of South Carolina* (London, 1856), 169-170; Johann David Schoepf, *Travels in the Confederation*, trans. and ed. Alfred J. Morrison, II (Philadelphia, 1911), 160; Robert L. Meriwether, *The Expansion of South Carolina, 1729-1765* (Kingsport, Tenn., 1940), 94, 106, 167; Leila Sellers, *Charleston Business on the Eve of the American Revolution* (Chapel Hill, N.C., 1934), 164. It is not possible to determine the extent of backcountry contributions to South Carolina's extensive indigo exports. See Charles Joseph Gayle, "The Nature and Volume of Exports from Charleston, 1724-1774," South Carolina Historical Association, *Proceedings* (Columbia, S.C., 1937), 29, 33; *Boston Chronicle*, Nov. 14, 1768, in H. Roy Merrens, ed., *The Colonial South Carolina Scene: Contemporary Views, 1697-1774* (Columbia, S.C., 1977), 247; William Bull to Lord Hillsborough, Nov. 30, 1770, Records in the British Public Record Office Relating to South Carolina, Transcripts, XXXII, 393-396, 402-403, hereafter cited as S.C. Transcripts; D. Huger Bacot, "The South Carolina Up Country at the End of the Eighteenth Century," *American Historical Review*, XXVIII (1923), 693-698; South Carolina Commons House of Assembly Journal, July 5, 1769, hereafter cited as Commons Jour.

[8] *South Carolina Gazette* (Charleston), July 12, Aug. 30, 1760, Feb. 2, 1765; Bull to Hillsborough, Dec. 17, 1765, S.C. Transcripts, XXX, 300, and Nov. 30, 1770, XXXII, 393-396; Joseph A. Ernst and H. Roy Merrens, " 'Camden's turrets pierce the skies!': The Urban Process in the Southern Colonies during the Eighteenth Century," *William and Mary Quarterly*, 3d Ser., XXX (1973), 560-

In various ways, South Carolina's backcountry settlers revealed their growing interest in commercial agriculture. They called upon coastal leaders to pass tobacco and flour inspection laws, and inundated the assembly with petitions for ferries and road improvements. During the 1750s, wagon traffic between Charleston and the frontier had grown to such an extent that a village (Moncks Corner) grew up on the primary trade route. Enterprising tavern and storekeepers were able to profit from the influx of travelers. In December 1771, the *South Carolina Gazette* reported "no less than 113 waggons on the road to Town, most of them loaded with two Hogsheads of Tobacco, besides Indico, Hemp, Butter, Tallow, Bees Wax and many other Articles who all carry out on their 360 Return, Rum, Sugar, Salt and European goods."[9]

As frontier producers entered the colony-wide trade, they demanded increasing numbers of slaves. During the 1760s—a period for which we are fortunate to have aggregate tax records—inland residents owned only a small fraction of the colony's slaves, but the number was growing rapidly. By 1768 about 8 percent of South Carolina's slaves lived in the backcountry, where they composed about 19 percent of the population.[10] Interested observers were quick to notice this trend. Henry Laurens, Charleston's

---

564; Ernst and Merrens, *The South Carolina Economy of the Middle-Eighteenth Century: The View from Philadelphia,* West Georgia College Studies in the Social Sciences, XII (Carrollton, Ga., 1973), 16-29; Charleston Inventories, RR-&.

[9] Commons Jour., July 6, 1759, May 21, 1762, Jan. 29, 1766, Mar. 4, 1767, Jan. 27, 1768, Mar. 15, 1768, July 5, 1769, Aug. 3, 1769, Dec. 6-8, 1769, Jan. 10, 1770, Feb. 15, 1770, Feb. 8, 1771, Feb. 2, 1775, July 10, 1775, Feb. 3, 1789; Thomas Cooper and David J. McCord, eds., *The Statutes at Large of South Carolina* (Columbia, S.C., 1836-1841), IX; *S.C. Gaz.,* Dec. 5, 1771; Alexander Gregg, *History of the Old Cheraws* ... (New York, 1867), 155-156; George D. Terry, " 'Champaign Country': A Social History of an Eighteenth-Century Lowcountry Parish in South Carolina, St. Johns, Berkeley County" (Ph.D. diss., University of South Carolina, 1981), 206-208.

[10] Using militia rolls for 1770 and multiplying by the conventional figure of five, Richard M. Brown estimated the backcountry population at between 30,000 and 35,000 in 1765. Brown relied on Robert L. Meriwether's calculations when he suggested that slaves composed about 10% of the total population. Because Meriwether was referring only to the piedmont, Brown's 10% estimate is far too low. I have assumed that the total inland population was about 35,000 by the late 1760s, but I have used tax records to arrive at the slave population. Brown, *S.C. Regulators,* 182; Meriwether, *Expansion of S.C.,* 260; Public Treasurer, General Tax Receipts and Payments, Account of the General Tax Collected for the Charges of the Government, 1768. Of the 143 surviving backcountry inventories filed during the 1760s, 98 (69%) included slaves. Of all slaveholders, 51 (50%) included fewer than five slaves while only five (5%) included 20 or more slaves. The inventories are heavily weighted to the wealthier segment of backcountry society, but they do suggest that ownership of a few slaves was quite common among more prosperous frontiersmen. Charleston Inventories, T-Y.

leading merchant, wrote in 1762 of "a large field for trade [in slaves] opening in these colonies." He pointed to the "vast number of people seting down upon our frontier Lands," who would "with a little management . . . take off almost insensibly a Cargo by one or two in a Lot." According to Laurens, it was "from such folks that we have always obtain'd the highest prices & hitherto we have had no reason to be discourag'd from dealing with them on Account of bad debts."[11]

Purchase was not the only way to "take off" slaves. Lowcountry owners accused frontier settlers of being less than zealous in returning runaways. In 1763 James Parsons denounced a "pernicious custom" whereby "backsettlers when they meet with run away negroes, and . . . some of the magistrates and others in the back parts of the country when such negroes are brought to them [d]o publish purposely blind advertisements for a short time of them, and afterwards keep them at work for themselves." Three years later, a runaway notice declared it "a customary thing for the back settlers of this province, to take up new negroes, and keep them employed privately."[12]

Frontier planters who acquired slaves often engaged in multiple economic pursuits. The cost and difficulty of transport and land clearance limited profits to be gained from farming. Many of those men who emerged as leading slaveowners and political leaders began their careers not only as planters but as store or tavern keepers, millers, and surveyors. Leading Regulators were involved in a variety of such moneymaking activities. Morris Murphy and Claudius Pegues, both prominent Peedee slaveowners, were listed on pre-Revolutionary deeds as merchants. James Mayson, a substantial slaveowner and magistrate in the western piedmont, had a store, mills, and a distillery at his home plantation. Another Regulator, Joshua Dinkins, operated a tavern. Ownership or control of toll roads and ferries offered additional commercial advantages. Although the toll was small, the location could afford excellent opportunities for a store or tavern. Five Regulators were or later became ferry operators.[13]

[11] Henry Laurens to Richard Oswald & Co., Feb. 15, 1763, Philip Hamer *et al.*, eds., *The Papers of Henry Laurens* (Columbia, S.C., 1968-), III, 260. Writing during the early 1770s, Peter Manigault, a wealthy Charlestonian, observed that "the great Planters have bought few Negroes within these two Years. Upwards of two thirds that have been imported have gone backwards. These people some of them come at the Distance of 300 miles from Chs Town, & will not go back without Negroes, let the Price be what it will." Manigault to William Blake, n.d. [probably written in Dec. 1772], in Maurice A. Crouse, ed., "The Letterbook of Peter Manigault, 1763-1773," *South Carolina Historical Magazine*, LXX (1969), 191. See also Patrick S. Brady, "The Slave Trade and Sectionalism in South Carolina, 1787-1808," *Journal of Southern History*, XXXVIII (1972), 601-620.

[12] *S.C. Gaz.*, Jan. 29, 1763; *South Carolina Gazette; And Country Journal* (Charleston), June 17, 1766.

[13] Rachel Klein, "The Rise of the Planters in the South Carolina Backcountry, 1767-1808" (Ph.D. diss., Yale University, 1979), 24-33.

Ambitious men who lacked the capital necessary to establish a store, tavern, or distillery had other alternatives. Eager to attract inland settlers, the colonial government allowed a free fifty-acre headright for each household head, family member, and slave. Enterprising men could sell headright lands at an absolute profit while continuing to live on inherited, purchased, or additional granted property. Many sold land within months of receiving their grants.[14] Such small-scale speculation enabled settlers to accumulate capital with which to purchase improved lands, tools, or slaves.

362   Of all known Regulators, Moses Kirkland had the most complex (and shady) business interests. After migrating from Virginia during the early 1750s, Kirkland operated a store and tavern near Camden, where he was accused of harboring runaways and selling rum to the Catawba Indians. He later moved to the lower forks of the Broad and Saluda rivers, where by 1765, he maintained a large grist mill, several sawmills, and a brewery, and ran a ferry. By 1767 Kirkland had entered into a partnership with several wealthy lowcountrymen who planned to build sawmills on the Edisto River. That year he joined three other Regulators in presenting the Remonstrance to the assembly. In 1770 Kirkland nearly succeeded in defrauding settlers in the township of Saxe Gotha of a portion of their commons land. As a loyalist refugee after the Revolution, he claimed compensation for 33 slaves, 152 cattle, 24 horses, and 255 hogs. Kirkland held over 10,000 backcountry acres, including a 950-acre indigo plantation.[15]

Although aspiring frontiersmen were quick to seek profits through commercial activities, they apparently regarded planting as the more desirable and respectable occupation. Inland merchants and entrepreneurs were among the largest landholders and slaveholders of their region, and many who were involved in trade preferred to call themselves planters. Laurens described the prevailing attitude when he advised his associates to establish themselves as planters before opening a frontier store. To enter immediately into retail trade would, he observed, "be mean, would Lessen them in the esteem of people whose respect they must endeavour to attract." Only after they were "set down in a Creditable manner as Planters" could Laurens's partners "carry on the Sale of many specie of

[14] Charleston Deeds, WPA transcripts, vols. 200-208.

[15] Audit Office, Transcripts of the Manuscript Books and Papers of the Commission of Enquiry into the Losses and Services of the American Loyalists Held Under Acts of Parliament of 23, 24, 26, 28, and 29 of George III preserved amongst the Audit Office Records in the Public Record Office of England, 1783-1790, LIII, 223-230, New York Public Library, New York City; Council Jour., Nov. 15, 1752, Dec. 16, 1754, Oct. 10, 1770; Commons Jour., Mar. 15, 1765; S.C. Gaz.; Country Jour., Oct. 23, 1770; Brown, S.C. Regulators, 128-129. I am indebted to Professor Brown for allowing me access to his unpublished prosopography of the Regulators. See "Prosopography," 77-89.

European & West Indian goods to some advantages & with a good grace."[16]

Backcountry entrepreneurs were not operating on the scale of their rice- and indigo-producing coastal counterparts, but they were beginning to acquire slaves in the apparent hope of becoming planters. Their sons and grandsons would emerge in subsequent decades as leading South Carolina planters and political figures. Such men were not concerned simply with the establishment of law and order; they were struggling to establish a particular type of order consistent with the needs of hard-working farmers and rising slaveowners. The Regulator movement united frontiersmen in an effort to make their region safe for planting and property, particularly property in slaves.

363

By the mid-1760s backcountry settlers confronted a growing threat to their lives and property. Gangs of robbers, supported by other alienated members of the inland population, were plundering the frontier. Although Regulators and Regulator sympathizers indiscriminately referred to their opponents as horse stealers, cattle stealers, banditti, or vagabonds, it is possible, in retrospect, to identify different groups whose actions undermined the society and values that the Regulators sought to uphold.

The fundamental social division was between those who did and those who did not rely primarily on hunting for their subsistence. South Carolina leaders expressed concern about the wandering or "strolling" hunters described by one observer as "little more than white Indians." In 1750 the Speaker of the assembly told of the "many hundred men whom we know little of and are little the better, for they kill deer and live like Indians." William Bull made a similar observation in 1769 when he wrote of those "back inhabitants who choose to live by the wandering indolence of hunting than by the more honest and domestic employment of planting." Regulators complained in their Remonstrance of people who "range the Country with their Horse and Gun, without Home or Habitation."[17]

Not all hunters were wanderers; some were squatters or even owners of land who were unable or unwilling to undertake the strenuous labor of clearing and farming. Charles Woodmason, the Anglican minister who

[16] Laurens to Oswald, July 7, 1764, in Hamer *et al.*, eds., *Papers of Henry Laurens*, IV, 338; Klein, "Rise of the Planters," 40-41.

[17] Commons Jour., Feb. 27, 1766; Council Jour., Apr. 1, 1751; Andrew Rutledge to James Crocket, June 6, 1750, S.C. Transcripts, K, 1; Bull to Hillsborough, Oct. 4, 1769; *ibid.*, XXXII, 108-109; Hooker, ed., *Carolina Backcountry*, 226. In 1786 a settler living in the upper piedmont referred to many "who depend wholly on hunting for a subsistence and have supplied nature's calls out of the forest without attending to cultivation." *Charleston Morning Post, and Daily Advertiser*, July 3, 1786. See also S. F. Warren to Dr. [James] Warren, Jan. 22, 1766, in Merrens, ed., *Carolina Scene*, 233-234.

emerged as spokesman for the Regulators, observed one such hunting community near the Broad River. The people, he wrote, were "so burthen'd with Young Children, that the Women cannot attend both House and Field—And many live by Hunting, and killing of Deer." The Vagrant Act that finally passed the assembly in 1787 identified this nonplanting population. In defining "vagrant," the act referred not simply to wanderers but to "all persons (not following some handicraft[,] trade or profession, or not having some known or visible means of livelihood,) who shall be able to work, and occupying or being in possession of some piece of land, shall not cultivate such quantity thereof as shall be deemed . . . necessary for the maintenance of himself and his family." The first part of this definition derived directly from British precedent; the second, which identified vagrants as occupants or possessors of land who did not provide a subsistence, represented an adaptation to a particular American condition.[18]

364

Conflicts between hunters and planters were not confined to South Carolina's frontier. In 1749 Moravians in the Shenandoah Valley of Virginia observed "a kind of people . . . who live like savages. Hunting is their chief occupation." North Carolina's act of 1745 to "prevent killing Deer at Unreasonable Times" described the "Numbers of idle and disorderly Persons, who have no settled Habitation, nor visible Method of Supporting themselves by Industry or Honest Calling . . . and kill Deer at all Seasons of the Year." The Georgia statute of 1764 referred to people who had "no kind of property or visible way of living or supporting themselves but by Hunting being people of loose disorderly Lives."[19]

Writing in 1786, Benjamin Rush of Pennsylvania gave clear expression to the social conflict that pervaded frontier society during the eighteenth century. He observed that the original type of settler was "nearly related to an Indian in his manners." Such hunters built rough cabins and fed their families on Indian corn, game, and fish. Their "exertions," according to Rush, "while they continue, are violent, but they are succeeded by long intervals of rest." Of a "second" type of settler Rush noted that "the Indian

[18] Hooker, ed., *Carolina Backcountry*, 39; Cooper and McCord, eds., *Statutes*, V, 41-45; "An Acte for the punyshment of Rogues Vagabonds and Sturdy Beggars," 39 Elizabeth c. 4, *The Statutes of the Realm*, IV (London, 1819), 899-902; Statute 12 Ann. c. 23, listed under "vagabonds" in Giles Jacob, *The Law-Dictionary: Explaining the Rise, Progress, and Present State, of the English Law . . .*, VI (London, 1809).

[19] Robert D. Mitchell, *Commercialism and Frontier: Perspectives on the Early Shenandoah Valley* (Charlottesville, Va., 1977), 134-135; William Waller Hening, *The Statutes at Large; Being a Collection of the Laws of Virginia . . . from the First Session of the Legislature, in the Year, 1619*, VI (Richmond, Va., 1819), 29-33; Walter Clark, ed., *The State Records of North Carolina*, XXIII (Goldsboro, N.C., 1904), 218-219, 435-437, 656; Allen D. Candler, comp., *The Colonial Records of the State of Georgia*, XVIII (Atlanta, Ga., 1910), 588.

manners are more diluted," but it was, he insisted, "in the third species of
settler only that we behold civilization completed." Rush portrayed the
farmer as a "conqueror" whose "weapons . . . are the implements of
husbandry" and whose guiding virtues were "industry and economy." The
struggle between hunters and farmers was, according to Rush, "a new
species of war."[20]

The conflict became particularly acute in South Carolina. Hunters may
have been attracted to the colony because it had neither a vagrancy act nor
local government on the frontier. Regulators insisted that their country
was swarming "with Vagrants—Idlers—Gamblers, and the Outcasts of
Virginia and North Carolina." The disruptive Cherokee War of 1760-
1761 also fostered the growth of South Carolina's hunting population.
Settlers fled their farms for frontier forts; Indian attacks left orphans
wandering through the woods. Militiamen went unpaid, and officers
complained of dissaffection among their troops. Distressed and dislocated,
many settlers probably turned to hunting in order to survive.[21]

In various ways this hunting population interfered with and offended
the more settled members of frontier society. Not surprisingly, hunters
lacked notions of respectability common among farmers and rising

365

[20] Benjamin Rush to Thomas Percival, [Oct. 26, 1786], L. H. Butterfield, ed.,
Letters of Benjamin Rush, I (Princeton, N.J., 1951), 400-405. After traveling
through North America during the 1760s and 1770s Crèvecoeur observed that
"our bad people are those who are half cultivators and half hunters; and the worst
of them are those who have degenerated altogether into the hunting state. . . . If
manners are not refined, at least they are rendered simple and inoffensive by tilling
the earth; all our wants are suppled by it, our time is divided between labour and
rest, and leaves none for the commission of great misdeeds. As hunters it is
divided between the toil of the chase, the idleness of repose, or the indulgence of
inebriation." J. Hector St. John Crèvecoeur, *Letters from an American Farmer* (New
York, 1904 [orig. publ. London, 1782]), 69. See also James Axtell, "The White
Indians of Colonial America," *WMQ*, 3d Ser., XXXII (1975), 55-88.

[21] Hooker, ed., *Carolina Backcountry*, 246; Commons Jour., June 20, 30, 1760,
July 23, 30, 1761; S.C. Gaz., Feb. 16, 1760; David Ramsay, *History of South
Carolina from its first Settlement in 1670, to the year 1808* (Newberry, S.C., 1858),
119-120. For an account of the Cherokee War see Brown, *S.C. Regulators*, 1-12.
The violence and disruptions associated with the Revolution had a similar effect on
the frontier population. During the 1780s, settlers issued repeated complaints
against wandering hunters. In 1785, petitioners from the backcountry Little River
District noted that "the late war having given some people habits of idleness and
vice . . . we petition therefore that some mode of vagrant law may pass in order to
curb idleness and vice." Two years later, the Edgefield County Grand Jury
presented "as a great Grievance that a number of Strolling persons are allowed to
pass unnoticed often to the great Injury of the peacable Inhabitants of this
Country." Petitions no. 105, 1785; House of Representatives Journal, Feb. 7,
1787, 84. See also General Assembly, Grand Jury Presentments, County of
Edgefield, 1786-1787. The Camden District Grand Jury issued a similar complaint
in 1785. *State Gazette of South Carolina* (Charleston), Dec. 12, 1785.

slaveowners. They were, wrote Woodmason, "very poor—owing to their extreme Indolence for they possess the finest Country in America, and could raise but ev'ry thing. They delight in their present low, lazy, sluttish, heathenish, hellish Life, and seem not desirous of changing it. Both Men and Women will do anything to come at Liquor, Cloaths, furniture, &c. &c. rather than work for it—Hence their many Vices—their gross Licentiousness, Wantonness, Lasciviousness, Rudeness, Lewdness, and Profligacy." While backcountry planters grew cotton for their clothes, hunting families went scantily clad. Of the Broad River community Woodmason observed that "it is well if they can get some Body Linen, and some have not even that."[22]

366

Hunters did more than challenge the Regulators' standards of respectability. By hunting or squatting on Indian lands, they exacerbated frontier tensions. In 1769 William Bull complained of their "frequent intrusions on the Indian hunting grounds, and other injurious practices." Creek Indians in Georgia also pointed to "those who live chiefly by Hunting, wandering all over the Woods destroying our Game," and Georgia's vagrancy act suggested that hunters "frequently Tresspass on the Lands and Hunting Grounds of the Indians and Occasion Quarrels and Disturbances among them." In 1770 the Cherokees in South Carolina "expressed great Uneasiness on account of Encroachments on their Hunting Grounds. ... They also complained of the Number of White Hunters who destroy their Game." By angering neighboring Indians, hunters also threatened planting communities.[23]

Particularly disturbing was night- or fire-hunting. Adopted from the Indians, the practice enabled hunters to curtail the chase by blinding the deer with torchlight, but night-hunters also endangered livestock and people. They easily mistook cattle and horses for deer, and sometimes set fire to the woods in order to force out game for slaughter. In 1770 settlers on the Edisto River petitioned "on behalf of themselves and the rest of the Inhabitants living in the Interior parts of this Province" against those who "set fire to the woods" and thereby "destroy the range for Horses and Cattle." A South Carolina act of 1778 provided that any person convicted of fire-hunting was to be deemed a "vagrant." Finally, in 1789 the legislature passed an additional "ordinance for the Preservation of Deer" that prohibited the "practice of hunting with fire in the night time, whereby great numbers of deer are unnecessarily destroyed, and the cattle and other stock of the good citizens of this state are frequently injured."[24]

[22] Hooker, ed., *Carolina Backcountry*, 39, 52.
[23] Bull to Hillsborough, Oct. 4, 1769, S.C. Transcripts, XXII, 108-109; Candler, comp., *Colonial Records of Ga.*, VIII, 167, XVIII, 588; *South Carolina and American General Gazette* (Charleston), Apr. 27, 1770.
[24] Commons Jour., Jan. 24, 1770; Cooper and McCord, eds., *Statutes*, IV, 410-413; *Chas. Morning Post, Daily Advert.*, Feb. 16, 1786. See also Council Jour., Oct. 30, 1773; *Columbian Herald* (Columbia, S.C.), Apr. 16, 1789; Thomas J. Kirkland

Hunters who sold fur and deerskins caused additional problems. An early frontier storekeeper wrote of "many people who avoid work and prefer to wander around in the woods . . . in order to catch in their traps beavers which they later sell to the hatters. They also shoot bears and deer, only for the skin and fat, although meat from the fat young bears is also used occasionally." Backcountry settlers complained about men who took skins, "leaving the flesh to rot, whereby wolves and other beasts of prey are brought among the stocks of cattle, hogs and sheep, to the great annoyance and damage of the owners thereof." Regulators demanded "that Hunters be put under some Restrictions, and oblig'd not to leave Carcasses unburied in the Woods."[25]

While hunters depended on an open range, farmers and rising planters hoped to establish their rights to private property. By the 1760s, the supply of game had noticeably diminished in the more populated areas, and settlers wanted to safeguard a supply for themselves. In 1769 the assembly responded to backcountry grievances by passing an act for the preservation of deer that protected private ranges by restricting hunters to areas within seven miles of their residence.[26]

Settlers insisted that hunters pilfered livestock, and indeed farmers made livestock theft relatively easy by branding rather than fencing their cattle and horses. Animals wandered freely over uncleared lands. Backcountry petitioners insisted that "numbers of Idle Vagrant Persons . . . after the season of hunting is over, Steal Cattle, Hogs and Horses." Georgia's vagrancy act made a similar connection by observing that hunters "do also Trafick much in Horses which there is great Reason to believe are frequently Stolen." In their Remonstrance, Regulators told of "large Stocks of Cattel" which were "either stollen and destroy'd" and of "valuable Horses . . . carried off." They asked that cattle and horse stealing laws be made more effective.[27]

---

and Robert M. Kennedy, *Historic Camden*, I (Columbia, S.C., 1905), 96; Brown, *S.C. Regulators*, 47-48; and General Assembly, Grand Jury Presentments, Orangeburg, 1783. In 1786 Patrick Calhoun (the father of John C. Calhoun) urged that wolves and other "noxious animals" be killed "by inducing such persons as were employed in fire hunting to turn themselves to killing wild beasts." It was, Calhoun added, "always best to let a thief catch a thief." *Chas. Morning Post, Daily Advert.*, Feb. 16, 1786.

[25] Walter L. Robbins, trans. and ed., "John Tobler's Description of South Carolina (1753)," *S.C. Hist. Mag.*, LXXI (1970), 159; Adelaide L. Fries, ed., *Records of the Moravians in North Carolina*, I (Raleigh, N.C., 1922), 50; Cooper and McCord, eds., *Statutes*, IV, 310-312; Hooker, ed., *Carolina Backcountry*, 231. See also Commons Jour., Jan. 7, 1768.

[26] Cooper and McCord, eds., *Statutes*, IV, 310-312.

[27] Lewis Cecil Gray, *History of Agriculture in the Southern United States to 1860*, I (Gloucester, Mass., 1958), 200-201; *American Husbandry*, I, 459-460; Harvey Toliver Cook, *Rambles in the PeeDee Basin, South Carolina* (Columbia, S.C., 1926);

Prosperous frontiersmen had more to fear than theft of livestock. During the 1760s, organized gangs of inland bandits not only robbed families of cash and valuables, but often inflicted torture on the victims. When a gang near Pine Tree Creek robbed a man named Charles Kitchen, they also "beat out one of his Wife's Eyes, and then burned the poor Man cruelly." Bandits in the same area "met with one Davis, whom they tied, and tortured with red hot Irons." After Davis revealed the location of his money, the gang "set fire to his House, and left the poor Man tied, to behold All in Flames."[28]

368   Most striking was the case of John ("Ready Money") Scott, a prosperous frontier entrepreneur. As a storekeeper, slaveowner, and magistrate living on the Savannah River across from Augusta, Scott acquired his nickname because he reportedly would accept only cash for payment. When bandits demanded that he deliver his valuables, Scott initially "offered them some half pence." According to a newspaper report, the bandits then covered Mrs. Scott's head with an empty beehive, "tied her up in a blanket, ran a brands end of fire into her face, filled her eyes with ashes, and then threw her into the chimney corner." When Scott continued to resist, "they held him to the fire till his eyes were ready to start out of his head, burnt his toes almost off, heated irons and branded and burnt him . . . and then made him swear three times on the bible that he had no more money."[29]

Bandits probably acted in groups that included no more than twenty members, but separate gangs became part of a larger network. The opposition they encountered from the Regulators apparently strengthened their determination to coordinate their activities. A report from the backcountry in 1767 referred to "the gang of villains . . . who have for some years past, in small parties, under particular leaders, infested the back parts of the southern provinces." The correspondent suggested that the "villains" consisted "of more than 200, [and] form a chain of communication with each other, and have places of general meeting, where (in imitation of councils of war) they form plans of operation and defense." Several months later, another report told of "banditti" who were "so powerful, as to cause magistrates who have been active in bringing

---

Hooker, ed., *Carolina Backcountry,* 214; Commons Jour., Jan. 7, 1768; Candler, comp., *Colonial Records of Ga.,* XVIII, 588. North Carolina's "Act, to prevent Killing Deer at Unreasonable Times" also made an explicit connection between hunters and horse stealers. Clark, ed., *State Records of N.C.,* XXIII, 218-219. In 1773 the Cheraw District Grand Jury presented as a grievance "the Want of a Vagrant Act; the District being infested with many idle and disorderly Persons, who, having no visible Means of Subsistence, either plunder the industrious Inhabitants or become chargable to the Parish." *S.C. Gaz.,* May 31, 1773.

[28] *S.C. Gaz.; Country Jour.,* July 28, Aug. 4, 1767.

[29] *S.C. Gaz.,* Aug. 25, 1766; John A. Chapman, *History of Edgefield County from the Earliest Settlements to 1897* (Newberry, S.C., 1897), 386-392.

692 WILLIAM AND MARY QUARTERLY

674 WILLIAM AND MARY QUARTERLY

some of their gangs to justice, to be seized, carried before them, and tried by a jurisdiction of their own forming." Among these unfortunate magistrates was the Regulator James Mayson, who was taken from his house at night and "dragged and insulted all the way to about eighty miles distant." What happened at the ensuing "trial" remains a mystery, but its occurrence attests to the organization and power enjoyed by Mayson's accusers.[30]

These violent robbers cannot simply be identified with South Carolina's hunting population. Several gang members who were mentioned by name in newspaper accounts and court records appear to have been typical and even prosperous farmers before they became criminals. For example, the several Moon and Black brothers, members of a brutal group of robbers, had been part of an early Quaker settlement at Camden. At his death in 1771, James Moon had three slaves and fifteen cattle. George Burns, executed for having robbed a store, also appears to have been an unexceptional frontier farmer. His estate included fourteen cattle, four sheep, thirty-seven hogs, farm tools, and a "parcel [of] old books." The Moon and Black brothers were all married, as was their fellow gang member Benjamin Spurlock. Some were second-generation settlers who, like the Moons and the Blacks, had familial ties to farming communities.[31]

369

The motives of such men remain obscure. Some were simply carrying to an extreme the acquisitive impulse that characterized many frontiersmen. In the absence of local courts and jails, banditry could be an easy way to quick money. The "notorious" bandit, Anthony Duesto, was a prosperous landowner who, before the Regulator uprising, had made a substantial profit by small-scale land speculation. For Duesto and men like him, banditry was but an extension of an earlier pursuit of gain.[32]

But other landowning bandits had suffered hard times before their entry into lives of crime, and resentment born of misfortune may help to account for the gratuitous violence often perpetrated by frontier gangs. At least six "notorious" bandits had fought in the Cherokee War and doubtless suffered war-related disruptions; one was a deserter. Three severe droughts in 1758, 1766, and 1768 made it that much harder for struggling planters to recoup.[33] At least one leading bandit had gone

[30] S.C. Gaz., Aug. 3, Oct. 19, 1767.
[31] Indenture between James Moon and Joseph Kershaw, Oct. 19, 1765, Chestnut-Miller-Manning Papers, South Carolina Historical Society, Charleston, S.C.; Charleston Inventories, & 1772-1776, 7, 18-19; Commons Jour., Apr. 9, 1767; Council Jour., Apr. 1756; S.C. Gaz.; Country Jour., Oct. 20, 1767, Feb. 2, 1768; Colonial Plats, Aug. 21, 1756, V, 465, June 14, 1766, XVIII, 325, July 1767, X, 88, Kirkland and Kennedy, Historic Camden, I, 74-75, 366. Charleston Deeds, HH, 341; RR, 369; YY, 404; GGG, 161; QQQ, 389.
[32] Charleston Deeds, YY, 357, 367, BBB, 485-491; Index to Colonial Grants.
[33] The following bandits served in the militia during the Cherokee War: Isaac Edward Wells, George Underwood, Edward Walker, William Lee, James Moon, and Jeremiah Joyner. Militia Rolls, Cherokee Expedition, 1759-1760.

heavily into debt before he became a criminal. In 1761, six years after selling his entire 100-acre tract to the future Regulator William Boykin, Thomas Moon became indebted to the Camden merchant Joseph Kershaw for £640. Kershaw took Moon to court in 1765 and won his suit for the portion of the bond that was due. Several months earlier, James Moon had sold 131 acres to Kershaw. The sale, which apparently left Moon landless, suggests that he, too, may have been indebted to the merchant. James Moon had served in the Cherokee War and probably suffered losses as a result.[34]

Whether or not their greed was reinforced by a sense of grievance, backcountry bandits succeeded in winning support from hunters who had their own reasons for resenting respectable frontier society. Woodmason insisted that the nonplanting population gave its support to wandering bandits, thereby enabling robbers to roam the country without fear of capture. In 1766 efforts to suppress a gang of horse thieves were obstructed because "most of the low People around had connexions with these Thieves, [and] this gave them the Alarm." The following year, a letter from Augusta told of "a gang of notorious horse thieves" that "consisted of upwards of twenty men, and had settled a correspondence through the whole country with others that secretly supported them."[35]

Some hunters became actively involved with bandit gangs. Benjamin Burgess, member of a large and violent horse stealing ring, belonged to a hunting and trading community located between the Broad and Saluda rivers. In 1751 after stealing 331 deerskins from the Cherokees, he sought refuge with the Indian trader John Vann. Some years later, Vann himself appeared in court for horse stealing. Referring to Vann's settlement, one South Carolina official observed that "not three families on Saludy wou'd Suffer any one of them to Remain Four & Twenty Hours on their Plantation." Nimrod Kilcrease, who belonged to a gang accused of "robbing a dwelling house," was John Vann's neighbor.[36]

370

[34] Indenture between Moon and Kershaw, Oct. 19, 1765, Chestnut-Miller-Manning Papers, S.C. Hist. Soc.; Charleston Deeds, RR, 369, YY, 343, 404; Court of Common Pleas, Judgement Rolls, Oct. 17, 1765, 62A 119A. James Moon took out another warrant in 1767 for 150 acres, but Thomas Moon probably remained landless after he sold his acreage to Boykin. Colonial Plats, July 14, 1767, X, 88; Brown, *S.C. Regulators*, 29-30.

[35] Hooker, ed., *Carolina Backcountry*, 10; *S.C. and Amer. Gen. Gaz.*, June 5, 1767. Although bandits drew support from the disaffected segment of the population, there is no evidence to suggest that they behaved like European social bandits. See E. J. Hobsbawm, *Social Bandits and Primitive Rebels: Studies in Archaic Forms of Social Movement in the 19th and 20th Centuries* (Glencoe, Ill., 1959), 13-29.

[36] Meriwether, *Expansion of S.C.*, 121-122, 134n; Charleston Court of General Sessions, Journal, Oct. 19, 1770; Charleston Deeds, H-5, 160; James Francis to Gov. Glen, Apr. 14, 1752, in William L. McDowell, ed., *Documents Relating to*

An examination of bandit landholdings provides further evidence of the association between hunters and bandits. Of approximately 165 backcountry horse stealers, robbers, or banditti, more than half never purchased land or applied for headright grants.[37] Even under the headright system, land acquisition required considerable effort, but there is no indication that settlers who wanted land were unable to get it. Those who lacked influence with local deputy surveyors probably had some difficulty obtaining the land of their choice since, by the time of the Regulation, the most desirable spots were already well populated. Moreover, South Carolina frontiersmen were required to record their grants in Charleston. Although some probably sent their warrants to town with more prosperous neighbors, others were forced to make the long and costly trip. Regulators and other backcountrymen demanded more convenient mechanisms for processing grants and deeds, but the several impediments to land acquisition did not prevent the insurgents from acquiring farms. More than 90 percent of all known Regulators purchased land or received headright grants. That 50 percent of all known horse stealers or bandits failed to take advantage of the colony's free land-grant policy suggests not only that some were new arrivals, but that they did not regard land ownership and planting as primary goals.[38]

371

Strengthened by their ties to the hunting population, bandits posed a terrifying threat to frontier settlements. Prosperous men, with cash on hand, naturally had most to fear. As the crime wave swept the backcountry, a correspondent observed that "the lowest state of poverty is to be preferred to riches and affluence, for the person who by his honest labour has earned £50 and lays it up for his future occasions, by this very step endangers his own life and his whole family." Regulators put the matter succinctly in their Remonstrance. Frontier life, they insisted, provided "not the least Encouragement for any Individual to be Industrious. . . . If we save a little Money for to bring down to Town Wherewith to purchase

---

Indian Affairs: May 21, 1750–August 7, 1754, Colonial Records of South Carolina, I (Columbia, S.C., 1958), 250-251; Brown, *S.C. Regulators*, 201-202.

[37] A list of backcountry bandits will appear in the author's forthcoming book, *The Rise of the Planters in the South Carolina Backcountry, 1760-1808*. In the present account, horse stealers and bandits were identified in newspaper accounts, the Council Journal of 1768 and 1769, and the Charleston Court of General Sessions Journal, 1769-1776. Those found "not guilty" were excluded as were those who could, with some assurance, be identified as coastal residents.

[38] "Account of Sundries," May 1772, Joseph Kershaw Papers, Southern Historical Collection, Chapel Hill, N.C. Woodmason wrote that at Rocky Mount, a settlement on the Wateree River, the people were "already crowded together as thick as in England." In 1749 Rocky Mount had been the scene of a land riot. Hooker, ed., *Carolina Backcountry*, 22-23; Meriwether, *Expansion of S.C.*, 107. See also Merrens, ed., *Carolina Scene*, 234. For Regulator landholdings I have relied on Brown, "Prosopography."

Slaves—Should it be known, Our Houses are beset, and Robbers plunder Us, even of our Cloaths. If we buy Liquor for to Retail, or for hospitality, they will break into our dwellings, and consume it. . . . Should we raise Fat Cattle, or Prime Horses for the Market, they are constantly carried off tho' well Guarded." The Regulators' call for local courts and jails was, above all, an effort to make the backcountry safe for property holders. "Every Man of Property . . . ," declared an inland correspondent, "is a Regulator at Heart."[39]

Bandits posed another less obvious danger: they threatened the emerging backcountry slave system. Commentators noted the interracial character of bandit gangs. In 1768 the *South Carolina Gazette* reported that a group of Regulators had met near Lynches Creek after some of them had been "roughly used by a Gang of Banditti consisting of Mulattoes—Free Negroes & notorious Harbourers of run away Slaves." Woodmason thundered against the "Gangs of Rogues . . . composed of Runaway negroes, free mulattoes and other mix'd Blood." The thieves Winslow Driggers and Robert Prine were black, and newspapers described Edward Gibson as a mulatto. An early observer wrote that the Indian trader John Vann had "no less than three Negroes, one Mulatto, and a half-bred Indian now living with him," in addition to the white bandit Benjamin Burgess. The mulatto had escaped from prison, and "one of the negroes" had been "burnt on the Cheek for his Practices."[40]

Reports accused bandits of stealing slaves, but one suspects that some runaways voluntarily sought refuge with the gangs. Clearly, escaped slaves were making their way inland. During the 1760s, the *South Carolina Gazette* reported 49 slaves captured in the backcountry. The number rose to 132 during the 1770s, or about 8 percent of all captured slaves. A runaway notice of 1767 offered £100 for a slave who had escaped from a Savannah River plantation "and was seen . . . on Savannah River in company with Timothy Tyrrell, George Black, John Anderson, Anthony Distow, Edward Wells and others, all horse thieves." Several months later, Regulators captured two members of the same gang, along with four "stolen" slaves. In 1770 an inland planter advertised for a "very sensible and smart" young slave who was "supposed to be enticed away or stolen by some villain or villains."[41]

372

[39] *S.C. and Amer. Gen. Gaz.*, Aug. 7, 1767; Hooker, ed., *Carolina Backcountry*, 226-227; *S.C. Gaz.; Country Jour.*, Mar. 28, 1769.

[40] *S.C. Gaz.*, July 25, 1768; Charles Woodmason, "Memorandum," Sermon Book, IV, New-York Historical Society, New York City, 22; Hooker, ed., *Carolina Backcountry*, 277; *S.C. and Amer. Gen. Gaz.*, Dec. 12, 1766; Francis to Glen, Apr. 14, 1752, in McDowell, ed., *Documents Relating to Indian Affairs*, I, 250-251; Meriwether, *Expansion of S.C.*, 120-122.

[41] *S.C. Gaz.*, Oct. 26, 1767; *S.C. Gaz.; Country Jour.*, Mar. 8, 1768. I am indebted to Philip D. Morgan for providing me with his analysis of runaway notices published in the *S.C. Gaz.* before 1780.

The danger was obvious: slavery could not be made secure in a region where bandits captured or offered refuge to slaves. In his characteristically exaggerated style, Woodmason hit the main point. "The Lands," he wrote, "tho' the finest in the Province [are] unoccupied, and Rich Men afraid to set Slaves to work to clear them, lest they should become a Prey to the Banditti."[42]

Angered by the threat to their lives and property, Regulators not only called for local courts and jails but demanded the establishment of public schools, the lack of which had enabled "A Great Multitude of Children" to grow up "in the Greatest Ignorance of ev'ry Thing, Save Vice . . . For, they having no Sort of Education, naturally follow Hunting—Shooting—Racing—Drinking—Gaming, and ev'ry Species of Wickedness." Fifteen years later, a backcountry judge echoed Regulator demands for free schools by suggesting that the spread of "knowledge & learning thro' the land wd have this good effect, the Youth in our Back Country wd become valuable useful men, instead of being, as they are at present, brought up deer-hunters & horse thieves, for want of Education."[43] Regulators and other backcountrymen also demanded a vagrancy act, the want of which "hath sent such a gang among us, that it hath been in a great measure the Occasion of the Regulators laying themselves open to the Law." Reports from the backcountry in 1770 referred to a new influx of "horse Thieves and other Vagabonds, from whose Depredations and Outrages they fear they can never be completely relieved, "till a Vagrant Act is passed."[44]

In the absence of such an act, Regulators tried to force hunters to plant. In 1768 a large meeting of "the most respectable people" of the backcountry adopted a "Plan of Regulation" and were, according to an inland correspondent, "every day excepting sundays, employed in this *Regulation Work*." They whipped and banished many of the "baser sort of people." But those they thought "reclaimable they are a little tender of; and those they task, giving them so many acres to attend in so many days, on pain of Flagellation, that they may not be reduced to poverty, and by that be led to steal from their industrious neighbors." Farming was to be the foundation of social respectability and order.[45]

Regulators disbanded in 1769 having achieved considerable, if incomplete, success. The assembly's Circuit Court Act of 1769 established a system of courts, jails, and sheriffs in four newly created backcountry judicial districts. Also in 1769, the assembly adopted an act for the preservation of deer. One year earlier, Regulators had marched to the

373

[42] Hooker, ed., *Carolina Backcountry*, 27.
[43] *Ibid.*, 226; Aedanus Burke to Arthur Middleton, July 1782, in Joseph W. Barnwell, ed., "Correspondence of Hon. Arthur Middleton, Signer of the Declaration of Independence," *S.C. Hist. Mag.*, XXVI (1925), 204.
[44] *S.C. Gaz.*, Apr. 19, 1770; Commons Jour., July 4, 1769.
[45] *S.C. and Amer. Gen. Gaz.*, Sept. 2, 1768.

polls and elected six candidates to the assembly. During the same year, Parliament had finally consented to the creation of two backcountry parishes, St. David and St. Matthew.[46] Hunters and bandits would continue to annoy inland settlers, but with the establishment of courts and jails they would never again throw the region into a state of upheaval.

That Regulators succeeded as well as they did testifies not only to their considerable influence in the backcountry but also to the fundamental sympathy of the coastal elite. William Bull had been sensitive to backcountry grievances even before the uprising. As early as 1765 he had informed the Lords of Trade that "the inhabitants settled from 250 miles west from thence [Charleston] lie under great hardships for want of that protection of their persons and their property which the law affords." Bull was not alone in his sentiments, for in November 1767, within a week of receiving the Remonstrance, the assembly effectively legalized Regulator attacks upon bandits by establishing two backcountry ranger companies. The two captains and many of the rangers were already involved in the Regulation. During the same session, the assembly began work on the court and vagrancy acts. The Charleston Grand Jury of 1768 demonstrated its agreement with at least one key Regulator demand by urging the establishment of "Public Schools in the back parts of the province for the education and instruction of the children of poor people." Finally, in 1771 Governor Montagu issued a general Regulator pardon.[47]

As Brown has shown, the struggle with England interrupted the coastal response to Regulator grievances. A dispute with Parliament concerning the tenure of judges delayed passage of the Circuit Court Act for nearly two years. Preoccupation with the growing colonial controversy also led the assembly to suspend action on the public school and vagrancy acts. But such neglect did not signify antagonism to Regulator demands. William Bull cut to the heart of the matter when he observed that the insurgents were not "idle vagabonds, the canaille, the mere dregs of mankind." By the standards of coastal planters, Regulators were men of property whose leaders were beginning to acquire slaves. In their efforts to secure their possessions they supported, rather than challenged, prevailing values.[48]

A growing trade between the two sections also fostered contacts and linked the interests of the elites in each. During the third quarter of the eighteenth century, leading backcountrymen were beginning to establish business associations with planters and merchants on the coast, and

---

[46] Brown, *S.C. Regulators*, 60-82; Cooper and McCord, *Statutes*, IV, 298-302, 310-312; *S.C. Gaz.*, Oct. 10, 1768; *S.C. and Amer. Gen. Gaz.*, Sept. 28-30, 1768.

[47] Bull to the Lords of Trade, Mar. 15, 1765, S.C. Transcripts, XXX, 251; Brown, *S.C. Regulators*, 41-44, 58-60, 159-160; *S.C. Gaz.*, Feb. 1, 1768; Commons Jour., Nov. 11, 1767.

[48] Brown, *S.C. Regulators*, 64-111; Bull to Hillsborough, Sept. 10, 1768, S.C. Transcripts, XXXII, 39-40.

prominent lowcountry residents extended business and planting interests to the frontier. Henry Laurens was quick to see the advantage of circuit courts for his own substantial inland holdings. The acreage would, he suspected, "from an increase of inhabitants & from an expected establishment of Circuit Courts . . . become valuable very soon."[49]

This is not to minimize the suspicion that existed between the sections and dominated state politics until cotton transformed the frontier. Not until a greater proportion of inland settlers held a considerably larger number of slaves would coastal leaders give in to demands for a fundamental reapportionment of legislative representation. But the seeds of social and political unification were already present in the Regulator period. Woodmason expressed the situation clearly when he admonished coastal leaders "who treat Us not as Brethren of the same Kindred—United in the same Interests—and Subjects of the same Prince, but as if we were of a different Species from themselves."[50] Regulators insisted that they were not a different species and that the leading figures of both sections had basic interests in common. The backcountry would not be a plantation society for years to come, but aspiring planters had already begun to mold the frontier in their own image.

375

[49] Laurens to Oswald, Apr. 17, 1768, in Hamer *et al.,* eds., *Papers of Henry Laurens,* V, 665.
[50] Hooker, ed., *Carolina Backcountry,* 222.

The publisher and editor gratefully acknowledge the permission of the authors and the following journals and organizations to reprint the copyright material in this volume; any further reproduction is prohibited without permission:

The Journal of American History & Organization of American Historians for material in the *Journal* and *The Mississippi Valley Historical Review*; the Economic History Society for material in *The Economic History Review*; *The William and Mary Quarterly*; the Economic History Association for material in *The Journal of Economic History*; the *American Journal of Legal History*; *The Journal of Interdisciplinary History* and MIT Press for material in the *Journal*; the *American Quarterly*.

CONTENTS OF THE SET